Immigrant Protest

SUNY series, Praxis: Theory in Action

Nancy A. Naples, editor

Immigrant Protest

Politics, Aesthetics, and Everyday Dissent

Edited by

KATARZYNA MARCINIAK

and

IMOGEN TYLER

Published by
STATE UNIVERSITY OF NEW YORK PRESS
Albany

© 2014 State University of New York

All rights reserved

Printed in the United States of America

No part of this book may be used or reproduced in any manner whatsoever without written permission. No part of this book may be stored in a retrieval system or transmitted in any form or by any means including electronic, electrostatic, magnetic tape, mechanical, photocopying, recording, or otherwise without the prior permission in writing of the publisher.

For information, contact
State University of New York Press
www.sunypress.edu

Production, Laurie D. Searl
Marketing, Anne M. Valentine

Library of Congress Cataloging-in-Publication Data

Immigrant protest : politics, aesthetics, and everyday dissent / edited by
    Katarzyna Marciniak and Imogen Tyler.
        p. cm. — (SUNY series, Praxis : theory in action)
    Includes bibliographical references and index.
    ISBN 978-1-4384-5311-8 (hardcover : alk. paper)
    ISBN 978-1-4384-5310-1 (pbk. : alk. paper)
    ISBN 978-1-4384-5312-5 (ebook)
    1. Immigrants—Political activity.   2. Illegal aliens—Political activity.
3. Protest movements.   4. Immigrants—Political activity—Case studies.
5. Illegal aliens—Political activity—Case studies.   6. Protest movements—
Case studies.   I. Marciniak, Katarzyna, 1963– , author, editor of compilation.
    II. Tyler, Imogen, author, editor of compilation.
    JV6255.I56 2014
    322.4086'912—dc23   2013044072

10 9 8 7 6 5 4 3 2 1

Contents

List of Illustrations   vii

Acknowledgments   xi

Introduction: Immigrant Protest: Noborder Scholarship   1
    Katarzyna Marciniak and Imogen Tyler

I. The Aesthetic Performance of Immigrant Protest

1. Dare to Wear—a Mosque! Immigrant Protest as Cross-Cultural Pedagogy   25
    Azra Akšamija

2. The Political Aesthetics of Immigrant Protest   45
    Rozalinda Borcilă with Katarzyna Marciniak and Imogen Tyler

3. Becoming British: Exploring Citizenship through Arts Practice   63
    Lena Šimić with Imogen Tyler

4. Border Disorder   81
    Alex Rivera with Katarzyna Marciniak

5. Loving the Alien: Indigenous Protest and Neo-Colonial Violence in James Cameron's *Avatar*   97
    Bruce Bennett

6.	Pedagogy of Rage *Katarzyna Marciniak*	121

II. In the Field: Acts of Immigrant Protest

7.	On Israel/Palestine and the Politics of Visibility *Simon Faulkner*	147
8.	Everyday Acts of Resistance: The Precarious Lives of Asylum Seekers in Glasgow *Teresa Piacentini*	169
9.	Pushing the Boundaries of Asylum: Everyday Resistance in Swedish Clandestinity *Maja Sager*	189
10.	Subjects that Matter? Nonidentitarian Strategies of Pro-"Migrant" and "Migrant" Protest in Germany *Petra Rostock*	209
11.	Gender and the Politics of Anti-Racist and Immigrant Protest in Greece *Alexandra Zavos*	225
12.	Immigrant Protest and the Courts of Women *Marguerite Waller*	243
13.	Migrant Resistance and the Anti-Raids Campaign in London 2012 *Anti-Raids Campaign Coalition*	267
14.	Afterword: The Human Waste Disposal Industry *or* Immigrant Protest in Neoliberal Times *Imogen Tyler and Katarzyna Marciniak*	277
	Notes on Contributors	291
	Index	297

Illustrations

	Bullchete, 2011. Courtesy of Alex Rivera	xiv
Fig. I.1.	*Machete*, DVD cover, 2011	2
	Welcome to Gringolandia, 2006. Courtesy of Xico Gonzalez and Center for the Study of Political Graphics	22
Fig. 1.1.	*Survival Mosque*, 2005. Courtesy of Azra Akšamija	24
Fig. 1.2.	(Left) Switzerland's anti-Minaret campaign poster from 2009; (Right) anti-Islam poster by the British National Party	26
Fig. 1.3.	*Wearable Mosques*, 2005. Azra Akšamija	27
Fig. 1.4.	*Nomadic Mosque*, 2005. Azra Akšamija	30
Fig. 1.5.	*Dirndlmoschee*, 2005. Azra Akšamija	32
Fig. 1.6.	*Dirndlmoschee* (video stills), 2005. Azra Akšamij	34
Fig. 1.7.	*Dirndlmoschee* (details), 2005. Azra Akšamija	35
Fig. 1.8.	*Survival Mosque*, 2005. Azra Akšamija	36
Fig. 1.9.	*Survival Mosque* (bag constellation), 2005. Azra Akšamija	37
Fig. 1.10.	*Survival Mosque* (bag constellation), 2005. Azra Akšamija	38
Fig. 1.11.	*Mirror*, 2005. Azra Akšamija	39

Fig. 1.12.	*Speak*, 2005. Azra Akšamija	40
Fig. 1.13.	*Convertible Veil*, 2005. Azra Akšamija	41
Fig. 1.14.	*Nomadic Mosque*, 2005. Azra Akšamija	42
Fig. 2.1.	*We are not alien, we are awesome*, 2011. Developed collaboratively during sign-making event, written by ten-year-old Josue Herrera. Image by Sarah-Ji	44
Fig. 2.2.	Flyers for "Shut Down ICE," May 15–21, 2012	53
Fig. 2.3.	*If one is deportable, we are all exploitable—Si uno es deportabile, todos somos explotabiles*, 2011. Sign made collaboratively. Image by Brett Jenelik	55
Fig. 2.4.	*End of three day walk to the site of a proposed Immigrant Detention Camp in Crete, IL*, 2012. Image by Juan Ibarra	57
Fig 2.5.	*Signs carried for three days, left at the site of a proposed Immigrant Detention Camp in Crete, IL*, 2012. Image by Juan Ibarra	59
Fig. 3.1.	*Becoming British*, 2007. Courtesy of Lena Šimić	62
Fig. 3.2.	Lena as Medea, in *Medea/Mothers' Clothes*. Courtesy of Lena Šimić	70
Fig. 3.3.	Lena performs in *Blood & Soil*. Courtesy of Lena Šimić	76
Fig. 4.1.	*Sleep Dealer*, DVD cover, 2008. Alex Rivera	80
Fig. 4.2.	*Love on the Line* (from *The Borders Trilogy*), 2002. Alex Rivera	85
Fig. 4.3.	*A Visible Border* (from *The Borders Trilogy*), 2002. Alex Rivera	94
Fig. 5.1.	"I see into you": the ethnographic spectacle of *Avatar*	96
Fig. 5.2.	Sully is prepared for the avatar link	99
Fig. 5.3.	Sully's identity is uploaded to his avatar in the film's final shot	101
Fig. 5.4.	The multiethnic visual coding of the Na'vi	103
Fig. 5.5.	Becoming alien: the subjective experience of the avatar link	107
Fig. 5.6.	The heteronormativity of interspecies sex: Neytiri with Sully's avatar	111

Illustrations

Fig. 6.1.	*Who's the Illegal Alien, Pilgrim?* 1978. Courtesy of Yolanda Lopez and Center for the Study of Political Graphics	120
Fig. 6.2.	*Frozen River*'s landscape	125
Fig. 6.3.	Ray and Lila after the rescue	128
Fig. 6.4.	Ray at Yankee One Dollar	134
Fig. 7.1.	*Admit None*, 1999. Courtesy of THINK AGAIN and Center for the Study of Political Graphics	144
Fig. 7.2.	The 2010 Avatar demonstration in the West Bank village of Bil'in. Courtesy of Oren Ziv	146
Fig. 7.3.	Khaled Jarrar, "At the checkpoint" exhibition at the Hawara checkpoint, 2007. Courtesy of Rula Halawani	152
Fig. 7.4.	Khaled Jarrar assembling his exhibition at the Hawara checkpoint, 2007. Courtesy of Rula Halawani	155
Fig. 7.5.	Activists in Bil'in make a banner, 2006. Courtesy of Jacob Ketriol	157
Fig. 7.6.	Mock ship used in demonstration in Bil'in, June 2010. Courtesy of Simon Faulkner	162
Fig. 7.7.	David Reeb, *Facebook Painting*, 2010	163
Fig. 8.1.	*We Belong to Glasgow*, 2010. Courtesy of Cameroonian Association and Sympathizers in Scotland (CAMASS)	168
Fig. 9.1.	*Everydayness*, 2011. Fia Persson	188
Fig. 10.1.	The original photograph of Konstablerwache, Frankfurt am Main, Germany taken and uploaded by User Melcom on http://upload.wikimedia.org/wikipedia/commons/b/bf/Konstablerwache%2C_Frankfurt.jpg. Accessed June 21, 2012. Graphic: Carmen Losmann/Petra Rostock	208
Fig. 11.1.	*No to Racism from the Baby's Cot*, 2005 campaign. Collage by Alexandra Zavos	224
Fig. 12.1.	At the Court of Women on Poverty in the U.S. (May 2012), the all-woman *bomba* ensemble, *Las Bomberas de la Bahia*, performed songs and dances of protest created by seventeenth and eighteenth-century African slaves in Puerto Rico, 2012. Austin-Long-Scott	242

Fig. 13.1. Solidarity Leaflet (front), 2012. Courtesy of
The Anti-Raids Campaign in London . . . 266

Fig 13.2. Migrant Bust Card (front), 2012. Courtesy of
The Anti-Raids Campaign in London . . . 269

Fig. 13.3. Migrant Bust Card (back), 2012. Courtesy of
The Anti-Raids Campaign in London . . . 270

Fig. 13.4. Migrant Bust Card (front, Spanish), 2012.
Courtesy of The Anti-Raids Campaign in London . . . 271

Fig 13.5. Migrant Bust Card (back, Spanish), 2012. Courtesy of
The Anti-Raids Campaign in London . . . 272

Fig. 13.6. Solidarity Leaflet (back), 2012. Courtesy of
The Anti-Raids Campaign in London . . . 273

Fig. 14.1. *Report Non-Humans*, 2009. A *D-9* movie bus bench
poster. Photo courtesy of Kamil Turowski . . . 276

Fig. 14.2. Wan Yun Ji and Alfred Islami contemplate another
day in "Dungwood" Immigration Detention Centre in
Scotland. Still from *Asylum*, 2011, directed by
Joern Utkilen . . . 278

Fig. 14.3. Zombification in detention. Still from *Asylum*, 2011,
directed by Joern Utkilen . . . 279

Fig. 14.4. Dungwood Removal Centre. Still from *Asylum*, 2011,
directed by Joern Utkilen . . . 280

Fig. 14.5. Wan Yun Ji reads his poem "Shit Hole" to zombified
detainees in the English Language Class at "Dungwood"
Immigration Detention Centre . . . 281

Fig. 14.6. A photocopy of job description produced by Serco for
Immigration Detainees, published online at "Yarl's
Wood echos H-Block and Attica" http://stopdeportations.
wordpress.com/2012/09/10/yarls-wood-echos-h-block-
and-attica . . . 284

Acknowledgments

This edited collection on "immigrant protest" has been a labor of love involving various intensive cross-border collaborations, negotiations, and translations. Our aim in bringing together this eclectic mixture of academic, activist, and artistic work was to highlight the question of the politics of migrant representation. In particular, we wanted to explore how xenophobic politics, which pivot on the "problem of migration," is being troubled and contested through creative projects and everyday practices of resistance around the world. We owe a debt of thanks to the contributors to this book for going on this journey with us and for sharing intellectual passions and a belief in the power of oppositional, antiracist practices to effect social change.

Our special gratitude goes to the artists who generously permitted us to reproduce their images: *Bullchete* by Alex Rivera, *Welcome to Gringolandia* by Xico Gonzalez, *Who's the Illegal Alien Pilgrim?* by Yolanda Lopez, and *Admit None* by the THINK AGAIN Collective. The images by Gonzales, Lopez, and THINK AGAIN came from the collection of the Center for the Study of Political Graphics in Los Angeles and we thank the director of CSPG, Carol Wells, for facilitating permissions. The book cover, *Survival Mosque*, shared with us by one of our contributors, Azra Akšamija, speaks to the politically playful spirit of our collection.

We thank the Migrancy Research Group, the Sociology Department, and the Centre for Gender and Women's Studies at Lancaster University in UK for inviting Katarzyna in 2010 to participate in the workshop on Immigrant Protest, an event that precipitated our collaboration.

At SUNY, we thank Beth Bouloukos and Rafael Chaiken for their invaluable assistance. Special appreciation goes to Nancy Naples who, as a series editor of Praxis: Theory in Action at SUNY, accepted our project as part of the series. We are also grateful to anonymous reviewers for helpful insights.

Ohio University has been very supportive in helping us bring this project to publication. For the subvention assistance, Katarzyna thanks Dean Robert Frank at the College of Arts and Sciences and Dr. Joseph Shields, the Vice President for Research. For the financial help with image permissions, thanks go to Senior Associate Dean Howard Dewald at the College of Arts and Sciences.

Immigrant Protest

Bullchete, 2011. Courtesy of Alex Rivera

Introduction

Immigrant Protest

Noborder Scholarship

KATARZYNA MARCINIAK AND IMOGEN TYLER

In April 2010, Arizona governor Jan Brewer signed into law what was touted as the nation's "toughest bill" yet on illegal immigration, *Support Our Law Enforcement and Safe Neighborhoods Act* (commonly known as Arizona SB 1070). This controversial legislation made multiple ostracizing stipulations, including requiring immigrants to carry their documents at all times—which makes Latina/os especially (documented or not) vulnerable to surveillance and identity checks.

Shortly afterward, on Cinco de Mayo, a holiday that celebrates Mexican heritage, Chicano filmmaker Robert Rodriguez released an online trailer for the now cult "Mexploitation" action film *Machete* (2010): a cinematic announcement that might be read as a direct response to the punitive Arizona legislature. The trailer is introduced by the film's title character "Machete," played by frequent Rodriguez collaborator Danny Trejo. An intimidating figure, his body scarred and tattooed, he looks sternly at the camera and speaks angrily: "This is Machete with a special Cinco de Mayo message . . . to ARIZONA!" In the fast-paced scenes that follow, we see Machete performing over-the-top revenge on those who wronged him and we hear a voiceover: "They soon realized . . . they just fucked with the wrong Mexican!"

Machete rampages through the film like a Mexican Terminator, equipped with multiple steel knives attached to his body. Alongside him, armies of Mexicans with machetes and guns march out to kill white people. Highlighting what Bruce Bennett in this volume terms "an eye-jabbing aesthetic," *Machete* is a thoroughly violent spectacle in which the protagonist insists on using his machete, ensuring that each killing is tactile. Slashed bellies, dripping blood, cut-off hands, gouged eyes, dangling intestines—the relentless stabbings, dismemberments, and beheadings—are visual tropes that dramatize immigrant rage.

These revenge killings are mirrored throughout the film by multiple scenes of anti-immigrant violence. In one of the early moments in the narrative, Von Jackson (Don Johnson), a vigilante leading the Border Patrol,

Figure I.1. *Machete*, DVD cover, 2011

nonchalantly shoots a pregnant Mexican woman at the border, saying, "You know, you trespassing, on my daddy's land." This brutality parallels the speeches by Senator John McLaughlin (Robert de Niro), a politician campaigning against undocumented crossers: "Make no mistake, we are at war. Every time an illegal dances across our border, it is an act of aggression against the sovereign state, an overt act of terrorism."

In the history of cinema there has been a long-standing preoccupation with the fragile eye both as a literal object and as a privileged figure for vision, comprehension, and meaning (see, e.g., Clover 1993; Marks 2000; Tobing Rony 1996). In the famous opening scene of Luis Buñuel and Salvadore Dali's 1929 silent surrealist film, *An Andalusian Dog* (*Un chien andalou*), a man, (played by Buñuel himself), slices open a woman's eye with a razor, a scene purposefully offered in a close-up. An exemplary avant-garde film, *An Andalusian Dog* demonstrates the modernist conviction that art should not just entertain but should shock and disturb and open up new ways of seeing. *Machete* reworks this cinematic history; the motif of a jabbed eye, a blinded eye, underlines the ocular discomfort that characterizes the narrative as the film plays with the idea that eye jabbing enacts both immigrant and anti-immigrant rage. We see the evocative development of this idea in three scenes that feature either an immigrant or a "native" eye being stabbed: Machete stabs an attacker in the eye with a corkscrew; Shé (Michelle Rodriguez), an organizer of a legendary Network that helps people cross and finds them jobs in the United States, is blinded when Von Jackson shoots her in the eye, saying, "How about an eye for an eye?"; Agent Sartana Rivera (Jessica Alba), a conflicted Chicana immigration officer who eventually collaborates with Machete, stabs an attacker in the eye with her high-heel shoe. These visceral eye-jabbing moments might be read as metaphors for the *historical* and *cultural blindness* that characterizes public discourses of immigration politics in the United States.

While *Machete* is a fictional film about migrant revenge, it foregrounds the existing conditions of hostility, suspicion, and violence faced by many irregular migrants in the United States. Self-conscious of the pathologizing politics of alienhood (Marciniak 2006a), the narrative presents the inflammatory rhetoric that portrays Mexican border crossers as vermin and underscores the anti-immigrant violence and vigilante border policing this xenophobia incites. As Senator McLaughlin states in a TV campaign commercial in the film: "The aliens, the infiltrators, the outsiders, they come right across by day or night. They'll bleed us, they're parasites. They'll bleed us until we as a city, a county, a state, a nation are all bled out." During one of these ad spots, we see a close-up of writhing maggots, an image that evokes physical repulsion, as a voiceover declares: "The infestation has begun!" The maggots are then juxtaposed with the images of Mexicans crossing through fields and rivers: "Parasites have crossed our borders and are sickening our country, leeching off our system, destroying us from the inside!" screams the ad. A further close-up of cockroaches is accompanied by the message: "No amnesty for parasites. John McLaughlin wants to protect you from the invaders."

Conflating the images of crossers with the repulsive close-ups of bugs, *Machete* highlights familiar U.S. anti-immigrant rhetoric, offering all the customary denigrating tropes associated with the figure of the irregular migrant: invasion, parasitism, and disease. The film taps into the historical roots of anti-immigration sentiments, stretching back to the turn of the twentieth century when, rather than the U.S.-Mexico border, Ellis Island was a processing station and the symbolic site of the troubled history of migrant struggles to cross into the United States. The 1997 History Channel documentary *Ellis Island* details the humiliating bodily inspections that the newly arrived were subjected to. As political scientist Aristide Zolberg explains in the film, "There was a kind of fixation on disease as being something that an immigrant brought in" (*Ellis Island*). While speaking of the ideological impact of the national origin quotas established in the 1920s, historian Virginia Yans comments:

> It is very clear that the effort was to limit people who were not thought to be of the same level of culture and civilization as resident Americans. What they [those establishing anti-immigrant laws] wanted to do was maintain the predominance of white Anglo-Saxons in the country. . . . There was a tremendous fear that people who came in from Southern Europe, from Eastern Europe, would pollute the blood of American population. (*Ellis Island*)

The U.S. postcolonial imaginary suppresses both this history of migrant processing and a longer history of nation formation achieved through the colonalization and genocide enacted upon its many indigenous inhabitants. As Ali Behdad argues, "Both the benign discourse of democratic founding and the myth of immigrant America deny that nationhood has been achieved, at least in part, through the violent conquest of Native Americans, the brutal exploitation of enslaved Africans, and the colonialist annexation of French and Mexican territories" (Behdad 2005, xii). One of the climactic scenes in *Machete* addresses this history directly as Agent Rivera, torn between enforcing the law and honoring the Network's revolt, in a moment of epiphany, jumps on the hood of a car, raises her fist and shouts, addressing the migrants: "Yes, I am a woman of the law. And there are lots of laws. But if they don't offer us justice, then they aren't laws. . . . We didn't cross the border, the border crossed us!"

We began our introduction with Rodriguez's *Machete* because it so effectively *dramatizes* immigrant rage, presenting the audience with "images of racial anger, revolt, and empowerment," which arguably break sanitized Hollywood narratives of the "birth of the nation" more powerfully than "positive" multicultural representations of minorities (Shohat and Stam 1994, 203). Indeed, *Machete* speaks to both the history and the current fervor of anti-immigrant politics in the United States.

By 2011, Arizona SB 1070 was no longer the nation's "toughest" immigration bill as the states of Alabama and Georgia issued even more stringent bills that essentially legalized racial profiling. For example, Alabama's new measures, in addition to allowing law enforcement officers to arrest and detain anyone they suspect of being in the country illegally, introduces new rules for educators, landlords, and businesses: The new legislation makes it a crime for landlords to knowingly rent to undocumented immigrants and for citizens to offer a transport to "illegal" immigrants, while schools are required to collect citizenship information about their students, thus building databases of undocumented children. In all three of these U.S. states, these extreme anti-immigration measures have been met with passionate street protests about these new exclusionary and racist laws, which are creating a profoundly uncomfortable climate on the streets for all people of color regardless of their legal status.

Beyond the United States, the staggering economic inequalities effected by neoliberal globalization have led to an increase in migrations and often perilous border crossings around the world, particularly from the former communist bloc and the Global South toward the more affluent countries of the Global North. Migrant protests are forms of response to the deteriorating conditions for refugees, asylum seekers, economic and other unwanted and irregular migrants on the ground. Indeed, the last decade has witnessed a global explosion of "immigrant protests," political mobilizations by irregular migrants and pro-migrant activists. Indicative examples include: the rise of the Sans-Papiers movement in France (see McNevin 2006), the spectacular protests of millions of undocumented Latin American workers in the United States in Spring 2006, under the banner "A Day Without Immigrants" (see De Genova and Borcilă 2011; Marciniak 2013), events which, in turn, inspired the "A Day Without Us" marches and strikes in Italy, Greece, Spain, and France in 2011. This upsurge in immigrant protest is a consequence of the intensification of border security measures across the globe in recent decades, the abjectifiying effects of which have been well documented by scholars and activists. In the face of the incremental militarization of national and regional borders and the emergence of a "lucrative political economy of border policing and immigrant detention" (De Genova and Borcilă 2011), immigrant protests constitute critical counterpolitical movements, highlighting and protesting deteriorating conditions for irregular migrants and refugees, exposing the violence engendered by border controls, and challenging the abstract and fetishized political rhetoric of "illegal immigration."

New media, such as the Internet, 3G mobile video phones, Weblogs, social media, and instant messaging have inordinately strengthened migrant politics. These technologies are employed to coordinate the swarming of bodies on the streets, to capture and upload videos of protests and police violence and to generate publicity for struggles. The advent of these digital communication systems means that protests staged in one physical place are now transmitted across borders so that even smaller-scale protests such as riots, fires, and hunger strikes by immigration detainees, and individual anti-deportation campaigns have the potential to resonate internationally (Cottle 2011). International coalitions such as the *European NoBorders Network* and the *No One is Illegal* movement have emerged as important horizontal umbrella networks for protesters to connect and coordinate across borders, transforming online spaces into supra-national "common spaces" (see Papadopoulos and Tsianos 2013). These movements for migrant rights and visibility are often moving and inspirational but they are also politically and ethically complex as they make us think about the forms of solidarities and alliances that are possible and impossible between citizens and noncitizens (see Rigby and Schlembach 2013).

Immigrant Protest is the first volume to explore the rise of immigrant protest in a transnational context. With a specific focus on the centrality of aesthetics to migrant resistance movements, the project examines dissent, resistance, and revolt against the conditions and social attitudes faced by regular and irregular migrants, asylum seekers, refugees, and other unwanted "illegal" persons, within a range of national and regional border zones. Introducing the work of a group of international scholars, visual and performance artists and activists, the collection offers a rich series of accounts and analyses of protests and protest materials, which foreground the relationship between visibility, power, representation, and political agency, an arena that is underrepresented and underexplored in migration studies. Alongside contributions that analyze protest and resistance "in the field" in the context of Germany (Rostock), Greece (Zavos), Sweden (Sager), UK (Piacentini, The Anti-Raids Campaign Coalition), Palestine (Faulkner), and women's human rights (Waller), the book engages cinema, media, and performance and installation art as sites where migrant political struggles converge with aesthetic practices. This focus on political aesthetics and issues of in/visibility is critical for us as it connects work on aesthetics with work on politics and social movements.

The chapters variously document and examine protest in a range of mediums and theoretical dimensions, toward a shared goal of reimagining foreignness beyond the xenophobic logic of negativity, inadequacy, and deficiency. Within this framework, the individual contributions address immigrant protest in everyday, local, and wider national and transnational contexts. Employing a variety of feminist, transnational, and postcolonial methodologies, they explore forms of social, political, and aesthetic engagements in migrant politics. The contributions focus on vast array of themes, including desire and neocolonial violence in film, visibility and representation, pedagogical function of protest, and the role of the arts and artists in the explosion of political protests that challenge the intense precarity of migrant life in Global North. Other topics include shifting practices of boundary making and boundary taking, changing meanings and lived experiences of citizenship, embodied and affective dimensions of nationalism, and the many intersecting axes (class, race, gender, ethnicity, nativism, status) through which daily lives are lived, endured, and protested.

In/Visibility

The majority of contributions to this book are concerned with the ways in which migrants and their activist allies engage in political strategies of visibility in order to "make public" their specific concerns and grievances. Indeed, making migrant experiences visible and audible is often the overarching aim of immigrant protests. As Peter Nyers suggests, migrant struggles are often not only concerned with "legal status" and "justice" but are often also struggles "for recognition as someone with an audible and corporeal presence that can be described as 'political'" (Nyers 2007, 3). As noncitizens, migrants have few routes to self-representation available to them and often have no autonomous public voice. Madjiguène Cissé, for example, a spokeswoman for the Sans-Papiers movement notes, "In France up until now our fate as immigrants was: either take part in the Republic's process of integration, or be deported like cattle. . . . We have made ourselves visible to say that we are here, to say that we are not in hiding but we're just human beings. We are here and we have been here a long time" (Cissé 1997). However, it is not that undocumented or irregular migrants are invisible in the public domain; on the contrary, "immigrants" and the topic of "immigration" are "hypervisible" (see Tyler 2006). As Rodriguez's *Machete* reveals, the figure of the immigrant is invoked continuously in overdetermined, stereotyped, and stigmatized forms within mainstream media and political rhetoric. It is precisely the visibility of "the immigrant" and particularly the production of the "illegal immigrant" as a "national abject" which screens the realities of migrant lives from view and silences migrant voices (Tyler 2013). Grappling with social paradoxes of in/visibility in relation to her immigrant life in Canada in the 1970s, writer Bharati Mukherjee, for example, observed: "The oldest paradox of prejudice is that it renders its victims simultaneously *invisible* and *over-exposed*. I have not met an Indian in Canada who has not suffered the humiliations of being overlooked (in jobs, in queues, in deserved recognition) and from being singled out (in hotels, department stores, on the streets, and at customs" (Mukherjee 1981, 36; our emphasis).

Hostile political and public discourses depict immigrants as a dehumanized and undifferentiated foreign mass, mobilizing images of natural disaster (floods, plagues) to communicate the "crises" of migrancy. To counter these depictions, the representational strategies adopted by movements such as Sans-Papiers and, in more problematic ways, by various humanitarian organizations on behalf of migrants, provoke publics to recognize "the human face" of specific migrants. Indeed, a favorite device of humanitarian publications is the use of photographic close-ups of migrant faces and first-person accounts of their experiences. These affective technologies of the "close-up" aim to move the reader in ways that will enable citizens to identify with migrants as "human beings" (see, e.g., Hesford and Kozol 2005; Marciniak and Turowski 2010; Tyler 2006). In other words, these strategies attempt to counter the dehumanizing rhetorics by "humanizing" refugees and irregular migrants as *subjects who matter*, "like us." These kinds of publicity strategies, whether they are appeals made by agents or agencies on behalf of migrants, or whether, they are made by migrants themselves, can be extremely effective. As the contributions to *Immigrant Protest* suggest, the works of artists, writers, and filmmakers not only document immigrant protest but are a form of protest in their own right. The underlying assumption of the forms of "art-activism" presented in this book is that the work of creating alternative forms of visibility, or disrupting prevailing norms of representation, clears the ground for the political agency of migrant populations, denaturalizing xenophobic ideologies.

In his influential writing on politics and aesthetics, Jacques Rancière argues that "politics is aesthetic in that it makes visible what had been excluded from a perceptual field, and in that it makes audible what used to be inaudible" (Rancière 2003, 226). Rancière's thesis speaks to long-standing debates about visibility and audibility in postcolonial studies. The question of in/visibility is, for example, at the heart of Edward Said's project in *Orientalism*, which details "the crude, essentialized caricatures of the Islamic world" that underpin European and North American art, literature, and scholarship depicting the Middle East (1980). Imperialistic representational frames screen colonized and former colonized populations from viewing and, in so doing, curtail the political agency of subjugated populations (see Said 1979). For Gayatri Chakravorty Spivak, it is the question of the "audibility" of subjugated populations that is central. In her essay "Can the Subaltern Speak?" she argues that first world's attempts to ameliorate the conditions experienced by subaltern populations, through for example "acts of translation," often reinforce the inaudibility of "waste populations" (Spivak 1985). As both Said and Spivak variously suggest, a series of risks and tensions unfold from political strategies of visibility and audibility. In very material ways, "becoming visible" exposes irregular or undocumented migrants to the full force of state border controls. Hence, for many migrants, making themselves visible is an activity engaged in only as a last resort.

The punishing effects of visibility have led Dimitris Papadopoulos and Vassilis Tsianos to argue that "visibility, in the context of illegal migration, belongs to the inventory of the technologies for policing migrational flows" (Papadopoulos and Tsianos 2008). As they state, "This is the end of the politics of representation. And the decline of representation means simultaneously the end of the strategy of visibility. Instead of visibility, we say imperceptibility" (ibid.). Nevertheless, migrant activism reveals that "becoming perceptible" is also sometimes a necessary *survival strategy*. In this regard, it is of critical importance that we examine the ways in which migrants negotiate the contradictions and losses and gains of in/visibility in their interactions with sovereign power. It is the capacity for counter-representational practices to generate uncertainty about "commonsense" understandings of belonging that we want to insist upon here. Whether we understand migrant protests as forms of "fight back" against the exclusions of sovereign states or as marking the emergence of a new form of global citizenship against the inequalities and injustices of neoliberal capitalism, the visibility of these struggles is enacting new forms of political community on the streets.

Part I: The Aesthetic Performance of Immigrant Protest

One of the distinguishing contributions of *Immigrant Protest* is that it opens up a dialogue between a diverse range of scholars and artists, and tracks the important relation between theoretically oriented work and art activist practices. Indeed, the first section of the book focuses on the aesthetics of protest and the central role of artistic practice, visibility, recognition and representation to migrant social and political movements. The first three chapters form an exciting forum for a new generation of artists (Akšamija, Borcilă, Šimić) working in art installation, performance, and visual art whose narratives are intensely preoccupied with transcultural themes of mobility, displacement, and migrant experiences. These artists and art-activists variously examine what it means to be an immigrant other in a series of national contexts.

In "Dare to Wear—a Mosque! Immigrant Protest as Cross-cultural Pedagogy," Sarajevo-born Austrian artist and architectural historian Azra Akšamija explores increasing conflicts over the building of mosques in Europe and North America. As Akšamija argues, it is increasingly the case that, if a planning application for a new mosque is to be allowed, "this is only acceptable as long as the proposed mosque does not look like one." Conflicts around the building of mosques have led Akšamija to consider the creative means through which Muslim diasporas in the Global North might protest stigmatizing anti-immigrant and anti-Islamic propaganda. Through a series of provocative art projects she collectively titles "Wearable Mosques," Akšamija develops a visual and design-inspired approach to Muslim xenophobia. Her art practice makes a critical comment on the limits imposed on Muslims to exercise their legal rights to visibility and religious practice in public spaces.

The second chapter, "The Political Aesthetics of Immigrant Protest," is an interview with the Romanian artist and Chicago-based migrant activist Rozalinda Borcilă. In this interview we explore with Borcilă her past work on borders and migrancy and her recent activist work with young migrants in Chicago. In her various performance projects Borcilă experiments with and obsessively tests the limits of the citizen/foreigner binary in the U.S. context. This interview also opens up a series of theoretical questions that are pertinent to this book as a whole, namely, the relationship between art and activism, and between singular and collective modalities of resistance and protest, and the question of what "political aesthetics" means, for example, in terms of thinking about the ways in which "art" shapes creative strategies for resistance that "conventional" modes of protest might learn from and draw upon.

This artist interview is followed by another dialogue, "Becoming British: Exploring Citizenship through Arts Practice," between Imogen Tyler and the Croatian performance artist and political activist Lena Šimić. This chapter focuses on Šimić's ongoing art project "Becoming British" which began with Šimić applying for British citizenship as an "art protest" against what she described as "the social injustices of border controls." Šimić's intention was to reveal the contradictions between her position as an artist, a precarious but nevertheless valued middle-class "cultural worker" from Eastern Europe, and as a stigmatized migrant other.

Erik Swyngedouw uses the term *governance innovation* to describe the ways in which the expansion of purportedly democratic forms, such as citizenship, operate as mechanisms of neoliberal ideologies, as freedoms are retracted from individuals and communities and wealth and power concentrated in the hands of social and political elites and global corporations (Swyngedouw 2005, 1992; Tyler 2010). A "reality gap" has opened up between normative political rhetorics of "deepening democracy" through citizenship (including the exporting of "liberal democracy" through the "war on terror"), and the abjection of "illegal" populations from the rights and protections of citizenship through the enforcement of often brutal and inhumane immigration controls. This "liberal paradox" is further complicated by the incongruity between the opening up of international borders to flows of capital and the simultaneous "damming" of states and regions to "undesirable" migrants from the Global South: a migratory pull that is paradoxically fueled by market demands for cheap unregulated migrant labor in the Global North (see de Hass 2007; Hollifield 2004). By knowingly submitting herself to legal regimes of British citizenship, and by engaging with citizenship as a performative practice, Šimić's intention was to examine the paradoxical effects of these contradictory forces. She set out to document, expose, trouble, and protest the incongruity of different technologies and regimes of citizenship operating within the British state from the perspective of migrant experience. As the "Becoming British" project develops, however, it comes to encompass many other migrant experiences. By organizing a series of workshops in a local community center, Šimić began working collaboratively with a disparate group of migrant artists to document their different experiences of coming to citizenship. This "Becoming British" arts collective included Pa Modou Bojang, a Gambian poet, journalist, and then "failed asylum seeker" facing imminent deportation. The involvement of Pa Modou introduced refugee politics and the local vibrant anti-deportation and asylum advocacy movements in Liverpool to the project, and for a period transformed "Becoming British" into an anti-deportation campaign, as the group campaigned and raised funds for his legal appeal.

The last three chapters in this section focus on cinema and representational affectivities of protest. In "Border Disorder," Alex Rivera speaks with Katarzyna Marciniak about his stylistically original film projects in the context of Latino/a politics and the Mexico-U.S. border. Reflecting on the conceptual development of his films, Rivera traces his engagement in border politics since 1990s against the background of various influential and deeply contradictory historical moments: the introduction of NAFTA, an "open border" policy for trade and the promise of borderless economy, the creation of the first border wall, the rise of the Internet, the initiation of Operation Gatekeeper, which started to fortify the U.S.-Mexico border, and more recent national initiatives such as Secure Communities, a deportation program that engages federal, state, and local law enforcement agencies. In a series of films, Rivera explores the satirical idea of "tele-migration" as an original "solution" to the migration "problem." His *Papapapá* (1995), the 1997 mockumentary *Why Cybraceros?* and his award-winning *Sleep Dealer*, hailed as the first "Third World science fiction," offer a representation of a long-distance farm worker, one whose body physically remains outside the United States while his hands perform work inside the nation. As one of the characters in *Sleep Dealer* states, "We give the Americans what they have always wanted—all the work and none of the workers."

Film scholar Bruce Bennett's contribution to the book, "Loving the Alien: Indigenous Protest and Neo-Colonial Violence in James Cameron's *Avatar*," moves the discussion away from more independent productions such as Rivera's work into the commercial world of Hollywood cinema. The chapter starts with Cameron's provocative comment that "we are all alien," a point that the director sees as the narrative premise of *Avatar*. Interrogating this authorial intent to disrupt the native/alien binary, Bennett's analysis reveals *Avatar* as an intriguing case study in the potential and limitations of mainstream science fiction cinema as social criticism. In orienting its account of the violent conflict between the colonizing/immigrant minority and the indigenous majority around the perspective of a boundary-crossing protagonist, who is branded a race traitor, the chapter discusses *Avatar* as a self-reflexive film offering a powerfully affective but ultimately ideologically ambiguous account of the structural relationships between imperialist brutality and Western consumer culture. The chapter specifically examines the ways in which Cameron's film dramatizes issues of indigenous protest, immigration, and colonization and attempts to trouble the alignment of the spectator with particular positions, employing an immersive aesthetic to emphasize this disorienting sense of destabilized boundaries. The discussion ends with a foray into real life protests in the Palestinian border village of Bil'in where various activists, dressed as Na'vi characters from the film staged an "Avatar Protest." In moving his examination from a narrative analysis into public space, Bennett explores the film's political resonance for indigenous rights: "As a particularly visible attraction of contemporary entertainment culture, *Avatar* becomes available to colonized peoples as a tool which allows for active forms of political consciousness raising through the re-performance of violence and injustice in the neo-colonial political present tense."

Like the opening chapter by Akšamija, Katarzyna Marciniak's "Pedagogy of Rage" too has a distinctive focus on pedagogical function of oppositional art. Her essay begins with the conviction that to write about immigrant protest means to write about immigrant rage. Especially within U.S. media culture, rage is typically coded negatively as an emotion that needs to be treated or healed and when expressed by a migrant, it is considered intolerable, offensive, and insulting. In order to prove adequate and acceptable, the migrant is required to occupy the place of a metaphorically "clean" subject—humble, disciplined, grateful, and thus only tenuously vocal and politically barely visible (see Marciniak 2006b). Against such complexities, she recalls students' affective responses while studying Courtney Hunt's 2008 border film, *Frozen River*, and reflects on the possibilities and limits of enacting "immigrant protest" and "immigrant rage" in the classroom. Her interest lies in rage as a political category of intervention, one that can influence students' sensibilities and open them up to new ways of thinking resistance to oppressive forms of phobic nationalisms and exclusionary practices of citizenship. The chapter weaves the analysis of anger performed by two central female characters in the film, a Mohawk Indian and "low-class" white American, both engaged in smuggling the migrants' bodies across the Canadian-U.S. border, with wider and highly contradictory manifestations of the politics of rage in the U.S. culture. Drawing upon theories of affect in relation to pedagogy, the analysis culminates in a meditation on the "pedagogy of rage" as a potent philosophical platform to teach from. It is a pedagogy that has the power to challenge students and teachers by creating spaces for provocative encounters; a pedagogy that "demands that we think about politicized anger in nuanced ways and recognize that the 'rage of the oppressed is never the same as the rage of the privileged'" (hooks 1995, 30).

Part II: In the Field: Acts of Immigrant Protest

The second section has a focus on activism and everyday protest, struggles over the legitimacy of migrant voices and experiences, rights to political subjecthood, and strategies of dissent. Organized around the theme "acts of protest," a concept developed from Engin F. Isin and Greg M. Nielsen's "acts of citizenship" (2008), it explores the diverse forms that protest takes and considers how even small acts of protest and resistance can grant marginal populations political voice and recognition.

Simon Faulkner's contribution, "On Israel/Palestine and the Politics of Visibility," explores the relationship between politics, aesthetics, and protest through a focus on the strategies of resistance employed by Palestinians and their activist allies in the occupied territories. While not formally "migrants," Faulkner highlights the ways in which Palestinians find themselves in the situation of extreme precariousness (for example, in terms of rights of residence and belonging) that characterizes the struggles of disenfranchised populations in the multiple border zones explored in this book. Palestinians in the occupied territories face the same conditions of "inclusive exclusion" as many migrant populations, in which subjugated people are subject to sovereign power whilst being excluded from the rights and protections of citizenship. The relationship between indigenous and migrant forms of struggles against sovereign and corporate forms of displacement and disenfranchisement is an important one—which complicates easy understandings of "illegality" (see also Tyler 2013).

In this chapter, Faulkner examines the ways in which the Israel/Palestine conflict is fundamentally bound up with ways of seeing and perceiving the subjugation of the Palestinian people both "within the geographical space of Israel/Palestine and the broader international context." Foregrounding the problematic of in/visibility, Faulkner introduces a series of nonviolent resistance projects all of which focus on *transforming the perceptual frames* through which the struggles of the Palestinian people to justice and the rights of self-determination are understood. To this end, he details the activism of the Israeli journalist Michel Warschawski—who founded the Alternative Information Center (AIC), a joint Palestinian-Israeli nongovernmental organization in 1984; the interventions made by Ramallah-based Palestinian art-activist Khaled Jarrar through his checkpoint photography and temporary "exhibitions" at border zones and the theatrical image-making border activism of the *Bil'in Committee of Popular Resistance* in the West Bank village of Bil'in (see also Bennett this volume). As Faulkner details, in the case of Bil'in, this is a population who have been engaged in several years of struggle against "the confiscation of their land for settlement construction and the building of a section of the West Bank Barrier." What is exemplary about the struggle in Bil'in is the ways in which resistance is forged through practices of "image making," which, both in the moment of the event and in the documentary afterlives of these protests, refuse the construction of Palestinians as either passive "victims" or as illegitimate subjects. Drawing throughout on Jacques Rancière's work, Faulkner assesses the limits of these forms of protest to effect political change on the ground, but concludes optimistically by arguing that "the demonstrations in Bil'in affirm . . . the fact that it is possible to create interventions into the occupation regime that problematize and disrupt the given order of things and generate new meanings and possibilities."

In "Everyday Acts of Resistance: The Precarious Lives of Asylum Seekers in Glasgow," Teresa Piacentini draws upon the seminal work of James C. Scott (1985, 1990) to develop an account of "migrant resistance" that focuses not on explicit public acts of protest but on the more subtle and banal forms of everyday resistance employed by disenfranchised and marginalized migrants on the ground. Drawing on rich empirical data from her ongoing ethnographic study of asylum seekers' support networks in Glasgow, Scotland, Piacentini examines how "chance encounters" and everyday informal interactions enable migrants to come together, forging friendships and thick networks of mutual support. These informal modes of care and assistance among migrant populations work against the "isolating effects of displacement and invisibility" but also, she argues, transform conditions of exclusion into positive forms of "cultural and social belonging." Over time, as she details, informal networks develop into more formal structures and groups with "aims, objectives, and constituted members." Through close analysis of these developing processes of mutual support, Piancetini argues that everyday acts of resistance, characterized by care, support, and commonality of experience, "chip away, in often imperceptible ways at prevailing power relations and *over time* can and do effect important social change."

In "Pushing the Boundaries: Everyday Resistance in Swedish Clandestinity," Maja Sager, like Piacentini, draws upon original ethnographic research to examine the ways in which asylum seekers in Sweden engage practices of everyday resistance in order to survive as rightless people in a foreign land. Sager's essay focuses on a population she terms "clandestine asylum seekers": those migrants who "stay in Sweden after their asylum applications have been rejected and who consequently 'hide' from the police and the authorities in order to avoid deportation." What Sager argues is that many clandestine asylum seekers in Sweden are not, as popular media depictions of "illegals" suggests, in "hiding," but are, on the contrary, "actively underground," employing multiple strategies of survival. As Sager details, undocumented migrants organize themselves as social and political actors employing both formal and informal methods and creating networks of family, friends, NGOs, and activists to access welfare services such as healthcare, education, and childcare. As in the case of Glasgow, what Sager discovers is that for these migrants their clandestinity can become a source of positive commonality and community formation. In other words, a status that seemingly marks this population as "abject outsiders" can become a source of positive counterpolitical identification and community formation on the ground.

In "Subjects that Matter? Nonidentitarian Strategies of Pro-'Migrant' and 'Migrant' Protest in Germany," Petra Rostock examines two pro-migrant organizations in Germany: the feminist group *FeMigra*, which is based in Frankfurt and Main, and *Kanak Attak*, which has networks across several West German cities. These organizations, both founded in the 1990s, contrast with many of the mainstream NGO migrant organizations in Germany in assuming an open-borders, antinational philosophy. In particular, both these groups reject an identitarian political framing, in which citizens are pitted against migrant illegality. As Rostock details, the common concern of these two organizations is "to make migrants visible as integral part of German history and present." To further this aim, both groups employ different strategies: *FeMigra* intervenes in the public sphere "through lectures and the distribution of publicity materials, targeting organizations and events focused on women and migrant politics and antiracist events and conferences," while *Kanak Attak* employs theoretical and artistic strategies that call for the granting of citizenship to all while, at the same time, undermining the essentialist notions of belonging on which German citizenship is grounded. As Rostock argues, both these organizations understand resistance in terms of the labor of politicizing processes of exclusion and inclusion from below—troubling "who may—or can—speak for whom when, where, and how." What is useful about Rostock's analysis is that as well as detailing how these two organizations antagonize and disrupt nationalist and racist discourses of citizenship and illegality, she exposes the limits of these activist interventions and the difficulties of achieving lasting solidarities between citizens and noncitizens.

In "Gender and the Politics of Antiracist and Immigrant Protest in Greece," Alexandra Zavos undertakes a close analysis of the materials and protest events of pro-migrant antiracist activists in Athens. Weaving together accounts of three protests, she details the ways in which Greek gender politics and pro-migrant politics collide. In particular, she examines how the parentalistic discourses of the Greek antiracist movements work to produce often problematic depictions of migrants as "feminized, subordinate, and dependent" subjects. Zavos focuses on the ways in which migrant women are "discursively invoked though stereotypical roles such as courageous mothers, dependent wives, or, exploited sex objects" and how migrant women both draw upon and resist these stereotypes as they attempt to intervene as political actors within migrant political struggles for rights and residency. Zavos argues for the need for Greek activists to create spaces for migrants within antiracist struggles for their own emancipation, highlighting the need for collations, such as those detailed by Rostock in Germany, in which migrants, and in particular migrant women, are able to be conceived as political actors in their own right.

In "Immigrant Protest and the Courts of Women," Marguerite Waller explores a paradigm of transnational human rights activism that originated in the Global South. The "Courts of Women," a project begun in the early 1990s, were created to circumvent statist logic and the ways it does and does not bring into visibility the manifold forms of violence against women for which there are no legal remedies on local, national, or international levels. Over a quarter of a century, this series of public hearings and the years of planning they entail, have been organized transnationally by networks of activists addressing interlocking issues of migration, property rights, HIV, trafficking, development, sustainability, and many others. The Courts were an outgrowth of the work of the Asian Women's Human Rights Council, and galvanized early on by its participation in the Tokyo Tribunals on the Japan's use of military sexual slaves or "comfort women" during World War II. Originally based in Bangalore and Manila, and directed by Corinne Kumar and Nelia Sancho, the model of the Courts of Women came to the Arab World and sub-Saharan Africa when Kumar, a lifelong women's and indigenous rights activist, became the secretary general of El Taller International in Tunis. Partnering with more than five hundred other organizations, including the World Social Forum, more than thirty-eight Courts of Women have been convened since 1992. Offering a detailed account of the work of the Courts, Waller argues that the practices and strategies they implement open spaces for thinking about immigrant protest that puts the violence of sovereignty and the logic of citizenship on trial. Notably, while initially located and coordinated in the Global South, the Courts of Women came to the United States in 2012, with a Court of Women on Poverty: Disappeared in America, held in Oakland, California. As a particular form of protest, the practices and choreography of the Courts illuminate the nature of the epistemological and empirical violence exercised against indigenous, migrant, and immigrant women as well as the ways in which different "Souths," including those in the North, can work together to claim political subjectivities despite their social marginality and cultural invisibility.

On February 25, 2012, at a concert at "The Coronet," a music venue in Elephant and Castle, South London, mostly attended by Latin Americans, a massive immigration raid took place which saw numerous police and immigration officers checking the papers and the migration status of those queuing to get into the venue: by the end of the evening, ninety people were detained in immigration removal centers, some of whom were deported a few days later. We have chosen to end *Immigrant Protest* with the work of the "Anti-Raids Campaign Coalition in London" which formed in direct response to this raid. The Anti-Raids Campaign is a network of community-based groups composed of migrants and precarious workers in response to immigration raids by the UK Border Agency and the police in London. The "Anti-Raids Campaign Coalition in London" focuses on developing materials, such as the bust card and solidarity leaflet included here, to enable migrants to know their rights if they are arrested and detained. The short text that accompanies these materials captures the conditions of urgency that often face migrant and art activists on the ground as they seek to intervene within often brutal immigration and border control regimes, and protect lovers, friends, and co-workers from detention and deportation.

Conclusion: No Border Scholarship for a Noborder Politics

While there has been much recent scholarship on the changing ideologies of citizenship, the growth of detention landscapes, and border securitization in various national contexts (see, e.g., *Beyond Walls and Cages, Acts of Citizenship, Rallying for Immigrant Rights, Taking Local Control: Immigration Policy Activism in U.S. Cities and States, Art in the Lives of Immigrant Communities in the United States*), not enough attention has yet been paid to the significant role of mass immigrant protests that have arisen in response to these enforcement measures in a transnational context. Even fewer authors consider the aesthetics and technologies of these burgeoning social movements and the artists so central to their successes. Moving across both sovereign and disciplinary borders, this collection offers a series of scholarly essays, interviews, art, and activist projects, which detail an array of mainstream and marginal artistic, cultural, and political engagements with migrant and indigenous protest and resistance movements against the exclusionary logics of border controls. The collective aim of the authors and artists in *Immigrant Protest* is to open up the question of what counts as protest and to explore the ways in which political activism, art, and popular culture can work to challenge the multiple forms of discrimination and injustice faced by displaced peoples. What ties this project together is a concern with forms of political aesthetics that seek to confront forms of "common sense" and "status quo" around migration. The book contests those forms of knowledge, politics, and representations which rely upon and continuously reproduce the idea of migration as a foundational problem.

Rancière argues that "nothing is political in itself," but anything may become political if it gives rise to a meeting of two logics, namely the logic of the state and the logic of equality (Rancière 1999, 32). In his account, the political is located not within the official workings of government or the hegemonic aesthetics of mass media, nor in the "event" of protests themselves, but rather in the "dissensus"—or the "third space"—such protests can open up in the public sphere. Rancière suggests that what matters is the *interruption* that "fearless speech" gives rise to and the disputes which unfold from them. Such disputes, Rancière suggests, can produce new inscriptions of equality "and a fresh sphere of visibility for further demonstrations" (ibid., 40). What we might understand by this is that "the possibilities of resistance to migrant abjection lie not in singular acts of resistance but in the building of wider communities of struggle that question the inclusive/exclusive logic of citizenship, the economics of illegality and the global marketization of migration" (Tyler 2013). The case studies explored in this book testify to the ways in which the "theatricalization of political rage" (Butler 232) can trouble prevailing forms of common sense about the meaning of democracy and rights. So, while local forms of migrant protests or the art projects that attempt to represent them might register as little more than minor disturbances within the public sphere, the restaging and repetition of these acts form part of a critical practice of countermapping, which creates a transnational fabric of political resistance.

Pondering the politics of immigration scholarship, Ruben Andersson writes: "To capture the paradoxes of today's migrations, which seem to pound against the walls of our reality, we might similarly need to break through the conventions that have defined so much research, activism, art and journalism concerned with migration" (Andersson 2008). He argues that it is necessary to focus on "the energy, creativity and determination of migrants themselves" as well as to engage in what he terms "stylistic and methodological promiscuity" in order to break through the limits of disciplinary research. Andersson's point about "stylistic and methodological promiscuity" most compellingly describes the spirit of our book. The energy of the collection is driven precisely by immigrant voices that actively resist mainstream representations of immigrants as bodies without emotional complexities, too often boxed into binaries such as "passive" or "criminal." The authors go beyond eschewing such superficialities and instead mock them, from artistic play with the veil to ironic representations of migrant labor, to outrageous performances of "good citizen" and "bad migrant." From the outset, our intention has been to create a project that, like Rodriguez's *Machete*, is an unapologetic fusion of styles that provoke with the breadth of disciplinary employment and depart from ways of creating knowledges that too often rely on one theoretical paradigm, discipline, or region. Through its form and content, the book argues for a noborder politics which has to be enacted through a noborder scholarship.

Noborder scholarship must push through the limits of disciplinary boundaries, must honor intellectual messiness, demand agility, fluidity, situationality; it must create new conceptual bridges. The building of such new bridges is always about methodological innovations and thus about methodological pleasures and risks. And noborder scholarship must embrace those risks. Bridges demand that we resist the temptation to think of knowledge in territorial ways. The productive risks associated with such methodological "promiscuity" entail dislodging the fields of study from their accepted boundaries and from the defenses of those boundaries.

An interdisciplinary and multiperspectival hybrid situated at the intersection of migration studies, transnational studies, and media studies, both stylistically and methodologically, this project enacts cross-pollination by opening up a dialogue between diverse discourses in the humanities and social sciences, tracking the relations between empirical, theoretical, and art activist practices. Through this interdisciplinary approach, *Immigrant Protest* develops a comparative, non-nationalistic approach to immigrant protest, foregrounding the importance of breaking the silence that often accompanies im/migrant experiences and, in doing so, offers counternarratives to anti-immigrant actions and politics in various geopolitical contexts where im/migrant struggle is predominant.

Works Cited

Andersson, Ruben. 2008. "Migrant Visions." ASA Globalog. http://blog.theasa.org/?cat=49. Accessed May 10, 2009.

Behdad, Ali. 2005. *A Forgetful Nation: On Immigration and Cultural Identity in the United States*. Durham: Duke University Press.

Butler, Judith. 1993. *Bodies That Matter: On the Discursive Limits of "Sex."* London, New York: Routledge.

Cissè, Madjiguène, 1997. "The Sans-Papiers: a Woman Draws the First Lessons." http://www.bok.net/pajol/madjiguene2.en.html. Accessed January 15, 2012.

Clover, Carol. 1993. *Men, Women, and Chain Saws*. Princeton: Princeton University Press.

Cottle, Simon. 2011. *Transnational Protests and the Media*. New York: Peter Lang.

De Genova, Nicholas, and Rozalinda Borcilă. 2011. "An Image of our Future: On the Making of Migrant 'Illegality.'" *AREA Chicago*. http://www.areachicago.org/p/issues/immigrations/image-our-future/. Accessed January 3, 2012.

DiMaggio, Paul, and Patricia Fernández-Kelly, eds. 2010. *Art in the Lives of Immigrant Communities in the United States*. New Brunswick: Rutgers University Press.

Ellis Island. 1997. History Channel Greystone Production. A & E Home Video, New York. Video Group.

Haas, de Hein. 2007. "The Myth of Invasion: Irregular Migration from West Africa to the Maghreb and the European Union." International Migration Institute. http://www.imi.ox.ac.uk/pdfs/Irregular%20migration%20from%20West%20Africa%20-%20Hein%20de%20Haas.pdf. Accessed February 17, 2012.

Hesford, Wendy, and Wendy Kozol, eds. 2005. *Just Advocacy? Women's Human Rights, Transnational Feminisms, and the Politics of Representation*. New Brunswick, Rutgers University Press.

Hollifield, James F. 2004. "The Emerging Migration State." *International Migration Review* 38 (3): 885–912.

hooks, bell. 1995. *Killing Rage: Ending Racism*. New York: Henry Holt.

Isin, Engin F., and Greg M. Nielsen, eds. 2008. *Acts of Citizenship*. London: Zed Books.

Loyd, Jenna M., Matt Mitchelson, and Andrew Burridge, eds. 2012. *Beyond Walls and Cages: Prisons, Borders, and Global Crisis*. Athens and London: University of Georgia Press.

Marciniak, Katarzyna. 2006a. *Alienhood: Citizenship, Exile, and the Logic of Difference*. Minneapolis: University of Minnesota Press.

———. 2006b. "Immigrant Rage: Alienhood, 'Hygienic' Identities, and the Second World." *Differences: A Journal of Feminist Cultural Studies* 17 (2): 330–63.

———. 2013. "Legal/Illegal: Protesting Citizenship in Fortress America." *Citizenship Studies* 17 (2): 260–77.

Marciniak, Katarzyna, and Kamil Turowski. 2010. *Streets of Crocodiles: Photography, Media, and Postsocialist Landscapes*. Bristol: Intellect.

Marks, Laura U. 2000. *The Skin of the Film: Intercultural Cinema, Embodiment, and the Senses*. Durham: Duke University Press.

McNevin, Anne. 2006. "Political Belonging in a Neoliberal Era: the Struggle of the Sans-Papiers." *Citizenship Studies* 10 (2): 135–51.

Mukherjee, Bharati. 1981. "Invisible Woman." *Saturday Night* (March): 36–40.

Nyers, Peter. 2007. "Introduction: Why Citizenship Studies?" *Citizenship Studies* 11 (1): 1–4.

Papadopoulos, Dimitri, and Vassilis S. Tsianos. 2008. "The Autonomy of Migration: the Animals of Undocumented Mobility." In *Deleuzian Encounters: Studies in*

Contemporary Social Issues, edited by Anna Hickey-Moody and Peta Malins. New York: Palgrave.

———. 2013. "After Citizenship: Autonomy of Migration, Organizational Ontology, and Mobile Commons." *Citizenship Studies* 17 (2): 178–96.

Rancière, Jacques. 1999. *Dis-agreement: Politics and Philosophy*. Translated by Julie Rose. Minneapolis: University of Minnesota Press.

———. 2003. *The Philosopher and His Poor*. Translated by John Drury, Corinne Oster, Andrew Parker. Durham: Duke University Press.

Rigby, Joe, and Raphael Schlembach. 2013. "Impossible Protest: Noborders in Calais." *Citizenship Studies* 17 (2): 157–72.

Rodriguez, Robert, dir. 2010. *Machete*. 20th Century Fox Entertainment.

Rony, Fatimah Tobing. 1996. *The Third Eye: Race, Cinema, and Ethnographic Spectacle*. Durham and London: Duke University Press.

Said, Edward. W. 1979. *Orientalism*. New York: Vintage Books.

———. 1980. "Islam through Western Eyes." http://www.thenation.com/article/islam-through-western-eyes#. Accessed July 18, 2012.

Scott, C. James. 1985. *Weapons of the Weak: Everyday Forms of Peasant Resistance*. New Haven: Yale University Press.

———. 1990. *Domination and the Arts of Resistance: Hidden Transcripts*. New Haven: Yale University Press.

Shohat, Ella, and Robert Stam. 1994. *Unthinking Eurocentrism: Multiculturalism and the Media*. New York: Routledge.

Spivak, Gayatri Chakravorty. 1985. "Can the Subaltern Speak?" In *Marxism and the Interpretation of Culture*, ed. Carry Nelson and Lawrence Grossberg. London: Macmillan.

Swyngedouw, Erik. 2005. "Governance Innovation and the Citizen: The Janus Face of Governance-beyond-the-state." *Urban Studies* 42 (11): 1991–2006.

Tyler, Imogen. 2006. "'Welcome to Britain': The Cultural Politics of Asylum." *European Journal of Cultural Studies* 9 (2): 185–202.

———. 2010. "Designed to Fail: a Biopolitics of British Citizenship." *Citizenship Studies* 14 (1): 61–74.

———. 2013. *Revolting Subjects: Social Abjection and Resistance in Neoliberal Britain*. London: Zed Books.

Varsanyi, Monica, ed. 2010. *Taking Local Control: Immigration Policy Activism in U.S. Cities and States*. Stanford: Stanford University Press.

Voss, Kim, and Irene Bloemraad, eds. 2011. *Rallying for Immigrant Rights: The Fight for Inclusion in 21st Century America*. Berkeley: University of California Press.

Welcome to Gringolandia, 2006. Courtesy of Xico Gonzalez and Center for the Study of Political Graphics

I

The Aesthetic Performance of Immigrant Protest

Figure 1.1. *Survival Mosque*, 2005. Courtesy of Azra Akšamija

I

Dare to Wear—a Mosque!

Immigrant Protest as Cross-Cultural Pedagogy

Azra Akšamija

When controversies erupt over plans to build new mosques in countries such as Austria, Germany, United Kingdom, Netherlands, Norway, Italy, Slovenia, or United States, it is revealing that the planning application is less provocative to public opinion, and more likely to be passed, as long as the proposed mosque does not look like one. The moral panic about the visibility of the mosque is at the forefront of ongoing debates over the visibility of Muslim immigrants in Western Europe and United States; the codes in which the issue is discussed reveal the persistence of xenophobic and Orientalist thinking in developed countries where the Muslim population is in minority. Conflicts around the building of mosques have led me, as an artist, to think about how Muslim diasporas in the "West" might protest creatively against the increasing anti-immigrant and anti-Islamic propaganda, of which the mosque debates are symptomatic, and about how art could inspire and re-empower the increasingly alienated Muslims, allowing them to exercise their rights to visibility in public spaces.

Over the past four years, these questions have inspired me to develop a series of art pieces that I collectively label "Wearable Mosques." A wearable mosque is a piece of clothing that can be fashioned into a minimal prayer space. It provides Muslim immigrants in Western Europe and United States with the capability to transform any place into a prayer space, turning the tables on the binary visibility/invisibility under which mosques have been discussed. At the same time, these projects provide Muslim immigrants with means to reclaim their democratic right to religious and cultural expression,

Figure 1.2. (Left) Switzerland's anti-Minaret campaign poster from 2009; (Right) anti-Islam poster by the British National Party

subverting the established stereotypes and, I hope, disarming the prejudices of the public.

The conceptual foundation of these pieces is the idea that protest art can serve as a cultural pedagogy facilitating transformative conflict mediation. Instead of the problem-solving approach to conflict mediation, which aims at resolving conflicts, its premise is to enable the conflicting parties to identify the most pressing issues, recognize each other's positions, and find tools for resolving their differences on their own. The "Wearable Mosques," in this context, provide an understanding of cultural conflicts as a potentially creative force, whose negative aspects can be transformed through the catalysis of art into factors leading toward a positive outcome.

Mosque ≠ Dome + Minaret

To begin with, "Wearable Mosques" undermine the fundamental premise of the mosque building controversy: the widely accepted idea that the mosque has a rigid Gestalt, as a specific building type recognizable on the basis of two main architectural features: the dome and the minaret. Historically

Figure 1.3. *Wearable Mosques*, 2005. Azra Akšamija

speaking, this assumption cannot be sustained, since, as a glance at Islamic history shows, the mosque has never been explicitly identified with a particular architectural structure.

The Arabic word *mesjid* translates into "the place to prostrate in front of God." Prayer is one of the "Five Pillars of Islam"; the devoted Muslim prays five times a day. But prayer can be performed anywhere, at home or in a dedicated space.[1] The Prophet Muhammad himself, according to a *Hadith* (narrations about the deeds and sayings of the Prophet) understood the entire world as a mosque, by which he meant that any space where prayer is performed would automatically become a "mosque" for the duration of that prayer.[2] If the believer prays in the desert, for example, he or she can perform the ritual ablution by using sand instead of water. No architectural framework is needed to sanctify the spot. In praying, the only important spatial aspect is the worshipper's orientation toward Mecca.[3]

Although a built structure is theoretically not necessary if a prayer is to be performed, mosques quickly became part of Islamic culture. The reason for the mosque's prominence has to do with its multifaceted functions as a space for the community, as a provider of diverse social services and education, and as a means of representation (of a community or a ruler). The first mosque, or the first prayer space for Muslims, was the house of the Prophet Mohammed in Medina. This house was presumably a very simple rectangular structure with a courtyard, which had a palm tree shading alone one side.[4] The early mosques built in the first Islamic cities took up the plan of this first mosque, changing its basic outline according to new needs of the community, different site conditions, and available resources.

Over the course of Islamic history, the mosque was adopted to highly diverse architectural forms and typologies that reflected different interpretations of the initial idea of the mosque, as well as the open-endedness of the prescribed prayer space as per the nature of Islamic spatial regulations. The wide variation in mosque types is also due to the geographical spread of Islam and the assimilation of different cultural influences and local architectural languages. Although particular elements and forms of the mosque are neither specified in the Quran nor in the *Hadith,* a range of functional and symbolic elements gradually established themselves in the Islamic community, which has in turn been shaped by the cultures of various powerful Islamic polities. Domes or minarets, for example, which are so much a part of Mediterranean and North African city life, have taken on a representative and identifying role for Muslim communities, particularly for immigrant communities.

Challenged by new cultural contexts, Muslim diasporic communities tend to fearfully hold on their cultural or religious traditions. Identity becomes a burden, subjecting diasporic Muslims to a process of an internal "cultural purification," to use political theorist Anthony Smith's phrase to describe a group's attempt to preserve its identity when challenged by other groups (Smith 1996, 448–49). Groups under challenge, as minority groups are in host countries, or countries are by imperial powers, often produce an identity culture in which community opinion creates spoken and unspoken norms defining what is original and distinctive in its own culture, religion, and history. It is against these norms that deviants from the group can be judged. We can trace, in the current impoverished vernacular of mosque architecture, the results of this "cultural purification": Muslim groups are as liable to fall prey to Orientalist imagery, taken as positive, as are anti-Muslim groups, who take the imagery as negative. Those who are familiar with the architecture of mosques in the United States and Europe may recall the frequent use of the easily recognizable stylistic signifiers such as Ottoman domes and the minarets, for example, as though the community were somehow religiously committed to one framework of mosque design. This, in spite of the fact that, as I pointed out above, from the point of view of the Koran and the Hadith, the mosque is never defined as requiring a certain architectural form.

Thus, on the one hand, Muslim immigrants press for the inclusion of these architectural symbols, understanding them as essential markers of their religious and cultural backgrounds, while "mosque opponents," on the other hand, are just as adamant about rejecting these symbols of what they fear is the "Islamization" of host countries, arguing that domes and minarets do not fit into the local traditions or the landscape of their respective cities.

Common to both sides is a reductive understanding of the mosque as a building defined by a dome and a minaret. This understanding goes against the early, more fluid conceptual definition of the mosque, contradicting the mosque's multifaceted formal possibilities as they are known from history. The tremendous diversity of mosques worldwide, as they have developed in different social, cultural, and political contexts since the late seventh century, are witnesses to the latent richness of Islam's religious architectural vocabulary. Instead of transplanting a mosque design that is the standardized product of one branch of architectural tradition, the diasporic mosque could represent a resource for development of new ideas for mosque designs at present that better meet the needs of the community.

Given that both xenophobia and "cultural purification" have fastened on architecture and clothing to engage in symbolic battle, these two forms of representation became the central media of my projects. Wearable Mosques, in this context, question the territoriality and formal rigidity of the contemporary mosque architecture, both of which may reflect religious and/or cultural inflexibility of an immigrant community. My projects favor a more fluid spatial concept and more formal diversity, and engage with the other routes of Islamic religious design as it evolved in many cultures through history.

For example, the *Nomadic Mosque* is a female suit that takes seriously the early Islamic idea that any secular space can be transformed into a religious one through prayer. The suit reveals the ephemeral nature of the mosque, which—unlike the church, which is an institutionally sanctified place—is sanctified via the performance of the religious ritual. This performativity is referenced by the suit, which is simultaneously worn as clothing and embodies the mosque.

Because they can be worn for different functions—both as everyday clothes or places of worship—wearable mosques point to the multifaceted functions of the mosque beyond providing a space for prayer. Taking this idea as my motif, I aimed to challenge the Orientalist roots of the perception that mosques are exclusively used for Islamic worship, and as such, exclusively useable by Muslims.

The inspiration for this component of the project draws from the real religious practice of Muslim immigrants in the United States and Western Europe, whose mosques do not only serve as prayer spaces, but also centers for community's various social and educational needs. Large mosques mainly serve educational and representational purposes, while the social needs of Muslim immigrants are facilitated mainly by smaller mosques.

Regardless of the size, immigrants' mosques are supposed to bind Muslims together and strengthen their interconnections. As embodiments of social practices, they play an important role in defining a community's

Figure 1.4. *Nomadic Mosque*, 2005. Azra Akšamija

internal identity. At the same time, they also reflect a community's relationship to its non-Muslim context and represent its cultural and ethnic origins (Grabar 1973, 106). Mosques located in larger facilities such as airports or universities provide the smallest prayer spaces and the best proof of the elasticity of the mosque concept in Europe and America, where they are a part of a larger non-Muslim milieu. As such, these spaces seem to encourage spontaneous contacts between local Muslims, international Muslims and non-Muslims. Although their constantly changing worshippers' structure may present an obstacle to long-term community, it also provides a space for meeting and interaction of very diverse people.

All of these contemporary phenomena, including the reuse of major sport facilities to accommodate the Friday prayer or other larger religious gatherings, for instance, point to the programmatic flexibility of the mosque and its capacity to host both secular and religious functions. These contemporary phenomena echo the first centuries of Islamic practice, when the mosque was not yet limited to the religious or representational functions. A mosque served as a community meeting place where administrative and political announcements were made, assimilating the classical agora or forum as the main gathering center in the city. Mosques and mosque complexes also fulfilled various other social functions. They often doubled as hospitals, courtrooms, treasuries, council chambers, sanctuaries, soup kitchens, and even prisons. In some mosques, books were commonly "published" by being recited out loud (Grabar 1973, 58).

It is only with the advent of the modern state that the welfare function of the mosque was partially taken care of by specialized institutions, and that the mosque space became increasingly identified with religious functions (Grabar 1973, 59). Still, the mosque is not a "sacred space" in the Christian sense of the concept—the idea of a consecrated sacred space does not really have a corresponding spatial concept in the Islam context. The closest equivalent to "sacred space" in Islam revolves around the notion of purity—cleanliness and segregation—which distinguish the mosque from other places. The perception that a mosque is a sacred space in which only Muslims are allowed to enter contradicts the very notion of a mosque as a space where prayer is performed, but also where other secular activities, such as reading, learning, lecturing, discussing, playing, laughing, and even sleeping, can take place.

For example, during the Islamic parade in New York City, when people pray out on the street, the act of prayer gives the street a new meaning: for the duration of prayer, this space is transformed into a mosque (Grabar 1973, 205). What distinguishes the space of the mosque from the rest of the street is the volume of human bodies and direction of prayer: the mosque is minimally defined by the worshiper's orientation toward Mecca and the amount of space a person occupies when performing a prayer.

It is exactly this elasticity of symbolic space that represents an important affordance for my wearable mosque projects. While it can accommodate the ritual prayer of at least two worshippers, the wearable mosque functions as a tool for communication on different levels. First, it provides for a spiritual communication of worshippers with God at any place. Second, unfolding and closing up the dresses fosters the mutual interaction of worshippers, thereby instantiating one of the most important functions of the mosque—the making of a community. Finally, the design of the wearable mosque expresses the multilayered identities of the person wearing it and reflects the cultural context in which they are worn. As "personal facades," the wearable mosques represent the specific experiences and needs of Muslim immigrants living in different geographical, cultural, and political contexts.

Figure 1.5. *Dirndlmoschee*, 2005. Azra Akšamija

Islam Is Not a Monolithic Structure

The wearable mosque project evolved from my conceptual understanding of the mosque as an ephemeral space, which can switch programmatically from a secular to religious functions. The stylistic and programmatic transformations of the minimal mosque are thereby anticipated as an inner quality of its spatial system, which can change depending on the context and time.

Each wearable mosque piece is based on a site- and person-specific prototype design, which emerges from the discussions I have had about its conceptualization with different people in different places. These discussions are aimed at creating a critical engagement that relates to both Muslims and non-Muslims, inasmuch as the former should be incited to a more active sense of the meaning and responsibilities entailed by their visibility and integration in the West. At the same time, the varied interpretations and changing meanings of these pieces, including the very fact that they exist, should raise awareness about the diversity of Islamic cultures in the West and increase an understanding of the social dynamics between Muslims and non-Muslims.

This emphasis on the representation of individual—rather than collective—identity is particularly important to the work, since the project aims to undermine the common assumption that "Islam," the "Middle East," or the "West" are monolithic entities. It is thus crucial to find ways to present the cultural diversity of Muslim communities across the world, as they instantiate religious belief in a wide spectrum of different geographical and cultural contexts, which, in turn, creates a variety of religious and social practices. The different wearable mosque pieces point to the tremendous variety of Islamic identities, emphasizing the fact that people who associate themselves with Islam may have diametrically opposite worldviews.

Following this idea, the Wearable Mosques aim to disarm the argument that mosques represent the alien Other to western European and/or American culture. For example, the project *Dirndlmoschee* (*Dirndl-Dress-Mosque*, 2005) explores the possibilities of cultural enrichment that result through interaction between cultures and their provisional moments of mergers. The work functions as a hybrid device that connects the local Austrian traditions and the Turkish immigrant culture in the small town of Strobl/Wolfgangsee, Austria. The piece is inspired by the nomadic principle of transposing qualitative characteristics of an alien place into one's own familiar context to the point that the familiar changes, effecting a moment of cultural enrichment.

The design of the garment is based on a traditional Austrian dress made of locally found materials and souvenirs, and the apron can unfold into a prayer rug large enough for three worshippers. In the mosque configuration, the traditional shoulder scarf opens up into a veil. The silk decoration at the

Figure 1.6. *Dirndlmoschee* (video stills), 2005. Azra Akšamija

scarf edge playfully references a person's hair, which is actually hidden by the veil. The belt carries a compass with a carabiner attached, from which prayer beads are strung. The prayer beads are decorated with little multi-tool Swiss Army knives, locally sold mementos from which the crosses were not removed, but re-symbolized as a decoration.

In a conversation with an Austrian journalist, the use of these little multi-tool Swiss Army knives that I attached to the prayer beads was

Figure 1.7. *Dirndlmoscheee* (details), 2005. Azra Akšamija

described as threatening, despite the fact that these 3 cm (ca.1 in.) long knives are not functional as any sort of tool or cutting device. The journalist's interpretation was diametrically opposed to my reasons for including the knives, which was to provide a reference to the location in which the dress was made by decorating it with local souvenirs. In this sense, the work functions as a mirror of interpretations, a mirror that reflects how people's fears are shaped by the predominant political discussions in different places.

Muslim Does Not Mean Terrorist

Reacting to the insults and physical violence against Muslims in the United States that followed the tragic events of September 11, I designed the *Survival Mosque* (2005) and *Nomadic Mosque* (2005).

Survival Mosque (2005) addresses specific problems of Muslims living in the contemporary United States. Informed by problems many Muslim communities have been facing after September 11, as well as the flag-burkas developed during protests in France, the design of the *Survival Mosque* is intended as protective infrastructure.

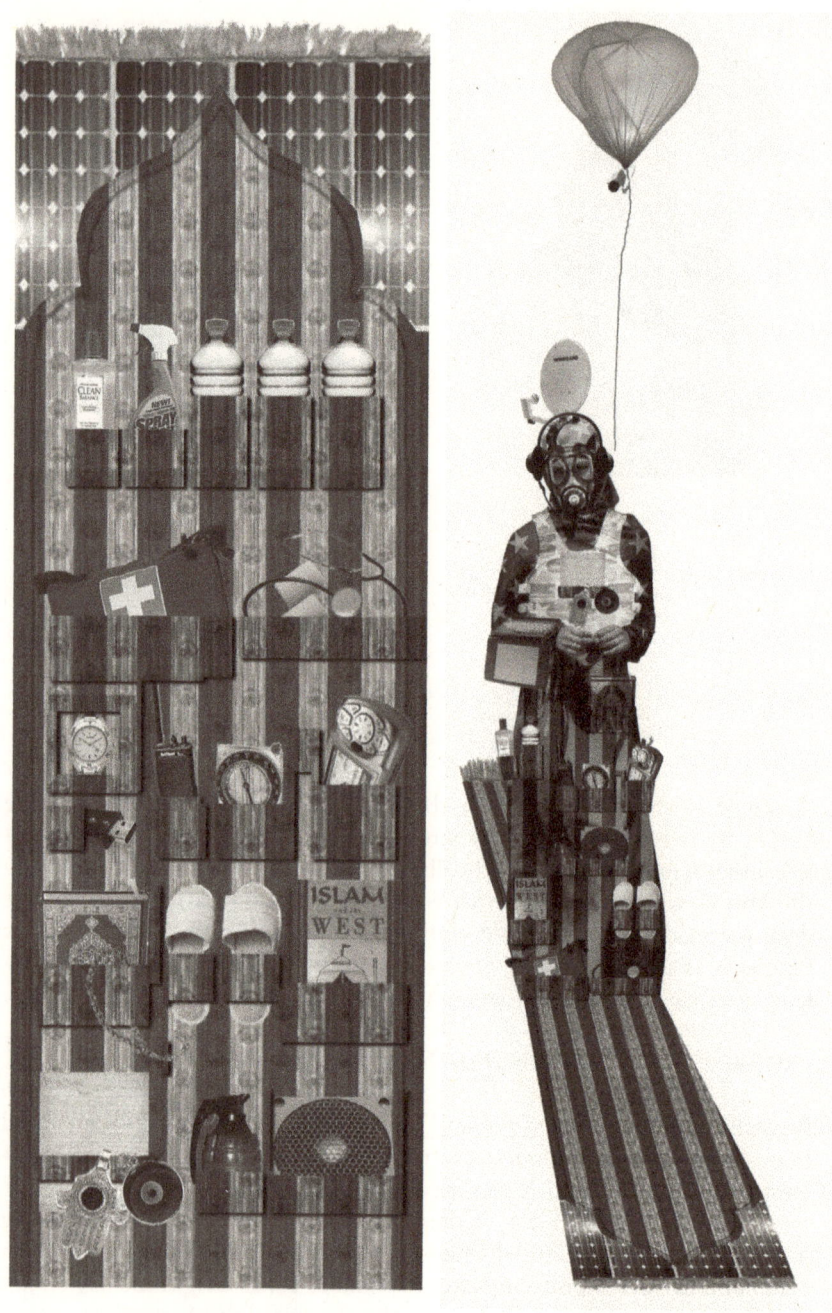

Figure 1.8. *Survival Mosque*, 2005. Azra Akšamija

Dare to Wear—a Mosque! 37

Figure 1.9. *Survival Mosque* (bag constellation), 2005. Azra Akšamija.

The survival kit contains elements for self-protection such as the American flag as a "façade" that communicates patriotism, a gas mask, nose filters, and an umbrella that protects one's back. The *Survival Mosque* is self-sufficient; the prayer rug is supplied with photovoltaic solar cells to produce its own energy. Inspired by Krzysztof Wodiczko's "alien devices" in his series *Xenology: Immigrant Instruments* (1992) (see Léger 2011), the *Survival Mosque* also carries different liturgical and practical features that can be useful to immigrants in their new, often challenging environments: a washing solution for ablution and for cleaning for occasions when the Muslim worshipper is spit on, ear plugs against insults, and an American Constitution for proof of the right of American Muslims to religious liberty, multireligious amulets, a loudspeaker with speech on tolerance held by President George W. Bush, ablution slippers, Quran, educative books, and diverse communication devices.

The *Survival Mosque* can be transformed into bags that camouflage its nature; the bags communicate with each other via Bluetooth technology. The bag-speakers reflect paranoia spreading messages, but they can also function as muezzins, calling for prayer at particular prayer times.

The Veil Does Not Equal Oppression

The increasing alienation of Muslims provoked by the terrorist attacks of September 11 particularly affected easily recognizable veiled women, whose veiling practices were considered a public provocation.

Adding to this problem, the veil itself is now "dramatically overburdened with competing symbolism," as cultural scientist Reina Lewis argues,

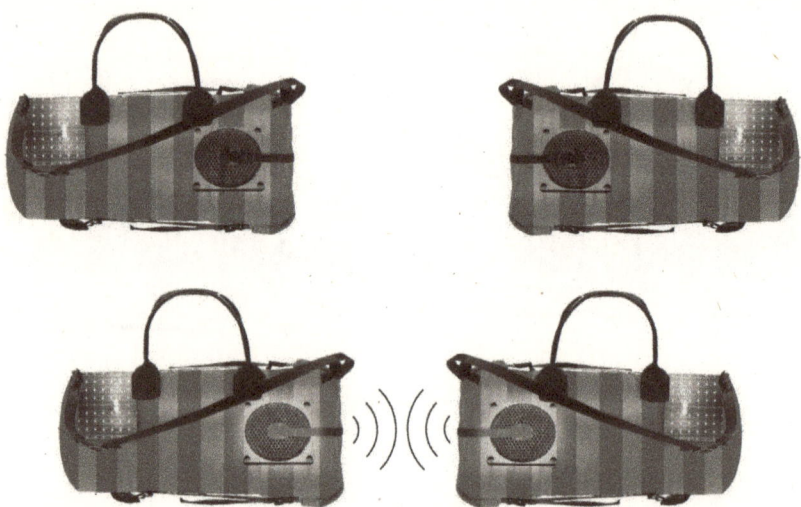

Figure 1.10. *Survival Mosque* (bag constellation), 2005. Azra Akšamija

assuming "new significance in the context of the world wide debate of multiculturalism" (Lewis 2003, 8). Indeed, over the course of the past twenty years, the veil (or the *hijab*) increasingly became one of the central vehicles to discuss the degree of immigrants' integration in the dominant society. Given this context, the veil can no longer be understood as a mere component of Muslim clothing. As a symbolically charged carrier of different meanings, it has become a reminder, as Lewis writes, of "Europe's constant struggle to come to terms with cultural diversity and social inclusion" (ibid.).

The wearable mosques tackle the question of gender in Islam and the stereotypes related to the veiling of women. Notwithstanding the fact that subjection of women exists in Islamic societies as well as all others, an understanding of the veil (*hijab*) as a form of oppression represents a simplistic way of looking at the position of Muslim women. It also represents a one-sided approach to the feminist politics.

While the questions about Muslim women's rights are important to be raised today, these questions need to include more complexity. Rather than focusing only on the veil, the debate about the situation of the Muslim woman in European or American society could be concerned with other important issues, such as the discrimination against Muslim women at work or legislative regulations of inequality in Muslim family laws.

Figure 1.11. *Mirror*, 2005. Azra Akšamija

While female employment in Islamic countries has been dramatically increasing in recent years, the notion of veiling still poses obstacles to the employment of Muslim women in the West. In her book *American Muslims: The New Generation*, Asma Gull Hasan argues that she would be very careful about wearing the *hijab* other than for prayer, considering the disadvantages this would cause, especially in view of the problematic treatment of veiled women by non-Muslims (Hasan 2000, 38). According to Hasan, Muslim women in America often face discrimination both in and outside their work. In response to such insulting and discriminatory situations, they tend to either compromise their veiling practice, covering themselves only for Islamic functions, or they become marginalized (ibid., 39).

The critique of veiling often involves the paradox of oppressive mechanisms that are ostensibly intended to oppose oppression. This insight allows us to understand additional dimensions of the veiling controversy, linking it to social rather than religious behavior. A dress code that is prescribed by a religious practice involves, on the one hand, the internally generated meaning ascribed to the clothes, and on the other hand, the signalization of social difference, which can effect social and spatial exclusion. In "Outsiders in Society and Space," David Sibley positions the notion of social or cultural difference in relation to the organization of space. Sibley connects the classification of space to the rejection of social groups who do not conform to some particular majoritarian standard or group. Consequentially, social segregation is intimately linked to the spatial exclusion, which reproduces social differences and encourages further spatial exclusions.[5] The post–September 11 marginalization of Muslim women in the United States represents a very convincing demonstration of this thesis.

Muslims often take the position, within the veiling debate, that the *hijab* is an extension of the Prophetic tradition of protecting women, or even as a statement against seeing women as sexual objects. Although I agree that *hijab* can to some degree condition women's empowerment—for example, if we think of acceptance and respect young Muslim women are able to gain with a *hijab* within their communities—I find the argument of being judged for "what one is rather than for what one wears" not applicable in regard to the Islamic dress code: a Muslim woman will face a dress code discussion regardless of whether she wears or does not wear the *hijab*. As argued by Kecia Ali, "Stereotypes of Muslim women as uniquely oppressed bear little resemblance to reality" (Ali 2002, 91). In both cases, she will find herself pressed to explain her personal position in regard to veiling within her Muslim and non-Muslim environment.

Nevertheless, wearing *hijab* in the West signals that the wearer has a "special status" as a Muslim woman; furthermore, this is one of the strong determinants that shape her interaction with her social and religious context.

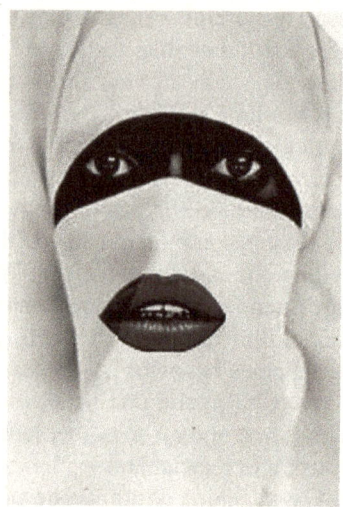

Figure 1.12. *Speak*, 2005. Azra Akšamija

Within the community, it reflects a Muslim woman's religious identification with Islam. Depending on the manner of veiling, *hijab* can communicate a belonging to a particular cultural and ethnic community, it can signal belonging to different Islamic sects or represents class status. Such factors as the degree of visibility and the way of covering one's body can function as an evaluative device for Muslims to judge each other's religiosity. This will certain play a role in the wearer's self-evaluation of the *hijab*. It may mark the wearer's fervor, or it may mark her position within her Muslim community (Ali 2002, 92–93).

On the other hand, *hijab* carries a message to the non-Muslim community. This is a message of identity with the Muslim community as against the influences of a purportedly secular dominant culture. Regardless of this meaning, the right to veil as a personal choice is a basic right in the Western legal framework, and especially in the United States, which was one of the first nations to embed that right in its founding documents—the Constitution itself.

The Wearable Mosques provide a tool for Muslim women to fearlessly assert their constitutional rights to religious expression. By wearing a *Nomadic Mosque*, a Muslim woman can both reveal her religious identity and, if necessary, camouflage it. The suit can also represent a person's cultural background, social status, and professional affiliation. As such, it can express a Muslim woman's versatile identities, beyond the religious one. The design of this wearable mosque also integrates cultural elements of the dominant

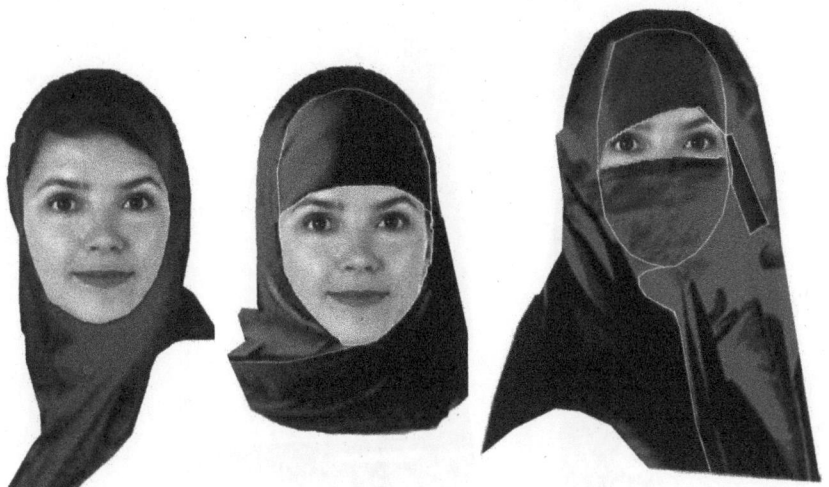

Figure 1.13. *Convertible Veil*, 2005. Azra Akšamija

American society, and thus opens up novel possibilities for a spatial negotiation between traditional and modern Islamic societies.

The Wearable Mosques are intended to exhibit and negotiate the tension between the purported secular and rights-based framework of Western society and the place of Islam within it. They allow for creative engagement of Islamic religious and social practices with emphasis on pluralism and acceptance of difference (Udel-Lambert, 100). These projects shape an interactive space though which immigrants and hosts could learn to coexist by, for one thing, discarding stereotypical views of Islamic piety. When learning from each other though Wearable Mosque, a fertile social milieu can be created that will not only make the "commitment to being a Muslim" more comfortable, but it may contribute to a communal effort to adapting the Islamic traditions to the contemporary environments in Western Europe and the United States.

The *Wearable Mosque* infuses an understanding of Islam as a non-static, non-monolithic religion into an architectural expression of Islamic religious practice. Addressing the new young Islamic community, the Wearable Mosque is meant to be both a pro-vocative claim to democratic rights and an immigrant protest against prejudice. However, the success of this protest to induce a productive dialogue among cultures is dependent on the process of wearing, which can only happen if Muslims themselves shake off a fixation on contingent forms of piety to recognize the basic ideological

Figure 1.14. *Nomadic Mosque*, 2005. Azra Akšamija

elasticity of Islamic traditions, which not only allow, but also call for their own change and development.

Notes

This text represents an expanded version of my article "Echo of Islam in the West: Reactions to the Wearable Mosque," first published in *ArteEast Online*, ed. Diana Allan, March 1, 2009. http://www.arteeast.org/pages/artenews/art-engagement/205/.

1. The other four pillars are: almsgiving, fasting, pilgrimage to Mecca, and remembrance of God.

2. Prayer can be performed anywhere except for spiritually impure places such as toilets or cemeteries.

3. The notion of orientation is also elastic in this case. If the exact direction to Mecca is unknown, the prayer can still be performed in any direction. It becomes more a matter of intention of a direction.

4. The first purposefully built mosque was modeled after the house of the Prophet; it was erected in 638 in what is today the city of Kufa in Iraq. See Irwin 1997, 58.

5. Sibley also examines how cultural difference is then often mediated through stereotypes that are used to construct the otherness by setting parameters of judgment for normality. In this context, social difference and further social exclusion that result out of this construction are strongly linked with the role of media in producing stereotypes.

Works Cited

Ali, Kecia. 2002. "Rethinking Women's Issues in Muslim Communities." In *Taking Back Islam*, edited by Michael Wolfe. Emmaus, PA: Rodale.

Grabar, Oleg. 1973. "Islamic Religious Art." In *The Formation of Islamic Art*. New Haven and London: Yale University Press.

Hasan, Asma Gull. 2000. *American Muslims: The New Generation*. New York and London: Continuum.

Irwin, Robert. 1997. *Islamic Art in Context: Art, Architecture, and the Literary World*. New York: Abrams Perspectives.

Léger, Marc James. 2011. "Xenology and Identity: Krzysztof Wodiczko's Immigrant Instruments." http://legermj.typepad.com/blog/2011/10/xenology-and-identity-krzysztof-wodiczkos-immigrant-instruments.html. Accessed June 6, 2012.

Lewis, Reina. 2003. "Preface." In *Veil: Veiling, Representation, and Contemporary Art*. London: Institute of International Visual Arts.

Sibley, David. 1992. "Outsiders in Society and Space." In *Inventing Places: Studies in Cultural Geography*, edited by Kay Anderson and Fay Gale. Melbourne: Longman.

Smith, Anthony D. 1996. "Culture, Community and Territory: The Politics of Ethnicity and Nationalism." *International Affairs* 72 (3): 445–58.

Udel-Lambert, Miriam. 2002. "Born in the U.S.A." In *Taking Back Islam*, edited by Michael Wolfe. Emmaus, PA: Rodale.

Figure 2.1. *We are not alien, we are awesome*, 2011. Developed collaboratively during sign-making event, written by ten-year-old Josue Herrera. Image by Sarah Jane Rhee

2

The Political Aesthetics of Immigrant Protest

Rozalinda Borcilă with Katarzyna Marciniak and Imogen Tyler

> 1994. I am at the U.S.-Canadian border, attempting to travel with only a Romanian passport and no visa. I have been in the U.S. for a year, and am acutely aware of being visibly marked as other. My body betrays itself almost immediately: I was asked to give evidence of my identity with a passport and was quickly denied passage. A few years later, I have rehearsed the American body, its costume, accent, license. In order to *pass through*, I must *pass for*. It becomes necessary to be re-marked, to court disappearance, invisibility—and to strategically consider crossing recognition thresholds. The border agent assumes I am American, and asks only for a driver's license. The test is complete in this moment of strategic mis-recognition. I re-enact this and other tests repeatedly, compulsively, to the dismay of my friends, for whom the license of the white American body is naturalised.
>
> —Rozalinda Borcilă, "Tracking Down, or What to Do With a Disturbing Body"

The border-crossing experiment described here was part of a series of performances titled "Tracking Down, or What to Do With a Disturbing Body," undertaken by Rozalinda Borcilă, a Romanian-born, U.S.-based art activist during 2001–02. As she describes it, this particular performance was a staging of "passing for" an American: a migrant masquerading as a citizen and a test of the legal/illegal binary. "Passing through" the border was enabled by Borcilă's mastering of the grammar of the "white American body." This "passing" was aided by the misrecognition of Borcilă's ethnicity—her Eastern European whiteness was read by the border guards as a generic whiteness. Borcilă writes on this project that "to explore the production of the American national subject, it is necessary to theorize it *through* the body of the foreigner" (Borcilă 2002).

Over a decade, Borcilă has had dozens of solo exhibitions and is amassing a growing body of written, video, installation, and performance work. "Tracking Down, or What to Do With a Disturbing Body" (2001–02) reveals Borcilă's critical concern with the relationship between power and aesthetics, violence and categorization. She explores the questions of who gets to be seen and heard and, in particular, the question of who has *border mobility*. In many such performances, she has utilized her own body in what she terms "violent acrobatics." As she notes:

> I deploy these strategies in the gallery and also in what are often called private performances, what I term simply every day experiments. I have begun the process of applying for US residency, placing myself in the contexts that most strongly situate me as other. At the same time, by eliminating all recognizable markers of an other/foreign identity (mode of dress, accent, etc), I have been experimenting with "passing as a citizen." In these experiments, I again deliberately place myself in contexts where the citizen-foreigner line is clearly drawn, but this time produce myself in such a way as to be mis-recognized. I have engaged in illegal border crossings, unauthorized employment and other activities, not by claiming to be a citizen, but by allowing others to mis-recognize me as one. (Borcilă 2001)

Much of Borcilă's art practice responds to the racialized politics of migrant "illegality," which became entrenched within the United States and Europe in the 1990s. As Alessandro De Giorgi argues, this was the decade in which migration was systematically "*produced* as a 'problem': as an invasive and incorrigibly 'foreign' menace to national sovereignty, as a racialized contagion that undermines the presumed national 'culture,' as a recalcitrant 'criminal' affront to national security" (De Giorgi 2010, 163). In the United States, the emergence of a new grammar of migrant illegality nurtured an escalating anti-immigrant hostility which was concretized through punitive immigration and citizenship laws, and the development of a massive for-profit global immigration detention estate. In engaging with this political culture, Borcilă sets out to map and subvert the landscape and grammar of migrant/citizen visibility. For example, in a series of performances and photographs titled *This is a Test* (2001–03), she performed the roles of a gymnast and the mail-order bride, utilizing Western tropes of Romanian border-crossing subjectivities. She writes about her work on alienhood and citizenship:

> My sources come from sites in which I find the relationship of citizen and foreigner is articulated most clearly and most explicitly: immigration law, travel guides, military technology, TV coverage of American military operations and Olympic TV coverage. In these sites, the citizen/American national subject is produced around a certain way of watching the other. This always presupposes a way of accessing, recognizing and naming the other, all of which are acts of privilege and power. My strategies have been to experiment with this process of recognition, the process of identification as a performative act—taking on not only the identity of the foreigner, but also of the citizen. (Borcilă 2001)

Borcilă's current counter-cartographical work "Riding the Zone" (Borcilă 2012) develops this earlier work through a focus on unmapped zones and places of exception, including Foreign Trade Zones and U.S. military installations. In this work, she draws attention to the ways in which the military-industrial complex is not a secret ideology or technology, but is "hidden in plain sight." The problem for the artist is how to depict or document what we already in effect "know" through processes of estrangement, the creation of sensory fabrics, which pierce the prevailing regimes of perception. In this vein, Borcilă calls for forms of disruption and the generation of "social conflict" as a response to everyday modalities of illegality. She rather beautifully describes this *aesthetics of conflict* in the following way:

> transgression or trespass—considered not for their value as individual acts, but for the potential of their accumulation. The dynamic buildup of infinitely small disturbances changes structure into movement, being into becoming, a thing into a current. As this dynamic develops and builds, representation moves, strains against its surface, swells and eventually breaks. (Borcilă 2005)

Theoretically speaking, Borcilă's work is reminiscent of Jacques Rancière's writing on political aesthetics, which describes "the role of art or the practice of art [as] a transformation of a certain state of relations between words and things, between words and the visible, a certain organization of the senses and the sensory configuration of what is given to us and how we can make sense of it" (Rancière 2008, 174). Aesthetics in these terms is concerned not with "beauty" or with the marketization of art objects as objects of value and exchange, but conversely with art as forms of potentially disruptive forms of practice that trouble and disturb prevailing regimes of perception. Political aesthetics is concerned with questions of in/equality and is what we might understand as declassificatory practices, which refuse or attempt to undo given forms of "knowing" and "perceiving" (see Tyler 2013). Indeed, Rancière argues that "nothing is political in itself," but anything may become political if it gives rise to a meeting of two logics, namely the logic of the state and the logic of equality (Rancière 2008, 32).

In Rancière's account, the political is located not within the official workings of government or the hegemonic aesthetics of mass media, nor in the "event" of protests but rather in the "dissensus"—or the third space—such protests can open up in the public sphere. Rancière suggests that what matters is the *interruption* which "fearless speech" gives rise to, and the disputes that unfold from fighting words. Such disputes, Rancière claims, can produce new inscriptions of equality "and a fresh sphere of visibility for further demonstrations" (Rancière 2008, 40). In this context we might understand that the possibilities of resistance to migrant abjection lie not in singular acts of resistance but in the building of wider communities of struggle that question the inclusive/exclusive logic of citizenship, the economics of illegality, and the global marketization of migration.

Borcilă's recent work has concentrated on local activism and the forms of "social conflict" it engenders. During 2010 and 2011 she has been developing collective art-activist and education projects in Chicago in collaboration with AREA (Art, Research, Education, Activism). Founded in 2005, AREA Chicago has developed as a community newspaper and Web publishing platform, a series of events and a distributed research/learning project. AREA is focused on supporting and connecting Chicago-based autonomous or self-organized practices directed at building a more socially just city. Through her work with AREA and other autonomous collectives such as Mess Hall and Compass, Borcilă has been seeking to develop her longstanding interest in collaborative practice, exploring shared capacities for radical imagination and action through art and pedagogy. She also works within migrant justice groups, exploring the possibility for "interventionist tactics" to disrupt "the privileged spaces of neoliberal globalization—the smooth spaces where social conflict is rendered invisible" (Borcilă 2010). The focus of much of this recent work has been "illegality," and "deportability," and it includes the editing of an issue of AREA's magazine titled: *Im/migrations: a local reader about how borders are made, experienced and challenged through human movement (or this whole illegals thing is bullshit)*.

In what follows, Borcilă, Katarzyna Marciniak, and Imogen Tyler discuss her past and current work, the relationship between art and activism, and the possibilities and limits of collective practice and the aesthetics of immigrant protest.

Katarzyna Marciniak and Imogen Tyler: Before we speak about your current projects, let's return to your earlier work in order to offer the readers a better context for your artistic practice. In two thousand eight when we first spoke, you offered me [KM] your materials, which I used for my graduate seminar on *Transnational Aesthetics and Politics*. I thus first experienced your work in a pedagogical setting. In this course, students analyzed theory, cinema, and performance art to probe the contemporary terrain of transnational productions focusing on complexities of immigration, foreignness, alterity, and legitimacy in different national contexts. The artist whose work was initially most inspirational for the class was Guillermo Gómez-Peña and his bold experiments with "reverse anthropology" and "Chicano cyber-punk art" [Gómez-Peña 2005, 10]. So he was my students' favorite until they saw and read your work and immediately started making connections between his and your performance pieces. They thought you were an Eastern European female Gómez-Peña! In fact, you use his writing in your projects—can you tell us about his influence on your practice? Simultaneously, I want to complicate this question by telling you that while my students claimed they "understood" his Latino "rage" (even though the majority of them were white Americans) as a conceptual basis for his border aesthetic, they were surprised to experience your immigrant rage in relation to border experiments. Was it because your art—involving East European female body—felt more "alien" to them than perhaps a more familiar Latino or Chicano art? Was it perhaps because they are not used to thinking about immigrant resistance in relation to East European identities in the U.S.?

Rozalinda Borcilă: Peña's work, in its totality, was incredibly inspirational to me. However, I referred to his work primarily because I understood it to dominate a certain arena of performance and writing in relation to the space of the border and the body of the migrant. He, not just his work, but his persona, his presence, his image, became a compulsory reference for anyone whose work dealt with the politics of identification and with normative understandings of the body and of citizenship in dominant U.S. culture. I felt I needed to acknowledge this directly. It raised a series of important questions about racialization in relation to migrant illegality, and challenged me to be explicit about working through a body considered to be "white on arrival." At the same time, there is a political economy to migration—and its illegalization—that I feel is important to at least gesture towards, if not explore and theorize through artistic means. I was specifically working with feminized migration as neoliberal capital expands globally post nineteen eighty-nine—therefore the repeated uses of the gymnast, the mail order bride, the interest in the domestic(ated) body as a site of consumption. I was also considering the role of visibility—and of lines of sight, of the politics of appearance and dis-appearance—in policing/ marketizing the migrant female body, and in the transgressive acts of migrants who collectively produce global spaces that resist visibility. My whiteness is a process that unfolds through specific historical conditions. It is part of a series of complex equations that has to do with stratification in relation to reproduction and power relations. At the same time, the increasing "emancipation" of middle-class Western white women, produces (or is predicated upon) the emergence of a global underclass of migrant domestic servants and other reproductive laborers, the most marketable of whom can also be racialized as "white." In other words, Eastern European migrant women become highly marketable in the global circuits of exploited reproductive labor—from sex work to childcare—as long as they could "pass as white." In the nineteenth century, eugenics played a significant role in the emancipation of middle-class white women in the U.S., whose potential to produce middle-class white babies became a strategic, speculative asset (to project neoliberal rationality backwards), linking citizenship, race, and class. Today, the relative privilege of "white" Eastern European women on the market of exploitable reproductive labor also hinges on racialized understandings of class reproduction—simply put, a nanny that looks white capitalizes, and socializes, differently. Their racialization has to do with the reproduction of highly differentiated and stratified spaces, populations and regimes of mobility.

I also referenced Peña's work because I wanted to trouble the relationship or distinction between art and life sometimes made in reference to his writing. This has been a concern in my work, especially of the last ten years in relation to the distinctions between art and activism.

KM and IT: The issue of East European whiteness you raised is one of increasing importance in transnational feminist and media discourses as recent scholarship begins to pay attention to the need to de-homogenize whiteness precisely by recognizing the crucial historical differences between, say, Western whiteness and more invisible East European whiteness [Bardan 2008; Marciniak 2008; Murawska-Muthesius 2006]. You mentioned the challenge to be explicit about working through the body that is viewed "white on arrival"—can you tell us a bit more about this challenge?

RB: Living on both sides of the spatiotemporal nineteen eighty-nine divide, I found myself racialized in conflicting and confusing ways that required some interrogation. I had to try and understand empirical evidence and embodied knowledge in relation to more systemic political and economic equations. Pre nineteen eighty-nine, Romanian whiteness was produced and normalized primarily via tropes of Latinity and via differentiation from Roma populations, who were, and continue to be, perceived as illegitimate and abject subjects in all national regimes. The end of nineteen eighty-nine is seen as the end of the Cold War, most present in the popular imagination as the fall of the Berlin Wall. But in the nineteen nineties the wall between East and West becomes, of course, reconstructed through other technologies and mechanisms, above and below national regimes. The production of "globalized" space reconfigures stratification through a series of new processes, and produces a set of new scales (at once more vast and more molecularized), along historically familiar vectors (race, gender, citizenship, and so on). You mentioned the "fear of contagion" that becomes characteristic of Western discourses in the nineties, and the production of the racialized migrant as a criminal category under the guise of national security. In the case of migration from the former Soviet bloc, this was also specifically a fear of the contagion of "communism," which linked national security with capitalist exchange. Capitalism became equated with national interest, and we begin to see racialization playing a significant role in a changing state form and its articulation with global markets.

Neoliberal capitalism imposes itself as the only planetary logic in the early nineties. In the course of the systemic devaluation and dismantling of domestic economies of the nineteen nineties, increasing numbers of Romanians are forced to migrate for work. Upon arrival in Western and Northern Europe they find themselves "illegalized." Over the course of this decade, Romanians in particular are racialized as gypsy or Roma. The space (economic, juridical, political) that we now call Europe is a construction that hinges on a number of stratifications, including the racialization and illegalization of migrant groups, which simultaneously determines its margins. In the U.S. however, it is migrants from Central and Latin America who constitute the primary flexible labor market and who are racialized as nonwhite. By distinction, many migrants from East Europe arriving in the U.S. during the nineties are both illegal and "white" on arrival.

But Eastern European racialization as white is volatile, slippery, "flexible" due to the role of chronotype and the importance of vision—of visual markers, and technologized visualization that characterize neoliberal regimes of subject formation. And vision is a learned process, it is political, it is relational. Of course, racialization is not about skin color, it is about relations of domination and subjugation. Neoliberalism, in this specific example, appears as an adaptive logic, as a range of technologies that "optimizes" existing conditions, creating hierarchies of migrant populations within capital markets.

Different communities of illegalized migrants and refugees have developed highly nuanced and sophisticated ways of "surfing" regimes of visibility and invisibility. Eastern Europeans in particular are keenly aware of the tactical importance of "passing as white" while at the same time maintaining spaces that are densely "invisible" to the state and to the market. In the same ways that so-called black markets operate both outside of, and within, the logic of "legitimate" markets, the invisiblity of Eastern European illegality requires the production of a visible whiteness.

However, when displaced and illegalized communities become highly politicized and, more importantly, self-organized, the contradictions inherent in these flexibilized and speculative ways of being are exploded, explicitly articulated, and challenged. It is here that the possibility of an "outside" to these regimes is collectively articulated and practiced.

KM and IT: The story you are telling about the complex intersections of whiteness, neoliberalism and il/legality is both a fascinating and an important one. The focus on Latino/North American and African/European modalities of border crossing and migrant illegality within academic scholarship, and within critical art practice, often obscures the nuances of the production and negotiation of "white" migrant illegality—and the "shades of whiteness" produced through both racializing bordering regimes and through migrant negotiations of these regimes.

Could you tell us about some of your current work with migrant youth in Chicago?

RB: I have been working within the *NoName Collective*, a countercapitalist, antiracist group of mixed-status immigrants who come out of various experiences in migrant justice work and grassroots organizing. The primary public face of the collective and its initiatives is the Moratorium on Deportations Campaign, which is a kind of meeting place for a shifting constellation of migrant justice, antiwar and anticapitalist groups and individuals. Over the last two years we have developed a series of actions and formalized a set of practices—some self-consciously performative—that articulate a set of shared critiques of, and desire to experiment with, dominant forms of organizing and social movement work. Our practices include workshops and teach-ins, bike caravans and durational walks, speak-outs and collective writing. While doing this work, my expectations as an artist were swept aside by the very new (to me) conditions under which we were working. I have found it important not to determine in advance the forms the work will take, or to author individual projects, images, or text. Rather, we have collectively developed many texts, performative events, images, as well as forms of "territorial research" and moving seminars, which involved people using their experiences and bodies to develop a collective visualization of a larger, dynamic geography. I see this as a kind of collective theorizing and articulation that seems to gesture towards the possibility of dissolving both art and organizing into a more generalized social process of oppositional learning and being. Curiously, these were the very questions I had been exploring in my artwork for some time, particularly in the performances developed with the collective BLW,[1] and in my critiques of the institutionalization, and marketability, of "social practices" or "relational" art. In my own development as an artist, this exploration led me to practices that exceed what is recognizable as art, and to collaborations within social bodies that are excluded from the circuits of the art market [see Borcilă 2009].

It is maybe banal to say, but one of the main distinctions between art and social movement work hinges upon questions of authorship and attribution of methods, objects, or images, upon identifying rights over objects within a process of exchange. In other words, these differentiations

Figure 2.2. Flyers for "Shut Down ICE," May 15–21 2012

are produced in the mobilization of art within the circuits of capital—and therefore cannot be overcome within it. Collectivism can be a significant challenge to this distinction, but only as part of a significant, long-term countercapitalist project.

At the same time, the more I work as an organizer, I have learned that it is also important to maintain a space of relative autonomy for the "artistic" sphere—as it allows social movement work to escape from dominant political forms and imaginaries, such as campaign organizing. In the *NoName Collective*, we trespass into the domain of "art," but it is a kind of "art drag" that allows us to stage heightened social conflicts in real life, with real risks, under the guise of art or performance. It also allows people whose legitimacy in the U.S. is denied, to claim a different position, both individually and collectively. For instance, we developed an intervention into a meeting conducted by Immigrations and Customs Enforcement (ICE) through a series of written statements and manifestos, interviews, and actions collectively called "Shut Down ICE"—interpreted by officials as a plan to blockade or force entrance into ICE headquarters. In fact, we used the slippage between "ICE" and "ice" to march across the city with a hundred-pound block of ice, and to stage a confrontation with it upon arrival at the main ICE headquarters in the financial district. This was lot like street theatre, but it was directed at escalating a social conflict within incredibly asymmetrical and hostile conditions. It is surreal to enact something like this with participants who are undocumented and facing deportation. "Shut Down ICE" played out within mainstream media channels as a very real blockade and as a political crisis for state representatives in the struggle around a new proposed Immigrant Detention Center. For us, this shift or slippage between ICE and ice, between the symbolic and the "real," was a way of dealing with the political as aesthetic through engaging performative practice.

The *NoName Collective* also developed sign-making workshops where people could think critically about what a collective sign—such as a flag—is. These workshops enabled us to work towards a collaborative articulation of our identity as a migrant collective. For me, this was artistic and political work, as complicated and intellectually challenging as anything I have ever been involved in, somewhere between popular education, performance art, and movement building. As the signs became objects, put into action in protest events, replicated and multiplied, they were photographed and became circulated and sold as authored images in both media and artistic spheres. So all our activities produced discrete images but none were of my authorship. It is somewhere along this fault line that the irreconcilable conflict between the role of organizer, and the role of art worker as author of images or events, makes itself most felt by me at this point.

Figure 2.3. *If one is deportable, we all are exploitable—Si uno es deportabile, todos somos explotabiles*, 2011. Sign made collaboratively. Image by Brett Jenelik

KM and IT: There is a vital tension emerging here between "art" and "activism" and between "the singular" and "the collective." As I (IT) see it, this is not a conflict which you seek or should seek to resolve in your work, but is rather a description of a form of "life practice" which engages with "sore spots"—sites of pressure and weakness—which you/I must continuously seek out. At the heart of all this work, what it has *in common*, is what Judith Butler terms the "theatricalization of political rage" [232]. In my own work (IT) as a scholar-activist (rather than an art activist), I am also interested in maximizing these spaces of tensions. In writing about migrant protests in the UK, for example, I am interested not in the singularity of protests as "events," but in their documentary "afterlives" and residues, and the forms of alternative story-lining of the political present tense which they enable. It is for me, the capacity of acts and events of protest, be they nominally "aesthetic" or more recognizably "political" in orientation, to be transformed into *political parables* which trouble prevailing forms of common sense about the meaning of democracy and rights which is most important. For it is the vitalization and proliferation of acts of resistance *within* their many documentary afterlives that allows for the weaving of alternative political imaginaries with which to perceive differently the state we are in. So, while protests like "Shut Down ICE" might register as little more than minor disturbances within the public sphere, the restaging and repetition of these acts, in spaces which include publications such as this book, form part of a broader critical practice of *countermapping*, which is creating an unravelable fabric of political resistance across borders. It is the accumulation of "small acts" which strain against the invisibility and inaudibility of abject lives constituted by sovereign power. Perhaps this sounds too hopeful, but in what are for many the current dark days and perhaps end days of neoliberal capital, it seems to me that the intellectual and the political challenge is precisely about the necessity of working at the borders of older and different genres and forms of practice as a means of reinventing "from the scene of survival, new idioms of the political, and of belonging itself" [Berlant 2011, 262]. In a more practical register, survival also means being strategic as well as making compromises, including perhaps the necessity of taking up given names of value, such as "artist" or "academic," as a means of making interventions which are "registerable" within the public domain.

Given the forms of generic and disciplinary *border crossing* with which your current art and activist practice is engaged, we wonder how you position your work in the broader context of the upsurge in similar forms of art activism around the globe, as a response to the democratic deficits, staggering economic inequalities and laissez-faire violence which have been effected by neoliberal globalization [Federici 2011]. In particular, we wonder how or if you imagine the "glocal" implications of your work with AREA in Chicago in relationship to the current upsurge of "space-hacking" forms of protest against austerity, best illustrated by the wave of pro-democracy revolts in North Africa and the Middle East (the "Arab Spring") in twenty-ten and twenty-eleven, and the North American and European Occupy movements against austerity that were inspired by these revolts? We are thinking in particular here of the activism and scholarship which thinks with notions of "the commons" and which seeks to think connections between seemingly disparate forms of *resistance from below* in relationship to the broader frameworks of neoliberal disenfranchisement.

RB: You mention the ways we intervene, strategically leveraging our positions, while understanding that we live irreconcilable contradictions. This does indeed seem like our only option. But the goal to me seems to be to create the conditions for a collective exodus, a withdrawal that can constitute something else . . . otherwise, we are stuck juggling tactics, we are stuck trying to leverage what we have towards what we understand as a

Figure 2.4. *End of three-day walk to the site of a proposed Immigrant Detention Camp in Crete, IL, 2012. Image by Juan Ibarra*

collective project, even as we remain in the battle for cultural capital and legitimacy that sees us competing against each other for the same jobs, the same contracts, the same grants. And we see this in the recently institutionalized markets of socially engaged and relational art practices. What does it mean when autonomous or resistant practices are marketized? What are the mechanisms through which collectively generated value becomes converted into private capital, and what role does the art worker play in this? We live this contradiction as artists and academics because, even as we resist, our economic self-interest coincides with the perpetuation of the prevailing economic and political system. To seek to undermine it is self-destructive.

To shift the terrain it is necessary to ask how a more collectivized exodus is possible, how questions about intervention or oppositionality might be *socialized* differently. That is to say, how might we live differently, how might we feed ourselves and each other, how might we collectivize our reproduction?

Let me back up to your provocative suggestion that actions, images, events have numerous afterlives, through the example of "Shut down ICE." When Homeland Security announced a public meeting on a new detention center project in Crete, Illinois, something we had been organizing against for many months, our process called for direct action. "Shut down ICE" grew out of years of thinking and doing collectively, and appeared to us as somehow self-evident. I do not think we saw it as symbolic; it was our full intention to challenge the legitimacy of this "public meeting" and of official claims to public consultation and transparency, to actually, not symbolically, *shut it down*. By necessity this meant to manifest, to constitute another public, to invent and enact different forms of what a public meeting could be, to make real the alternative, at any cost. We had developed techniques for leveraging mainstream and alternative media channels not merely as a platform to amplify, but also to test out the possibility of inserting radical formulations within official discourses and spaces, to produce a set of surreal performances. (As when a local evening news anchor finds herself citing deportation as a form of state terror.) The system response was swift—Homeland Security and Congressman Jesse Jackson Junior (who we see simultaneously as targets and partners in a strange unfolding dance), called off the public meeting citing security threats from protesters, effectively shutting themselves down. We immediately announced a public meeting with ICE at their main headquarters downtown Chicago—at the same time as the originally scheduled official meeting. Again the response was swift: hundreds of robocops of all jurisdictions were called in to barricade the building, and once again the news media presence was overwhelming—as was the presence of people who arrived to participate. It is under these conditions that "Shut Down ICE" unfolded. The event itself is part of a process that greatly exceeds it, that takes place over many years and that builds structures, relations, networks, and a kind of improvisational "groupthink."

Often, in art as in organizing, the focus is on producing an event, an image. Your reflections on afterlives finds a corollary in a simpler organizing notion that social change has to do with community building, that is to say constructing stories, forms, relations, temporalities, sensations: Understanding communities as living systems within larger ecosystems.

"Shut Down ICE" was one of many efforts to stop the detention center—from NGOs pushing legislative initiatives, to suburban citizen NIMBY campaigns, to our own teach-ins, educational campaigns, and durational walks. But there was no alliance, no way for these different tactics, and positionalities, to speak to each other. The success of our efforts in ultimately stopping this detention center suggests something very provocative: that overlapping—and often incompatible—efforts, forms, and tactics is at the moment a more realistic model than alliance building or the rather thin understandings of "solidarity" we manage to practice within the relative

Figure 2.5. *Signs carried for three days, left at the site of a proposed Immigrant Detention Camp in Crete, IL, 2012. Image by Juan Ibarra*

safety of privileged positions. In this fight we did not work together—we did not coordinate, bridge or even translate well across the different efforts and organizations, recognizing a set of incommensurabilities and asymmetries that we felt we could not overcome. We tried instead to push others into the fight, to rattle the bushes. Somehow, the sheer density of these efforts created the conditions for overlapping effects, a kind of accumulation that resonated for me with Graciela Carnevale's notion of building nets that can hold us as we resist reality [Carnevale 2009]. In the radical movements of the 1960s, in the Global South and in the North, social change was imagined as a break. Today we are looking more at building alternative structures that can sustain us, from within which we can produce realities, something we see perhaps most strongly in the U.S. not in the recent movements against austerity, but rather in the ongoing grassroots work in a place like Detroit, so clearly articulated by the work of Grace Lee Boggs [see Lee Boggs and Kurashige 2011]. We are experimenting and learning how to build such structures—spaces, relations, practices, languages—and we are often surprised and humbled by what we find. Carnevale suggests art can be understood in terms of its effects, as "a critical doing that tends to invent ways of life more human and just" [Carnevale 2009]. If this is so, what art might become may surprise us as well.

Notes

1. BLW is an arts collective, which stands for the last names of the artists, Rozalinda Borcila, Sarah Lewison Lewison, and Julie Wyman, and it is also an acronym for *BeLikeWater* and *BeLoW*.

Works Cited

Bardan, Alice. 2008. "Welcome to Dreamland: The Realist Impulse in Paweł Pawlikowski's *Last Resort*." *New Cinemas: Journal of Contemporary Film* 6 (1): 47–63.
Berlant, Lauren. 2011. *Cruel Optimism*. Durham: Duke University Press.
Borcilă, Rozalinda. 2001. "Citizen/Foreigner in Recent Installation and Performance Art." http://www.gradnet.de/papers/pomo2.papers/Borcilă00.htm. Accessed June 7, 2012.
———. "Tracking Down, or What to Do with a Disturbing Body." borcila.com/archive/tracking_down.html. Accessed July 7, 2012.
———. 2005 6+: A Women's Art Collective. http://www.6plus.org/borcila.html. Accessed June 7, 2012.
———. 2009. "In Search of Liberation." *Maska, Performing Arts Journal* XXIV (120–21) (Spring). http://borcila.com/In_Search_of_Liberation.htm.
———. 2012. "Riding the Zone." In Compass Collaborators. *Deep Routes, the Midwest in All Directions*, edited by Rozalinda Borcilă, Bonnie Fortune, and Sarah Ross. Iowa City: White Wire. Available at http://www.commonplacesproject.org/borcila/blog/?p=290.
Butler, Judith. 1993. *Bodies That Matter: On the Discursive Limits of Sex*. London, New York: Routledge.
Carnevale, Graciela. 2009. "Radical Imagination: Ruptures and Continuities." http://radical.temp.si/wp-content/uploads/2011/07/Graciela-Carnevale-Radical.pdf. Accessed July 18, 2012.
De Giorgi, Alessandro. 2010. "Immigration Control, post-Fordism, and less Eligibility: A Materialist Critique of the Criminalization of Immigration across Europe." *Punishment and Society* 12 (2): 147–67.
Gómez-Peña, Guillermo. 2005. *Ethno-Techno: Writings on Performance, Activism, and Pedagogy*. Edited by Elaine Peña. New York: Routledge.
Federici, Silvia. 2011. "Feminism and the Politics of the Commons." *The Commoner*. http://www.commoner.org.uk/?p=113. Accessed July 3, 2012.
Lee Boggs, Grace, and Scott Kurashige. 2011. *The Next American Revolution: Sustainable Activism for the Twenty-First Century*. Berkeley: University of California Press.

Marciniak, Katarzyna. 2008. "Foreign Women and Toilets." *Feminist Media Studies* 8 (4): 337–56.
Murawska-Muthesius, Katarzyna. 2006. "1956 in the Cartoonist's Gaze: Fixing the Eastern European Other and Denying the Eastern European Self." *Third Text* 20 (2): 189–99.
Rancière, Jacques. 1999. *Dis-agreement: Politics and Philosophy*. Translayed by Julie Rose. Minneapolis, London: University of Minnesota Press.
———. 2008. "Aesthetics Against Incarnation: An Interview by Ann Marie Oliver." *Critical Inquiry* 35 (Autumn): 174–90.
Tyler, Imogen. 2013. *Revolting Subjects: Social Abjection, Resistance, and Protest in Neoliberal Britain*. London: Zed.

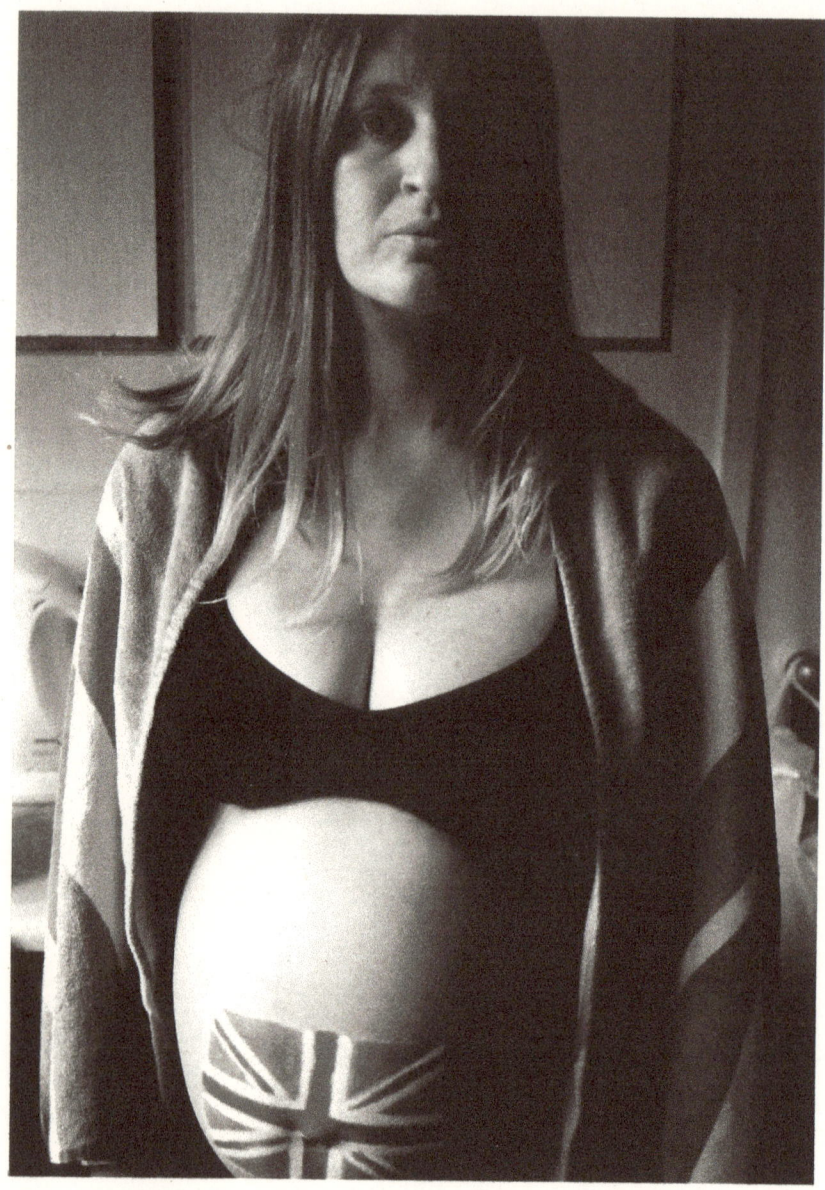

Figure 3.1. *Becoming British*, 2007. Courtesy of Lena Šimić

3

Becoming British

Exploring Citizenship through Arts Practice

Lena Šimić with Imogen Tyler

The Croatian-born, Liverpool-based performance artist Lena Šimić has produced an extraordinary body of artistic work since 2003. Lena's performance-oriented arts practice variously explores citizenship and immigrant experience, postsocialism, anticapitalism, climate change, social class, the sexual and domestic politics of family life and motherhood. In collaboration with her partner, the artist Gary Anderson, and their children, Lena co-organizes *The Institute for the Art and Practice of Dissent at Home,* an artist-activist initiative run from the spare bedroom of their family home in Everton, Liverpool. *The Institute* engages in what they term "family activism": "A practice which politicizes everyday living by thinking critically through our immediate contexts." Everton is one of the most deprived wards in Britain, with unemployment at 50 percent and the average household income well below the national average, a situation arguably exacerbated by the diversion of funds to the city center for "cultural regeneration" of the city. Indeed, *The Institute for the Art and Practice of Dissent at Home* was set up in 2008 to coincide with, and in response to, the Liverpool 08 European Capital of Culture, or what *The Institute* and other opponents termed "Culture of Capitalism," "C®apital of Culture," and "Capital(ism) for Vultures" in protest against the neoliberal project at the heart of the European City for Culture program (a project that in the case of Liverpool 08 saw the selling off of large parts of the city center to commercial developers, the demolition of inner city housing and the eviction of local residents).[1] *The Institute for the Art and Practice of Dissent at Home* describes itself as a space for dissenting "the capitalism of culture." Indeed, Lena's arts practice is fundamentally *a protest practice*, which engages with anticapitalist social movements seeking to not only examine, but to generate forms of cultural praxis that are resistant to forces of neoliberal marketization.

Since 2009, Lena has been engaged in a project that was originally titled, *Becoming British: exploring citizenship through arts practice* and it is this project which I set out to document in my conversations with her over a two year period. Lena described the motivations of *Becoming British* in the following way:

> I am a "foreigner," a Croatian, resident in the UK for the last ten years. I am married to a British citizen and have an Indefinite Leave to Remain visa in my passport which allows me to enjoy most of the privileges of British citizenship, except the right to vote, participate in juridical activities (like be a member of a jury), having a British passport and staying out of Britain for more than three consecutive years. I am eligible to become British. My three children have dual citizenship, British and Croatian. I have however been deferring my citizenship application in order to make it into an arts project—a process and an event which is interrogative and activist. I am planning to Become British in twenty-ten. This project will mark my ten years of living in the UK.

I was particularly interested in thinking about Lena's project in relation to the theme of this book, "immigrant protest." For what motivated the art project *Becoming British* was Lena's immigrant frustration as she experienced being processed and captured through the British immigration system. What follows is an edited transcription of several conversations I have had with Lena about the *Becoming British* project over the course of one year. Some of our conversations took place on e-mail; some took place face to face when I visited *The Institute*. The first part of this conversation focuses on the early stages of the project as Lena began to conceive of the project, and this first stage culminated in Lena taking the "Life in the UK" citizenship test and attending a citizenship ceremony. The second part details Lena's collaboration with fellow art activist Jennifer Verson and their community workshops with fellow migrants in Liverpool, which culminated in a performance event entitled *Blood & Soil: we were always meant to meet* . . .

Becoming British

Imogen Tyler: Lena, I would like to begin our conversation about *Becoming British* by inviting you to describe the background to the project. I am interested in what motivated you to develop it and, in particular, the fury you have previously documented that you experienced in becoming an "immigrant wife."

Lena Šimić: *Becoming British* is about collapsing my life with arts practice. This particular project continues my investigation of the theme of foreignness and otherness. In two thousand four, I worked on two performance pieces: *Medea/Mothers' Clothes* and *Magdalena Makeup*, both of which played with the notion of what it means to be different, but at the same time worked from and within the local communities of Liverpool. Both of these performance pieces re/presented me as the Other through makeup, costume, language, and stage appearance. *Becoming British* builds on that theme conceptually, but at the same time asks its audiences/recipients (humorously and critically) for a kind of impossible "normalization" and acceptance of myself, as a subject, now that I am/will be British. I would like to note that I am still in the process of becoming British—my application is being considered. Furthermore, I never thought about becoming British without it being an arts project—there is something performative about citizenship, and it is that which I want to disclose through my arts practice. Citizenship is constructed, nationality is constructed, identity is constructed. From the moment I started thinking about *Becoming British*, I realized that the piece is as much about me as it is about others, those who define me as non-British. *Becoming British* starts with a request to my family, colleagues, friends, and neighbors, most of the people I have met during my last ten years while living in the UK, to advise me how to become British. All these "others" are my accomplices in this arts project, and the others speak, whilst I am quiet. I listen and I obey. I perform for them. There is passivity in becoming British, both in the actual formal process and in my art project. You do what you are told.

Being marked as "other" is difficult. My otherness is apparent through my speech, my nuanced English. It is through language that I am marked as other and that I find myself explaining my "otherness." Through explaining I attach myself to my husband—the one who brought me "here." I am therefore defined as "immigrant wife." This explaining usually happens in ordinary, everyday situations (for example, in a taxi or shopping queue), and hardly ever in arts and academic contexts where people are too conscious of being politically correct. In arts and academic contexts, my difference becomes my trump card. It might be interesting to attempt to "erase" (and stage that erasure) my difference (such as nuanced accented English) in *Becoming British*. Officially, I will not gain my citizenship on the basis of being married to my British husband but on the basis of five year residence in the country. I could have claimed my citizenship via my marriage (with three years residence), but that would have meant that our wedding certificate (which is in Slovak—we got married in Slovakia) would need translating into English. This is an unnecessary expense. It is expensive to become British—it cost seven hundred thirty-five pounds for the application and sixty pounds for nationality check service. The cost of the British passport is seventy-eight pounds. I applied to Arts Council England to fund the project; I am waiting for their decision on funding. I would love it if the state [Arts Council England] decided to pay for my British citizenship. We'll see.

When entering the UK on January thirty-first, two thousand, with my "wife visa" (which does not allow me to have access to any public funds), I was asked if I was pregnant at the Heathrow airport entry. I answered: "Not to my knowledge." I was pregnant at the time, but I did not know it then. I suspected it. The first year of my living in the UK, I was very much "immigrant wife," with no rights or benefits. My husband could claim jobseeker's allowance and housing benefit while I couldn't. Once the baby was born, Gary claimed the child benefit for the baby as I couldn't. After a year's residence in the country, I obtained Indefinite Leave to Remain. I have lived with ILTR and with "Other Nationalities" queues at the airport for the last ten years. Gary, my husband, and our three children, all "proper" British citizens always join me in the queue. We stand and wait, children often misbehave and we feel marked as "other"—there is something powerful and provocative in having that status. However, I am aware of our privilege. We cannot be refused an entry into the UK. Our "otherness" while standing at the airport queue is performative in the same way as my *Becoming British* arts project is. But, it is through both of these actions that we can comment on social injustices of border controls.

IT: I love the story you are telling about this art project and its relationship to your lived experiences of "becoming British," applying for citizenship, passing through immigration controls and encountering everyday borders in your positioning as a foreigner and outsider. I want to return to your experience of being asked if you are pregnant at the border. This question to you, from a border official, is such a powerful and revealing one, I think. He is asking, "Are you smuggling a child in? Are you concealing an alien life?" This experience resonates with my research on the maternal body as a border body and what I describe as the securitization of reproduction [Tyler 2013]. In government policy, and "border handling guidelines," pregnant women have been identified as and are specifically targeted as "a threat" to Britain's borders, and suspected pregnancy is managed in immigration policy, in much the same way as smuggling drugs or carrying a weapon. For example, women are subjected to body searches to ascertain whether or not they are attempting to "smuggle" unborn foreign nationals into Britain. What does it mean when "life itself," the capacity to create life, becomes subject to the kinds of border interrogations you describe? More rhetorically, the figure of the "reproductive migrant" who threatens to populate "our country" with "foreign children" contributes to a rising nativism by proliferating fears about loss of ancestry, a demise which, it is imagined, threatens the existence of the nation-state itself. Your description of waiting with your British-born children in the "other nationalities" queue speaks to the nativist ideology which drives or rather legitimates the securitization of borders we have seen over the past few decades. It also, I think, reveals the centrality of maternity to your thinking and practice, to your work as an artist and an activist.

The relationship between your position as a maternal subject and your performance of becoming British is encapsulated for me in the provocative photograph which you made of yourself at the beginning of this project [opening image]. This image of you, a foreigner noncitizen pregnant with a child who is a British citizen, provocatively stages the dissensual relationship between maternity, nativism, nationalism, and citizenship. Your body is the border here. Draped in a Union Jack towel, with a Union Jack painted on your pregnant belly, this image also speaks to a particular moment in the neoliberalization of Britain in the 1990s, which is symbolized with the rise of "Brit Pop," and the deepening capitalization of art associated with "Young British Artists" (YBAs) under New Labour and interestingly by the rise of a new visual culture of pregnancy, and the postfeminist sexualization of maternity [Tyler 2011].

In terms of *Becoming British*, I would like to dwell a little bit on the relationship between art and experience, and the ways in which the activist or politics of your work emerges in their relation. For example, you describe citizenship as performative, rather than a status or property of self. Citizenship is in some senses always enacted in that it emerges only in encounters with borders of some kind, including those banal everyday experiences of the border, such as a question or look from a taxi driver, or a polite refusal to acknowledge your foreignness in bourgeois spaces such as a theatre or academic context. I want to explore what this performative account of citizenship means in relation to your performance practice. Your description of citizenship is reminiscent of Engin Isin's influential account of citizenship as acts. By "acts," Isin means the practices through which subjects transform themselves into citizens [Isin 2008, 18]. The activities through which individual subjects and groups "constitute themselves as . . . those to whom the right to have rights is due" [Isin and Nielsen 2008, 2]. This is a radical break from formal definitions of citizenship and indeed from citizens per se, to those "performances, enactments and events" [Walters 2008, 192] which produce *relations of citizenship* in any given moment. Isin cites the examples of the hunger strikes of British Suffragette Marion Wallace Dunlop in nineteen hundred and nine and the Montgomery Bus Boycott in nineteen fifty-five, to argue for the transformatory potential of "momentous acts" of citizenship [see Isin 2008, 18]. Such acts, he suggests, have the capacity to rupture hegemonic social convention and be a catalyst for social transformation. However, your account of citizenship as perfomative punctures the optimism of Isin's account. Indeed, *Becoming British* invokes a much more cynical account of citizenship as a drag act, a parodic enactment of subjection to state sovereignty and governmentality. For example, you state that *Becoming British* is about staging an erasure of your foreignness, yet it is, of course, also the opposite of this, in applying for citizenship, and turning this into an art project, you are in fact drawing attention to your status as foreign. It is also significant, I think, that you imagine citizenship as a passive project, to the extent that you imagine *Becoming British* as an art project in which you are "the object," shaped and directed by others, a robotic practice without agency. It might be interesting to think about this configuration of passivity, performance, and direction a little more. In order for us to further open up this question of citizenship and performance, could you describe some of the specific components of *Becoming British* in more detail? In what respects are your performances of *Becoming British* a protest against citizenship itself as a mode of governance?

LŠ: I am not sure if my performance/s of "becoming British" are a protest against citizenship per se; ultimately the project is a comment about social injustice. From commenting and representing I hope to get to "challenging and changing." I do not have a political solution, but I feel, as an artist/activist, it is my obligation to "speak out." As an artist, I am in a relatively privileged position to create a different, temporary space, which is striving for utopian encounters with others. Isin describes "momentous acts of citizenship" in relation to certain groups of people who have been denied that right/privilege that comes with citizenship. My aim with the *Becoming British* arts project is to expose the injustices and, hopefully, move from artistic representation to action (therefore my calling of myself as artist/activist). "Being passive" is my methodological performance-making tool. I feel that the official process of "becoming British" puts you in a passive position—you are obliged to do as you are told. For example, while waiting to do "Life in the UK" test, we, the applicants, were put in a small waiting room and were not allowed to leave the building for the duration of the testing process. First you register, then you go into a small room, which does not even have enough chairs for all of us, then we are called one by one into the testing center, then are collectively instructed about the test, then we take the test, then we go back to the small waiting room, then we are called one by one from the waiting room to receive our result: pass or fail. The whole process takes about three hours. The test itself is only forty-five minutes. In this kind of environment I felt I was unable to speak with my fellow applicants. It is almost as if we were all in competition with each other, inviting a thought: "Who is more British, me or you?" It was a very oppressive space. I felt disabled and passive. I would like to expose that passivity in my performance making. However, in my role as an artist, I am not passive: I am organizing this project, I have applied and received Arts Council funding for it (more on this later on), I will collaborate with others, and finally present it at West Everton Community Council (WECC). Hopefully, the space at WECC will become a discursive, critical and open space where the public performance will open up a debate about citizenship and immigration and combat racist ill-informed views on the issues, like the ones you mention about fears about loss of ancestry. In my work as a pedagogue, I do that with my students through my lectures and discussions. Arts practice also has that potential to effect change.

IT: I think we should pause to say more about the "Life in the UK" citizenship test that is now required for settlement (indefinite leave to remain) in the UK. The test was introduced in two thousand five, as part of an ever-evolving raft of requirements for migrants trying to obtain indefinite leave to remain, or naturalization as a British citizen. Before you can apply for citizenship, you must now take the "Life in the UK" test often in combination with English for Speakers of Other Languages (ESOL) courses and citizenship classes (depending on external assessment of your English Language proficiency) in order that you have demonstrated "sufficient knowledge of life in the United Kingdom" and in the case of the ESOL, "sufficient knowledge of the English Language." As you have noted, Lena, the whole process is itself "a market in citizenship" which proves prohibitively expensive for many people.

LŠ: I attended my Citizenship Ceremony on November seventh, two thousand ten, with my two sons, Neal [10] and Gabriel [8], dressed up in my Medea costume [Figure 3.2]. In two thousand four I developed a performance piece entitled *Medea/Mothers' Clothes*, which looks at intervening into socially accepted Mother norm as well as juxtaposing two Liverpool toddler group mothers with anti-mother archetype and barbarian Medea who kills her two sons as a revenge for her husband Jason taking on a new younger bride. Attending the Citizenship Ceremony in my Medea costume is tongue in cheek: a barbarian is becoming civilized. Of course, no one asked me about my costume. My dress was not perceived as a costume: to ask me why I was dressed that way would be politically incorrect; my difference would be acknowledged. And yes, by attempting to erase my difference, I am drawing attention to it. I can think of my act of wearing the Medea costume at the Citizenship Ceremony as passive, unnoticed, gentle, but there is a life for it after the ceremony, for example, in this conversation with you or mentioning it in my public *Becoming British* performance at WECC.

Figure 3.2: Lena as Medea, in *Medea/Mothers' Clothes*. Courtesy of Lena Šimić.

IT: When you wrote about *Medea/Mothers' Clothes*, the idea of costume was central to the performance. You noted that "[p]utting a costume on makes you into a character, into someone else, into pretence. Costume is like a mask." It is interesting, I think, that you went with your children to the citizenship ceremony dressed as Medea, a mythological sorceress (and that nobody thought this was strange!). In the Greek play, Medea, of course, sent a poisoned dress to Jason's wife—a gift of death. There is not time for us to explore the meaning of this further here, but I want to challenge your argument here that this was a "passive act," given the many ways in which the politics of clothing was such a considered part of your Medea performance [see Simic 2009].

Blood & Soil: We were always meant to meet . . .

LŠ: *Becoming British* needed to evolve as a collaborative project so that it wasn't just about my own journey, and I began working with Jennifer Verson to expand the project. I told you about my application to the Arts Council. Well, I did receive four thousand two hundred pounds from the Arts

Council England for this project. I originally asked for five thousand eighty pounds, but the ACE refused to pay eight hundred eighty pounds in citizenship costs. I was rather disappointed about this as I wanted the citizenship application process to be paid for by the state or at least institutionalized. *The Institute for the Art and Practice of Dissent at Home* will cover the eight hundred eighty pounds citizenship costs, but it would have been stronger if ACE did. Now, part of the project is to spend four thousand two hundred pounds ethically. *Becoming British* is about meeting others and creating networks of citizens and noncitizens, natives and foreigners. A friend of mine and a collaborator on *Becoming British*, Jennifer Verson, a U.S. citizen, is currently applying for Indefinite Leave to Remain. Jennifer's partner Rob is British and they have a British daughter. Both Jennifer and Rob are currently unemployed and do not have the nine hundred pounds to pay the fee (and are exploring their limited legal options). Another collaborator, a refugee journalist and poet from Gambia, Pa Modou, is also fighting for his right to stay in the UK. Some friends of mine are organizing campaigns to raise the money for his legal battle costs. With four thousand two hundred pounds received from the ACE, I plan to pay for both my citizenship and Jennifer's ILTR and some of Pa Modou's legal costs, even when these will be called "artistic costs" on activity report I need to produce afterwards. I cannot think of a better way to spend the money. Of course, some of the expenditure will go into producing a catalogue and thus documenting the process. Furthermore, while talking about creating connections, one of the new British citizens who I met at the ceremony, Dejan, befriended me over Facebook. It is interesting to see how a small network of people is already forming and being formalized through my *Becoming British* project. In my catalogue that will accompany the public performance as well as in the actual performance I will try to air Pa Modou's, Jennifer's, Dejan's and all the other stories of citizenship I gather, in addition to my own.

IT: I want to introduce Jennifer for the readers. Jennifer describes herself as a performance activist who "trains people in the art of politically subversive theatrical performances." As Lena notes, she is Jewish American and a mother of a Liverpudlian child, who is trying to obtain leave to remain. Jennifer has been central in the recent period of North American and British art activism. She has worked as part of *The Laboratory of Insurrectionary Imagination*, helping found the Rebel Clown Army (CIRCA) who featured heavily in the protests surrounding the two thousand five G8 summit in Scotland. CIRCA has become an iconic feature of twenty-first-century antiglobalization movements, with "swarms of clowns" now a regular feature in anticapitalist, environmental, antiwar, and noborders protests across the world. Jennifer describes CIRCA in the following terms:

> Rebel clowning [is] an emergent form that combines the ancient art of clowning with the practice of non-violent civil disobedience.... Rebel clowning is partially a tactical weapon against the sheer stupidity of capitalism and war, and partially a tool to free the self from the tremendous damage that capitalism has done to our bodies and our minds. (Verson 2006, 183)

This clowning performance of carnivalesque disobedience takes me back to your Medea costume at the citizenship ceremony, Lena, and makes me think of the ways in which "acting" and "acting out" are central features of *Becoming British*, and your strategies of "submission" to the processes and practices of citizenship.

LŠ: When I started working with Jennifer, we began by thinking more about the ways in which we could reach other noncitizens, others who were journeying to British Citizenship. We set up three workshops called "Becoming British" at a local community center, but they did not recruit very well. We think this was because of the title "Becoming British"; this just did not work to attract people to come, particularly in the context of Liverpool which has a long history of imagining itself as somehow separate and in a kind of politically adversarial relation to the British state. So we changed tactics and got in touch with a local college and began working with migrant women who were enrolled on an ESOL for citizenship course. Now we had participants for our workshops, but it still was not working in the way we imagined. What we had wanted to do was bring together immigrant communities and immigrant artists, with the people who were the users of WECC, who are predominately white working-class Liverpudlians of various ages (pensioners, carers, parents, and young people engaged in training courses). This was a utopian idea, of course, that we could facilitate some kind of "social mixing" through arts practice. Everton is a very white working-class area; people speak about the area as "hard" and it is the kind of area which is often attributed with a certain kind of prejudice and mistrust about immigrants. There is Liverpool Province Loyal Orange Lodge on Everton Road which holds regular parades and displays loyalist flags. The neighborhood around the Orange Lodge feels British. The WECC does not; it is project-managed by Paula Kearns, who is Irish; the Board whom I encountered when I first approached the center about doing my arts project there was very welcoming and supportive of my idea of working in the center around the questions of immigration and identities, probably because many of them come from immigrant families. Nevertheless, at one of the first encounters I had with users of the WECC center, I was confronted with a story about Yugoslavs (or are they Polish?) who run car wash "here" now. In this situation I became "responsible" for influx of Eastern European immigrants into not only the UK, or Liverpool, but specifically Everton. "Becoming British" workshop did not attract participants, and yet there was still some unease about "immigrants" in the center. Clearly, no center has one set of "immigration feelings" and there are complex issues at play around "old immigrants" not liking "new immigrants," for example. The women from the ESOL course who came to work with us had never been to this area of Liverpool before. Our idea of "mixing" did not work, as the white working-class community did not participate in the workshops. What happened is that we ended up working with the ESOL students in a more conventional way. On the ESOL course they are studying English but they also learn about Britain. It was difficult to be critical in the workshop since, if you are doing the "Life in the UK" test, you need to memorize a lot of information, facts about Britain, which is mostly irrelevant knowledge. Therefore, we ended up trying to assist the women with that but, at the same time, trying to think about what they might need to know to live here, make a life here, in a more practical sense. Essentially, we became a part of the ESOL course, for what these women wanted to learn was "the facts" they needed, instrumentally, to know about Britain in order to gain ILTR or citizenship status. That learning was done somewhat more creatively through games, drawing of a map of Britain on the floor, and working physically through movement.

IT: That is really interesting because in a way you and Jennifer found yourselves in a comic position. You set out to critically examine the processes of becoming British, both in terms of the informal and formal legal processes of obtaining citizenship, but also in more abstract terms what it means to be "foreign," and yet you became co-opted into what you might describe as State sanctioned "citizenship pedagogy": instructing foreign women on how to "become British."

LŠ: We were compromised, and yes, it was comic and there was an element of "co-option" in the workshop. However, it was not a "failure" because even bringing the ESOL group on buses into Everton, into a community in which they had never been, felt like an achievement. At the end of the workshops, we had a round of sharing our own migrant knowledge about the UK, sharing what we have learnt as foreigners. It was an attempt to introduce a more experiential element, sharing migrant experiences, taking this in our own hands, and making something with it together outside of the knowledge for the test. It was after these workshops that we decided to change the name of the project to *Blood and Soil*. This came about because we were thinking, myself, Jennifer and a small group of migrant artists (Yoel,

Pa Modou, Dejan, and Adam) about what citizenship is, and how you get it. Citizenship is granted through blood or through soil.

IT: Of course, you are also identifying the fact that in most states citizenship has, historically, been legally granted through blood or soil: *jus soli* (right of soil), is the legal term for birthright citizenship and *jus sanguinis* (right of blood) describes citizenship granted by parentage. But "Blood and Soil" was also a Nazi slogan "Blut und Boden," used by the Nazi Ministry of Food and Agriculture to communicate ideas of Aryan ethnicity as grounded in both genetic bloodlines and in the moral virtues of agricultural society (in contrast to the perceived corruption of modern urban life). Yet here you are, a disparate collective of migrant artists, deciding that "Blood and Soil" is a useful way of troubling ideas of belonging as always tied to the state and notions of citizenship! It is difficult to imagine forms of belonging which do not conjure some problematic notions of nationalism, ethnic singularity, and nativism. I confess that I like the title "Becoming British" because it invokes not only the ways in which citizenship is a receding category for many migrants in the UK, as it becomes more difficult to obtain, but also because the notion of "becoming" underscores the historical instability of notions of Britishness: as we know, these categories are continually being struggled over and redefined in both formal and informal settings.

LŠ: I think, the point for us was, through the making of the project, to map our different stories about coming to British citizenship and, in doing so, to problematize the idea of citizenship as belonging. We became particularly involved with the story of one of the group, Pa Modou Bojang, who was an asylum seeker from Gambia, or rather "a failed asylum seeker" who was appealing against the decision of the immigration tribunal and was threatened with deportation from the UK, and, as such, was caught into a much more difficult process of "becoming legal" to the rest of us artists from Eastern Europe, the U.S., France, and Ireland.

IT: For the readers, Pa Modou was a journalist in Gambia and had spoken out against the Government; death threats had been made against him. He came to Britain in two thousand nine and continued to work as journalist in online news forums [see http://jamano.wordpress.com/]. Despite what many felt was a clear-cut case for refugee status under international law, Pa Modou found himself detained in an immigrant prison in July two thousand ten, a month after his claim for asylum was refused. The flight to deport Pa Modou to Gambia was only canceled at the last minute, after the high court accepted an injunction, and he was given leave to appeal.

LŠ: As a group we wanted to reach deeper underneath Pa Modou's asylum story, and we explored with him what ideas of inheritance and generation meant in Gambia; his ideas of belonging and forced displacement were all grounded in an oral family history, stories of blood and soil.

IT: You included some text from your work with Pa Modou in the *Blood and Soil* performance document. It is really a moving poetic account of his family's history, in which he imagines himself in dialogue with his ancestors.

LŠ: Yes, and through our work with him, we became involved in his appeal fund and campaign for leave to remain as a refugee in Britain. He came to talk to my students, in Liverpool Hope University, where I work. During his time in Liverpool, Pa Modou had become an activist for an organization called asylum-link and was a passionate campaigner and speaker for human rights. Through the making of the project, stories like Pa Modou's revealed the different ways migrants come to citizenship, and the specifically punitive nature of the asylum process in the UK. When Pa Modou was granted leave to remain as a refugee, it was a great moment.

The next stage was to move the project into a performance. It was such a brilliant mix of audiences, migrants, users of the center, people from the communities and local churches, artists, students . . . just what we had hoped for the first workshop. We designed the performance as a test, an exam. The audience had to sit at desks and take the "Life in the UK test" while Jennifer and I read out the stories we had collected and written during the project so far. We took different roles in the performance. I was "blood" and I moved and danced between the desks, walking on a gymnastic beam [Figure 3.3]. Jennifer was "soil" and she took the more static role of "the teacher" at the front of the class, reminding the audience how long they had before the time of the test (forty-five minutes) ran out.

IT: Lena, you have described the performance in the following way:

> *Blood & Soil: we were always meant to meet* . . . is a performance event by Lena Simic and Jennifer Verson which sought to problematize notions of citizenship and belonging current in the application process for becoming British in the UK. *Blood & Soil* took place at West Everton Community Council in Liverpool, April 2011 (funded by Arts Council England).
>
> The piece was conceived as a "community exam", where the audience members took the "Life in the UK" test—an obligatory test for all immigrants applying for British citizenship and for Indefinite

Figure 3.3. Lena performs in *Blood & Soil*. Courtesy of Lena Šimić

Leave to Remain. Throughout the performance/test, two performers map their stories of multiple belongings to this isle. The performance event addresses the question of how texts regulate, map, and shape real living bodies. The piece juxtaposes the memorizing of the facts and figures of the "Life in the UK" test alongside the fictionalized poetic narration of "nearly-lost," "almost-forgotten" identities of the performers—in this case as a "Yugoslav" and a "Jew."

An explicit aim of the performance was to unpack and trouble different notions of citizenship: citizenship as pedagogical (about testing, learning, passing), ideas of a citizenship from above (granted and governed by the state), and migrant paths to citizenship from below (about personal memories, and embodied experience). In particular, you wanted, I think, to expose the contradictions between these different versions of citizenship in order to challenge the instrumentalization of belonging in the form of the "Life in the UK" test.

LŠ: Working in a community center is not easy. So actually, the emphasis on the classroom as the stage for the performance, and the idea of testing the audience, was partly a consequence of the space but it worked really well conceptually.

IT: What happened is that you gathered people who are trying to obtain citizenship, who are in the process and are going to have to take test, together with people who are never going to have their citizenship questioned, who will never go through the test.

LŠ: On the one hand, the test was fun. Of course, most people did not pass the test (and most of the "British" in the audience failed). We talked about what it meant to pass and fail and then we started to question the questions of the test themselves as the audience disputed the answers. The other message is that for some people, like Pa Modou, "becoming British," passing often arbitrary tests to remain in the country, can be a life and death situation. By the way, the Guardian has run Life in the UK test for its readers on the blog: http://www.guardian.co.uk/uk/blog/quiz/2011/oct/11/uk-citizenship-test-quiz.

IT: So *Blood and Soil* was about acting out the absurdity of regimes of citizenship. What happens next in the *Becoming British* project?

LŠ: Well, while there are currently no concrete plans for continuing the work through the *Becoming British* project, the critical thinking behind it around the notions of immigration and protest continues. As a part of the project, I started exploring questions of nationalism, migration, and citizenship in relationship to conflict, and to this end, I have begun to work with some British soldiers who have been involved in recent conflicts overseas, particularly in the Balkans in the nineteen nineties. Furthermore, Jennifer and I conducted creative writing and photography workshops for MRANG (Merseyside Refugee and Asylum Seekers Pre and Post Natal Group) [http://www.mrang.co.uk/]. What for me has been developing from the project is thinking about different communities, like that of soldiers, on the one hand, and that of refugees and asylum seekers, on the other, and trying to understand how/why they are such separate groups. Jennifer and I might continue our work with MRANG provided there is interest from the women in the group and hopefully some financial backing. Jennifer has set up Migrant Artists Mutual Aid network and its first fundraising event in December twenty eleven, with the support from the Lantern Theatre in Liverpool, raised funds for Fatoumata Sowe, a Gambian mother claiming asylum to protect her two-year-old British-born daughter from FGM. In March twenty twelve Migrant Artist Mutual Aid staged a production of *Vagina Monologues* for VDay twenty twelve—A Global Movement to End Violence Against Women [http://www.vday.org/home]. The three performances involved a number of performers, professional and amateur, and took place at the Lantern Theatre and Unitarian Church Hall (usually toddler group). The event raised awareness about FGM and Fatoumata's case. Both Fatoumata and her two-year-old daughter were present. I was involved in both events as a performer and as a pedagogue. Furthermore, together with Jennifer and colleagues at Liverpool Hope, I am currently organizing creative event "Cartographies of Justice" (due to take place in December twenty twelve at Liverpool Hope University). The event will include student performance (directed by Migrant Artist Mutual Aid), migrant story slam, invited performances, long table discussion, and migrant feast.

Notes

1. The effects of Liverpool 08 on local people and artists have been documented in the film *Liverpool 08—Capital of Vulture* (dir Jürgen Cyranek, Rebecca Cyranek, and Claudia Christen, City Pictures, 2011).

Work Cited

Isin, Engin. 2008. "Theorizing Acts of Citizenship." In *Acts of Citizenship*, edited by Engin F. Isin and Greg M. Nielsen. London: Zed Books.
Šimić, Lena. 2009. "'On Medea/Mothers' Clothes: A Foreigner Re-figuring Medea and Motherhood." *Feminist Review* 93 (1): 109–15.

Tyler, Imogen. 2013. "Naked Protest: The Maternal Politics of Citizenship and Revolt." *Citizenship Studies* 17 (2): 211–26.

———. 2011. "Pregnant Beauty: Maternal Femininities under Neoliberalism." In *New Femininities: Postfeminism, Neoliberalism, and Identity*, edited by Rosalind Gill and Christina Scharff New York: Palgrave.

Walters, William. 2008. "Acts of Demonstration: Mapping the Territory of (Non-) Citzenship." In *Acts of Citizenship*, edited by Engin F. Isin and Greg M. Nielsen. London: Zed Books.

Verson, Jennifer. 2006. "Why We Need cultural activism." In *Do It Yourself: A Handbook for Changing Our World*, edited by Kim Bryan, Paul Chatterton, Alice Cutler. London: Pluto.

Figure 4.1. *Sleep Dealer*, DVD cover, 2008. Alex Rivera

4

Border Disorder

Alex Rivera with Katarzyna Marciniak

With my work in film and video I try to address and reflect the experiences of the Latino community through a language of humor, satire, and metaphor. This is easy since our reality these days is increasingly becoming a dark, surreal comedy.

—Alex Rivera

This is the American Dream. We give the Americans what they have always wanted—all the work and none of the workers.

—Node factory operator, *Sleep Dealer*

Alex Rivera, the director of *Sleep Dealer*, which premiered at the Sundance Film Festival in 2008, winning the prestigious Waldo Salt Screenwriting and Alfred P. Sloan awards there, describes his film as a "Third World science-fiction," and a "cyberpunk of the south." In stylistically innovative ways, the narrative engages the politics of the Mexico-U.S. border, highlighting the intersecting themes of migration, labor, and technology. It offers a dystopic vision of the future where a coyote is transformed into a "coyotek," where crossing the border on foot is perceived as obsolete: "[My uncle] crossed the border in the old days by foot. Before nodes that's how they used to do it. Unbelievable." In *Sleep Dealer* people from the south connect with the prosperous north via nodes. Instead of "Want to cross?" the question now is "Need a connection? Want to connect, baby? Looking for a node job?" The nodal "connection" is the new "crossing;" Tijuana is branded the city of the future; Tijuana Node Bar is one of those cool sites where one can initiate the desired transaction.

The opening shots of *Sleep Dealer* fragment protagonist Memo Cruz's body—we see his face, his glazed eyes, his moving hands attached to nodes, his mouth covered by a futuristic, pilot-like gear. In this opening sequence, the "nodal hands" remain most evocative, recalling a memorable scene from Gregory Nava's film *El Norte* (1983) when the character Arturo Xanax tells his son, Enrique: "For the rich all peasants are just a pair of arms to do their work."

In *Sleep Dealer*, Memo's arms perform the work, a hypnotic dance of sorts, which the audience cannot possibly comprehend until Memo reveals that through the nodal technology he is actually working in the United States while his body physically remains in the factory in Tijuana. His voiceover informs us: "We call the factories 'sleep dealers' because if you work long enough you collapse." Being a node worker one can pick oranges in Florida, work a construction job in New York, or be a nanny in California—all from hyper-connected factories in Mexico, or any of countless sites around the globe. It is certainly a different kind of labor, a disembodied work; as Memo eventually claims, "My energy was being drained, sent far away." Several times we see memorable long shots of the inside of the factory, which punctuate the narrative. In a long hallway, connected through endless wires, human bodies perform a robotic, rhythmical movement, recalling similar "working" scenes from the factory in Fritz Lang's 1927 *Metropolis* and thus making an intertextual connection with a longer cinematic history of social critique.

When Memo gets the desired nodes, his own cybernetic implants, and plugs in for the first time, he reflects: "Finally, I could connect my nervous system to the other system—the global economy." The moment of connection feels hallucinatory: Memo armors his body and finds himself operating a robot somewhere in California, on a construction site. We hear his heavy breathing, we share the first wobbly moments of Memo trying to steady himself as, uncannily, he finds himself simultaneously in two different spaces. He looks down—and the audience shares his point-of-view—and realizes that, as a robot, he is positioned high up. This initial connection is thus figured as a moment of dizziness and also one of curious emptiness and physical disengagement as his body performs the work long-distance without actually touching anything on the other side. The fact that "real touch" is not permissible underlines the film's poignant argument: the futuristic politics of the U.S.-Mexico border is a violent anti-immigrant fantasy—the border is sealed and uncrossable, but the labor from the south can still flow, carefully orchestrated by "sleep dealers" that, of course, reference the contemporary *maquiladoras*.

While at the factory, Memo wears a blue vest stamped with the word *cybracero*, referencing Rivera's 1997 mockumentary *Why Cybraceros?*, the short film that paved the way for *Sleep Dealer*. *Why Cybraceros?* cleverly utilizes and reconfigures an original 1959 promotional film by the California Grower's Council titled *Why Braceros?* to make a historical connection. On the one hand, the viewers hear about the bracero (meaning "a man who works with his arms and hands") program, one instigated by the U.S. government to bring in skilled Mexican farmers to work in the California fields. On the other hand, weaving archival footage, animation, and computer-generated graphics, the original documentary is formally and conceptually reworked into a mocking farce: "Under the cybracero program, American farm labor will be accomplished on American soil but no Mexican workers will need to leave Mexico. Only the labor of Mexicans will cross the border; Mexican workers will no longer have to." As the cheerful female voiceover delivers this message, we see an animated figure of the Mexican worker jumping across the imaginary border—except that his armless body stays behind and only his arms are permitted on the other side. The innovative idea is "cybracero," a long-distance farm worker, one that operates a computer with a joystick and uses high-speed Internet connection to act as the telecommuting laborer who, via robots, can work in the orchard and pick the fruit: "To the worker it's as simple as point and click to pick; for the American farmer it's all the labor without the worker."

In November 2011, while Rivera was a visiting artist at the Occidental College in Los Angeles, we sat down to talk about immigration, protest, anger, and oppositional art.

Katarzyna Marciniak: Anger is a potent political motivator that can lay ground for radical, nonhegemonic representations, like your work. My students and I screened *Why Cybraceros?*—they recognized the irony that is embedded in the narrative and thought that the film could be interpreted as an indictment of a violent exploitation, a critique of the uneven "global flow," that is, the fact that the goods and labor can cross but people cannot. They thought the film successfully undermines the euphoric narratives of globalization.

Alex Rivera: One of my deep beliefs is that for many, many people on the planet to be able to exist and express themselves as complete humans would take radical transformation, meaning that the global economic system right now is very effective at moving millions of people around and into positions in which they are only able to express themselves in very limited ways, often through their labor, but not supposed to express themselves in other ways that we would think about as the most essential to being human—not able to access education, unable to vote, having to live in fear in order to access health services. In the case of the United States, with its community of between twelve and fifteen million undocumented workers, I really view that community as a presence that is very real, material, embodied in millions of people—many of them my friends and family—but also a community that is in a position where their full humanity is constantly being denied by the context in which we live. The work that I do often uses satire or documentary, trying to get at that violent contradiction of being and not being. There is an underlying anger that needs to course through that.

KM: I was telling my students who did not attend your talk about the tension that you articulated between, on the one hand, the rise of new media technology and the sense of movement, openness, and borderlessness and, on the other hand, the obsessive tightening of the border—patrolling the border, aggressive militarization of the border. Speak to this incongruence vis-à-vis your work.

AR: I started to make film and video work in nineteen ninety-three and ninety-four and, through my family and my father's story, I got interested in immigration and, through the national political conversation in the mid-nineteen nineties, I became further interested in it. In the mid-nineteen nineties, primarily in California, there was a really powerful and vocal anti-immigrant movement that motivated statewide propositions like Proposition one-eighty-seven, which targeted immigrant youth in public schools and disputed their access to health care. A similar climate existed at the national level, evidenced by President Clinton who began Operation Gatekeeper to fortify the U.S.-Mexico border in unprecedented ways. There was a powerful anti-immigrant discourse in the nation in the mid-nineteen nineties. But nineteen ninety-four was also the year that NAFTA was signed and implemented so there was this counter, parallel discourse around free trade, and that somehow an emergent borderless economy would produce benefits for everybody. That borderlessness was crystallized in the phrase "the global village," and embodied by the Internet. It was an interesting moment to start to care about borders and immigration because there were very conflicted and contradictory messages coming through the ether.

In my first film *Papapapá* (1995), I made reference to the contradiction between NAFTA's "open borders" policy for trade, on one hand, and the militarization of borders for working people, on the other. I was struck by the stark contrast on display in nineteen ninety-four. It made me wonder—Where are we going? Is it free trade, integration, or is it separation? Which is it? And it turns out it is both. It is free trade for products and flows of capital and it is militarism and criminalizing for flows of workers, or people. Now in twenty twelve, the critique seems fairly obvious, but nineteen ninety-four—the year NAFTA took effect, the year the border wall was first built—was a special historical moment, unique and powerful in how visible those contradictions were. So, when I started to make films, that is what I wanted to explore.

KM: *The Borders Trilogy* [2002], a triptych you showed here, is fascinating in terms of these contradictions and tensions between borderlessness and tightening of the border. In the first one, *Love on the Line*, there is a series of haunting images of humans touching each other across the bars on the Tijuana beach that form the official border. The bars are thick and form a barrier yet people put their arms between to reach out, to be able to make a connection through touch. So, like in *Sleep Dealer*, the audience is again asked to contemplate the trope of touching as crucial for the politics of the border. Looking at the bars, one of the men there says: "This is solid, you cannot cross through. But there are things that aren't solid and they can cross through" [Figure 4.2]. The film offers a visual meditation on touching,

Figure 4.2. *Love on the Line* (from *The Borders Trilogy*), 2002. Alex Rivera

yet not being able to be together. I thought that was a really compelling visualization of the kind of cruelty that the border symbolizes.

AR: The U.S.-Mexico border is a very unique border because it is a land border between the so-called third world and first world, or the developing and the developed. However you want to phrase it, it is a unique border because it is a land border whereas in the Straits of Gibraltar you have a lot of migration between Northern Africa and Southern Europe. A family that is divided perhaps between a resident in Spain and a resident in Morocco cannot meet at the Straits of Gibraltar and embrace. But the U.S.-Mexico border, because it is a land border, has created fascinating and heartwrenching visuals, including, of course, the wall that runs now for thousands of miles and out into the Pacific Ocean, and these transnational families that gather there to reconnect, through the bars. Visually, these encounters look like jail visits because there are people meeting, separated by a barrier, and yet on both sides nobody has done anything wrong.

KM: And they are free to move on each side.

AR: And they are free on either side, but just not free to cross. The first time I saw these families divided by that fence I thought maybe they were performance artists, or I thought it was a conceptual statement because the border beach in Tijuana is a place that for a long time has attracted many artists, so I thought that these families might be . . .

KM: Part of border art.

AR: Yeah. But it turned out just to be border life, which is more surreal than most border art.

KM: Of course, what interests me most is the relation between your work and the idea of immigrant protest. In a different interview, you commented on the dangers of visibility that protest in general might engender: "With any gesture to express power, to organize, or to make noise, you have the threat of deportation looming over you. Reality sets the stage for transnational movement. . . . It is a process of becoming powerful in the context of being told to disappear" [Decena and Gray 2006, 132]. So protest as such is already contingent, ridden with ambivalence and undecidability [see Tyler and Marciniak 2013] and yet, as Jacques Derrida has argued, "ethics and politics . . . start with undecidability" (66). The English word *protest*—"to declare publicly"—derives from a Latin verb meaning "to testify, give witness." Immigrant protests are certainly acts of public declaration that testify to and contest various forms of social abjectification, but, the very performance of protest exposes the protestors thus making them potentially vulnerable to all kinds of punitive measures. The underpinning sense of "ethical undecidability" is crucial to keep in mind in order to forestall a romanticization of protest as an unproblematic social revolt. Given this context, you made an interesting observation during your public talk—that the way we think of the border is indicative of the way we think of the nation.

How might we relate this point to the discussion of protest and its undecidability?

AR: In terms of the concept of the border and protest, when I started to work on immigration, the border was being fortified with the wall in Operation Gatekeeper. I knew the border as a place and a metaphor. Through writers like Gloria Anzaldúa and performance artists like Guillermo Gómez-Peña, I was aware of a mental borderland that people could live in no matter where they happened to be. "The nation" has two sets of borders that we must examine to understand the existence of the nation, and the ways in which immigrants challenge it.

The first, and easiest to understand, are geographic borders. Lines on maps, lines on the ground. These are still remarkably fluid, and change over time as a result of war, revolution, and sometimes in other surprising ways. I love the story of the Chamizal border dispute. For half of its length, the U.S.-Mexico border follows the Rio Grande, a natural border. Seems like a simple and stable arrangement. But the section of the river called the Chamizal kept changing, because the river would flood, and run a new course, and so landowners who were in Mexico for decades perhaps, after a flood, would find themselves all of a sudden on the other side of the river, now in the United States, or vice versa. The land itself kept crossing the border. Geographical borders, can, in surprising ways, become slippery and contested.

But the more important border system, in a sense, refers to the national borders wrapped around our bodies. Even though a group of a hundred people might be inside the United States' land borders, that, obviously, does not make them all citizens. Inside that group there may be citizens, temporary guests, permanent noncitizen residents, undocumented people, etcetera. And the "border system" that regulates which bodies have access to which types of power and permanence inside the nation is a system that is highly fluid because it exists in our imaginations and memories, and it is the system that the immigrant is contesting when she engages in protest. The undocumented immigrant is trying to expand the nation, and create flow and fluidity in the system of regulation of bodies.

It is interesting to look at this second border scheme historically. I have been reading Mae Ngai's book, *Impossible Subjects*, and she talks about the very first year in the nineteen twenties when the border patrol was first funded, so they were first charged with apprehending undocumented immigrants and deporting them. There was immediately a conversation of "Where is the border?" because everyone knew the Border Patrol was not going to stand right on the border. The border itself is not even a millimeter thick. It is a point of contact, it has no width, only length, and the border patrol cannot literally patrol only the border. The patrol is going to necessarily occur one foot or ten feet or ten miles inside the nation. So when this new enforcement regime was invented, there was public confusion about how far into the nation would these officers be going? And how will they decide who is documented and who is not without violating protections against unreasonable search and seizure?

The border patrol is a kind of phantom within the nation-space, tasked with having to separate bodies into groups of legal and illegal and to do so based on suspicions and hunches. In order to make contact with someone who is inside the borders of the nation (which is everyone the border patrol will encounter), the agent needs to assume their guilt. The "border" that is being enforced is inside the mind of the agent as he or she assumes for one reason or another that an individual is likely undocumented or not.

So from the very founding of the Border Patrol there were questions around jurisdiction and process and those questions were never really answered in a clear way—questions around immigration status to this day exist in a separate legal zone. Furthermore, thanks to our politics and thanks to advances in information sharing and new technologies, you have the integration of local police into the border patrol through programs like "Secure Communities," which mandates that local police forward the fingerprints of anybody they arrest to immigration so that any contact with law enforcement can lead to deportation for the undocumented. You have all these cases of people who were driving with a broken taillight, get pulled over by the cops, who send the fingerprints to ICE, and then this family that might have been here for twenty years is then, all of a sudden, separated. The cause of deportation being driving with a broken taillight, perhaps in Iowa, or a state far from the physical border, is a new reality.

KM: And you are also probably thinking about the new laws in Arizona, Georgia, and Alabama?

AR: Well, Secure Communities is a national program that began under the Bush administration and has been strengthened under the Obama administration. It is separate from the state-by-state programs. In Arizona and Alabama and other states, what they have been empowering the police to do is to look across the street and say, "Oh, I suspect that person. I'm going to go check their papers." The law in Arizona was infamous for allowing that. They basically told the cops they could walk up and say, "Can I see your papers?" Secure Communities is about a database, and just saying "Once a person is detained by the police, arrested and fingerprinted, forward those fingerprints to immigration." They are in the system, so they have not been necessarily profiled or singled out, but they end up in the system for any number of reasons and then the police are connected to immigration, but the net effect has been the border-ification of the entire country. Every inch of the nation has become also its border.

KM: This induction of fear, the perpetuation of a culture of national anxiety about immigration and thus the ongoing production of what Engin Isin calls "the neurotic citizen" [2004] has been historically contested by various transborder art projects coming from Latino/a and Chicano/a communities. You have mentioned Anzaldúa's and Gómez-Peña's work, and whenever I teach their texts and performances, my students always end up discussing anger and protest in relation to the biopolitics of the border. Anzaldúa movingly writes about the violence of the first world meeting the third world, the border as a "shock culture" [11], as an ongoing national wound, unable to heal itself: "The U.S. Mexican border *es una herida abierta* where the Third World grates against the first and bleeds" [11]. And Gómez-Peña and his group La Pocha Nostra, artists who are engaged in "Conceptual Institute of Hybrid Art" [http://www.pochanostra.com], embrace border aesthetics as one of impurities and radical possibilities and even defiantly call themselves "border citizens" devoted to experiments with identity [*A World of Art*]. I see their influence in your films but the innovative and interventionist part that is unique to your work centers on the idea of a "tele-migrant." You fuse immigration and technology in a way that is oppositional to anti-immigrant digital rage that has been vigorously developing online [see Doty 2007; Marciniak 2013]. Anti-immigrant online activism—groups such as the well-known Minuteman, or Grassfire, ProjectUSA, National Organization for European American Rights, and many others—has been on the rise and the new media has become a powerful organizational tool for the coherence of the nation that anxiously imagines its own white extinction and acts on that fear.

AR: There is the Internet as an organizational tool; people talk about the essential role it played in Arab Spring. And whether that is true or not, it is definitely talked about, as well as the role its playing in the Occupy movement right now. The Internet is also fundamental to the world social forum and to all kinds of progressive activism globally. Parallel to that, the Internet has obviously been a space where the skinheads, neo-Nazis, and border vigilantes have been exerting themselves, and in some cases, the border vigilantes have really been visionary in their use of the digital space as a performative space, where they have been performing fantasies of security, whether it is putting cameras on the border and streaming it, or flying remote control airplanes with little cameras and streaming that to the Internet. Either way, they have used the digital space as a space to say, "We have better technology than the government," and to shame the government into investing more and more money into border security. And it has been kind of fascinating to watch as an artist because in a sense they have been using the techniques of performance art to create a public disturbance and to move people's emotions and produce very material results in terms of this extraordinary investment in so-called security, which is a fantasy of its own. The more money that is spent on border security, the larger and larger the community of undocumented folks in the U.S. grows. It is almost a parallel chart in terms of the amount of money spent on border security and the size of the undocumented community in the U.S. It is amazing to watch the vigilantes put up their fantasies of security, the government invest billions of dollars in security, and then the actual material result is simply more and more migration.

KM: And these public disturbances, as you put it, of the online anti-immigrant activism have been widely successful in mobilizing citizens who get seduced by the national narrative of security and by the fantasy of purity and wholeness of a nation that needs to be ongoingly protected from the perceived invasion. You refer to this as "border disorder."

AR: You know, it is tempting to think their success is because of the downturn in the economy but I remember the mid-nineteen nineties when the economy was booming. The vigilantes were also successful then, so the currency of the anti-immigrant narrative is not dependent on the economy at all, up or down. There is something else that is happening there. To me, the question of "Do people deserve to be here or not?" and how it is simply put . . . even asking that question is all about asserting power and privilege over the national space and asserting a kind of dominance.

KM: These discourses are ultimately about the possession of the nation, about ownership, and thus about a neurotic policing of that ownership. Your representation of a "tele-migrant" both playfully acknowledges and disturbs this national fantasy. On the one hand, the worker is across the border and thus poses no threat to those inside the nation. On the other hand, this figure exposes deep-seated hypocrisies and contingencies that underpin what Nicholas De Genova, for example, calls "the border spectacle" [2011].

That is, these passionate anti-"alien" actions and declarations produced by anti-immigrant activism obliterate the fact that while many crusade against undocumented workers, or documented dark-skinned immigrants, simultaneously such workers are willingly employed by "legitimate" Americans as a cheap labor force to care for their children, clean their houses, or do their gardening [see Hondagneu-Sotelo 2001]. Given these paradoxes, tell us how you came up with this figure of a tele-migrant in *Why Cybraceros?* What is the film's connection to the idea of protest and anger?

AR: I just want to finish a thought from before because I have been dwelling on it, and then I will get there. One thing I want to say is that in the anti-immigrant rage, you really do sense that the idea of the American nation is inherently unstable because it is—in our myth system—a nation of immigrants. Who is and who is not American is always a shifting terrain, so I think that uncertainty that is built into our national myth system is a definite motivator for people who need to patrol its edges and decide who is inside or out. It is uncertainty that is on full display by the people who want to make it so fixed and so clear.

The idea of the tele-migrant. . . . The back-story of it is that in the 1990s I was reading about the idea of telecommuting in *Wired* magazine, and *Wired* offered up this vision of the future where everybody could work from home, and there would not be any traffic on the highways, no one would be in the subways any more because we would all be at home, telecommuting to our offices. I was joking around with a friend of mine because my family has had to "commute" from Latin America to the United States to work, traveling four thousand miles from Peru to New York to work in factories and landscaping, so I thought, "What if they could telecommute? Could they have a place in this utopian fantasy?" And so I came up with this idea of the telecommuting immigrant, and at that time, in that moment of anti-immigrant hysteria in the U.S., I said "Wow, that actually would be the perfect solution—the economy could receive the labor without receiving the workers." It was a joke over a beer, but then I started to talk to people about the idea, and I went to see a show at the Museum of the Moving Image in New York where this archival film was presented. The film was called *Why Braceros?* It was produced in the nineteen fifties by the California Growers Association, so it was made by the owners of California farms who were defending the bracero program.

KM: And who were also obviously benefiting from the program, right?

AR: Yes, it was in defense of using Mexican labor on American farms, and the film expressed all the ways in which having migrant labor benefits the farm owners, and what is good for the farm owner is good for the economy.

Broadly, that was the argument of the film. I took that film and recut it and used its voiceover and its title and its images as a template for an updated version called *Why Cybraceros?* which proposed the tele-migration solution, a high-tech solution to the immigration crisis.

KM: That was such a brilliant conceptualization—the migrating hands without the body; we get the labor but not the worker. In other words, we get the hands.

AR: It is weird how sometimes ideas come out of you, and then you stare at them, whether you are a painter or a writer or what have you. You know there is a moment when you create something, and then it is sort of not yours anymore. It just sits there, and you can look at it and see things that sometimes you did not even put in it, that are there. So this idea, which was really a joke about telecommuting and a critique of Internet utopianism, the idea sat there with me and started to talk back at me, and the idea became a reflection on labor in general, just the alienation of labor and working for a wage, putting your life energy into something that rarely you get to own. That condition is exaggerated for the undocumented immigrant who puts her labor into a system and a society that she is unable to access in countless ways. It became a meditation on the logic of the global economy, which is that as technology advances, it collapses distance, and that allows powerful interests, corporations, for example, to slide around the globe and either move their factories to look for lower wages, to look for weaker environmental regulations, and also to use the digital matrix to create new and bizarre and hyper-profitable configurations of capital and labor. So you can have service sector workers working in call centers in India, beaming their labor into the American consumer, so you are billing the American consumer in dollars in this economy, but paying people rupees in that economy in ways that were unimaginable fifteen years ago. The metaphor of the tele-migrant has kind of become everything to me. I can see into it like looking into a diamond; the more detail I look at, the more I see all these other kinds of ideas and reflections in it that I never even intended when I came up with it. It has been a fun idea to play with.

KM: And the concept of the cybracero, the hybrid you have imagined—the Mexican farmer with the joystick.

AR: It is my dad playing that character!

KM: For the readers, tell us a bit about your family background; you mentioned that your father is Peruvian.

AR: I was born in New York City. My mom was born in Brooklyn; she is Irish-American. My dad was born in Lima, Peru, in a rough neighborhood there called La Victoria. For readers who might know Mexico City, it is like the Tepito of Lima. He came to the U.S. in his early twenties and worked in New York City in factories and restaurants. He was drafted into the army and was in the infantry. Through that he started to put himself through college. He met my mom. I was born in New York and raised in upstate New York; my mom worked at IBM in upstate New York.

KM: Did you have a sense of growing up in a bilingual, binational family?

AR: Well, my father learned English when he came to the U.S., but I think his whole life he felt like he suffered because of his accent and lost opportunities because of his accent. He was worried that I would have an accent if he spoke Spanish to me, so he did not speak Spanish to me when I was young, and so I grew up very assimilated. My awareness of Peru was from a kind of Peruvian grab-bag around the house: Inca Cola, Inca Pisco, images of Peru, and then hearing my grandmother's voice on the phone occasionally, who I could not speak to because she spoke Spanish and I spoke English. But through my dad I knew there were Maoist revolutionaries laying siege to Peru, and that my grandmother's life was at risk because everybody's life was at risk at the time of the Sendero Luminoso. So it was an odd Latino experience in the sense that I was in a bubble in upstate New York, protected and assimilated, and yet there was still this rumble offscreen where I knew there was another place that was night to our day and I was connected to it by blood. I think the idea of this other place that was intimately connected to my life, but somehow also invisible, expresses itself in my work in terms of notions of connectivity and trying to humanize and visualize those invisible linkages—the linkages that our political/economic system needs to have invisible and benefits by having them invisible.

KM: During your talk about *The Borders Trilogy*, you commented on the idea of dead labor and living labor; you spoke about how we want the product but do not want to think about the labor that goes into the creation of this product. Explain how this point is reflected in your films.

AR: In *The Borders Trilogy* [2002], I tell three stories of three different borders. The first, *Love on the Line*, takes place at the U.S.-Mexico border where you can see the wall; you can see how material it is as families that are divided due to complications in immigration law make pilgrimages to the wall, one member of the family on the north side and the rest of the family on the south side. They both cannot cross and so they reunite through the bars. The second film, *Container City*, is set in Newark, New Jersey, which is a big port for the northeast, and it tells the story of these shipping containers which are used for moving products from one country to another. Shipping containers are basically the little blood cells of the global economy; they allow for international trade to occur. The film focuses on the-port-as-a-border of sorts for commerce. You can see how massive the movement of products is into that port. In the final segment, *A Visible Border*, I focus on a single, haunting image. It is an image produced by backscatter x-ray technology, which is a new x-ray technology that they are using at airports as well as at borders to scan your body before you enter an airplane or to scan entire trucks before they enter the U.S. [Figure 4.3]. In that image, you see a shipping container filled primarily with bananas, but contorted and hidden in some secret compartments underneath, you see several bodies of the migrants. So in that third segment, I try to bring the two previous ones together by showing how when you have these militarized, violent borders for people, but these wildly open borders for commerce, a natural response for these people is to seek the same freedom as the product. So you have people in a shipping container hoping to cross with the same facility that the bananas will cross.

My occasional collaborator, filmmaker David Riker, introduced me to Marx's theory of living and dead labor. Living labor is the type of labor that expresses itself in the act of cleaning a floor or washing a dish or taking

Figure 4.3. *A Visible Border* (from *The Borders Trilogy*), 2002 Alex Rivera

care of a child, mowing a lawn, the kind of labor where there is a service provided by the body and a wage is offered in compensation. The worker is present and needs to be cared for, her children need to be educated, they need to be housed—this labor comes with needs. The counterpoint is dead labor, labor where in a factory environment, the labor is embedded in a product, let's say a shirt and that shirt is moved to a distant point where it is sold, so at the moment the value of the labor is realized in a sale, the labor is already embedded in the product and the laborer is now invisible. In the shipping container filled with bananas and migrants, you have both types present. The bananas reflect all the thousands of hours of agricultural labor inside the bananas and that labor is welcomed across the border. But the migrant bodies that are also present, perhaps even the people who once picked the bananas; that type of labor is not welcomed across the border. This frames our current immigration and economic policy as a kind of contradiction between a policy that welcomes dead labor under the rubric of "free trade" while it problematizes and criminalizes living labor. To me that was a useful and elegant and frightening way of looking at the status quo and how hard it is to change it.

Works Cited

Anzaldúa, Gloria. 1987. *Borderlands/La Frontera: The New Mestiza*. San Francisco: Aunt Lute Books.

De Genova, Nicholas, and Rozalinda Borcila. 2011. "An Image of Our Future: On the Making of Migrant 'Illegality.'" *AREA Chicago*. http://www.areachicago.org/p/issues/immigrations/image-our-future/. Accessed July 12, 2011.

Decena, Carlos Ulises, and Margaret Gray. 2006. "Putting Transnationalism to Work: An Interview with Filmmaker Alex Rivera." *Social Text* 24 (3): 131–38.

Derrida, Jacques. 1999. "Hospitality, Justice, and Responsibility: A Dialogue with Jacques Derrida." In *Questioning Ethics: Contemporary Debates in Philosophy*, edited by R. Kearney and M. Dooley. New York: Routledge.

Doty, Roxanne L. 2007. "States of Exception on the Mexico-U.S. Border: Security, 'Decisions,' and Civilian Border Patrols." *International Political Sociology* 1 (2): 113–37.

Hondagneu-Sotelo, Pierrette. 2001. *Doméstica: Immigrant Workers Cleaning and Caring in the Shadows of Affluence*. Berkeley: University of California Press.

Isin, Engin, F. 2004. "The Neurotic Citizen." *Citizenship Studies* 8 (3): 217–35.

Marciniak, Katarzyna. 2013. "Legal/Illegal: Protesting Citizenship in Fortress America." *Citizenship Studies* 17 (2): 260–77.

Ngai, Mae. 2004. *Impossible Subjects: Illegal Aliens and the Making of Modern America*. Princeton: Princeton University Press.

Tyler, Imogen, and Katarzyna Marciniak. 2013. "Immigrant Protest: An Introduction." *Citizenship Studies* 17 (2): 143–56.

A World of Art: Works in Progress: Guillermo Gómez-Peña, The Temple of Confessions. 1997. S. Burlington, VT: Annenberg/CPB Project.

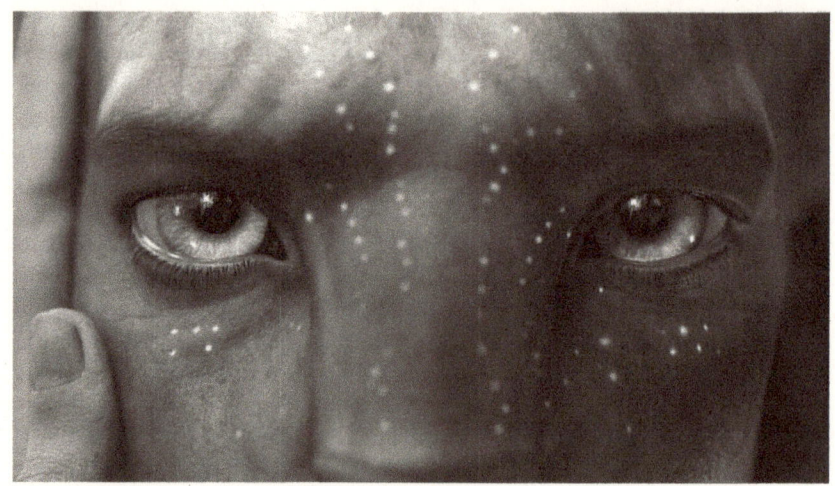

Figure 5.1. "I see into you": the ethnographic spectacle of *Avatar*

5

Loving the Alien

Indigenous Protest and Neo-Colonial Violence in James Cameron's Avatar

BRUCE BENNETT

What is the relationship between the imaginaries of mainstream cinema and migrant protests? This is a slightly strange and slightly awkward question, but what this chapter seeks to explore is the sometimes unexpected ways in which popular culture can provide materials and spaces for critical self-reflection around issues of colonization, capitalism, and the displacements it effects. Further, as we shall see in the case of *Avatar* and the *Avatar*-activism that it enables, popular culture is an important source of what Tyler (2013) describes as "political parables," which travel and sometimes trouble prevailing forms of common sense about the meaning of democracy and rights.

Among the hours of supplementary material included with the 2010 "Extended Blu-Ray Collector's Edition" of *Avatar* (Cameron 2009) is a feature-length promotional documentary, *Capturing Avatar* (Bouzereau, Grane [producers] 2010), which comprises a detailed account of the film's development and production. Interviewed in the documentary, Cameron explains that the narrative premise of *Avatar* is that "we are the aliens." This apparently simple inversion of an opposition that structures the drama of many science fiction and fantasy narratives is the basis for the film's critique of racism and colonial violence, corporate greed and self-interest, and the environmentally destructive effects of mining, deforestation, and industrial "progress." In narrating the transgression of the interface between human and alien, the film invites the viewer to identify with (and to identify herself as) an abjected, racialized other; the politicizing "alienation effect" associated with critical film and theatre is literalized here in the most striking way. In orienting its account of the violent conflict between the colonizing/immigrant minority and the indigenous majority around the perspective of a boundary-crossing protagonist, who is branded a race traitor by a colleague, this self-reflexive, transnational film offers a powerfully affective but ultimately ideologically ambiguous account of the structural relationships between imperialist brutality and Western consumer culture. *Avatar* offers an intriguing case study in the potential and limitations of mainstream fantasy cinema as social criticism, a question that, Cameron makes clear, exercises him in relation to this film:

> The question remains, "How much does a piece of entertainment—a movie—actually change the way people act?" One can hope that if people feel that twinge of conscience, that little sense of responsibility, it can only be a movement in the right direction. I just don't want to feel that I'm going through this process of making these movies just entertaining people and that it has no higher purpose. I'll settle for a small change.

This chapter will examine the ways in which Cameron's film dramatizes issues of indigenous protest, immigration, and colonization and attempts to trouble the alignment of the spectator with particular positions, employing an immersive aesthetic to emphasize this disorienting sense of destabilized boundaries.

Avatar is one of a number of recent science fiction films to explore, in more or less direct ways through the narrative device of encounters between humans and aliens, issues of invasion, immigration and exploitation, catastrophic climate change, and the global war on terror. It is also one of a number of recent films that experiment with the aesthetic possibilities of stereoscopic cinematography and exhibition through narratives that deal with exploration and journeying, from documentaries such as *Cave of Forgotten Dreams* (Herzog 2010), which details prehistoric cave paintings in France, to an action-adventure film like *Sanctum* (Grierson 2011) depicting a disastrous cave-diving expedition in Papua New Guinea, or the anachronistic science fiction adventure, *John Carter* (Stanton 2012), in which the nineteenth-century protagonist is transported to Mars. *Avatar* is a contemporary example of what film theorist André Bazin termed the "exotic film," in which we see "the Western mind as it were taking over a far-off civilisation and interpreting it after its own fashion" (Bazin 1967, 155). *Avatar* stands apart, however, for its technical complexity, the global scale of the project (with production distributed across Europe, New Zealand, and the United States), and its hypervisibility as an example of contemporary Hollywood cinema.

Set in the middle of the twenty-second century, *Avatar* tells the story of Jake Sully,[1] a former marine, now disabled, who is dispatched to a distant Earth-like planet, ominously named Pandora, to participate in the exploitation of the planet's reserves of a highly valuable metal called "unobtainium." He is taking the place of his twin brother, a scientist who had trained to operate an "avatar," a genetically engineered remotely controlled replica of one of the planet's indigenous, blue-skinned "humanoid" inhabitants, the Na'vi. The story is thus built around the premise of a marvelous prosthetic, prophylactic technology that extends the physical capacities and the mobility of the operator in this environment with low gravity and unbreathable atmosphere. This is also a representational technology that projects the operator/viewer in a sensorially convincing environment—a fantasy of Bazinian total cinema—although the mechanism allows the operator, lying unconscious within a coffin-like capsule, the "avatar link" (see Figure 5.2), to interact with the environment in real time from a distance, like the pilot of an "unmanned aerial vehicle" or drone (see Bazin 1967, 17–22).[2] The film's title is thus a judicious reference both to the Hindu concept of a deity's use of a physical body to move around on earth, to the animated figures used to represent individuals within game environments, and to the narrative function for the spectator of a film's protagonist, but it also refers to the panoptic technologies of military surveillance and reconnaissance.

Figure 5.2. Sully is prepared for the avatar link.

The role of the scientists who operate the avatars is to mediate between the mining company and the natives in order to gain access for the humans to the planet's mineral reserves—to find what the company executive Parker Selfridge terms euphemistically, "a diplomatic solution" since, with regard to corporate public relations, "killing the indigenous looks bad." Headed by botanist Grace Augustine, the scientists are also engaged with a parallel form of nonconsensual "resource extraction," using this opportunity to undertake anthropological, botanical, and geological research, but, like "civilizing" European missionaries or colonists in Africa and Southeast Asia engaged with the acculturation of other peoples, they have also taken it upon themselves to educate Na'vi children in writing and speaking English, building a school in the forest.

Sully is persuaded by Colonel Quaritch, a brutal, prominently scarred security officer working for the mining company's private army (and another ex-marine), to feed him information directly about the geography of the environment and the culture of the Na'vi that he later uses to plan military assaults upon the Na'vi and their habitat. However, over the course of the narrative, Sully falls in love with a Na'vi princess, Neytiri, after she rescues his avatar when it becomes lost in the forest. At the same time, he is initiated into her community, learning to speak Na'vi, learning to track and hunt, and learning to ride a horselike "Pa'li" and, later, a flying lizard called an "Ikran." He becomes more attracted to her culture and the unspoiled, edenic natural environment she lives in, which is the spectacular focus of the film's intricate visualization of a new planet (and is contrasted with the suffocating urban sprawl depicted in the opening scenes).[3] When the mining company locates a huge reserve of unobtainium beneath a colossal centuries-old "Home Tree" that is the physical and spiritual focus for the tribe, Selfridge and Quaritch ignore the objections of Jake and his boss, Grace Augustine, and fell the tree in a spectacularly destructive sequence that recalls the sinking of the *Titanic* in Cameron's previous fiction film. This atrocity prompts the disaffected Jake, acting through his avatar, to rally the various "clans" of the Na'vi in fighting back against the mining company declaring, "This is our land." He secures his role as leader by taming a huge predatory flying lizard, the Toruk (which resembles the flying dragons of Anne McCaffrey's novels) and, in so doing, becomes only the sixth person ever to become the legendary "Toruk Makto," which grants him messianic status.

After a ferocious battle on the ground and in the air between the excessively armed humans and the Na'vi, armed only with spears and arrows and traveling on foot or mounted on horseback and banshee, the film concludes with surviving humans being escorted onto spaceships to be expelled from the planet. As Jake explains on the voiceover, marking his total identification with the Na'vi, "The aliens went back to their dying world." This transfer of allegiance is made permanent in the film's final scene in which Jake's human body is laid alongside his inert avatar's body at the base of the "tree of souls," which is the hub of a network of rhizomatic electro-chemical connections that run across the surface of the planet (see Figure 5.3). The bodies are enveloped in glowing cilia while hundreds of Na'vi dance and sing in Busby Berkeley–like unison and, in the film's final shot, which reiterates the film's thematic preoccupation with sight, the eyes of Jake's avatar open, his identity having been uploaded from one body to the other without the cumbersome technology of the avatar link. He has become alien.

Racial Cinema

The preoccupation of science fiction cinema with more or less conscious allegories of race is well established but it has a particular pertinence in relation to Cameron's cinema since one of his early professional assignments was redrafting the screenplay of *Alien Nation* (Baker 1988). This satirical film, subsequently developed into a TV series, depicts a near-future Los Angeles in which alien immigrants, "Newcomers" or "Slags," live and work uneasily alongside humans and, reprising *In the Heat of the Night* (Jewison 1967), the narrative has an alien detective assigned to partner a xenophobic human policeman. As Adilifu Nama observes:

Figure 5.3. Sully's identity is uploaded to his avatar in the film's final shot.

The tenet of America as a land of immigrants and, in the wake of the civil rights movement, a model of racial tolerance is stretched to its metaphorical limits by a narrative which a quarter of a million humanoid aliens, slaves on another planet, are given asylum in the United States. (Nama 2008, 132)

In particular, the film characterizes the alien asylum seekers as Latin American immigrants so that, Nama suggests, the film "views Los Angeles as the literal and symbolic frontline of a multicultural transformation sweeping across America wherein 'the aliens' of the film also signify a growing anxiety with the possible economic impact that Latino immigration could have on America" (Nama 2008, 133).

Despite its setting in a distant future and imaginary world—a gesture of allegorical outsourcing, perhaps—*Avatar* is no less specific with regard to the metaphoric significance of the Na'vi as an amalgam of indigenous peoples. In terms of their culture, habitat, and their spoken language, they are a representational synthesis of native Americans, Africans, Maoris, and Aborigines from Australia and New Zealand (where much of the film was shot in a motion-capture studio), South American indigenous peoples, Southeast Asian and Pacific peoples (see Figure 5.4). Unlike the technologically advanced and monstrous aliens encountered by humans in much contemporaneous science fiction cinema, however, such as *Transformers* (Bay 2007), *District 9* (Blomkamp 2009), *Skyline* (2010), *Battle: Los Angeles*[4] (Liebesman 2011) or *Super 8* (Abrams 2011), the Na'vi are initially coded as "primitive." This problematic characterization of the Na'vi is acknowledged by the highly self-conscious film, as Quaritch describes them as "savages" while Selfridge calls them the "blue monkeys." However, at the same time that the film displays a postcolonial anxiety, or what Gayatri Chakravorty Spivak terms "reverse-ethnic sentimentality," with regard to this depiction of a racialized other, it is clear that among the genre elements that make up this self-referential and self-consciously authorial hybrid text, is the classical ethnographic film with its anxious racial fascination (Spivak 1988, 289).

As Fatimah Tobing Rony observes in a historical study of ethnographic film and photography, ethnographic films have been concerned with a restatement of difference:

> The people depicted in an "ethnographic film" are meant to be seen as exotic, as people who until only too recently were categorized by science as Savage and Primitive, of an earlier evolutionary stage in the overall history of humankind: people without history, without writing, without civilisation, without technology, without archives. (Rony 1996, 7)

Figure 5.4. The multiethnic visual coding of the Na'vi

While the frame narrative of *Avatar* is concerned with environmental destruction, colonial exploitation, and features some exhilarating action sequences, much of the film's attraction rests in its intricately detailed rendering of the topography of Pandora and of the bodies and culture of the indigenous inhabitants. In this respect the eye-jabbing aesthetic that "foregrounds" *Avatar*'s innovative 3-D technology is far from gratuitous but functions to heighten the spectator's immersion in this space and also provides an alibi for close, unrestricted observation. The promise of intimacy that is a property of cinema as a medium, renders film a particularly suitable format for ethnographic scrutiny. As Rony observes, in a comment that applies particularly well to *Avatar*'s exoticizing aesthetic:

> Cinema appears to bring the past and that which is culturally distant closer; likewise, anthropology, which posits that indigenous peoples are remnants of earlier ages has been largely concerned with the description and preservation of the spatially and historically distant. (Rony 1996, 9)

Stereoscopic cinema, which produces (with varying success) the effect of projecting the spectator into the diegetic space, or, alternately, of on-screen objects projecting into the viewing space, perhaps reinforces the sense that physical, historical, and cultural distance is collapsed or compressed in the experience of viewing a film. The play of distance and proximity is a feature of the film's technical spectacle as well as its narrative movements.

The promotional documentary (and other related material included with the "Collector's Edition" Blu-ray including interviews, outtakes, screen tests, and storyboards) stresses the painstaking care with which the fictional space and the alien culture were conceptualized in order to produce a convincingly authentic and comprehensively imagined world, drawing on academic consultants as well as technicians. For instance, an ethnomusicologist worked with the film's composer on the instrumentation, a linguist was employed to devise the alien language[5] (which was then further developed into distinct dialects) and an ethnobotanist was employed to design Pandora's plant life. The significance of this detailed production history is partly to heighten the spectatorial pleasure to be derived from the spectacle of technical virtuosity and colossal expense[6] that has become associated with Cameron's work, and also to stress the seriousness of purpose and the conscientious, methodical rigor with which the film visualizes this alien world, rebutting in advance criticism of careless stereotyping or "brutal racist undertones" (Žižek 2010).

Anthropological Cinema

Avatar is a film about anthropological research since it tells the story of the protagonist, Jake Sully's, investigation and exploration of this exotic, "savage" people and his transgression of scientific objectivity as he is "seduced" by the Na'vi. As anthropologist David Price observes, discussing the U.S. military's practice of embedding "Human Terrain Teams" of social scientists with occupying forces at the frontline of the global "war on terror": "It is worth noting some of the obvious parallels between these elements in this virtual film world, and those found in our world of real bullets and anthropologists in Iraq and Afghanistan" (Price 2009). However, in its expansive and exhaustively researched visualization of this alien culture at the expense of classical narrative economy, the film is also underpinned by a classical ethnographic fantasy of the reproduction of "a metonym for an entire culture" (Rony 1996, 7). Rony observes that the depiction of alien cultures in ethnographic films, as with ethnographic photographs, narratives, exhibitions, and demonstrations, tended to serve a dual purpose, or to address a variegated audience, functioning simultaneously as scientific evidence and popular entertainment: "Ethnographic footage purportedly obtained for research purposes was often used as entertainment (with an educational veneer) for mass audiences" (ibid., 64). In exploring the historical relationship between cultures of popular entertainment and academic research, Rony identifies an intriguing historical parallel between ethnographic documentary and the fiction film. Comparing *The Birth of a Nation* (Griffith 1915), the historical epic traditionally credited with the codification of the classical American cinema, with *Nanook of the North* (Flaherty 1922), a pioneering ethnographic account of a people outside history, Rony suggests that

> both impose a stereotyped vision of the meaning of the past, and both smooth over anxieties about difference through ideologies of race. The dominant subject position of the spectator, the ideal viewer of the films—white, masculine, the bearer of History—is alternately frightened and soothed by the narratives of the Ku Klux Klan as saviors of the nation, and of the Inuit hunter as raw-flesh-eating but smiling Savage. (Rony 1996, 12)

A connection with Griffith's cinematic ideologization of race is acknowledged indirectly in *Avatar* with the naming of one of the humans' airships that participates in the final battle, "Valkyrie," invoking the use of a passage from Richard Wagner's opera, *Die Walküre* (*The Valkyrie*) in the score of *The Birth of a Nation* to accompany the massing of the Ku Klux Klan to attack the African American former slaves. The reference exemplifies the self-reflexive ambivalence of the film, as it draws a self-promotional parallel between Griffith's film and *Avatar* as a similarly formally, technically, and commercially innovative event movie that might usher in a new period of mainstream stereoscopic post-cinematic cinema.[7] It also suggests a genealogical link between *Avatar* and Griffith's film that deals thematically with racial formation, slavery, exploitation, and racist violence. While the association of the xenophobic humans with the racism of Griffith's film and its protagonists might be intended as a disavowal, the allusion to *The Birth of a Nation* also implies a competitive comparison in which Cameron measures himself against "Griffith," the great industrial artist. It seems that race remains the territory on which this battle for mastery is fought. Just as in *The Birth of a Nation*, where "miscegenation" is the focus of anxieties around social transformation and possible futures, exemplified by the mixed-race governor Silas Lynch, *Avatar*'s romance narrative concerns the coupling of a human and an alien (or racialized other).

In its blend of anthropological exoticism and sumptuous hyperrealism, what *Avatar* resembles more closely still is the spectacular fantasy film, *King Kong* (1933), directed by former ethnographic filmmakers Cooper and Schoedsack and foregrounding elaborate, state-of-the-art photographic effects. *King Kong*, Rony suggests, "is a pastiche film about the making of an ethnographic film and hence offers a meta-commentary on 'seeing anthropology,' one which . . . foreshadows the fear of the postcolonial Other as monster" (Rony 1996, 15). The film recounts the story of an expedition to an island near Sumatra by an American film crew to shoot a film on location. While there, their lead actress is kidnapped by the indigenous islanders and offered as a sacrifice to Kong, the giant gorilla that is held at bay behind enormous gates; an interspecies romance is, similarly, at this film's dramatic core. The film crew set off into the jungle to rescue her where they encounter exotic and unfamiliar creatures—dinosaurs that belong to an earlier period in the earth's history, as well as the Brobdingnagian ape. Kong is subsequently captured and transported to New York where it is displayed as an entertainment spectacle in a theatre before breaking loose and escaping with the woman, seeking refuge on the summit of the Empire State building. The film thus parodies the narrative structure of the conventional ethnographic documentary's account of an anthropological expedition, as well as the ethnographic film's assertion of the historical and cultural distance between the object of study and the presumed spectator. This is literalized in *King Kong* with the explorer-filmmakers encountering prehistoric dinosaurs and monstrous creatures (in addition to the superstitious islanders adorned with body paint), and the film's final scenes parody the parading of colonial subjects in pens at European and American world's fairs. *Avatar* does not make any direct allusions to *King Kong*, but Rony's description of the film as itself "a monster, a hybrid of the scientific expedition and fantasy genres" applies equally well to Cameron's heterogeneous film (ibid., 160).[8] Situating *Avatar* in this cinematic history of ethnographic entertainment brings to the fore some of the problematic questions around representation in the literal and political senses posed by the film.

Politics and "Avatar Activism"

A second promotional documentary, *A Message from Pandora* (Bouzereau, Grane [producers] 2010), which is included with the supplementary material packaged with the collector's edition of *Avatar*, indicates that the preferred reading of the film qua allegory is that the aliens should be read as figures for exploited or oppressed indigenous peoples, although this is somewhat redundant since all the significant human characters in *Avatar* are white Americans. This invites us to understand *Avatar* more specifically as an allegory both for U.S. and European history and for the postindustrial West's relationship with the developing world. *A Message from Pandora* offers an account of the director's slightly awkward involvement—alongside his partner and two of the actors who play scientists in the film, Sigourney Weaver and Joel David Moore—with a campaign to prevent the construction of the Belo Monte dam complex in the Amazon rainforest in Brazil. Cameron is also shown speaking at the "International Forum for Sustainability" in Brazil and attending the ninth session of the "United Nations Permanent

Forum on Indigenous Issues."⁹ The humanitarian political framework with which Cameron attempts to manage and direct the reading of *Avatar* risks reproducing the invisibility of "indigenous people," denying them the opportunity or the stage on which to act and speak as political subjects on their own behalf. As activist, Hollywood filmmaker and entrepreneur, Cameron is drawing on his considerable celebrity, visibility, and political agency to "speak" on behalf of indigenous populations. Cameron employs technologies of visibility as a means of countering the absence of indigenous voices but, in doing so, he re-silences these voices, or at least limits how they might be heard as autonomous actors (see Tyler 2006). The problem with both humanitarian discourses and ethnographic frames is that they pivot upon a restatement of difference, a gesture of othering, an insistence that *they* are aliens, not *us*.

Within *Avatar*, the fantastic, magical technology of the avatar link is the means by which the film's narrative negotiates this limit in allowing Sully, to pass—not so much in disguise, as in "blackface" or drag—as a Na'vi. The projection of Sully's consciousness into the alien body is visualized as ecstatic, ejaculatory movement through space, a point-of-view shot racing through a colorful, glowing tube (like the "Beyond the Infinite" sequence of *2001: A Space Odyssey* [Kubrick 1968]) before fading to white (see Figure 5.5). Ultimately, the mysterious biotechnology of the planet's ecosystem allows him to become alien, collapsing this difference between human and alien entirely.

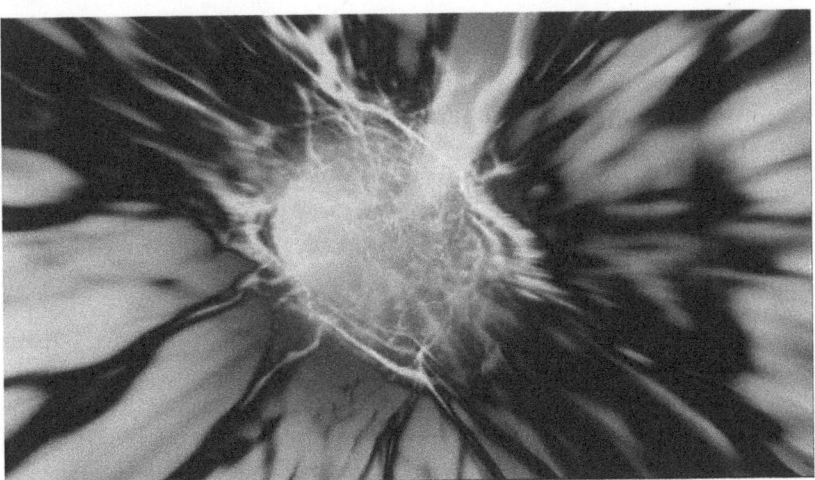

Figure 5.5. Becoming alien: the subjective experience of the avatar link

Of course, despite this climactic erasure of the boundary between human and racialized other, the film's reverse discourse or inversion of this relationship does not necessarily destabilize or deconstruct such an opposition. On the one hand, for example, the rhetorical use of the alien as an alienating or estranging device depends upon the maintenance of the human/alien distinction to have any power or purchase. On the other hand, it is notable that the film stops precisely at the point that Sully becomes alien. It seems that a limit of subjective articulation and communication is encountered so that, once Sully becomes alien, he can no longer speak or narrate.

The liberal fantasy underlying *Avatar*'s narrative is that surface appearance is deceptive and substitutable, and that if we could get past prejudices around superficial difference—even when confronted with a three-meters-tall, naked and hairless, blue-skinned, feline alien with a tail—rather than achieving an ethical acknowledgment of difference or alterity, a limit or boundary that cannot be crossed (which is the premise of the encounter between humans and the initially repulsive insect-like aliens of *District 9*), we would recognize a fundamental similarity. The Na'vi greet one another with the phrase, "I see you," and, as the aptly named scientist, Norm, explains, "It's not just, 'I'm seeing you in front of me,' it's 'I see into you.'" This idea of exploratory, penetrative, investigatory vision—a mode of looking with what Donna Haraway terms "fingery eyes"—underlies both the film's stereoscopic eye-jabbing aesthetic and continually mobile camera (emphasized visually by the recurring motif of a subjective point-of-view shot plunging through space). This mode of deep looking also underlies the film's conception of ethical relations with the other, relations that are premised upon deep knowledge and the effacement of boundaries (Haraway 2008, 5). "Good science," as the head scientist explains to Sully, "is good observation."

However, observation is inextricable from forced exposure, objectification, and possession in several senses that are figured more or less uncritically. Observation is violence—a self-interested practice of acquisition, surveillance and cartography, framing and meaning-fixing. As Nicholas Mirzoeff puts it in a historical account of practices of "visuality," the oppressive processes of classification, social segregation, and aestheticization of the resulting order, "In a sense, all visuality was and is imperial visuality, the shaping of modernity from the point of view of the imperial powers" (Mirzoeff 2011, 196). Scientific or anthropological observation is very clearly marked in *Avatar* as a mode of visuality that complements the military-industrial complex that stands, metonymically, for the United States or the West. Regimes of visuality are structured by an unequal configuration of visibility or exhibition, and abilities or rights to look. Looking is a means of surveillance and control and is therefore the exercise of power relations. Mirzoeff explains,

> The right to look is not about seeing. It begins at a personal level with the look into someone else's eyes to express friendship, solidarity or love. That look must be mutual, each person inventing the other, or it fails. As such, it is unrepresentable. The right to look claims autonomy, not individualism or voyeurism, but the claim to political subjectivity and collectivity. (Mirzoeff 2011, 1)

Sully's romance with Neytiri, mediated through his avatar, literalizes the unequal distribution of this right. Confronted with a synthetic body, the alien is denied the right to return Sully's gaze, to look back at him (until the final sequence where she rescues his suffocating human body from its damaged avatar link).

The scrutiny of Pandora and its inhabitants is undertaken by scientists who are apparently opposed to the forced displacement of the indigenous people that accompanies the mining operation, but, in a parody of anthropological or academic narrow-mindedness, are nevertheless enthusiastic participants in the business of resource extraction. In particular, it seems that, far from being concerned about the potentially destructive and empirically counterproductive effect of cultural contamination from contact with humans, the scientists are spearheading the acculturation of the Na'vi on the pretext of mediation between the mining company and the indigenous inhabitants. The clearest example of this is a sequence, which is absent from the original theatrical version of the film,[10] in which Sully visits the bullet-riddled and abandoned school that Grace built in order to educate the Na'vi children, teaching them to read and write English. The simple building, which, unlike the rest of the futuristic and militaristic human architecture, resembles a thatched wooden hut in a nineteenth-century equatorial plantation, raised off the ground on stilts, contains the teaching aids of a primary school including, with heavy irony, a discarded copy of the ecological fable, *The Lorax*, by Dr Seuss. Although reluctant to discuss it initially, Grace later explains to Sully that in response to the company's clear-cutting of the forest, some of the children had set fire to a bulldozer. The school was subsequently raided by the company's security men who shot the children responsible, and none of the surviving Na'vi pupils returned. The scene draws a distinction between the brutality of the mercenaries and the apparently benign compassion of the scientists, but also exemplifies the invasive threat posed by even the most well-intentioned intervention, neatly aligning the scopophilia and epistemophilia underlying the scientific investigation with the greed and xenophobia underlying the mining operation. In different ways these parallel operations are concerned with exposure and acquisition and are sustained by an ideology of progress and expansion.

This co-implication is embodied by the protagonist, Sully. Part-soldier, part-scientist, he epitomizes the violence and betrayal of colonial exploitation but, as a paraplegic, whose wheelchair-bound body with its CGI-rendered atrophied legs, is treated with open disgust by some of the soldiers. As an abjected, othered figure who no longer belongs fully with the humans, he is therefore presented as already aligned with, and therefore better able to identify with, the aliens. His liminality is established visually in the opening scene, set on earth, in which Sully is shown returning the camera's gaze, isolated at the center of a vast, bustling crowd of people in the streets of a dark, neon-lit metropolis that fills the frame and recedes into the distance. The images make clear his estrangement from the bodies around him and the dehumanizing environment, while on the accompanying voiceover it is made clear that Sully's lack of belonging is heightened by the fact that his injury means his economic value as a human resource is exhausted. His treatable injury does not warrant the investment: "They can fix a 'spinal' if you got the money; not on vet benefits; not in this economy. . . . I'm what they call 'waitlisted.'" At the same time, this characterization of Sully is ironized through the parallel drawn between Sully's damaged, prosthetically augmented body and the dependence of "able-bodied" humans upon a wide range of prostheses including breathing apparatus, vehicles, mechanical suits, and body armor.[11] More generally, the film highlights the absurdity of the economic and technical dependence upon this scarce mineral.

Going Native—Loving the Alien

Sully first makes contact with the Na'vi when his avatar is escorting the avatars of the scientists Grace and Norm into the jungle on botanical fieldwork. They are attacked by a huge "Thanator" and, fleeing from the creature, he becomes separated and lost. He is later rescued by Neytiri from a pack of dog-like "Nantang," and she is angry and impatient with Sully until his body is covered by "seeds from the sacred tree" drifting through the air. Shocked at this, Neytiri, who was taught English by Grace, tells him they are "very pure spirits," and this apparently marks Sully's difference. He is presented to the Omaticaya clan by Neytiri, and, impressed by this blessing, her parents, the clan leaders, who dub him "jakesully," instruct Neytiri to educate him. It is unclear exactly what status is accorded to Sully's avatar by the Na'vi and the extent to which they understand that these are remotely controlled meat puppets, but he is variously described as a "demon" and a "dreamwalker."[12] Receiving a parallel education from Grace and Norm when not in the avatar link, Sully learns from Neytiri how to navigate the jungle, how to fly an "Ikran," how to speak Na'vi and gains a knowledge of their history and culture.

While undergoing this cultural immersion, Sully continues secretly to relay "good, reliable intel" to Col. Quaritch, while also recording his field notes in comprehensive video logs under Grace's instruction.[13] Sully thus remains an ambivalent figure that plays a key narrative role in accelerating the violent and destructive conflict between the humans and the aliens crystallized in his relationship with Neytiri. His seduction by Pandora is interwoven with his seduction by/of Neytiri and this culminates in the two of them having sex in the forest. The anatomical specificities of avatar sex and alien sex are left modestly vague by the film, with the otherwise naked Na'vi all sporting loincloths, but sex begins with them interlinking the hair-like tendrils that grow from their heads, a biological equivalent to the avatar-link, that may be connected to other animals and also to trees, allowing them to access a database of dead souls[14] (see Figure 5.6). The consequences of this consummation are catastrophic within the film's melodramatic moral framework. This transgressive but decidedly nonqueer act of interspecies sex marks the abandonment of scientific or ethical distance, as well as the betrayal of Quaritch's confidence in him, and it also forecloses Neytiri's betrothal to the aggressive and suspicious young warrior, Tsu'tey. The transgression of, what Mirzoeff terms (in a different context), "a

Figure 5.6. The heteronormativity of interspecies sex: Neytiri with Sully's avatar

caesura of incommensurability between the 'indigenous' and the 'civilized'" is underscored by Sully's deception of Neytiri who does not yet know of his agenda (Mirzoeff 2011, 196). It is also emphasized melodramatically by the narrative shift that follows immediately afterward and is symbolically motivated by this encounter: lying in the arms of Sully's lifeless, disconnected avatar, Neytiri is woken from postcoital sleep by the sound of enormous bulldozers clearing a route through the forest to the Na'vi's "home tree."[15]

Like the colonial company agent Kurtz in Conrad's *Heart of Darkness*, Sully has succumbed to the spectacular and dark pleasures of the jungle, losing a sense of stable, geographically anchored, and racialized identity to undertake a sexual relationship with a local woman, and "go native." This disorientation is expressed on the voiceover where Sully explains that the relationship between the virtual experience of the avatar-link and material reality has been inverted: "Everything is backwards now, like out there is the true world and in here is the dream."

Protest and Representation

If we return to Cameron's insistence that this is a film intended to promote change and indigenous justice, then we need to ask how the film explores issues of representation and protest. Despite his betrayal of the Na'vi, they eventually accept Sully as a political and military leader and he is responsible for rallying them to retaliate against the company's security forces, despite being heavily outgunned. This acceptance rests on his assumption of the role of "Toruk Makto" upon capturing and taming the giant flying lizard, which accords him messianic status in the eyes of the Na'vi.[16] The narrative gratification offered by this retaliation lies partly in the halting of the environmental and cultural devastation caused by the company, and also in the punishment that is meted out to the xenophobic human settlers. John Rieder has suggested, for instance, that *Avatar* shares with *Inglourious Basterds* (Tarantino 2009) and *District 9* a "spectacularly violent racialized revenge fantasy" (Rieder 2011, 41):

> The spectacularly violent punishment of racist villains is not only a utopian moment in these high-budget, mass-circulation films, but also a tactically crucial means of achieving the emotional satisfaction demanded in the closure of such films. Thus the strong degree to which race continues to evoke violence and to demand identification or counter-identification would seem to me to be one of the primary conclusions about contemporary ideology to be drawn from these films. (ibid., 46)

However, what leaves the conclusion of *Avatar* somewhat unsatisfactory is an ideological ambiguity that runs through the film, leaving identification and counter-identification in play. Thomas Elsaesser has suggested that this ambiguity is a conventionally cynical commercial strategy of stratified address that allows the film to engage with multiple audiences simultaneously, and is evidence of Cameron's authorial and managerial mastery of the process of developing and releasing a superproduction. Criticisms of the film's disingenuousness, Elsaesser suggests,

> overlook the fact that Cameron systematically planned and provoked this false consciousness at all levels, making it the very principle of the film's construction, because—at the allegorical level—these are the objective conditions under which the USA maintains both its military supremacy and its cultural hegemony, the two locking together not (only) by reinforcing each other, but also by openly contradicting each other: the outlines of a double bind. (Elsaesser 2011, 254).

For Elsaesser, *Avatar* demonstrates an exceptional level of directorial control over the reception of a film wherein a carefully constructed textual ambiguity ensures that the film can address multiple, incompatible audiences internationally and simultaneously. This ambiguity is distinct from the uncontainable, inadvertent, or ironic polysemy of a classical Hollywood text to the extent that it is calculated and makes contradiction a commercial and aesthetic principle. Thus, Elsaesser claims, "these divergences and seeming contradictions were programmed into the film from the beginning, as part of the Cameron concept" (Elsaesser 2011, 252). This account of the film is striking partly for its defiantly reactionary insistence upon the gendered concept of directorial "mastery" (which defers to the promotional construction of the filmmaker as a technocratic creative genius), but also for its assertion that the film effectively disables ideological criticism through its strategic internal contradictions. However, for all its strategic semiotic innovation and judicious ambivalence, in its discourse of race the film remains thoroughly consistent. The contradictions lie more in the framing and reception of the film than in its narrative detail. As a white character, Sully is both raced *and* unraced, an avatar in another sense whose racialized body is an empty, material vessel, a substitutable chassis or skin that can be sloughed off or transcended, rather than a constituent of his identity. He epitomizes the dominant Christian-influenced dualist Western conception of whiteness outlined by Richard Dyer, as "involving something that is in but not of the body" (Dyer 1997, 14).

In this respect the disembodied, mobile spectatorial experience of 3-D cinema articulates a specifically racialized, or transracial subject position. As with ethnographic films that are produced to be viewed by audiences other than the people whose communities are documented or constructed on screen, so *Avatar* too is not directed toward "indigenous" viewers and in this sense does not offer what Elsaesser terms, "access for all" (Elsaesser 2011). The subject of Cameron's assertion that "we are the aliens" is the primarily white audience and, in response to criticisms of the film's racial politics, he has protested that the film's goal was not to "tell indigenous people how bad things are for them," but to generate a political awareness among viewers in the developed world. In response to the contention that the film offers a belligerent white savior as the solution to the problems outlined, Cameron has stated, "I understand the white messiah argument . . . but in this movie, I am trying to make everybody a white messiah, for everybody to have the sense of responsibility to help with the problem" (Lee 2010).[17] To some extent, this appears to respond to the political imperative identified by Dyer: "White people need to learn to see themselves as white, to see their particularity. In other words whiteness needs to be made strange" (Dyer 1997, 10). However, in the account of a human becoming alien, the potential strangeness of this transition—the horror of Gregor Samsa's metamorphosis—is always contained by the sense that the integrity of Sully's raced identity that is never under threat.

Discussing the historical and institutional roots of ethnographic film, Rony observes that classical anthropology was underpinned by a certain unreflective narcissism: "Anthropological discourse, with its roots in the exploration and colonization of the rest of the world by the West, is the discourse of the self. It defines itself primarily as the study of the other, which means that its selfhood was not problematic" (Rony 1996, 12–13). The consequence of this is to repeat the silencing of the "other" under scrutiny:

> One result of this ever-present division between Historical same—Western subjectivity—and Primitive Other is a speaking for and thus a silencing of the peoples depicted in ethnographic cinema, an assumption of voice made especially dangerous because of the perception that film is a window onto reality. In this setting the critic may become the unwitting propagator of a new postcolonial form of fascinating cannibalism, a reification that further entrenches the categories of Same and other, Western and Indigenous. (ibid., 13)

Avatar could not be mistaken for a documentary, of course, although it seems likely that, as Elsaesser suggests, Cameron "thinks of himself as much a documentary filmmaker as he is a storyteller, even though 'documentary' here clearly does not mean 'realism,' but the more probing, exploring mind of the scientist" (Elsaesser 2011, 255). In this respect, the adventuring filmmaker with whom Cameron has most in common is the director Werner Herzog, whose obliquely ironic "documentaries" and feature films display an ethnographic fascination[18] with sublimely wild landscapes, remote communities, colonial expeditionaries and scientists. While not a documentary, *Avatar* is no less affectively plausible in its hyperrealism and composite of familiar generic and narrative elements. In its depiction of the aliens as racialized others, rather than radically other, the film declares its disinterest in questions of mutual exchange and what the Na'vi see when they look back at humans. In its allegorical account of indigenous rage, channeled, authorized, and given agency by Sully as a latter-day Lawrence, instigating armed resistance, the film declares its disinterest in the question we might ask, after Spivak, "Can the alien speak?" As Peter Nyers observes on the historical tendency for refugees to be characterized as animalistic, this depends partly upon a philosophically conventional binary distinction between humans and animals in which "animals are presented as incapable of reasoned speech and so possess no independent will (only nature's command), no intelligence (only the dictates of instinct), and no immortal soul (only mere existence)" (Nyers 2006, 75). The corollary of this animalization is that "the banished individual not only loses claim to a political community and identity but is also banished from the space where political speech is audible. This displacement from meaningful discourse also involves a dislodging of their claim to be human" (ibid., 75). Indeed, rather than functioning as an avatar or ventriloquial figure for the Na'vi in order to give them a voice, like a filmmaker, Sully directs *them*.

Conclusion: Companion Species

There remains a potentially productive strangeness and affective power in *Avatar* in the theme of human/alien contact and communication, which is not entirely elided or foreclosed. This affect is attested to, perhaps, by the handful of examples of "avatar activism" in which protestors have appropriated *Avatar*'s imagery in ironic and satiric fashion to give voice to particular campaigns, as well as in the parodic reiterations of this imagery in various media (see Faulkner 2010). Rony suggests that an appropriately critical response to the ethnographic films is to work at viewing the images with an ironic "third eye," a term that carries echoes of Getino and Solanas's polemical third cinema (as well as foreshadowing the avatar eye through which the scientists perceive Pandora), and also draws our attention to the racialized optics of stereoscopic cinema (Getino and Solanas 1976). This third eye denotes the historically undocumented spectatorial perspective of the indigenous subjects of ethnographic films when presented with the films, and is a way of looking that, possibly, "can begin to bring the people who inhabit them out of their bondage of silence and into the present, one that acknowledges performance rather than empirically represented primitives in timeless Picturesques" (Rony 1996, 13).

In February 2010, the Bil'in Popular Committee, a group based in the Palestinian border village of Bil'in, organized an "Avatar Protest" in which Palestinian activists and their allies dressed as Na'vi characters (see Elsaesser 2011; Faulkner 2010; Jenkins 2010). This is one of several protests by the Bil'in activists to draw upon transnational popular culture as a resource with which to generate both publicity, but also to open alternative ways of looking and perceiving the politics of indigenous rights. As a particularly visible attraction of contemporary entertainment culture, *Avatar* becomes available to colonized peoples as a tool that allows for active forms of political consciousness raising through the re-performance of violence and injustice in the neo-colonial political present tense. In spite of the apparent ideological contradictions and narrative incoherencies, the allegorical film tells a very clear story of colonial violence and repression, one which is rendered in spectacular hypervisible, picturesque fashion. The counterpolitical appropriation of the film's imagery by the Bi'lin protestors to dramatize their colonial subjugation by the Israeli state is thus a particularly striking and literal realization of the process of critical reinterpretation advocated by Rony (see above). What is demonstrated by this protest-cum-performance is that the progressive political significance of *Avatar*'s account of colonial violence lies not so much in the text, but in its openness to political appropriations by those fighting against imperialism and for indigenous rights.

As Haraway suggests, in her reflections upon the relationships between "companion species":

> My premise is that touch ramifies and shapes accountability. Accountability, caring for, being affected, and entering into responsibility are not ethical abstractions; these mundane prosaic things are the result of having truck with each other. Touch does not make one small. It peppers its partners with attachment sites for world making. Touch, regard, looking back, becoming with—all these make us responsible in unpredictable ways for which worlds take shape (Haraway 2008, 36).

The final closeup shot of *Avatar*, in which the eyes of Sully's avatar suddenly flick open, his consciousness having been uploaded from the human body, and stare back at the viewer, invites us to imagine viewing the film through this third eye, a fingery haptic eye, perhaps, that reaches out to touch the apparently three-dimensional world on screen.

Notes

1. Sully's name is, perhaps, a reference to the contaminating or damaging environmental effect of humans.

2. This theme of virtual embodiment through a marvelous post-cinematic technology is explored in more detail in *Strange Days* (Bigelow 1995), which was co-scripted by Cameron and turns on the trading of contraband recordings made from the cerebral cortex using a SQUID apparatus.

3. The opening sequence that depicts a crowded noir-ish mega-city resembling the dystopian Los Angeles of *Blade Runner* (Scott 1991) is truncated in the original theatrical release.

4. *Battle: Los Angeles* is an interesting companion film to *Avatar* since its premise is that the earth is being invaded by aliens in search of a crucial natural resource—in this case, water.

5. See *Naviteri.org*, the blog by Paul Frommer who devised the Na'vi language (http://naviteri.org/).

6. See Bennett (2007) for an account of the pleasurable spectacle of consumption in Cameron's cinema.

7. Cameron has repeatedly referred to a "3-D renaissance" of film and television. See, for example Anon. 2010.

8. Incidentally, much of the digital effects work on *Avatar* was done at Peter Jackson's Weta Digital studios in New Zealand, the company responsible for the 2005 remake of *King Kong* (Jackson).

9. It is also notable that the "tie-in" publication to accompany the film's release is a fictional leaked scientific report on Pandora and its inhabitants entitled *Avatar: An Activist's Survival Guide*.

10. As with Cameron's earlier films, *Aliens* (1986), *The Abyss* (1989), *Terminator 2: Judgment Day* (1991), and *Titanic* (1997), several versions of *Avatar* are in circulation. As Charles Acland suggests, "What we think of as *Avatar* is in fact a mutable and varying entity, a work-in-progress" (2010).

11. Dana Fore proposes that "the film promotes a view of disability that is unusually nuanced for a Hollywood blockbuster, and one which complicates the nature and direction of its escapist fantasies. *Avatar*'s gallery of disabled, vulnerable, and consistently un-readable bodies transforms the film into an unsettling commentary on war movies, if not on war itself" (2011).

12. Dreams are another motif of the film alongside vision, inviting us to understand aspects of the film as fantastic.

13. The video logs are an expository device employed throughout the film through Sully's voiceover commentary.

14. Predictably enough, there is a parodic 3-D hardcore porn sequel to Cameron's film, *This Ain't Avatar XXX* (Braun 2010), which explores the mechanics of interspecies sex in familiar ways.

15. In the moralistic melodramatic universe of Cameron's films, sex often has a profoundly radical effect, from the lovers' kiss on the deck of the *Titanic* that "causes" the collision with the iceberg, to the coupling of Sarah Connor and Kyle Reese that leads to the birth of John Connor, the narrative focus of all the action in all four films and the spinoff TV series.

16. The messiah is a recurrent motif in Cameron's films; for example, Sully is prefigured by John Connor in the series of *Terminator* films initiated by Cameron.

17. Cameron may be referring here to a *New York Times* review of *Avatar* by David Brooks (see Elsaesser 2011, 249–50).

18. This is most evident in the first documentary he directed, *The Flying Doctors of East Africa* (1969), which celebrates the work of white European medics and nuns giving medical treatment to impoverished and "ignorant" African villagers.

Works Cited

Acland, Charles. 2010. "*Avatar* as Technological Tentpole." *Flowtv.org*. http://flowtv.org/2010/01/avatar-as-technological-tentpole-charles-r-acland-concordia-university/. Accessed May 15, 2012.

Anon. 2010. "*Avatar*'s James Cameron Says 3D Renaissance Has Arrived." *The Independent*, May 14, 2010. http://www.independent.co.uk/arts-entertainment/tv/avatars-james-cameron-says-3d-renaissance-has-arrived-1973307.html. Accessed May 15, 2012.

Bazin, André. 1967. *What Is Cinema?* Edited and translated by Hugh Gray. Berkeley: University of California Press.

Bennett, Bruce. 2007. "Towards a General Economics of Cinema." In *Fiction and Economy*, edited by Susan Bruce and Valeria Wagner. London and New York: Palgrave Macmillan.

Dyer, Richard. 1997. *White*. London and New York: Routledge.

Elsaesser, Thomas. 2011. "James Cameron's *Avatar*: Access for All." *New Review of Film and Television Studies* 9 (3): 247–64.

Faulkner, Simon. 2010. "Not Just Avatar Activism." http://simonsteachingblog.wordpress.com/2010/09/18/not-just-avatar-activism/. Accessed June 6, 2012.

Fore, Dana. 2011. "The Tracks of Sully's Tears: Disability in James Cameron's *Avatar*." *Jump Cut: A Review of Contemporary Media* 53. http://www.ejumpcut.org/currentissue/foreAvatar/index.html. Accessed April 25, 2012.

Getino, Octavio, and Fernando Solanas. 1976. "Towards a Third Cinema." In *Movies and Methods. An Anthology*, edited by Bill Nichols. Tucson: University of Arizona Press.

Haraway, Donna J. 2008. *When Species Meet*. Minneapolis and London: University of Minnesota Press.

Jenkins, Henry. 2010. "Avatar Activism and Beyond." http://henryjenkins.org/2010/09/avatar_activism_and_beyond.html. Accessed June 1, 2012.

Lee, Jessica. 2010. "'AVATAR' ACTIVISM: James Cameron Joins Indigenous Struggles Worldwide." *The Indypendent*. http://www.indypendent.org/2010/04/26/avatar-activism/. Accessed September 20, 2011.

Mirzoeff, Nicholas. 2011. *The Right to Look: A Counterhistory of Visuality*. Durham and London: Duke University Press.

Nama, Adilifu. 2008. *Black Space: Imagining Race in Science Fiction*. Austin: University of Texas Press.

Nyers, Peter. 2006. *Rethinking Refugees: Beyond States of Emergency*. New York and London: Routledge.

Price, David (2009) "Hollywood' Human Terrain Avatars." *counterpunch*, December 23 2009. http://www.counterpunch.org/2009/12/23/hollywood-s-human-terrain-avatars/. Accessed June 12 2012.

Rieder, John. 2011. "Race and Revenge Fantasies in *Avatar*, *District 9*, and *Inglourious Basterds*." *Science Fiction Film and Television* 4 (1): 41–56.

Rony, Fatimah Tobing. 1996. *The Third Eye: Race, Cinema, and Ethnographic Spectacle*. Durham and London: Duke University Press.

Spivak, Gayatri Chakravorty. 1988. "Can the Subaltern Speak?" In *Marxism and the Interpretation of Culture*, edited by Cary Nelson and Lawrence Grossberg. Urbana and Chicago: University of Chicago Press.

Tyler, Imogen. 2006. "Welcome to Britain: The Cultural Politics of Asylum." *European Journal of Cultural Studies* 9 (2):185–202.

———. 2013. Revolting Subjects: Social Abjection and Resistance in Neoliberal Britain. London: Zed Books.

Wilhelm, Maria, and Dirk Mathison. 2009. *James Cameron's Avatar: An Activist Survival Guide*. London: Harper Collins.

Žižek, Slavoj. 2010. "Return of the Natives." *New Statesman*. http://www.newstatesman.com/film/2010/03/avatar-reality-love-couple-sex. Accessed May 31, 2012.

Figure 6.1. *Who's the Illegal Alien, Pilgrim?* 1978. Courtesy of Yolanda Lopez and Center for the Study of Political Graphics

6

Pedagogy of Rage

KATARZYNA MARCINIAK

> Teachers often learn how to teach defensively to reduce controversy, student resistance, parental objections and administrative sanctions.
>
> —Julie Andrzejewski and John Alessio, "Education for Global Citizenship and Social Responsibility"

Can teaching be thought of as an act of "immigrant protest?" And even more boldly, can teaching enact "immigrant rage"? Knowingly or not, as teachers we bring our histories, sensibilities, and vulnerabilities to the classroom and to the process of teaching. All the visible markers of identity—our race, ethnicity, gender, age, accents, ability, the pigment of our skins, the very look of our bodies, the way they are carried, the way they sound—are always on display to be read, scrutinized, admired, or criticized. As bodies that actively perform the process of knowledge creation, exchange, and circulation with student bodies, we often find ourselves in challenging pedagogical situations, situations for whose volatility no number of lesson plans or careful training can possibly prepare us. Pedagogy, after all, is an interactive and dialogical performance, and as such it can never be fully scripted. As Krista Ratcliffe has remarked, "teaching is a lot like jazz" (Ratcliffe 2005, 141).

My interest lies in pondering pedagogical performance from the point of view of an immigrant teacher, or to use Sneja Gunew's apt term, "a serial immigrant critic" (Gunew 2003, 41), a foreigner who has moved through several stages of an institutionalized "immigration machine" that imprints the psychic predisposition of a teacher with a stamp of alienhood.[1] In this essay, I want to tease out the possibilities and limitations of immigrant protest through the activity of "immigrant teaching." I am not interested in "protest" or "rage" in any simple way, that is, as a process of acting out personal grievances or performing the role of an "angry teacher." What compels me is "rage" as a political category of intervention, which can influence students' sensibilities and open them up to new ways of thinking about resistance to oppressive forms of phobic nationalisms and exclusionary practices of citizenship. I am interested in rage as a pedagogical countermeasure to the often seemingly innocent, if not ignorant, complacency with which restrictive models of being are perpetuated. I want to pursue what Jayne Ifekwunigwe calls "an engaged and enraged" critique (Ifekwunigwe 2004, 399).

Such a critique is not easy to implement in the classroom. To begin with, rage is culturally frowned upon and, when expressed by a migrant or immigrant, it is considered intolerable, offensive, even insulting. To draw attention to this taboo, I take an inspiration from Eva Hoffman's 1989 autobiographical narrative, *Lost in Translation: A Life in a New Language*, which, in the context of her Polish-Jewish experiences in Canada and the United States, introduces the concept of "immigrant rage" as a defense against a "hygienic" immigrant identity.[2] The immigrant, in order to prove adequate, is required to occupy the place of a "clean" subject—humble, disciplined, quiet, grateful. With these givens, an immigrant teacher with a philosophical agenda of rage in the classroom becomes a rather tough proposition. Yet, Hoffman's provocative articulation of immigrant rage also invites us to think about the fact that "rage" has symbolically belonged to discourses of "rightful" citizenry and national purity, which aggressively invest in guarding the borders against immigrant "contamination."

The rise of anti-immigrant sentiment in the post-9/11 era in the United States, which singles out specifically nonwhite aliens as a source of national anxiety, has resulted in an excessive push to police and discipline those who are classified as questionable others. Rage is obviously an explosive proposition but, as I want to argue, also a necessary impetus for countering this push. Simon Critchley aids my argument here by describing anger as "the *emotion* that produces *motion*, the mood that moves the subject," and argues that anger is, in fact, "the first political emotion," and that "it is often anger that moves the subject to action" (quoted in Badiou 2009, 155; my emphasis).

But what happens when the economy of rage enters a classroom? Can this politicized rage be taught? I ask these questions because time and time again, my students, properly schooled in cultural protocols, have been uncomfortable with, and troubled by, the discourse of rage, even one employed for progressive political purposes. They claim that rage is anger and that anger is inappropriate and unscholarly. My students have a point: rage is indeed coded negatively as an emotion that needs to be eradicated, or "healed." In this respect, in media therapeutic culture, the *Dr. Phil Show* is one well-known cultural platform that presents rage as unhealthy, dangerous, and in need of treatment. Yet, this therapeutic ideology is one I work to complicate, showing my students that, in fact, rage is not a neutral mode of expression but a symptom of political gendered and racialized relations.

Thus, probing anger as the *mood* that *moves* the subject, I want to theorize my experiences of teaching Courtney Hunt's 2008 border film *Frozen River*, a directorial debut that garnered multiple awards and nominations in the United States and internationally.[3] The course in which I have used *Frozen River*, "Race, Immigration, Nation," brings together cinematic, literary, and theoretical explorations of these concepts and asks students to examine the complex subject positions of immigrant, migrant, and refugee identities in terms of their representation in the U.S. context. I have used a variety of films in this course, including features—Palestinian American director Cherien Dabis's *Amreeka* (2009), Iranian director Ghasem Ebrahimian's *The Suitors* (1988), and Tom McCarthy's *The Visitor* (2007); documentaries—Panamanian Anayansi Prado's *Maid in America* (2004) and *Children in No Man's Land* (2009), Carlos Bosch and Joseph Domènech's *Balseros* (2002); and a video essay, *Performing the Border* (1999), by a Geneva-based artist, Ursula Biemann. Wanting to offer my students a recent filmic context, I have also shown border-crossing scenes—either interrogations at the airports or crossings through rivers and sewer tunnels—in independent and Hollywood productions such as Gregory Nava's *El Norte* (1983), John Sayles's *Lone Star* (1996), Steven Spielberg's *The Terminal* (2004), Joshua Marston's *Maria Full of Grace* (2004), and Alejandro González Iñárritu's *Babel* (2006). This archive explicitly engages transnational subjectivity and transnational encounter, foreignness and citizenship, the politics of visibility, legality, and race. National borders emerge as both geopolitical constructs and, as abstractions related to ideas of difference, otherness, travel, migration, and cross-cultural translation.

These concepts also underpin Hunt's *Frozen River*. Set near a border crossing on the Mohawk reservation between New York State and Quebec, the film tells the story of two women—Lila Littlewolf (Misty Upham), a Mohawk Indian, and Ray Eddy (Melissa Leo), a white American, both single mothers living in dire poverty. Motivated by desperate circumstances, they become unlikely allies and partners in smuggling "third world" bodies of migrants across the Canadian-U.S. border, where it is formed by the Saint Lawrence River, which runs through the Mohawk community of Akwesasne.[4] In this respect, engaging both local and global dimensions, *Frozen River* is an unusual "trafficking" film. Unlike in so many other films of this genre—Michael Cory Davis's *Svetlana's Journey* (2004), Marco Kreuzpaintner's *Trade* (2007), or Lukas Moodysson's *Lilya 4-ever* (2002)—the smugglers are not ruthless and often violent males but women whose economic deprivation and need to provide for their children makes spectators empathetic and perhaps delays judgment or outright condemnation of such acts.

As the narrative sutures the audience into the escalating anxiety surrounding the numerous border crossings, the film implicitly asks challenging questions: Under what kinds of circumstances is it moral and just to perform "illegal" acts? How is state-defined and state-controlled legality at odds with Mohawk identity? What do the intersections of race, class, and gender reveal about complex discourses of poverty and deprivation in the film? Finally, how does the narrative's racial politics, which implicates all the main characters as motivated by resentment and prejudice, speak to the global manifestations of what Arjun Appadurai has called "the geography of anger"? He claims: "Until we understand how globalization can produce new forms of hatred, ethnocide, and ideocide, we will not know where to seek resources for hope about globalization" (Appadurai 2006, xi).

Frozen River in the Classroom: "White Trash"/"Alien Trash"

Frozen River offers a slow-paced opening sequence: the first shot reveals a vastness of winter space, frozen and white, an almost lunar space. This is a beautiful but harsh and frigid landscape. There are images of a barbed wire fence and of moving trucks that pass a sign saying, "Welcome to the USA. US Customs and Border Protection. Massena, NY. Post of Entry. Be Prepared to Show Identification. Declare All Articles." The sign locates the narrative geographically, anticipating the dynamic of border crossings and implicit discourses of legitimacy and (il)legality. Along with the barbed wire fence, it evokes, in Ali Behdad's words, the fact that "the border is not just a territorial marker of the modern nation-state—defining its geographical boundary—but an ideological apparatus where notions of national identity, citizenship, and belonging are articulated" (Behdad 1998, 109). The culmination of this sequence reveals Ray sitting hunched over in an open car, smoking, in front of her trailer. In striking close-ups, the camera stays close to Ray's body and lingers on her face—we see wrinkles, blotches, redness of her skin, her tears. Such spectatorial proximity to her skin, to her face, is unusual since her face is not aestheticized and alluring, but rather marked by the harshness of experience. The barren space that surrounds Ray and her trailer, her pink fuzzy robe, her chipped nails and an overall worn-out, haggard look betray her and her family's economic status and draw us into the discourses of "white trash."[5]

Figure 6.2. *Frozen River*'s landscape

Ray's tears are all about betrayal, disappointment, and anger. The husband and father, Troy, a compulsive gambler who never appears onscreen, has absconded with the money saved by the family for the purchase of a prefabricated doublewide, a luxurious trailer home that Ray and her two sons fantasize about. We learn that the family operates on a rent-to-own basis and is facing the loss of the down payment on the new trailer. Men who work for these rental places come to threaten to repossess the family's possessions (large flat-screen TV, for example) and treat Ray condescendingly. In turn, knowing her family's precarious situation, Ray keeps telling her boys that she expects a raise at Yankee One Dollar, a local "dollar store" where she works. The scene at the store, however, where she is subordinate to a much younger male manager, clearly shows that she stands no chance of receiving a raise. He is patronizing and dismissive; for him, Ray is an older female employee to be ignored as he is clearly interested in a young, perky blonde worker:

"I see you as a short-timer."
"What is that?"
"Not here for long, not really committed."

In *Not Quite White: White Trash and the Boundaries of Whiteness*, Matt Wray has theorized the category of "white trash" in the historical context of American culture, suggesting that it signals the "moral unworthiness of poor whites" (Wray 2006, 16): "The historical situation of poor whites has always been one of *ambiguity and liminality*, attributes shared by the identity—white trash—so frequently ascribed to them" (ibid., 17; emphasis added). In their introduction to *White Trash: Race and Class in America*, Wray and Annalee Newitz, argue that the term "helps solidify for the middle and upper classes a sense of cultural and intellectual superiority," and they quote John Waters who points out that " 'white trash' is not just a classist slur—it's also a racial epithet that marks out certain whites as a breed apart, a dysgenic race unto themselves" (Wray and Newitz 1997, 1–2). "Trash" signals economic waste, refuse, something to be rejected as worthless, a contaminated matter that needs to be discarded as unusable, a throwaway. In short, "white trash" has historically been used as an insult to denigrate lower-class whites, rendering them useless and metaphorically "dirty." The term has also carried specific undertones of moral failings.

Hunt's film is implicitly aware of these meanings. There are many scenes showing Ray's financial struggle, which subtly question her mothering practices without, however, condemning Ray as irresponsible mother. Rather, the audience is asked to ponder the poignant contingency of her situation. She is always scrambling for change whether she buys gas or gives lunch money to her sons. The breakfast she serves to the boys consists of popcorn and Tang, an artificial, powdered orange juice, a "low-class" food—as my students pointed out. When TJ, the older son, repeatedly offers to get a job, Ray always insists that his job is to attend school and take care of his younger brother when she is at work. Simultaneously, there are images—such as the one of "romance bath salts" on a rusty, old bathtub—which speak to Ray's perhaps dubious spending practices but also to her desire for a bit of luxury.

What is fascinating about the discourse of whiteness is that the film destabilizes its hegemonic meaning by representing whiteness as multilayered, as, at once, paradoxically, deprivileged and privileged. It is clear, for example, that Ray has not experienced the privileges of her whiteness until she begins risky border crossings with Lila. As she worries that the local trooper might stop them on their way, Lila says, "He won't. Just remember you are white. They are not going to stop you. You are white." To Ray's surprise, Lila repeats this at different moments during their crossings, validating Ray's whiteness as a protector and guarantor of their mutual safety. Thus, in many ways, Ray's whiteness facilitates their smuggling.

In a similarly complicated move, the film intensifies the notion of "trash," making an uneasy connection between poor whites like Ray and her sons and the "illegal aliens" smuggled in a trunk of the car driven by Ray and Lila, notwithstanding the fact that Ray herself repeatedly acts condescendingly toward those being smuggled. During the first crossing, when the women drive up to a shack on the Canadian side of the frozen river, the mise-en-scène speaks to this connection: we see piles of rubbish, used tires, waste, all resembling the dilapidated landscape around Ray's house, which her older son at one point refers to as a "tin crapper." During all four crossings, the film represents the migrants, Chinese and Pakistani, in a conflicted way: they are at once nameless throwaways and valuable cargo to Ray and Lila, who get paid for each smuggling. As Ray is probing Lila about the financial value of "those Chinese" locked up in a trunk, Lila reveals that "snakeheads," that is, the ones who orchestrate the smuggling on both sides of the border, get $40,000 to $50,000 per body, sums that the migrants have to work off to buy their freedom. Though none of them says it directly, it is clear that the migrants are, in fact, slaves, locked into indentured servitude. Ray cannot believe this: "They pay so much to get *here*? No fucking way." For her, this is not a land of opportunity but a harsh place of survival.

A heartwrenching sequence involving a Pakistani baby is perhaps most evocative in showing how "trashing" works, here quite literally. The crossers are a Pakistani couple who are carrying a bag. Seeing their different "look," Ray is nervous, spontaneously revealing her orientalist xenoracism: "Let's hope they are not the ones who blow themselves and everyone else up." Even though she had not objected to transporting Chinese men on a previous run, for her, the Pakistani couple (though she says she does not know where Pakistan is) immediately invites the suspicion of terrorism. Not knowing that the bag contains the couple's baby, Ray throws it out of the car during the crossing: "Nuclear power, poison gas, who knows what they might have in there." Only later, upon realizing that they have thrown

Figure 6.3. Ray and Lila after the rescue

away a baby, Ray and Lila return to the river to retrieve it. This successful rescue notwithstanding, the sequence shows the precarious volatility that affects the smuggled migrants, who can be tossed out as unwanted, if not dangerous, garbage.

(Il)legality and Borders: the Idea of Difference

The unlikely and tense alliance between Ray and Lila as smugglers points to the film's overt play with the concept of difference, akin to Trinh Minh-ha's proposal of a difference that is nondemonizing, nonseparatist, and nonreductive to the "simplicity of essences," a notion she terms "the non-apartheid type of difference": "Difference, in other words, does not necessarily give rise to separatism. There are differences as well as similarities within the concept of difference" (Trinh 2001, 930). For her, such a reconfigured idea of difference can be a potential "tool of creativity to question multiple forms of oppression and dominance" (ibid.). Indeed, in *Frozen River*, the idea of difference as nuanced and enmeshed with similarities forcefully emerges through Ray's and Lila's positions. Both women are on the fringes of society, both are poor, both live in trailers, both are single mothers, and both are angry. Both are "betrayed" by their families. Ray is left by her gambler husband; Lila, a widow, loses her baby who is taken from the hospital by her mother-in-law; as she explains, "She stole him from me. Tribal police don't get involved in stuff like that." Furthermore, it is clear that the film consciously privileges female experiences. When Ray first starts looking for her gambling-addicted husband, she finds Lila, who took his car instead. And, the plot never returns to the narrative about finding the missing father but stays focused on Ray and Lila's uneasy partnership and their attempts to function as caring mothers, albeit through unconventional means.

Despite these similarities, the different ethno-racial bearings of Ray and Lila, tied to their "national" belonging, begin to paint differences not as easily apprehended but rather as rife with certain incommensurabilities. The notion of incommensurability has come to be recognized as a potent critical nexus in feminist explorations (Imre, Marciniak, O'Healy 2007; Jaikumar 2007; Waller and Marcos 2005). As I have argued elsewhere, rather than seeking sameness through eliminating or minimizing difference, a feminist acknowledgment of incommensurability enables difference to be maintained *as difference* without denying its complex contexts. A strategic insistence on incommensurability circumvents the privileging of palatable difference, a domesticated difference that is deemed acceptable and consumable because it seems safe (Imre, Marciniak, O'Healy 2009, 387).

It is these incommensurabilities, in fact, that push the limits of our understanding, as my students realized. The women's first run across the river exposes profound ambivalences about the border and its elusive meaning:

RAY: That's Canada.

LILA: That's Mohawk land—the Res is on both sides of the river.

RAY: What about the border patrol?

LILA: There is no border.

While Ray is apprehensive about the border crossing ("I am not driving just anybody across the border. It's a crime"), Lila's understanding of the crossing as "a crime" is very different: "There is no border here. It's a free trade between nations." Ray dismisses such an idea, however: "This isn't a nation." Through their interaction thus all these concepts—"nation," "border," "legality," and "criminality"—supposedly transparent and obvious, emerge as polysemous and conflicted, pointing to the different epistemological paradigms that inform Lila's and Ray's experience and thinking, revealing residues of the colonization of indigenous peoples in the United States.

Lila's apprehension of the "nation" demands the conceptual dismantling of the officially sanctioned idea of the U.S. nation since the "Res" is a nation within a nation, a "contested jurisdiction border community," as Ruth Jamieson claims (1999, 259), something Ray does not seem to consider even though she lives near the "Mohawk Land" sign, buys gas at the Wolfmart station, goes to a casino looking for her husband, and so on. In fact, several times we see the sign—"Thank you for visiting the Mohawk Land"—a sign that has an ironic tonality because it subtly points to the separateness of the Mohawks but also to their confinement; ultimately, however, it marks the land as a tourist attraction. In many ways Ray's obliviousness exemplifies Behdad's argument about national historical amnesia: "The forgetful representation by the United States of its immigrant heritage is part of a broader form of historical amnesia about its violent formation. Both the benign discourse of democratic founding and the myth of immigrant America deny that nationhood has been achieved, at least in part, through the violent conquest of Native Americans, the brutal exploitation of enslaved Africans, and the colonialist annexation of French and Mexican territories" (Behdad 2005, xii).

Lila's at first incomprehensible comment about smuggling that is not really smuggling but "a free trade between nations" needs to be unraveled in the context of the Akwesasne Mohawks' historical situation. As Jamieson explains, the claims by the U.S. and Canadian governments to the border that Ray and Lila cross have always been contested by the Mohawks themselves:

> Much of what would be identified by established police and government authorities in Canada or the U.S. as "smuggling" is seen by the Mohawks of Akwesasne as routine, legitimate trading—a part of the normal everyday business of survival in Akwesasne. The Akwesasne Mohawks claim the right to travel freely with personal, community and trade goods "unrestricted by borders established

by non-Aboriginal societies." . . . Aboriginal spokespeople claim the right to cross the Canada-US border as an "Aboriginal right" pertaining to all First Nations. (Jamieson 1999, 261)

Thus, the issue of belonging to an "official" American nation as a Mohawk emerges as clearly fraught with tensions. In another film involving American Indians, Chris Eyre's 1998 *Smoke Signals*, hailed as "the first feature film written, directed and produced by Native Americans," there is a comic scene that speaks to this idea. When the protagonists, Victor and Thomas, leave the Coeur d'Alene Reservation, their female friend asks jokingly, "You guys got your passports?" Thomas is surprised: "But it's the United States," to which she replies, "That's as foreign as it gets." Undoubtedly, the bitter legacy of internal colonization and domestic ghettoization of indigenous peoples results in their status, in John Borrows's words, as "uncertain citizens" (Borrows 2001). Alain C. Cairns, in his study of citizenship regimes vis-à-vis the Indian peoples of Canada, succinctly summarizes this uncertainty: "Their allegiance to a state that has victimized them is problematic" (Cairns 2002, 209).

If the idea of national belonging in the film is represented as at best ambivalent, so is the practice of "smuggling," which also needs to be considered in the context of a dismaying environmental degradation. The Akwesasne Reservation occupies some of the most polluted land in North America (Jamieson 1999, 267–68): "Because the traditional economic activities of hunting, trapping fishing and farming are no longer available to the members of the community, they can no longer survive outside the cash and/or welfare economy even if they wanted to do so" (ibid., 268). Hence, what Ray considers illegal "smuggling" is, for Lila, a member of the Mohawk Nation, a legitimate practice of trading. The ice-covered St. Lawrence River, paradoxically a border for Ray but not a border for Lila, thus ultimately emerges in the film as a site of incommensurability, underscoring the arbitrariness of its meanings. The intricacies of this incommensurability can be productively approached only through a careful look at the history of indigenous confinement on the "Res" and its complicated socioeconomic aftermath. Among other things, in a twist of historical irony, this confinement relegates the Mohawks, at least in Ray's eyes, to the space of otherness, transgression, and criminality.

The Affect of Rage

Festival juror Quentin Tarantino, handing the Grand Jury Prize for Best Feature to Courtney Hunt at the Sundance Film Festival in 2008, reportedly said, "[*Frozen River*] put my heart in a vise and proceeded to twist that vise until the last frame" (Taylor 2008). Certainly, part of this "vise" feeling is the spectatorial experience of relentless racial prejudice, which, along with xenophobia, sexism, and ageism, underlies the entire narrative. The ethnic tensions between the Mohawks and the white working-class residents abound: Lila does not like to work with whites; Ray thinks Lila is "some Indian chick"; Ray's older son, TJ, wants to "kick some Mohawk ass"; in fact, without remorse, he scams an elderly Mohawk woman using her credit card. Furthermore, the trooper who comes to Ray's door clearly displays his prejudice against the Mohawks, wanting to warn her that Lila is a questionable character because she smuggles "illegal aliens." Ray acts falsely surprised: "She is?" Even the smuggled ones, although barely audible in the narrative, are motivated by prejudice, this time a gendered one, as the Chinese men do not want to get in a trunk upon seeing a woman driver, clearly an ironic, if not a subtly comic moment, given the fact that they want to be smuggled across the border but mistrust a woman to do the driving.

This particular all-encompassing aura of racism and xenophobia further extends the film's challenging of stereotyped villains and victims and prevents it from demonizing those who are prejudiced. It refuses to arrest meaning this way, it refuses to be didactic and to offer a facile reading of "right" and "wrong," infusing the narrative climate instead with acute moral ambiguity. Equally importantly, the film avoids arousing pity or sentimentalizing Ray and Lila as noble yet de-privileged mothers. There are some fleeting moments of tenderness in the film but even those do not necessarily lead to a cathartic sublimation. One such moment occurs during the women's first encounter by Lila's trailer. Shortly after Ray shoots a hole in the trailer, trying to figure out whether her husband is inside, she gets a phone call from her son. Amidst her anger, it is as if the entire "action" stops briefly, interrupted by familiar "kid" talk. "There is a boiled egg in the fridge. Take the yolk out," she says, clearly responding to TJ's not wanting to eat an egg. Another such moment, coming directly after the rescue of the Pakistani baby, is a juxtaposed scene inside Lila's trailer—a tiny, claustrophobic space that holds only her bed. It is clear that Lila misses her baby. In one of the previous scenes, she is allowed only to watch it from a distance, staying in the dark outside her mother-in-law's house, and lurking inside like a criminal. In the trailer, we watch her practicing the traditional way of carrying an infant on a cradleboard except that her infant is made of cloth, an uncanny simulation. She places the board on her back to see how it would *feel* to have her baby, and the audience, too, is left to contemplate this simulated feeling.

This avoidance of sentimentality is crucial to the effusion of anger and to the overall tone of economic bleakness, desperation, and deprivation that affects all the inhabitants of the area. Anger certainly navigates Ray and Lila's alliance, but they are by no means like the flamboyant transgressors in *Thelma and Louise* (Ridley Scott 1991), a well-known film about angry women-partners. Upon their first meeting, Ray is not afraid to use her gun; later, it is Lila who grabs Ray's gun and points it at Ray. They hit and kick each other; they are both ferocious fighters and, even as their partnership develops, the feeling of distrust never quite disappears. On their first run, Lila takes all the money. On the second one, it is Ray who does, saying, "Now we are even." There is no enactment of "sisterhood," no idealized "feminist solidarity" between the two, no romanticized "cross-cultural" alliance that the narrative strives to establish. In the narrative's end, when the two women are caught and Ray decides to turn herself in to the police to save Lila from a banishment from the Res, and when Lila moves into Ray's trailer to take care of her sons and her regained baby, we are reminded of Chandra Mohanty's point that "sisterhood cannot be assumed on the basis of gender; it must be forged in concrete historical and political practice" (Mohanty 2003, 24).

So, how can we read these tough complexities and the moral ambivalence, imbued with violence and anger, into which the narrative interpellates its spectators? It would be hard to separate this question from the wider discourses of globalization and the ensuing practices and experiences of increased migration, trafficking, poverty, and oppression. There is a relevant moment in the film that comments on the global flow of goods. The five-year-old Ricky comes to wake up Ray:

RICKY: Mommy, what's going to happen to our old house when we get our new house?

RAY: They are going to flatten it and send it to China.

RICKY: Then what?

RAY: They will melt it down and make it into new toys.

RICKY: Then what?

RAY: Then they will send them back here so that I can sell them at Yankee Dollar.

Figure 6.4. Ray at Yankee One Dollar

This is clearly a view of globalization from "below," from the local point of view of a mother who sells cheap toys at Yankee Dollar. In contrast to the conventional understanding of globalization as linked to ideas of democracy, freedom of movement, free trade, and "global community," the tale of their globalized trailer that Ray tells her son is analogous to the story of migrant bodies smuggled in a trunk to be *used* in a new economic environment. If the smuggled migrants are "human waste" to be put into service again, so is Ray's trailer.

Zygmunt Bauman's *Wasted Lives: Modernity and Its Outcasts* explicitly engages the metaphor of "waste" to apprehend the precarious positions occupied by the displaced ones: "Refugees, the displaced, asylum seekers, migrants, the *sans papiers*, they are the waste of globalization" (Bauman 1998, 58). Movingly writing about the production of "wasted lives" as a part of a larger framework of industrial waste in Western cultures ("Waste is the dark, shameful secret of all production" [ibid., 27]), he coins certain unforgettable phrases such as "human rejects" (59), "superfluous people"

(41), or "redundant humans" (71) to express both the fragility of such lives and the ostracism the displaced ones often experience. If *Frozen River* strives to suture its audience into the relentlessness of anger, into this "vise" feeling, it is also true that the diagetically expressed anger does not embrace the smuggled ones. They are, indeed, in the perilous position of "redundant humans" Bauman writes about. That is, the film subtly shows that "migrant rage" is disallowed as the smuggled migrants need to remain mute as it is their muteness and invisibility that are of paramount importance during the moment of crossing.

Rage and Pedagogy: "An Ethics of the Affective in the Classroom"

In "Imagined Violence/Queer Violence," which explores literary and cinematic representations of rage and its possibilities, Judith Halberstam has asked: "When and why and how did rage disappear from the vocabulary of organized political activism?" (Halberstam 1993, 189). If we agree with Halberstam that political activism has indeed been cleansed of angry contestation (as socially inappropriate, volatile, and potentially violent), it is also true that the contemporary social and cultural landscape is not free from multiple and deliberate manifestations of rage. It is enough to consider *The Jerry Springer Show* as just one indicative example, which thrives on eliciting rage from both the invited guests and the audience and, in fact, actively encourages foul language and screams and orchestrates onstage verbal attacks, physical aggression, and security guards' intervention. It is crucial, of course, to remember that the guests on this show, and others like it, are often people of color, or whites coming from de-privileged social strata. Many are severely overweight, many are working-class, many are single parents, collectively, then, creating an impression that "regular" folks do not do rage, just the "unfortunate" ones.

Beyond the arena of "trash TV" where depoliticized and gratuitous rage is staged as a national spectacle to be enjoyed, *anti-immigrant* activist rage flourishes in both the material and the virtual world. The by now well-known Arizona Minuteman Project and many other U.S.-based online and offline anti-immigrant groups thrive on righteous anger, which is often strategically evoked as a necessary emotion used in a battle to protect the nation. These are instances of culturally allowed, if not sanctioned, rage, which become powerful expressions of nationalism in the hands of, predominantly, white men.

I discuss such examples of sanctioned rage with my students to illustrate the highly contradictory manifestations of the politics of rage in U.S. culture. I show them how, on one level, rage is often feared and distrusted (especially coming from the "wrong" people), while on another level, rage has been widely used to shore up a particular identity for the nation. But, despite our best critical intentions, it is difficult to engage students in issues relating to rage, given the predominant ethos of pedagogical exchange via "productive engagement" that is currently promoted in academia. No matter what kinds of models circulate among us as teachers—"the student-centered classroom," "collaborative learning," or "multimodal pedagogy"—this productive engagement is often understood through the notion of the classroom as safety zone, an emotionally safe space.[6] That is, we are praised for challenging students but not necessarily for making them uncomfortable. This contention goes straight to the heart of the forms of affect that are considered appropriate to teaching—rage is certainly not one of them. It is also obvious that the anticipated affect is gendered; women are implicitly expected to be personable, kind, and nurturing. In my own teaching evaluations, students frequently comment on how initially, before they can appreciate the rigor, they find me "aggressive," "forward," and "blunt," which they interpret as a "turn off." And even if I try to convince myself that I am not being "aggressive" and that I am opposed to "teaching defensively," I have to admit that somehow I am failing the initial test of a personable teacher. Even so, I am fascinated by a "turn off" comment. Does this mean that the affect my body projects to my students, the way they "read" it, is translated into some toughness that kills the "turn on" button?

The issue of "emotions" generated by the affect of bodies in the classroom has been, in fact, an invigorating topic of pedagogical scholarship. Elspeth Probyn zeroes in on "the affective work of a text," the "affective reaction" it can produce and asks "what type of affective response is appropriate in the classroom context"? (Probyn 2004, 30). She acknowledges that such affective responses are "hugely complex" and wants us to think about "the messiness of bodies, experience, and affect" (ibid., 33). And, of course, the circulation of affect goes both ways. Melissa Gregg and Gregory J. Seigworth contend that "affect is in many ways synonymous with *force* or *force of encounter* and, referring to affect as "gut economies," they claim that "affect arises in the midst of *in-between-ness*: in the capacities to act and be acted upon" (Seigworth and Gregg 2010, 1–2).

To realize that the classroom itself is a ground of such "encounters" shaped by the complexities and force of affect—the gut economies, indeed, that happen *in-between*—certainly undermines the conventional emphasis on our *intended* pedagogical goals. I know that my teaching agendas are under constant negotiation and that the "learning outcomes" that we are institutionally asked to foresee often amount to mandated discursive exercises. Obviously, I am not advocating that we abandon any sense of agency, or that we give in to chaos in the classroom but rather that we recognize the necessary limitations of our planned "objectives." Megan Watkins speaks of pedagogy as "affective transactions" (Watkins 2010, 271) and, referring to Henry Giroux and Peter McLaren as primary theorists of critical pedagogy, contends: "Their vision of critical pedagogy is reliant on problematizing teacher authority and redirecting power into the hands of students, giving them responsibility for their own learning" (ibid., 272). I think many of us who are passionate about nonhegemonic versions of pedagogy might readily agree that we want our students to be actively responsible for their learning. As bell hooks says, the greatest gift she can offer her students is the ability to think critically, and this can happen only when students remain active agents (hooks 1997). However, the point about "redirecting power" feels too easy. If we take the claim that pedagogy involves "affective transactions" seriously, we also need to think about power dialogically, emerging *in-between*, in the space of *encounter*, and thus not in the hands of a teacher or her students.

The "affective reaction" Probyn wants us to consider is particularly potent when we engage films in the classroom, precisely because of the medium's sensory power, its "goose bump effect" (Probyn 2004, 29). Laura U. Marks, develops the metaphor of "the skin of the film" as a way to draw attention to film's materiality, and argues that "vision itself can be tactile, as though one were touching a film with one's eyes: I term this *haptic visuality*" (Marks 2000, xi). She emphasizes "the tactile and contagious quality of cinema as something we viewers brush up against like another body" (ibid., xii). A similar contention is present in Trinh Minh-ha's *Elsewhere, within here: immigration, refugeeism and the boundary event* in which she claims that "the eye hears, the ear sees" (Trinh 2010, 2). If we treat film as "another body," with a complex terrain of visuality and audibility that viewers brush up against, then the process of pedagogical encounter and affective transactions gets further complicated since the *in-between*, in fact, involves the triad of film, students, and teacher.

This is not a novel observation. Teachers know that the filmic texts they bring to the classroom have their own *power* and produce affect, impacting our sensorium, and, while the unpredictability of textuality itself is important to acknowledge, so is the specificity of cinema as a visceral medium that allows us to feel the tactile and kinetic force of the images and sounds. Vivian Sobchack, demanding that we think of embodied spectatorship and "the carnal sensuality of the film experience" (Sobchack 2004, 56), wants us to think about "the capacity of films to physically arouse us to meaning" (ibid., 57).

The unpredictability of textuality and "the capacity of cinema to physically arouse" meanings surprised me during the discussion of *Frozen River*.

Despite the fact that my students discursively disavow rage, many of them, in fact, got quite angry. They turned out to be a particularly compelling yet judgmental audience because many of them intuitively sensed the ambiguous positioning of "poor whites." A number of my students come from very poor, rural Appalachian communities. They intimately understand the pejorative notions of "white trash" and "trailer park families," and their environment has an uneasy relation to the notion of "white privilege." It is perhaps this specific background that offered my students a sense of authority as they reacted disapprovingly to the film's representations of poverty, revealing their spectatorial desire for a "proper" and "acceptable" depiction of deprivation. Ray's onscreen actions did not measure up to their expectations that she should display appropriate humility and acceptance of the experiences of privation. Both "engaged and enraged," they vehemently critiqued Ray's mothering practices ("she shouldn't have this large TV," "she is a consumerist," "she needs to feed her children first"), which they perceived as simply irresponsible.

This was a highly charged moment in my teaching *Frozen River*. I have realized that the politicized rage I hoped to focus on–immigrant rage about the "illegitimate bodies" locked up in a trunk and the racist and sexist inequalities the film reveals—got usurped, as it were, and transformed into a moral disapproval of the low-income white mother in the film. That is, my students performed what Beverly Skeggs refers to as "metonymic morality" (Skeggs 2009, 635), which, in this specific case, attacked the mother (already coded as "low-class" and "trashy") as a repository of failure in need of repair.

Coda

The topics raised in *Frozen River*—racial politics, national belonging, cross-cultural encounters, difference, the politics of anger—are the most frequently discussed themes in my courses. These topics challenge the students, requiring them to extend their intellectual curiosity well beyond familiar territory; they also challenge me as I try to demonstrate that we all participate in various forms of social injustice, if only indirectly or unconsciously. But how do we avoid "consumerist" emotionality in teaching such complex topics? How do we implicate the local in the global and encourage the students to see beyond their own borders of social and cultural contexts? In other words, how does one imbricate the transnational into one's pedagogical practice so that issues of foreignness, migration, and dislocation begin to feel pertinent and urgent?

These are hard questions. Though I do not believe that there are easy answers, I am convinced that, as educators, we have an obligation to grapple actively with such challenges, probing with the students the complexity of the uneven and multilayered ways in which globalization affects various quarters of the world, often fostering new regimes of oppression. If we agree that the classroom has the potential to become a site of political and ethical transformation, then the politics of politeness, often performed through tactics of appeasement that forestall pedagogical risk taking and encourage the students to "like us," is clearly a flawed, if not dangerous, way of thinking. Despite the fact that my students activated the rage button in a different direction than I had hoped for, revealing to me, yet again, that pedagogy is inherently contingent, I am still convinced that the "pedagogy of rage" is a potent philosophical platform to teach from. I still believe that such a pedagogy—one that demands that we think about politicized anger in nuanced ways and recognize that the "rage of the oppressed is never the same as the rage of the privileged" (hooks 1995, 30)—has the power to challenge students and teachers by creating spaces for provocative encounters, sometimes mediated by cinematic affect. This pedagogy also has the power to produce an "affective seepage" (Skeggs 2009, 640), unexpected responses that may rupture expected outcomes in the classroom.

On some level, the stories from the classroom I share here are aligned with an ongoing effort in contemporary U.S. academia to "globalize" education. Many universities have opened interdisciplinary institutes and offices that sponsor such initiatives. My own institution's Web page advertises our university as "the home of global perspectives." In the wake of this "globalization" push, we faculty members often hear that our prescribed role is to educate our students to become "global citizens." On the surface, the idea of students gaining the consciousness of "global citizens" appears to be desirable and warranted. We want our students to "be" both "local" and "global," to understand and to think critically about their own culture but also to have a sense of the world and its complexities well beyond the boundaries of their community, race, ethnicity, and nationality. The "global citizen" implies an ethical impetus toward an awareness of human rights and their violations across the world, a sensitivity to uneven processes of globalization, responsibility toward the others. It also potentially moves our students beyond restrictive, U.S.-centric, systems of knowledge. Yet, "global citizen" also implies a kind of unhindered mobility that harks back to the older, exclusionary paradigm of cosmopolitanism. As Bauman's poignant analysis of globalization reveals, for certain cosmopolitan inhabitants of the first world, "global businessman, global culture managers or global academics," state borders are permeable and fluid, "dismantled for the world's commodities, capital and finances." While such privileged members travel at will and freely, experiencing pleasures of mobility, those coming from the outside of the first world "travel surreptitiously, often illegally, sometimes paying more for the crowded steerage of a sinking unseaworthy boat than others pay for business-class gilded luxuries" (Bauman 1998, 89).

I am also compelled by Gayatri Spivak's punchy point: "The 'globe' is counterintuitive. You walk from one end of the earth to the other and it remains flat. It is a scientific abstraction inaccessible to experience. No one lives in the *global* village." She asks, "In what interest, to regulate what sort of relationships, is the globe evoked?" (Spivak 1998, 329). Considering such critiques of the master narrative of globalization and the contentious nature of the "global"—critiques carried out most forcefully in postcolonial, transnational, and feminist studies (see, e.g., Behdad 2005; Lionnet and Shih 2005; Mohanty 2003; Waller and Marcos 2005)—I want to trouble the concept of a "global citizen" and ask: What happens if, in such institutional circumstances of education, one (a teacher or a student) is not a citizen per se, or is marginalized vis-à-vis the privileges and rights of citizenship? What happens when we consider stateless people, those who live without basic freedoms, those who, often violently uprooted from their native lands, seek protection in the Global North but end up in detention centers and refugee camps? How might we bridge the discrepancy between the pedagogical ideals of "global citizenship" and the troubling limitations of this term? Isn't the idea of "global citizens" an elitist one? Isn't the very category of "citizens" a sanctioned yet a restrictive designator? Should we then perhaps understand the category of citizenship in those educational settings as fashionable slogans that need to be scrutinized and deconstructed? Slogans that demand a good dose of critical anxiety, one infused with the *mood* of anger that can *move* us to action?

Notes

1. I developed this discussion fully in *Alienhood: Citizenship, Exile, and the Logic of Difference*.
2. I developed this discussion in "Immigrant Rage."
3. The film won the Grand Jury Prize at Sundance, 2008; Melissa Leo was nominated for the 2008 Oscar for her role.
4. According to Schoemer, Hunt spent ten years researching the Mohawk tribe near the Canadian border, befriending a medicine woman and slowly gaining the insular community's trust. " 'It took me a long time to feel like I understood enough about that life to make a credible character,' she says" (2008).
5. As Hunt explains in one of the interviews, she is guided by a "realist" impulse:

> People are so jaded at this point by seeing only beautiful, big, toothy smiles, she says. Even if the characters are dirt-poor and desperate, they're gorgeous. I guess I'll be struck dead for saying this, but I didn't

like Erin Brockovich. I feel like we don't have to seduce everybody every moment. (Schoemer 2008)

6. For a development of this idea, see my "Pedagogy of Anxiety."

Works Cited

Appadurai, Arjun. 2006. *Fear of Small Numbers: An Essay on the Geography of Anger.* Durham: Duke University Press.

Badiou, Alain. 2009."Comments on Simon Critchley's *Infinitely Demanding: Ethics of Commitment, Politics of Resistance.*" *Critical Horizons: A Journal of Philosophy and Social Theory* 10 (2): 154–62.

Bauman, Zygmunt. 1998. *Globalization: The Human Consequences.* New York: Columbia University Press.

———. 2004. *Wasted Lives: Modernity and Its Outcasts.* Malden: Polity Press.

Behdad, Ali. 1998. "INS and OUTs: Producing Delinquency at the Border." *Aztlan: A Journal of Chicano Studies* 23: 103–13.

———. 2005. *A Forgetful Nation: On Immigration and Cultural Identity in the United States.* Durham: Duke University Press.

———. 2005. "On Globalization, Again!" In *Postcolonial Studies and Beyond,* edited by Ania Loomba et al. Durham: Duke University Press.

Borrows, John. 2001. "Uncertain Citizens: Aboriginal Peoples and the Supreme Court." *The Canadian Bar Review* 80 (1–2): 15–41.

Cairns, Alan C. 2002. "Citizenship and Indian Peoples: The Ambiguous Legacy of Internal Colonialism." In *Handbook of Citizenship Studies,* edited by Engin F. Isin and Bryan S. Turner. London: Sage.

Eyre, Chris, dir. 1998. *Smoke Signals.* ShadowCatcher Entertainment.

Gunew, Sneja. 2003. "The Home of Language: A Pedagogy of the Stammer." In *Uprootings/Regroundings: Questions of Home and Migration,* edited by Sara Ahmed, Claudia Castaneda, Anne-Marie Fortier, and Mimi Sheller. New York: Berg.

Halberstam, Judith. 1993. "Imagined Violence/Queer Violence: Representation, Rage, and Resistance." *Social Text* 37: 187–201.

Hoffman, Eva. 1989. *Lost in Translation: Life in a New Language.* New York: Penguin Books.

hooks, bell. 1995. *Killing Rage: Ending Racism.* New York: Henry Holt.

———.1997. *bell hooks: Cultural Criticism and Transformation.* Northampton, MA: Media Education Foundation (DVD).

Hunt, Courtney, dir. 2008. *Frozen River.* Sony Pictures Home Entertainment.

Ifekwunigwe, Jayne. 2004. "Recasting 'Black Venus' in the New African Diaspora." *Women's Studies International Forum* 27: 397–412.

Imre, Anikó, Katarzyna Marciniak, and Áine O'Healy. 2009. "Transcultural Mediations and Transnational Politics of Difference." *Feminist Media Studies* 9: 385–90.

Jaikumar, Priya. 2007. "Translating Silences: A Cinematic Encounter with Incommensurable Difference." In *Transnational Feminism in Film and Media*, edited by Katarzyna Marciniak, Anikó Imre, and Áine O'Healy. New York: Palgrave.

Jamieson, Ruth. 1999. "'Contested Jurisdiction Border Communities' and Cross-Border Crime—the Case of Akwesasne." *Crime, Law, and Social Change* 30: 259–72.

Lionnet, Francoise, and Shu-Mei Shih. 2005. "Introduction: Thinking through the Minor, Transnationally." In *Minor Transnationalism*. Durham and London: Duke University Press.

Marciniak, Katarzyna. 2006. "Alienhood, 'Hygienic' Identities, and the Second World." *Differences: A Journal of Feminist Cultural Studies* 17 (2): 33–63.

———. 2006. *Alienhood: Citizenship, Exile, and the Logic of Difference*. Minneapolis: University of Minnesota Press.

———. 2010. "Pedagogy of Anxiety." *Signs: Journal of Women in Culture and Society* 35 (4): 869–92.

Marks, Laura U. 2000. *The Skin of the Film: Intercultural Cinema, Embodiment, and the Senses*. Durham and London: Duke University Press.

Mohanty, Chandra. 2003. *Feminism without Borders: Decolonizing Theory, Practicing Solidarity*. Durham and London: Duke University Press.

Probyn, Elspeth. 2004. "Teaching Bodies: Affects in the Classroom." *Body and Society* 10 (4): 21–43.

Ratcliffe, Krista. 2005. "Listening Pedagogically: A Tactic for Listening to Classroom Resistance." In *Rhetorical Listening: Identification, Gender, Whiteness*. Carbondale: Southern Illinois University Press.

Seigworth, Gregory J., and Melissa Gregg. 2010. "An Inventory of Shimmers." In *The Affect Theory Reader*. Durham and London: Duke University Press.

Shoemer, Karen. 2008. "Little Miss Darkness: Courtney Hunt's First Film Won Sundance, but It's Hardly Cute." *New York*. http://nymag.com/movies/profiles/45293/. Accessed February 27, 2011.

Skeggs, Beverly. 2009. "The Moral Economy of Person Production: The Class Relations of Self-Performance on 'Reality' Television." *The Sociological Review* 57 (4): 626–44.

Sobchack, Vivian. 2004. *Carnal Thoughts: Embodiment and Moving Image Culture*. Berkeley: University of California Press.

Spivak, Gayatri Chakravorty. 1998. "Cultural Talks in the Hot Peace: Revisiting the 'Global' Village." In *Cosmpolitics: Thinking and Feeling Beyond the Nation*, edited by Pheng Cheah and Bruce Robbins. Minneapolis: University of Minnesota Press.

Taylor, Ella. 2008. "*Frozen River* Lays It on Thick." *Village Voice*. http://www.villagevoice.com/2008-07-29/film/frozen-river-lays-it-on-thick/. Accessed February 27, 2011.

Trinh T. Minh-ha. 2001. "Not You/Like You: Postcolonial Women and the Interlocking Questions of Identity and Difference." In *The Longman Anthology of Women's Literature*, edited by Mary K. DeShazer. New York: Longman.

———. 2010. *Elsewhere, within Here: Immigration, Refugeeism, and the Boundary Event*. New York: Routledge.

Waller, Marguerite, and Sylvia Marcos, eds. 2005. *Dialogue and Difference: Feminisms Challenge Globalization*. New York: Palgrave.
Watkins, Megan. 2010. "Desiring Recognition, Accumulating Affect." In *The Affect Theory Reader*, edited by Gregory J. Seigworth and Melissa Gregg. Durham and London: Duke University Press.
Wray, Matt. 2006. *Not Quite White: White Trash and the Boundaries of Whiteness*. Durham: Duke University Press.
Wray, Matt, and Annalee Newitz, eds. 1997. "Introduction." In *White Trash: Race and Class in America*, edited by Matt Wray and Annalee Newitz. New York: Routledge.

Figure 7.1. *Admit None*, 1999. Courtesy of THINK AGAIN and Center for the Study of Political Graphics

II

In the Field

Acts of Immigrant Protest

Figure 7.2. The 2010 Avatar demonstration in the West Bank village of Bil'in. Courtesy of Oren Ziv

7

On Israel/Palestine and the Politics of Visibility

SIMON FAULKNER

Although not concerned with people conventionally defined as immigrants, through the consideration of Israel/Palestine[1] and the situation of Palestinians living under occupation, this chapter does address conditions of precariousness in terms of rights and residence that often define the situation of the migrant. The chapter is also not explicitly about the political actions conventionally understood as protest, at least until its final section. However, it deals throughout with relationships between politics and aesthetics, and specifically with the way that the conflict between the Israeli state and the Palestinians is wrapped up with the question of what it is possible to see. The discussion is concerned in general with the politics of visibility within the geographical space of Israel/Palestine and the broader international context of the Israeli-Palestinian conflict. It addresses this subject via Jacques Rancière's ideas about the organization and disruption of given social orders. These ideas prioritize the sensible and aesthetic dimensions of the political. To begin with, the aim is to use Rancière's thinking as an approach that enables the drawing out of some general points relevant to the issue of visibility when it comes to the political differentiation of bodies and spaces within Israel and the occupied West Bank. This analysis is intended as a general frame for the consideration of political actions that are aimed at gaining visibility. It also suggests that Rancière's ideas need to be elaborated upon when it comes to visibility and protest in a highly mediated world through an engagement with images. Thus, the chapter continues by examining the role of iconic motifs in relation to the politics of visibility, focusing upon recurrent images generated by and in response to Palestinian struggle. The discussion ends with a consideration of demonstrations in the West Bank village of Bil'in where residents have been engaged in seven years of resistance against the confiscation of their land for settlement construction and the building of a section of the West Bank Barrier. These demonstrations are taken as exemplary of interrelationships between politics, visibility, and images in the context of Israel/Palestine.

Supplementing the Field of the Visible

According to Rancière, "politics is a question of aesthetics, a matter of appearances" (Rancière 1999, 74). A point he makes elsewhere, when he observes, "politics is first of all a battle about perceptible/sensible material" (Guénoun and Kavanagh 2000, 11). Politics always entails an intervention into the existing order of the seeable and the sayable that is one aspect of what Rancière defines as the "distribution of the sensible." This phrase refers to the relationship between the practico-material organization of social reality and the sense that is made of it. Hence, Rancière's observation that a "distribution of the sensible is a matrix that defines a set of relations between sense and sense: that is, between a form of sensory experience and an interpretation which makes sense of it" (Rancière 2009, 275). The distribution of the sensible involves a demarcation of roles, places, and times that is subject to sense-making practices that legitimize this structure, rationalizing it in terms of an ethos that ascribes to everyone a place and the need for them to be in their place. Through this relationship of sense and sense, the performance of particular roles is matched up with a perceived delimitation of capacities. A distribution of the sensible therefore involves a relationship between sense and sense that delimits people in terms of who they can be and what they can do. The sensible order of roles, places, and times presents certain things as visible and thus open to sense-making practices, while other things are rendered invisible. People are only visible in terms of the roles and places they have within the given order.

Closely linked to this is Rancière's concept of "the police order" that refers to the policing of the distribution of the sensible. The "police-principle" (Rancière 2010, 36) functions by showing and keeping people in their place, and by reinforcing the perception that there is nothing in excess of the given order. Thus, Rancière observes that the police order is "characterized by the absence of void and of supplement" (Rancière 2010, 36). This is not to suggest that the experience of the sensible is exhausted by the police-principle; rather, the function of the police is to try to exhaust the sensible in this way. Politics intervenes into the order of roles and demarcations that constitute the distribution of the sensible, creating what Rancière calls a "dissensus" that involves the introduction of a supplement to the given order of things. This does not replay existing divisions. Instead, it is something that problematizes the very divisions upon which such conflicts are based. If the distribution of the sensible is a division between what can be seen and heard and what cannot, then it is also a "sharing-out and dividing up of the sensory" (Davis 2010, 91) through which people are allotted a particular part of the sensible. This can be understood in terms of basic visibility: some people just have a greater sensible presence than others. It can also be understood in terms of how people are given visibility and what that visibility means in terms of the delimitation of roles and places. But the distribution of the sensible also involves the demarcation of the cultural field in terms of relationships between aesthetic practices and constituencies. This is why Rancière has argued, in his book *Nights of Labor*, that the decision of some workers in early-nineteenth-century France to take up writing at night instead of resting constituted a political act. This act revealed that, contrary to the police-principle, these workers could be more than one thing. They were, in Rancière's words, "beings to whom several lives were owed" (Rancière 1989, ix). Politics is therefore a break with the given rules of the game of conflict and involves people taking more, or a different share of the sensible to that which they have been apportioned. Such appropriations of the sensible are always about visibility and, in Rancière's terms, always about the creation of a "stage" upon which politics can be enacted (Hallward 2009; Davis 2010, 85–86). Such stages are places for interactions that would not normally happen between people who would not normally interact, or who would only interact in particular ways. They are also places for performances and spectacles that redefine what can be seen and what should be thought, talked about, and taken into account. These performances are what Rancière terms "world openers" (Rancière 1999, 58) that involve the imagining of another world within the one that currently exists. Underpinning this is Rancière's commitment to equality and the idea that politics is fundamentally something that declassifies the hierarchical divisions between groups of people and asserts an equality of intelligence manifested through a shared command of language. This means that what is political for Rancière is that which involves a demand for equality, involving either an assertion of greater visibility on the part of those who are uncounted, or the setting up of a stage upon which those who dominate are compelled to respond to those who are dominated.

Todd May has pointed out that there are many ways in which societies are hierarchical and divided and can therefore be approached via Rancière's thought (May 2010, 71). Indeed, May notes the relationship between Israelis and Palestinians as an example of this kind of division (May 2008, 56). But how exactly can Rancière's ideas be used to explore the relationship between Israel as an occupying society and the occupied Palestinian population that has been described as a condition of "inclusive exclusion" (Ophir, Givoni, and Hanafi 2009) through which Palestinians are ruled by the Israeli state but excluded from its protection? To answer this question we might start by focusing upon the power of the Israeli state to shape the sensible environment: to draw lines between populations and apply different modes of governance to them. This separation of the population is *the* primary element of the distribution of the sensible when it comes to Israel/Palestine and has been so since the foundation of the Israeli state.[2] If we think about Israel's rule of the West Bank since the period of the Oslo process in the 1990s, we can see that this establishment of dividing lines involves the differentiation of zones of governance and legality as well as a system of physical barriers, channels, and checkpoints that segregate spaces of movement and residence. This system of separation is made sense of in particular ways. The fundamental rationalization is a commitment to ethnic-national difference that is used to legitimize keeping populations apart on the basis of their essential incompatibility. This overarching notion is combined with the idea of Palestinians as an existential threat to Jewish Israelis and a belief in a deep territorial bond between Jews and the land of "Israel" that rationalizes the displacement of the Palestinians. Of course, such rationalizations do not go unopposed. If we can define a general Palestinian viewpoint, it is one that contests the inequality, subordination, and displacement enforced upon Palestinians by Israeli state power. However, this viewpoint does not usually challenge the maintenance of separation between Israelis and Palestinians and in a sense contributes from a subordinate position to the distribution of the sensible defined by the law of separation. It is part of what Rancière might define as the "consensual game of domination and rebellion" (Rancière 2009b, 9). Palestinian nationalism, premised upon a two-state solution, involves a rationale of equality to the extent that it demands citizenship for Palestinians in their own territorial state that is equal to that already experienced by Israelis, but it does not challenge or declassify the foundational division within the population of Israel/Palestine. This challenge to the "consensual game" is to be found in the politics of bi-nationalism that Israeli filmmaker Udi Aloni describes as a "specter" that "haunts the Middle East" (Aloni 2011, 19). In relation to these observations, it can be suggested that the police order in Israel/Palestine is that which maintains the separation and inequality between Israelis and Palestinians. Politics in this context arises when separation and inequality are disrupted by a supplement that makes visible other possibilities, when Israelis and Palestinians come together, or when a stage is created on which Israelis are compelled to interact with Palestinians on an equal footing. Two examples will give specificity to this argument.

The first example involves the arrest of the Israeli activist Michel Warschawski by Shin Bet (the Israeli general security service) in 1987. Although he was accused of specific offences (helping Palestinian "terrorist" organizations), Warschawski's real crime was to work with Palestinians as comrades and equals at the Alternative Information Center (AIC) in Jerusalem. The AIC was formed as a means of transmitting information across the linguistic and ideological border that divides Jewish Israelis from Palestinians under occupation. Those who worked at the AIC conceived themselves as taking up a position on the border and, in Warschawski's terms, functioned as "border runners" (Warschawski 2005, xvii and 5). In his autobiographical book, *On the Border*, Warschawski recounts how his Shin Bet interrogators made it clear that they could not accept any ambiguity when it came to the border between Israeli citizens and Palestinian noncitizens. This border had to function as an absolute partition. During one interrogation session they stated:

> Over there . . . there is no democracy, there is occupation. And we have a problem with people like you: where are you? Here, protected by democracy, or on the other side? On the one hand, you're one of us . . . but on the other hand, you bring with you Ali . . . and Hamdi . . . and they are not protected by democracy. So you have to choose: to be on this side of the border and be protected by democracy, or be with them and be treated the way we treat them. (Warschawski 2005, 120)

For the Shin Bet, as a representative organization of the police order, there is no middle ground, there is only an "us" and a "them." In this context and following Rancière's ideas, the most political thing about the practices of the members of the AIC was not necessarily the content of the information they communicated across the border, but the creation of the new context necessary to enable this communication to happen. This needed people usually separated by ethnically defined nationalism to come together on the border and become a novel transethnic collective political subject. It was this new space on the border that Shin Bet wanted to eradicate, for it was a space that not only allowed for cooperation and communication between Israelis and Palestinians, but also opened up possibilities for a bi-nationalism that would threaten partition as the fundamental logic of the police order. Border running was a practice and the border runner was a figure that made possibilities beyond the police order visible.

The second example, which takes us closer to the explicit subject of protest, involves an action undertaken by the Ramallah-based Palestinian artist Khaled Jarrar when he established a temporary "exhibition" of forty-one photographs of checkpoints and demonstrations in Bil'in at the Hawara checkpoint near Nablus on Saturday, February 3, 2007.

The photographs were hung on the fence that divides the entry and exit lanes on one side of the checkpoint. The exhibition began at 12:00 p.m. and lasted for three hours. It was unlikely to have lasted that long if Jarrar had not contacted representatives of international NGOs to attend the exhibition and had not been able to rely on interventions by members of the Israeli women's organization Checkpoint Watch to stop Israeli soldiers at the checkpoint from taking the photographs down. Jarrar considered the photographs to have a documentary function and the exhibition to have a revelatory role. Thus, he has observed that the exhibition was aimed at the foreign spectators present at the checkpoint and that he was concerned to "show people our tragedy through my art, the reality of the daily humiliation we suffer, how old people, women and children are treated at the checkpoints."[3] These intentions are entirely congruent with the dominant Palestinian mode of address aimed at foreign spectators during and after the second Intifada, which has involved the visual revelation of Palestinian suffering on the basis of a shared conception of human rights

Figure 7.3. Khaled Jarrar, "At the checkpoint" exhibition at the Hawara checkpoint, 2007. Courtesy of Rula Halawani.

(Allen 2009, 162, 165, 170–73). Framed in these terms, the exhibition entailed a novel mode for the dissemination of conventional documentary forms that are meant to make the occupation visible as a crime.

However, if we approach the exhibition via Rancière's ideas, we might think about the political nature of this action not in terms of Jarrar's stated concerns with a documentary revelation of reality, but in terms of how this action provided a supplement to the distribution of the sensible as manifested at the checkpoint. Although human interactions at Israeli checkpoints are not entirely uniform, on the whole, they are defined by a stark binary between those who are checked and those who check. This is a binary that is obviously also a power relationship between those who mobilize a militarized surveillant gaze and those who are the objects of this gaze. It is the Palestinian's allotted role within this order to be the person who is checked and nothing else. Jarrar's exhibition disrupted this situation by turning part of the space of the checkpoint into a location for a different kind of interaction between him and the soldiers than simply waiting to be checked and responding on command. In this sense it is not the content of the photographs that disrupts the distribution of the sensible, but how they are used, where, and by whom. The images have a representational function, but they are also kinds of talismans around which an enactment of a kind of equality ensued. Thus, the exhibition created a temporary and precarious "common stage" (Rancière 1999, 23, 26) between Jarrar and the soldiers that was normally ruled out as a possibility by the order of things at the checkpoint. This happened not only during the exhibition, but also when Jarrar was putting the photographs into the boot of a car. In both contexts soldiers came to talk to him and explain why they thought the photographs were misrepresentative and why Israel had to maintain the checkpoints.[4] As Jarrar observed in a written statement: "One of the soldiers, a young woman, suddenly felt she needed to defend herself and her comrades by saying they have to protect their country and that it is legitimate to fight terrorists."[5] Jarrar's action disturbed the checkpoint regime, creating an opening to an alternative world in which soldiers felt compelled to explain their position to a Palestinian. As with the worker-writers discussed by Rancière in *Nights of Labor*, Jarrar acted at the checkpoint as someone who could be two things at once rather than accepting the singular role allotted to him by the order of the checkpoint. Through his actions, Jarrar established that he was not only a body to be checked. He was also a thinking, creative subject who had political agency and voice.

The two examples of the practices of Warshawski and the AIC and Jarrar's exhibition are quite different, but each in its own way delineates something of the distribution of the sensible that structures the geographical space of Israel/Palestine. One attests to the power of the partition of the population within this space and the anxiety that accompanies any compromise of this division on the part of agents of the police order. The other indicates the power relations between the roles of the occupier and the occupied and the demarcations of modes of being that these relations entail. Both show how politics in this context involves a dissensual break with the order of partition, making something supplementary and new appear. As such, both examples amount to political interventions into the field of visibility: in one case making visible a collective subject that spans the border between Israelis and Palestinians while, in the other, indicating possibilities for Palestinians to gain a different kind of visible presence within the sensible order of the occupation.

The Iconic Order

So far, there has been no discussion of images outside of the example of Jarrar's exhibition at the Hawara checkpoint. This is in part because Rancière does not on the whole address visual images and their representational functions in addressing political themes. However, for the notion of the distribution of the sensible to be made workable in relation to contemporary social orders and to Israel/Palestine in particular, visual representations need to be taken in account. This is because the roles, places, and perceived capacities allotted to different people within any given order are often accompanied and enabled by images. With this in mind, it is possible to suggest that any distribution of the sensible is also partially an iconic order of established and stereotypical images.

One interesting place where Rancière discusses visual images in his more politically oriented writings is in *Nights of Labor,* where he contrasts what he calls the barely visible "shadow images" of the worker-writers who are the subject of his book with the "accepted images of the 'worker movement,' 'popular culture,' and the like" (Rancière 1989, ix). Rancière's use of the word *image* here is generic in its reference to images as things that can be mental, verbal, and visual, but it also refers to actual visual images of laborers. Indeed, in the first chapter of this book, Rancière discusses conventional visual images of blacksmiths in contrast to the dream of a writer-locksmith to become himself a painter and a producer of images (ibid., 5). What we have here is an indication of how the idea of an iconic order of established visual motifs might be worked into the notion of the distribution of the sensible. Conventional images of workers reinforce their allotted place in the given order, while alternative "shadow" images point to declassificatory possibilities. If we think about Jarrar's exhibition at the Hawara checkpoint, not only were visual images used to facilitate a political disruption of the given at that location, but the event was itself imaged and these images were circulated more widely. Photographs of Jarrar assembling the exhibition amounted to a new image of a Palestinian in the context of the checkpoint.

These points lead us to an important consideration about the mediating role of visual images in relation to the sensible order. What constitutes reality in contemporary societies is often visible through tele-mediation, meaning that many situations and events have a dual existence, as both "immediate and media-ted" (Routledge 1997, 362, 371). Kevin DeLuca and Jennifer Peeples, for example, have developed the notion of the "image event" as a means of theorizing this dual visual existence when it comes to political protests (DeLuca and Peeples 2002). Such protests are intended as actions that are to be seen both by eyewitnesses and from afar via photographic and video imagery. Being counted in political terms is therefore understood as significantly a matter of making oneself visible to others who are spatially separated from oneself. In this sense, Jarrar's exhibition was a form of image event that was immediate in its use of images at the checkpoint, but also media-ted through images. Although the exhibition lasted only three hours, it continues to have an afterlife through the latter images. When it comes to Israel/Palestine in general, this relationship between the

Figure 7.4. Khaled Jarrar assembling his exhibition at the Hawara checkpoint, 2007. Courtesy of Rula Halawani

immediate and the mediated also needs to be considered in terms of the intersecting geographical scales involved in the Israeli-Palestinian conflict; scales that are local, state-based, and international. This adds further complexity to the relationship between the distribution of the sensible and images in this context.

From here, it is useful to consider the general issue of the relationship between the mediation of Palestinian political struggle and the iconic order. Image making has been significant to the Palestinian national movement at least since the 1960s. Through acts of symbolic violence conceived as kinds of image events, Palestinian fighters thought they could use the media as a means of intervening into the international field of vision. This is demonstrated by the TV footage contained within artist Johan Grimonprez's 1997 film *dial H-I-S-T-O-R-Y*, about the history of skyjacking that shows Palestinian guerrillas at press conferences, or being allowed to speak to the press about their cause after they are arrested. For example, at a Popular Front for the Liberation of Palestine press conference in Amman in August 1970, Mouna Abdel-Majid stated: "For you westerners you don't understand, you have the Israeli propaganda, you think the Arabs, they are the dirty Arabs, and . . . we have to fight outside our territory and we have to bring the whole world to understand our case."[6] This was not just a fight elsewhere in the world, but also for international media attention and thus for the attention of the world. It was a fight that both acknowledged the need to turn media attention to the advantage of Palestinian resistance and placed a high level of faith in visual media as a means of connecting with empathetic audiences. Lori A. Allen points out that this faith in the imagined power of visual media is related to a crisis of Palestinian national politics, especially in recent decades (Allen 2009, 162). The less actual political power Palestinians have had to affect conditions on the ground the more they have committed themselves to finding salvation through mediation. This faith in visual media is revealed, for example, by a banner made by activists in Bil'in and carried during one of the weekly demonstrations staged in the village in June 2006 that depicted a giant still-camera against a white background and bore a slogan in English that declared: "Their eyes won't stop showing the Israeli soldiers crimes."

The slogan personifies the camera, suggesting that it has an eye that sees like a human being. At the same time, it suggests that this eye also shows the crimes of the Israeli state to other viewers. We might also consider a recent video of a demonstration in the West Bank village of Nabi Saleh, posted on YouTube by the Israeli painter and activist David Reeb that presents another video activist and resident of Nabi Saleh, Bilal Tamimi, speaking to the camera and discussing why he has been filming the demonstrations in the village. He states: "I would like to have a good future for my

Figure 7.5. Activists in Bil'in make a banner, 2006. Courtesy of Jacob Ketriol

family, for my children, for my village. Because of that I am photographing and recording everything that happened and spread it to all the people in all the world to let them know what's happening in Nabi Saleh and so hope to give us support to end the occupation."[7] In this statement we not only have a replication of the imagined possibility of speaking to "the world" articulated by Abdel-Majid in 1970, but also an affirmation of the belief that visual images allow for a kind of immediacy that connects people suffering under conditions of repression with far-flung spectators. Such a connection is imagined as a means of intervening into a field of vision within which the Palestinian experience of occupation lacks proper visibility.

Yet the issue here is not one of visibility alone. The way that visibility is attained or allotted is also important. Writing about his experiences among Palestinian refugees and fighters in Jordan in the early 1970s in his book *Prisoner of Love*, Jean Genet emphasized how the Fedayeen (guerillas) were turned into "stars" by the foreign news media. One Palestinian fighter is recounted as declaring: "Stars, that's what we were" (Genet 1986, 12). Another observes, however: "But you'd turned us into monsters, too. You called us terrorists! We were terrorist stars" (ibid., 13–14). Palestinian fighters could gain visibility, but it often came at a cost. Moreover, the terrorist is not the only image ascribed to the Palestinians within the internationalized iconic order. The other significant image is that of the Palestinian as victim. This image is partly the result of efforts on the part of Palestinians to gain acknowledgment from international observers in terms of their human rights. But the effects of this emphasis upon victimhood are not necessarily politically effective simply because the iteration of images of Palestinian suffering has the potential to naturalize this condition, encouraging a perception of Palestinians as those who *exist to suffer*. Even for those who are empathetic toward Palestinian plight, perceptions of Palestinians as essential victims do not encourage seeing them as equals. Palestinians thus come to be viewed as those who lack, not only human rights, but also political agency.[8] This is why the images of Jarrar setting up his exhibition at the Hawara checkpoint are so important, as is the footage of Bilal Tamimi talking about his work as a filmmaker/reporter in David Reeb's video. This imagery makes visible a different kind of Palestinian agency. But even this visibility can be defined as something that delimits Palestinian political agency. The roles adopted by Jarrar and Tamimi as image makers are that of documentarians who reveal the plight of their own people. Such acts of image making are important for the visibility of the Palestinian experience under occupation yet, at the same time, they also are framed by a particular delimitation of the relationship between Palestinians and cultural production that affirms a naturalized link between Palestinian image making and documentary media. This point can be further understood via an observation made by Rancière:

> The main enemy of artistic creativity as well as of political creativity is consensus—that is, inscription within roles, possibilities, and competences. Godard said ironically that the epic was for Israelis and the documentary for Palestinians. Which is to say that the distribution of genres—for example, the division between the freedom of fiction and the reality of the news—is always already a distribution of possibilities and capacities: To say that, in the dominant regime of representation, documentary is for the Palestinians is to say that they can only offer the bodies of their victims to the gaze of the news cameras or to the compassionate gaze at their suffering. That is, the world is divided between those who can and those who can-

not afford the luxury of playing with words and images. (Carnevale and Kelsey 2007, 263)

The political struggle over the sensible is therefore not just about bringing unseen suffering into the field of vision, but also about how this happens, what technologies and conventions of representation are used, and how representation frames and positions those being represented. When it comes to images, the distribution of the sensible also involves a demarcation of relationships between ways and genres of image making and groups of people that is also a way of defining and putting people in their place. This is not stated to suggest that Palestinians should not use documentary modes of representation, or that documentary forms are not important for highlighting specific events and situations related to the Israeli occupation. Rather, it is to suggest that the relationship between Palestinian suffering and its documentary representation as a form of Palestinian political expression is at one and the same time an effect and a delimitation of Palestinian agency. Within the distribution of the sensible and its iconic order, Palestinians are expected to suffer and to be seen to suffer through documentary representation. This means that a dissensual mode of Palestinian political agency would involve a break with both the role of the victim and the documentarian in some way, perhaps, as Rancière suggests, through play with cultural forms not usually directly related to the seriousness of political communication.

"It seems like you're living on a different planet."

How might the preceding discussions of the distribution of the sensible and the iconic order be related to the protests that have occurred in the West Bank village of Bil'in since 2005? For a start, these protests represent a particularly concentrated example of how Palestinian activists and their allies have intervened into the field of visibility related to Israel/Palestine since the second Intifada. The protests have involved a challenge to the silence and invisibility that the Israeli state has attempted to impose upon village communities affected by the construction of the West Bank Barrier since 2002. The villagers of Bil'in have courted the local and international media to project their voices beyond the spatial confines created by the occupation. Thus, at a basic level, the protests have involved a struggle over the seeable and the sayable when it comes to the colonization process within the West Bank. The relationship between the immediate experience of protest and the mediated dissemination of images of these protests has been crucial here. Additionally, the demonstrations in Bil'in have contested the place given to Palestinians within the regime of ethnic-national partition that came into being with the establishment of the Israeli state and was elaborated thereafter. The villagers have developed forms of "creative resistance"[9] against settlement construction and the West Bank Barrier that have also given Palestinians a new image and demonstrated that they have different capacities and can assume different roles to those prescribed by the given order of the occupation. Writing on this subject in 2008, also with reference to Rancière's ideas, Noa Roei observed that "the Bil'in demonstrations have brought about a new generic definition of what political resistance means in the Palestinian context" (Roei 2008). For her, the demonstrations and in, particular, the artifacts they involve create "a possible world where the colonizing parties are required to see the colonized in a light that they normally would have no reason to see" (ibid.). In these terms, the protests do not simply make the plight of the villagers more visible; they also function as world openers that bring into visibility a situation in which the villagers are not just those who suffer—though this is an aspect of what the demonstrations convey—but also those who create. The protests involve a nonviolent resistance that utilizes practices associated with art and theatre that also demonstrate that the villagers are cultural creators and sophisticated political beings. After years of protest, the demonstrations have become somewhat ritualized, with the demonstrators, the media, and the soldiers knowing and playing their respective parts. This means that an image has been established through the demonstrations of the villagers as those who both suffer and protest. However, the creative nature of the demonstrations counters this image by defining a world of possibility beyond the hierarchical separations of the occupation.

The demonstrations also bring together Palestinians and Israelis in collective struggle, producing a shared space on the border that, like the work of the AIC, contests the organization of the population of Israel/Palestine in terms of oppositions between the occupier and the occupied, citizen and noncitizen. For example, in December 2005 a container of the type often used on building sites as an office was moved using a crane to land privately owned by a member of the village close to the edge of Matityahu East, a settlement currently under construction on already confiscated village land. The villagers and their Israeli allies called the container the "Center for the Joint Battle for Peace" suggesting that it was not only a symbolic assertion of Palestinian ownership over the land, but also symbolic of a potentially different kind of relationship between Palestinians and Israelis that broke with the law of separation.

In other instances such interventions have not only involved Israelis and Palestinians working together, but have created situations where soldiers have had to momentarily address villagers as relative equals. In September 2006, the villagers installed a large sign announcing the future building of what they called the "Palestine Hotel" near the site of ongoing construction in Matityahu East. This action was planned as an event that would enable the video documentation of village activists interacting with soldiers and settlers. Mohamed Khatib a key member of the Bil'in Committee of Popular Resistance is recorded in a conversation with a soldier that involves him placing a demand upon the soldier to recognize a degree of equality between them. In the process, Khatib explains to the soldier that the Israeli Supreme Court had declared the villagers to be the legal owners of the land upon which the proposed hotel is to be built and that this legal ruling gives the villagers the right to forbid Jewish settlers from traveling across it. Such rhetorical assertions of Palestinian legal rights run counter to the manifest reality of the occupation as a regime that discriminates against Palestinians in favor of the settlers. This rhetorical performance creates an almost uncanny effect, something that the soldier responds to when he says: "Drop it. It seems like you're living on a different planet. What does it mean 'it's forbidden'?! Don't you recognize this reality? You don't know what is going on."[10] Of course, Khatib does understand the reality of the occupation; however, the statements he makes to the soldier are a refusal to see this reality as the only possible situation for people in Israel/Palestine. His point is to contest the legitimacy of the reality of the occupation regime, to separate sense from sense, and to bring into visibility a gap between what is and what ought to be. Thus, he counters the soldier's statement by making reference to the law, saying: "What reality? If you mean the occupation and the authorities I surrender, because I'm limited as compared to the army. I'm only standing here with my nonviolence in front of the army. . . . But if we are talking about court and law . . . so it depends on what we are talking about."[11] Khatib knows that the reality of the occupation is set against him, yet he seeks to set the ideal of the rule of law against this reality. This is only partly about persuading the soldier and viewers of the video of the legality of his claim. This legal claim is part of a performance re-presented through the video that is meant to create—to appropriate the words of the soldier—a "different planet" upon which the villagers are those who control the land where they and Orthodox Jewish settlers share an equality as interlocutors who discuss the possible merits of the proposed hotel in terms of how many stars it will have and whether or not it will be kosher.

The two interventions discussed above were planned as events that would be turned into images. However other, more conventional demonstrations in Bil'in have involved a more significant element of image making. Again, these image-making practices make visible the creative capacities of the villagers and involve attempts to take a different part of the sensible than that allotted to the villagers and Palestinians in general within the given order of things. As image events, the demonstrations also involve an attempt to build a bridge through images between the villagers and media spectators; a bridge that involves symbolic communication, but is also aimed at generating visual affects. Such affects constitute something close to what DeLuca and Peeples describe as "visual philosophical-rhetorical fragments, mindbombs that expand . . . the universe of thinkable thought" (DeLuca and Peeples 2002, 144). The demonstrations constitute interventions into the distribution of the sensible that confound expectations in terms of the standard sights of the occupation. For example, in early June 2010 village activists built a mock ship on top of a car for use in a demonstration in response to the Israeli military storming of the "Free Gaza" flotilla earlier that week. The ship was made out of board with spray-painted portholes and waves, and with a mast with a sail and numerous international flags on top.

The ship functioned as a spectacular element within the demonstration and became the focal point of an image event within which Israeli soldiers were provoked to play a part in the reenactment of the storming of the flotilla before the cameras of attendant media personnel. This performance referred to an actual news event, yet it provided a disruptive supplement to the sensible reality of the occupation. The images produced of this event in the media were not simply about a documentary revelation of this reality, but also a transmission of a dislocating visual effect.

Figure 7.6. Mock ship used in demonstration in Bil'in, June 2010. Courtesy of Simon Faulkner

A similar image event was organized in Bil'in in August 2010 in response to the media furor around a former Israeli soldier called Eden Abergil posting photographs taken during her army service of her posing with handcuffed and blindfolded Palestinian detainees on her publicly accessible Facebook wall. This posting of what Abergil thought to be unexceptional images led to a series of responses by activists, the local and international media, and the Israeli military. In Bil'in five activists staged a performance that involved them posing as handcuffed and blindfolded detainees in front of a line of soldiers near the West Bank Barrier. The soldiers became unwilling participants in a re-staging of the Abergil photographs. They also contributed the final element of the performance when they decided to drag off a Norwegian demonstrator, turning mock into real arrest. More than other protests in Bil'in, this particular action affirmed the essential role of the media in the demonstrations. Video footage of the event posted on YouTube reveals just how close members of the media are to the handcuffed and blindfolded activists and to the soldiers. It is as if we are witnessing the organization of a photo opportunity staged for the media with the willing participation of the army. David Reeb has pictured this situation in a painting he produced from a video still soon after the demonstration entitled *Facebook Painting* (2010).

Figure 7.7. David Reeb, *Facebook Painting*, 2010

This work presents three rows of people: at the back there are the soldiers, in front of them there are the sitting demonstrators, and then, barely in the picture, there are the usually unseen agents of mediation. In Reeb's video of the demonstration, a Palestinian activist also emphasizes that the action is about the production and use of images by making statements apparently aimed at the soldiers: "Now you get a picture, you can put it in your Facebook.... If any soldier has Facebook you take this picture to Facebook."[12] In practical terms these images would only be available to the soldiers through the media, but this is not the point. Rather, the intention is to make the image-making event as well as the resulting images public artifacts that refer to the Abergil affair in such a way that the perceived callousness of Abergil in posing for the original photos is transferred to the soldiers in Bil'in and to Israeli state policies in general. Reeb's painting also emphasizes the difference between the form of image-making involved in this particular event and the relationship between the represented scene and image maker involved in the production of most other press images. The former is very much a cooperative process between the demonstrators and media personnel involving a meeting point between their two sets of interests, whereas other press images often represent events where the relationship between the action and its visual mediation is incidental. This affirms the way that such a demonstration is very much a self-conscious staging of a political event with the aim of not simply gaining attention to a cause, but also affecting what and how people see. The demonstration was self-consciously made out of and functioned with reference to existing representational materials. The demonstration worked with familiar imagery of Palestinian suffering and Israeli oppression, but this imagery is enacted in a way that introduces an additional element of artifice and playfulness so that we, as viewers, might be able to take up a new perspective on the taken-for-granted-ness of the distribution of the sensible and its standard images.

The demonstrations in Bil'in affirm what has already been discussed to a certain extent in relation to Jarrar's exhibition, that is, the fact that it is possible to create interventions into the occupation regime that problematize and disrupt the given order of things and generate new meanings and possibilities. These demonstrations contest the law of separation that underpins the distribution of the sensible in Israel/Palestine in different ways: breaking Palestinians out of their established role and image as those who are either terrorists, or who simply exist to suffer and also bringing together Israelis and Palestinians in shared resistance to the occupation. On the face of things, this resistance is against the confiscation of village land and, beyond that, through the use of Palestinian flags in the demonstrations, against the denial of a Palestinian state. But running through this is a more unconventional politics of the kind identified by Ranciére that is about the unraveling of certainties of identity and difference of the kind that are played out through the struggle between Israeli and Palestinian nationalisms. This is a politics of dissensus and of world openers that point in directions yet unknown. The problem is how to make this kind of politics count; how to make the challenge to the established order of division and its standard images work in more than a fleeting way both on the ground in Israel/Palestine and beyond through the mediation of protest? This chapter has been about the complexity of this situation and the historic pitfalls of representation when it comes to the Palestinian resistance, but it is also about the power of creative resistance and the hope for a "different planet" that it entails. It is therefore worth ending the chapter where it began, with an affirmation that politics is always to a high degree a matter of aesthetics and a struggle over what is visible. This suggests that those who resist situations of hierarchical division and oppression should place a good deal of emphasis upon aesthetic effects in what they do. In the context of Israel/Palestine, this emphasis upon aesthetics may well need to depart more often than it does from the documentary revelation of suffering that is prevalent, or at least find ways of leading people to witness and understand this suffering without rendering Palestinians as mere victims. When it comes to the creation of new possibilities for Israelis and Palestinians to come together, as with the work of the AIC and the collective actions in Bil'in, this is also about contesting the image of the Israeli Jew as merely an occupier. Whatever happens, this struggle will need to involve the reconfiguration of the existing distribution of the sensible and the generation of new images of who and what people can be.

Notes

1. The phrase "Israel/Palestine" is used here instead of "Israel" and "Palestine" because a territorial state by the latter name does not currently exist and, more importantly, because historical processes of colonization and occupation mean that Israel "proper" and what remains of Mandate Palestine are utterly enmeshed. Israel/Palestine refers to this enmeshment while also signifying the structures of segregation and separation that exist between Israelis and Palestinians.

2. We might relate this to Ariella Azoulay's discussion of the establishment of a "dividing line" between Jews and Arabs around 1948, which she states is "still a central component of the Israeli regime's ruling apparatus" (Azoulay 2011, 9).

3. Quoted in a statement accompanying photographs of Jarrar's "At the Checkpoint" exhibition on Flickr.com: http://www.flickr.com/photos/excauboi/433395543/. Accessed May 14, 2012.

4. Conversation between Khaled Jarrar and the author, Ramallah, November 4, 2008.

5. Khaled Jarrar, written statement sent to the author by e-mail in 2009.

6. Film clip in Johan Grimonprez, *dial H-I-S-T-O-R-Y*, San Francisco: Other Cinema, 2004.

7. David Reeb, "Nabi Saleh 9. 3. 2012," YouTube: http://www.youtube.com/watch?v=2ry9alt26pc&list=UU5iIhK9vGdQ8Io8E-uP0rpQ&index=2&feature=plcp. Accessed March 20, 2012.

8. For a discussion along these lines in relation to African Americans and the civil rights movement, see Berger, 2011.

9. "Discover Bil'in": http://www.bilin-village.org/english/discover-bilin/. Accessed January 2, 2012.

10. Communichaoz, "Bilin—Hotel Palestine," uploaded to YouTube February 20, 2009. http://www.youtube.com/watch?v=PTeDLHv77p8&list=PL90C9A8DC4B329CB9&index=3&feature=plpp_video. Accessed January 5, 2012.

11. Ibid.

12. David Reeb, video of demonstration in Bil'in, August 20, 2010. http://www.youtube.com/watch?v=q-9BQ-CpS20&feature=plcp. Accessed March 20, 2012.

Works Cited

Allen, Lori A. 2009. "Martyr Bodies in the Media: Human Rights, Aesthetics, and the Politics of Immediation in the Palestinian Intifada." *American Ethnologist* 36 (1): 161–80.

Aloni, Udi. 2011. *What Does a Jew Want? On Binationalism and Other Specters*. New York: Columbia University Press.

Azoulay, Ariella. 2011. *From Palestine to Israel: A Photographic Record of Destruction and State Formation, 1947–1950*. London: Pluto Press.

Berger, Martin A. 2011. *Seeing Through Race: A Reinterpretation of Civil Rights Photography*. Berkeley, Los Angeles, and London: University of California Press.

Carnevale, Fulvia, and John Kelsey. 2007. "Art of the Possible: Fulvia Carnevale and John Kelsey in Conversation with Jacques Rancière." *Artforum* (March): 256–69.

Davis, Oliver. 2010. *Jacques Rancière*. Cambridge: Polity.

DeLuca, Kevin Michael and Jennifer Peeples. 2002. "From Public Sphere to Public Screen: Democracy, Activism, and the 'Violence' of Seattle." *Critical Studies in Media Communication* 19 (2): 125–51.

Genet, Jean. 1986. *Prisoner of Love*. New York: New York Review Books.

Guénoun, Solange and James H. Kavanagh. 2000. "Jacques Rancière: Literature, Politics, Aesthetics: Approaches to Democratic Disagreement." *Substance* 29 (2): 3–24.

Hallward, Peter. 2009. "Staging Equality: Rancière's Theatrocracy and the Limits of Anarchic Equality." In *Jacques Rancière: History, Politics, Aesthetics*, edited by Gabriel Rockhill and Philip Watts. Durham and London: Duke University Press.

May, Todd. 2008. *The Political Thought of Jacques Rancière*. Edinburgh: Edinburgh University Press.

———. 2010. "Wrong, Disagreement, Subjectification." In *Jacques Rancière: Key Concepts*, edited by Jean-Philippe Deranty. Durham: Acumen.
Ophir, Adi, Michal Givoni, and Sari Hanafi, eds. 2009. *The Power of Inclusive Exclusion: Anatomy of Israeli Rule in the Occupied Palestinian Territories*. New York: Zone Books.
Rancière. Jacques. 1989. *Nights of Labor: The Worker's Dream in Nineteenth Century France*. Philadelphia: Temple University Press.
———. 1999. *Disagreement: Politics and Philosophy*. Minneapolis and London: University of Minnesota Press.
———. 2009a. "Afterword/The Method of Equality: An Answer to Some Questions." In *Jacques Rancière: History, Politics, Aesthetics*, edited by Gabriel Rockhill and Philip Watts. Durham and London: Duke University Press.
———. 2009b. "The Aesthetic Dimension: Aesthetics, Politics, Knowledge." *Critical Inquiry* 36 (1): 1–19.
———. 2010. "Ten Theses on Politics." In *Dissensus: On Politics and Aesthetics*. London and New York: Continuum.
Roei, Noa. 2008. "Moulding Resistance: Aesthetics and Politics in the Struggle of Bil'in Against the Wall." http://home.medewerker.uva.nl/m.g.bal/bestanden/Roei%20Noa%20paper%20Moulding%20Resistance%20READER%20OPMAAK.pdf. Accessed January 5, 2012.
Routledge, Paul. 1997. "The Imagineering of Resistance: Pollok Free State and the Practice of Postmodern Politics." *Transcripts of the Institute of British Geography* 22 (3): 359–76.
Warschawski, Michel. 2005. *On the Border*. London: Pluto Press.

Figure 8.1. *We Belong to Glasgow*, 2010. Courtesy of Cameroonian Association and Sympathizers in Scotland (CAMASS)

8

Everyday Acts of Resistance

The Precarious Lives of Asylum Seekers in Glasgow

Teresa Piacentini

> I'm not allowed to work, but helping new arrivals, and the other people in my association, well, I treat that like my job. . . . I show a new person where everything is, the shops, the post office, how to buy in the supermarket . . . when you meet someone new, you don't think, Oh, another asylum seeker . . . no, you see a person first, a person who can think, who is an adult, but who just needs some help . . . and you know, when you help them, then they think, ah, I can help the next one I meet.
>
> —Annie, Ivorian woman, asylum seeker

Resistance is a concept not usually associated with asylum seekers. This is not because they are non-agentic beings, but because of the aggressive contexts of reception into they which they are accommodated in many European countries. These are characterized by extensive and regressive control mechanisms monitoring movement and consumption, which, superficially at least, would appear to leave little space to accommodate any form of action or opposition. The limited inquiry into resistance among asylum seekers might also be because the most commonly studied mode of resisting is material or physical, whereby attention focuses on visibly demarcated public activities such as "the election," "the strike," and "the demonstration." However, there are also cases whereby the state or other institutions are simply not present or powerful enough to "see" all aspects of social life (Scott 1998), or they do not consider certain aspects of life important enough to regulate. Focusing on these moments allows a movement away from formal acts of resistance and toward what Nyers describes as novel forms of political subjectification, when subjects constitute themselves as citizens (Nyers 2008, 174).

The understanding of resistance used in this chapter is informed by the influential work of the anthropologist and political scientist James C. Scott. Scott conceptualized everyday resistance as the ways in which the vulnerable work to stay invisible to the "powers that be," by hiding and obscuring identities and activities that the state or other powerful institutions prohibit (Scott 1985, 1990). This chapter seeks to add the voice of asylum seekers to debates on resistance by arguing that people seeking asylum accumulate multiple forms of resistance, often less visible and less documented, but which are everyday because of their commonplace and ordinary nature and that they make no headlines (Scott 1985, xvii). Drawing from ongoing research in Glasgow,[1] the actions explored here are conscious, subjective acts that are specifically intended to counter experiences of marginalization, segregation, and disempowerment and to effect change in how asylum seekers are treated and perceived. This resistance is accomplished through identity-talk, symbolic behavior, and cultural resistance (Scott 1998). In defining these acts as resistance, I recognize the core elements of action (verbal, cognitive, and physical) and opposition, as both explicitly and implicitly articulated (Hollander and Einwohner 2004). That these core elements are identifiable is critical to establishing meaning across cultures and for significance of actions to be understood as acts of resistance. I also identify a focus on intent rather than recognition and outcome (Scott 1985), as some actions intended to resist are purposefully concealed. This will demonstrate some of the ways in which (cf. Rubin 1996, 24); everyday acts *can* chip away in often imperceptible ways at prevailing power relations and *over time* effect important social change.

Asylum Seekers, Dispersal, and "Non-Settlement" as the Catalyst for Action

A basic premise that underlies my use of the term *asylum seeker* is that it is a legal category for a particular situation in which people find themselves. An asylum seeker is a person who has fled her country of origin for fear of persecution and formally applied for asylum in another country but whose application has not yet been concluded. She has made this application in accordance with the 1951 United Nations Convention Relating to the Status of Refugees. In the UK, a person is officially a "refugee" when her claim for asylum is accepted by the government. While in public and media discourse these terms are often (and problematically) used interchangeably, refugee status relates to a regularized position with concomitant rights and responsibilities, whereas the asylum seeker status is inherently temporary and highly restricted. The notions of transience and marginalization are useful starting points to illustrate the "incorporation regimes" that asylum seekers are subject to in the UK and consequently how their "abject identity" status (Tyler 2006) comes to be constructed by the state.

This marginalization is effected via multiple policy mechanisms, the very first of which is the constitution of the category of asylum seeker in British Law, which marks the beginning of this process of governance and control (Tyler 2006). When asylum seekers arrive in the UK, they are subject to a process of compulsory dispersal to a number of "regional" sites. Dispersal is underpinned by a rationale that is twofold: firstly to relieve "pressure" on public resources in areas of high incidences of asylum claims, namely South-East England; and secondly, dispersal is part of a "logic" of asylum governance that argues that the "fast and firm" processing of asylum claims substantially diminishes any meaningful need to tap into existing social networks and established migrant communities (Straw 1998; Temple and Moran 2005). Welfare support is administered through the National Asylum Support Service,[2] which removed asylum seekers entirely from mainstream welfare services. Through compulsory dispersal, no-choice housing, the withdrawal of the right to work and of support in cases of refused claims, prolonged processing times (in many cases taking many years), and the use of destitution and detention as key tools of deterrence (Bloch and Schuster 2005), this context of reception has gone farther to exclude asylum seekers over any other category of migrant. In real terms, this means that individuals are prohibited from working, from continuing education, from moving house, and forced into poverty for an indeterminate period of time.

Although often treated by policy discourse and media rhetoric as a homogeneous group, asylum seekers come from highly diverse nationalities and social backgrounds and the empirical research that this chapter draws from is highly indicative of this diversity, drawing from the experiences of asylum seekers from Cameroon, Democratic Republic of Congo, Ivory Coast, People's Republic of the Congo, Zimbabwe, and Uganda. These are women, men, professionals, students, academics, activists, and agitators. These are also men and women who are poorly educated, who may have never worked, but who have found themselves targeted because they belong to a particular social group. In short, they are ordinary people who have found themselves in extraordinary circumstances (Turton 2003). This arrival of such a diversity of new migrants in unprecedented numbers arriving from countries with a weak (if any) settlement history in the UK in predominantly "white" housing estates raised concerns over "cultural compatibility," fears of encapsulated migrant communities, and a multicultural society fractured by the existence of "parallel lives" (Cantle 2001), debates that echo the British "race relations" agenda of the 1970s and 1980s (Rex 1970; Miles 1993). The super-diverse (Vertovec 2006) nature of multicultural cities such as Glasgow also raised questions and concerns for integration with managed migration and border control now deemed central to attaining "cohesion." The nimbyism that is fueled by dispersal is also used to legitimize hostility and reinforce the undesirability of asylum seekers in the public consciousness (Hubbard 2005; Kundnani 2007). That "they" constitute a threat to the nation comes to be understood in a variety of ways through discourses of difference, ambivalence, entitlement, and eligibility. The exclusionary policies outlined above that segregate and degrade then legitimize hostility in public discourse and perception.

The undecided status of asylum seekers and their related ambivalence means that ethical responsibilities toward people in need come to be further eclipsed by this perceived threat that "they" now pose to "our" sense of identity and nationhood. From this perspective of similarity and difference, the stateless and status-less asylum seeker comes to be viewed as an aberration and a threat to national order (Malkki 1995; Eastmond 1998; Kuwee Kumsa 2006; Nyers 2008). This emphasis on their "out of placeness" pathologizes the asylum seeker and questions the moral bearings of displaced persons, feeding into discourses of the "deserving" and "undeserving" of state benevolence and the welfare bounty (Sales 2002; White 2004). Once reconstructed in this way, the moral case becomes about protecting "our" interests and needs over "theirs." Such aggressive contexts of reception, characterized by tightening border regimes, more restrictive immigration controls, and harsher punishments on asylum seekers throughout the process of claiming asylum necessitates a critical reconsideration of dominant discourses of "settlement," with their general focus on family formation, maturation of social networks, and labor market participation as fundamental in encouraging settlement. This position resolutely fails to capture the ongoing and long-term dislocating effects of existing in the liminal asylum space. Rather the concept of *non-settlement* better captures the limbo-like existence on the margins that is the common experience of asylum seekers (Piacentini 2008), whereby they become not people in need of "our" protection, but people "we" need protection from. Against this backdrop, what hope for resistance?

One of the unintended consequences of dispersal is that as a policy designed to "deterritorialize," it has resulted in processes of "reterritorialization" (Brun 2001), as dispersed asylum seekers and refugees began to engage not only in processes of placemaking and homemaking in dispersed sites, but also in processes of collective action to effect change and to challenge the prevailing perception of asylum seekers as passive and helpless. Recent scholarship has directly challenged the uncritical ways in which asylum seekers are often constructed using prefixes and suffixes of "dis" and "less": displaced, disorientated, disconnected, disadvantaged, powerless, stateless, rootless (Hajdukowski-Ahmed 2008); in terms of lacking something: lack of status, visibility, networks security (Nyers 2008); and as people who have things done to them not by them (Walters 2008). I agree that these "dis/less/lacking discourses" need to be critically challenged. However, I argue in this chapter that analyzing experiences through the tropes of action, resistance, and transformation reveals the various ways in which, through the collective, the asylum seeker identifies counternarratives to her "out of placeness," and how these can then come to be replaced with narratives of belonging and of asserting one's "in placeness" that importantly is recognized within a wider community of practice. While such actions of resistance and cooperation vary by site and by situation, they are most noticeable when, through the collective, the research participants in this study: engage in placemaking through cultural identity-talk and mobilization; develop an "insider expertise" that is transferred within and across groups; take "insider" action that is solitary but which increases visibility and is potentially high-risk; and then they "talk back" through the appropriation of and alignment to other social narratives of difference.

Placemaking through Identity-Talk and Mobilization

I met a Congolese woman at the hotel . . . we had been sent to Glasgow together. . . . I didn't really know Glasgow and she took me to the African shop Solly's . . . so one day I was on the bus going to Solly's and there were two women on the bus talking, they were talking French, Africans you know . . . and before getting off I said to one of them, you are from the Ivory Coast, the other I knew wasn't because of her accent, and she said yes. And that's how I met Annie . . . and she said to me we are putting together a small group, because we are on our own here. I gave her my number, and that's how I joined the group. When I went along to the first meeting, it was in Layla's flat in my own block, and I could see that these were all people who were feeling very isolated. . . . And the president at the time, she had said she wanted to create this group because she had also felt too isolated at the beginning, she knew others would feel the same and she didn't want to people to go through that . . . and that we were all asylum seekers too, and meeting was a way to come together, to try to enjoy ourselves together, eat our food, talk about home, listen to music . . . and to forget . . . but also to say, you know, I got this letter what does it mean, or, you know, if you needed to speak to your lawyer, or to know if your lawyer has a good reputation, or for advice or information, if someone has had the same experience, what they did, that kind of thing. (Joelle, Ivorian woman, asylum seeker)

Experience suggests that although the mass enforced dispersal to high-rise accommodation in designated urban areas marginalizes people, it simultaneously raises their visibility in these very spaces and creates possibilities for internal cooperation. Paradoxically, displacement through dispersal engenders an "emplacement," drawing people living under similar excluded conditions together to create and expand new networks and to establish new social and cultural practices. This supports my argument for extending the meaning of what constitutes a sense of "settlement" beyond labor market participation and family formation. Subsequently, asserting one's cultural identity and cultural "sameness" becomes a way to affirm alternative identities both publicly and privately. Being demarcated as asylum seekers within dispersal sites facilitated opportunities for sociability without incurring transport costs and in a way that meant safe movement in new areas in which they stood out as different, for example, within high-rise blocks or in local neighborhoods. Through everyday interactions—chance encounters at the bus stop, in shops, on the landings of the high-rise flats—not only do the challenges of homemaking come to be understood, met, and overcome, but we can see how the overwhelmingly isolating effects of displacement and invisibility as asylum seekers come to be resisted and renamed as processes of inclusion and cultural and social belonging. Joelle describes what happens on a practical level: mobilizing around informal meetings in each other's homes on a regular basis, and then gradually formally organizing into a constituted group with aims, objectives, and constituted members.

There is a growing body of work exploring the emergence and role of such groups, generally organized along national, ethnic, or language lines and generally described as Refugee Community Organizations (hereafter "RCOs") (*inter alia* Zetter and Pearl 2000; Griffiths et al. 2005; Kelly 2003). These analyses offer important insights into the processes of group formation among refugees. However, refocusing on action and opposition as the catalysts for mobilization offers fresh insights and a new critical perspective to understanding the agency of asylum seekers more specifically, a perspective often neglected. I argue that group formation is in and of itself a process of everyday resistance to the nonintegrative focus of dispersal, whereby the group is an opportunity to collectively resist the ascribed "asylum seeker label" through assertions of belonging to a wider community of practice. Homeland and the sense of "in placeness" that ensues can be a powerful, unifying symbol (Gupta and Ferguson 1992), but critically it also becomes a potent symbol for resisting negatively ascribed categorizations.

Moreover, individuals' interactions in their groups are not limited to nostalgic reminisces and imagined communities (Anderson 1983), but incorporate "identity-talk" that brings together "there" and "here." As suggested above and in what follows, this new collective space provides a critical asylum support mechanism, a safe place to discuss problems and concerns with asylum claims, sharing experiences of the asylum system, trading information on lawyers and on services, and working out collectively ways of coping with the daily struggle of uncertainty. This constitutes important social change in the conditions of living as an asylum seeker. This also reveals how the collective that emerges from dispersal has to negotiate the tension between resistance and accommodation. I understand this process as a critical experience of asylum seekers becoming social actors conscious of their state and who are acting consciously (Arendt [1946]1978).

Sharing Knowledge and Becoming "Insider Experts"

A number of scholars have described the different roles of an ethnic community in easing adaptation for new migrants: for example, diminishing the risks and costs of migrating (Massey et al. 1998); serving as buffers between the dominant society and the immigrant community (Portes and Rumbaut 1990); providing key advocacy, translation, and signposting services (Griffiths et al. 2005). For dispersed asylum seekers there is greater complexity to negotiating their "newness" because they lack immediate access to preexisting social networks and established communities. This was the experience in Glasgow, when in 2000 it became the only dispersal site in Scotland. This reinforced the immediacy for newly dispersed asylum seekers to mobilize into groups in order to share their expertise and transmit practical information and community standards to fellow asylum seekers and refugees. It might be argued that these are processes of accommodation rather than resistance, whereby individuals adapt to a social context without resolving conflict or underlying inequalities. However, as Hollander and Einwohner argue (2004, 549), resistance is never purely about resisting. Resistance has a dualistic nature; it is a movement both for and against, and this is particularly clear when the act in question constitutes both resistance, that is, resisting the negative label of the "unwanted asylum seeker," and accommodation, that is, carving out their own space in mainstream society. In the above and more explicitly in what follows, the communal experience of seeking asylum as highly instrumental not only to the emergence of these groups but also to the development of a consciousness of their marginalization and an expertise to better manage this becomes clear. What also emerges is how this is used to adapt to the new life environment of settlement. This raises two important questions: How is sharing insider expertise a form of resistance? How may this expertise produce transformative outcomes?

> I've got a lot of up-to-date information through the group of which I didn't know. . . . Through legacy, we have had lawyers come [to the drop-in] to explain the situation, on what grounds they are giving the papers to people. So in such a way, you would go to your lawyer knowing that I am asking A B C D, something already I know he is going to tell me, but I already know the answer myself. It's empowering, I have knowledge. 'Cos I would find my friends, people who don't come to the group, if I am talking about the legacy thing and what is happening, and a lot of people say "where did you get all this information, how did you manage to have this information?" That is really powering, really strong. (Julie, Zimbabwean woman, asylum seeker)

Being the "outsider" as an asylum seeker can mean lacking local knowledge and familiarity with the rules of engagement, which can seriously hamper how people survive their status as asylum seekers. Nonetheless, Julie presents an alternative perspective. As a group member, as an "insider" in her group, she asserts her "in placeness" as well as creates space for action for herself and importantly for others. Through regular and repeated engagement with her community group and through her own everyday practice and interactions, she develops a "feel for the game" (Bourdieu 1977), and this empowers her. Having become an "insider expert" on various aspects of the asylum process allows a degree of resistance to her abject status as she is able to question the process as an active subject. I believe this shows how her own practice is transformed by a sense not only of self-understanding but a sense of commonality and groupness with others.

When compared to Victoire's experience, a Cameroonian asylum seeker, the contrast is striking: "My lawyer always said no news is good news, I had never heard that before. I stopped calling him." Victoire feels disempowered by his individual attempts to actively engage with power relations whereas Julie felt enabled through the collective to not only ask certain questions, but also informed enough to be able to tell whether she was getting the correct advice. While during interviews, neither of them expressed any real institutional trust per se, Julie benefited from the social trust that had developed from her involvement in her group. This is illustrative of the critical space the collective provides for resistance: through its expertise and networks there is access to information and there are opportunities to adapt behavior, to discover rights and entitlements, to feel enabled to make decisions as active subjects rather than passive objects, and to create a space for a consciousness to emerge. Importantly, this knowledge marks a social change: taking Julie's example, through the benefits she has accrued from her involvement in the group and through critical reflection, she is able to reject a constructed picture of the world that requires a silent acceptance of and adherence to a set of behaviors: don't ask questions, sit and wait. Comparing Julie and Victoire's experiences highlights how access to varied social contexts impacts on interactions in multiple sites. The "RCO" network offers one such site and as a result individuals in groups attain opportunities for accumulation of various forms of capital relating to their rights and entitlements. As Victoire experienced, the "feel for the game" can be much more difficult for individuals to achieve on their own. It is predominantly through the "RCO" network that individuals become introduced to the logic of the asylum field and the various social fields radiating from this, for example, education, work, legal and political fields. Conceiving participation in the group in this way would suggest then that involvement in the "RCO" better endows individuals with critical knowledge of the conditions, structures, and relations of power of the new society. This suggests that the group may effect social change more effectively than the individual.

Furthermore, this reveals the transformative potential of collective action, not just for those inside the group, but also beyond its boundaries. When Julie talks about sharing her expertise with non-group members, she is providing those people located outside of the "RCO" boundary with ways to resist their construction as passive and silent objects of the asylum process. In communicating know-how across boundaries, via everyday practice of informal talk and social interactions, group members are generating a wider collective practice that is transformative and underpinned by a logic of resistance. As a result, there is a shift away from total dependency on state actors for the social facts:

> When you see the background of the group, it was at first only about helping asylum seekers, African women, who would arrive, who didn't know any English, help them go to see lawyers, register their kids in school, learn English. . . . And then gradually help those asylum seeker women who were being threatened by the Home Office . . . helping them finds ways of saying no to the Home Office, of not just sitting back, but learning to ask questions and demanding answers. (Pascaline, Congolese woman, asylum seeker)

Pascaline's defiance is illustrative of how communicative engagement and interactions between actors through the group can alter dispositions and expectations to great effect (Crossley 2001, 92) as well as generate a pressure for social change. There is a consciousness that, adhering to these behaviors, functions to maintain the status quo; active involvement in the group provides a space to reject this position. These are instances of resistance rather than accommodation because this collective action enables individuals to question the underlying inequalities they experience as asylum seekers. Importantly, then, participation in networks and groups is not only a practice of emplacement and inclusion but also of resistance where action and opposition can be identified. It is the conscious understanding of one's social position as an asylum seeker that individuals, through the "RCO," actively choose to respond to their categorization through action, via developing informal support networks that are proactive and focused on both individual and collective survival. Perhaps actions such as accompanying individuals to appointments, sharing information, advocating for others, and engaging with other support groups do not make headlines, but they are critical for developing a practical sense (following Bourdieu 1977) that is guided by the structural circumstances of the "host" country and the development of a mastery of the tacit rules of the new social world. Only then can conscious strategies develop to engage with relations of power.

Taking Solidary Action, Taking Risks

So far, I have explored different forms of solidary in action that resonate with other studies of "RCOs" across the UK. Less commonly investigated are acts of solidarity that carry with them a level of increased risk. One reason such acts feature less is that they may be less often reported to researchers for fear of reprisal, and this raises important ethical questions about producing knowledge about everyday acts of resistance, especially with particularly vulnerable groups. Engaging in any research on acts of resistance runs the risk of highlighting to the state the ways in which their rules are circumvented and thereby reduce space for life-saving creativity and flexibility in remaining invisible (Polzer and Hammond 2008, 418). How does academic research navigate the fine lines between knowledge production that enhances life chances but which might limit those very life-enhancing strategies? Between achieving understanding, making a difference and improving the situation of marginalized individuals, and worsening this by exposing their "hidden transcripts" (Scott 1990; Turton 2003)? Given their extreme exclusion, asylum seekers have to find inventive ways of surviving their increasingly regulated existence that often contravene the very conditions of their regulated temporary residence. On the one hand, studying these groups recognizes agency at an individual and collective level; on the other hand, highlighting such practices may also contribute to a tightening of systems to restrict such subversive behaviors. The ethics of rendering visible strategies of resistance serves as an important reminder of the role of social science research to explore and expose power relationships at play in society. While there is no clear answer to this ethical conundrum, only examples that have become "mainstream" practices now adopted by aid agencies, NGOs, and asylum seeker support groups will be reported, while acknowledging the genesis for these acts of resistance lie elsewhere.

As long as people are considered as asylum seekers, they receive state support through a separate welfare system (NASS) and are housed in dispersal accommodation. They are deemed non-bankable and are excluded from financial systems. Upon a positive decision they become "refugees" and are then eligible to access mainstream services. If their claim is refused, they enter a process of appeals, and when they become "appeals rights exhausted" (ARE), support is stopped completely and can be (but is not always) reintroduced in the form of "hard case" non-cash support, made available on condition of return. Known as Section 4 support, at the time of fieldwork it was provided in the form of luncheon vouchers, which may only be used in certain shops.[3] A common practice between asylum seekers has been to swap voucher support for cash and in some instances some group members described to me how they would routinely combine food vouchers in order to buy in bulk.

> You know I meet a friend every week, she gives me her cash and I give her vouchers, and I am scared for her. I don't want her to get into trouble, but she says that she won't get into trouble and that it is a small thing she can do for me. It's normal you know that she wants to help. . . . When I have money I go to Solly's [African and Caribbean food shop] and the Turkish food market place on Pollokshaws Road . . . the Asians on Albert Drive. (Virginie, Cameroonian woman, asylum seeker)

This practice is a particularly high-risk act of resistance because the exchange of vouchers for cash *between* asylum seekers is a breach of temporary conditions of stay. It is also an act of cultural solidarity as it resists a set of enforced behaviors: only being able to buy goods in designated shops, and thus consume certain products imposes a cultural hierarchy on the most vulnerable. Whereas having cash means individuals may shop where they like and purchase what they want. As with Julie earlier, the social capital individuals accumulate through their networks also extends to information sharing as to where culturally acceptable and familiar foods could be found in cheaper, local shops. These are actions intended to challenge the stigmatizing nature of vouchers that served to reinforce that asylum seekers are "different."

High-risk acts of solidarity extend to providing destitute asylum seekers with somewhere to sleep:

> When I was made destitute, and I was waiting for Section Four, my sisters in the group, they put me up, I would sleep on their floors, they said, we can't have our sister sleeping in doorways. But they also felt scared, you know if someone knocked at the door, was it the Home Office checking on them? So I would have to move around sleep one night here, one night there . . . but it was a risk for them, they wanted to take it, but it was a risk . . . I know that. (Elodie, Ivorian woman asylum seeker)

Having anyone stay overnight in NASS accommodation constitutes a breach of temporary conditions of stay. If caught, this can result in support being stopped, more regular reporting and, in extreme cases, detention. Other acts of collective resistance involve putting money aside weekly or monthly for what have become informal destitution funds, providing small cash handouts and one-off donations to members in need. Swapping vouchers for cash also allowed people an opportunity to save some money. More formal actions have evolved from these responses to combat financial exclusion, such as rotating savings and credit schemes which allow members to save and borrow and the setting up of microcredit. Although "hidden" publicly, these are practical, financial, and emotional acts of resistance and protest that are about circumventing state rules. They require courage and demand that persons who have claimed asylum be treated as human beings. What is damning is that, because these acts can constitute a breach of temporary leave of stay, what then emerges is a tendency for "solidarity" itself to be regarded as criminal. So an innocuous and humanitarian act such as housing and supporting the destitute becomes extremely high-risk. Despite the threat of exposure, these are potent illustrations of how "RCOs" challenge the marginalization and discrimination faced by asylum seekers. Such forms of "everyday resistance" are typical of the limited resources the powerless and vulnerable have to resist openly against their superordinates (Scott 1985).

Talking Back, Naming a Shared Reality

I have already explored a number of practices that counter the dominant perception of the asylum seeker as a passive object of the asylum system. Challenging such perceptions, providing alternative images, questioning categorizations are acts of defiance that constitute forms of "talking back" by reclaiming the subject and confronting the politics of domination (hooks 1989). Maintaining and affirming a sense of cultural connectedness through music, food, dance, through having access to shops and culture, through exercising choice is also a way of resisting an imposed cultural lifestyle and challenges a cultural hierarchy that dictates how, where, and when culture should be consumed and enjoyed. It is a public pronouncement of identity that is far removed from immigration status: it is a way of "talking back" and "taking back" pre-asylum self-identifications. For many respondents an awareness of either a shared history or experiences of marginalization as migrants allows them to articulate the connections and commonalities they have within their own boundaries of difference as well as across to other migrant communities. As has been argued, seeking asylum becomes a social connector of one kind. Being the more generic "migrant" is a social connector of another kind. It is a way of saying we are different but we are the same as others too:

> You know we are asylum seekers, yes, but we are Congolese first, we have our culture and you can't wipe out a culture. Look at the Indians here, the Pakistanis . . . their children speak their language, eat their food, you need to fight for it though. . . . I see the Indians get together, they help each other out, they go into their own pockets. They had to fight for it. They have big fancy houses . . . why not us? Where are we? We have to be about more than fighting deportation, there is more to us than that, you need to have a bigger picture in mind . . . the Pakistanis have the fast food restaurants, why not the Africans too? (Gregoire, Congolese man, refugee)

As an expression of his subjectivity, Gregoire explicitly aligns himself with alternative narratives of difference, not purely based on specific immigration status but on being "minority ethnic communities." This appropriation of alternative minority ethnic identities encapsulates a capacity for action, is future-oriented, progressive, and focused on social change, both internal and external. Other ethnic communities become the benchmark for what a "settled migrant community" can look like. In articulating his vision in this way and in aligning what he sees as "his community" with other established communities, he is resisting the liminal, transient space to which asylum seekers most often find themselves allocated. What is more, he is talking back from the margins, edging toward a more central social positioning. But it is a struggle to keep resisting the categorization as asylum seeker, even after a positive decision has been granted and one becomes another "other":

> I'll tell you the problem of who you are doesn't go away, I am still asked, "Are you an asylum seeker?" . . . So it's not even who you are it's who you were, that doesn't go away. So even if I was one

before, I am a refugee, they don't ask, "Are you a refugee?" No. It's always are you asylum seeker? . . . Like if you go to housing and ask for a housing list, they don't ask you your status do they? No . . . because you are Scottish, but me, they see me, my name, my skin, they hear my accent, and they ask me if I am asylum seeker. I don't answer [laughs]. . . . If you don't answer they think, "Ah, trouble maker," and then they think we are all like that. (Namutebi, Ugandan woman, refugee)

Namutebi resists her continuous categorization as "different" both through talking back and asserting herself as an individual with entitlements and rights *and* through her silence. Her refusal to answer questions does not constitute headline-grabbing protest but is protest nonetheless as she consciously seeks to question how she is being labeled by state actors. Her self-alignment with others who are applying for housing transcends boundaries of difference related to ethnicity, nationality, immigration status: she is simply someone in need of housing for a growing family. Namutebi expresses her self politically by not responding and this can be understood as, following Isin, an enactment as political without articulating directly her reason for acting as a citizen (Isin 2008; Nyers 2008). Furthermore, her actions lie closer to resistance than accommodation as she names and challenges the underlying inequalities at play. This alignment to other narratives is intended to counter anti–asylum seeker and anti-immigrant sentiment. Nevertheless, despite her changed immigration status, and her rapprochement to other narratives, her entitlement continues to be questioned by state actors: the discourse of deservedness prevails and being continuously interrogated on one's migranthood and entitlement as a specific type of migrant is in danger of undermining feelings of belonging. This directly challenges often oversimplistic understandings of immigration status about being either/or, or following some linear trajectory of asylum seeker to refugee to citizen migrant. The reality is that persons move in and out and between different degrees of legal status. This status fetishism exposes the way in which certain "others" continue to be categorized in fixed and unambiguous ways. But rather than being a remedy to their ambivalence and uncertainty, their ambiguity continues.

Concluding Comments

This chapter has sought to explore the different ways asylum seekers find to resist their marginalization through everyday acts of resistance. A number of processes have been identified: social emplacement facilitated by displacement and heightened visibility; a shift from individual consciousness to collective action; a transformation of practice that emerges from critical reflection as well as a transformation of the category of asylum seeker into a category for action. This is manifested through placemaking through identity-talk and mobilization; through the development of an "insider expertise" that is transferred within and across groups; through taking insider action that is founded on solidarity but is potentially high-risk; and through "talking back" through their appropriation of and alignment to other social narratives of difference.

These small everyday acts of resistance can be understood collectively as a response to policies that construct "the asylum seeker" as a category and, in doing so, demarcate boundaries of belonging and emplacement. The paradox of dispersal is that it renders asylum seekers both out of place *and* in place. I propose here that the very emergence of community associations in dispersal areas is in and of itself an act of everyday resistance to the social engineering project of dispersal that sought to keep people and social networks apart at worst and highly fragmented at best. The aim of dispersal was to destabilize; however, an unintended consequence has been the sustenance of links to a homeland "there" *and* "here," producing a sense of reterritorialization that fosters new belongings. The action-oriented responses presented here to processes of othering can be understood as constituting a form of transformative belonging through collective consciousness and action.

I have empirically explored what occurs when there is critical reflection at an above-conscious collective level which becomes the source of resistance and action. This challenges dominant "settlement" and "integration" discourses and highlights how such discourses have come to be uncritically and directly related to a hierarchy of migranthood that excludes the experience of asylum seekers. This also suggests extending understandings of settlement and the need to identify alternative indicators of adaptation that focus on bottom-up practices and actions. Mobilizing around the experience of being labeled the undesirable asylum seeker demonstrates the potential for transformation from exclusion and difference into inclusion, belonging, and action. In addition, the shift in focus onto group formation in itself as a form of resistance, as proposed in this essay, adds a new critical perspective to the existing literature on the emergence of "RCOs." I have also suggested that the collective can function as a critical space, which better endows the individual with knowledge to effect social change, while recognizing change is a long and slow process. Notwithstanding this transformative potential, the culture of disbelief asylum seekers face continues as they move in and out and in between different legal status. This means very real questions for asylum seekers and subsequently refugees in terms of how much to invest in an identity that is socially abject (Tyler 2006). Despite this, I hope to have highlighted that these sites of agency challenge notions of what extremely precarious lives *can* produce by exploring strategies of becoming other than "asylum seeker" and of self-identification in terms beyond "dis" and "less" (Nyers 2008).

This chapter focuses on both ends of the spectrum of resistance and accommodation by highlighting the ways that the African asylum seekers and refugees in this research assert their place in multiple sites in the home and the community. These individual and collective acts of internal cooperation can be seen as behaviors that challenge the dominant discourses of dependency associated with asylum seekers and which transform these discourses into the asylum seeker as active, involved, enabled, empowered, proactive (as Griffiths et al. 2005 argue, discourses normally reserved for refugees, not for asylum seekers). Redirecting attention on action and opposition in the everyday lives of asylum seekers not only brings to light some of the often invisible and unacknowledged forms of resistance people use to survive, but also adds their voices to debates and reveals some of the ways they are developing social narratives and subject positions of their own making.

Notes

1. This project draws upon reflections and findings from ethnographic research conducted with six Francophone-Anglophone African asylum seeker and refugee groups in Glasgow (2007–2010). This was part of ESRC-funded doctoral research completed in 2011 studying processes of community and identities formation and the development of social structures that influence the nature and quality of social survival in exile.

2. The National Asylum Support System (NASS) a key policy of the 1999 Asylum and Immigration Act. NASS is a UK agency that coordinates support for asylum seekers, until a decision is made about their asylum claim.

3. Vouchers have since been replaced with the Azure card which was piloted in Glasgow from November 2009 and functions as a type of debit card without a PIN number. Credit is topped up once a week—£35 for a single person—and then canceled from the card every Sunday. Single persons are allowed a £5 limit carryover; any additional remaining credit is lost. These cards may only be used in certain stores and they cannot be swapped for vouchers; the individual needs to call a free phone number to check the balance.

Work Cited

Anderson, Benedict. 1983. *Imagined Communities: Reflections on the Origin and Spread of Nationalism*. London: Verso.

Arendt, Hannah. [1946]1978. *The Jew as Pariah: Jewish Identity and Politics in the Modern Age.* Edited by Ron H. Feldman. New York: Grove Press.

Bloch, Alice, and Lisa Schuster. (2005) "At the Extremes of Exclusion: Deportation, Detention, and Dispersal." *Ethnic and Racial Studies* 28 (3): 491–512.

Bourdieu, Pierre. 1977. *Outline of a Theory of Practice.* Cambridge: Cambridge University Press.

Brun, Catherine. 2001. "Reterritorializing the Relationship Between People and Place in Refugee Studies." *Geografiska Annaler. Series B, Geography Studies* 83 (1): 15–25.

Cantle, Ted. 2001. "Community Cohesion: A Report of the Independent Review Team." London: Home Office. http://image.guardian.co.uk/sys-files/Guardian/documents/2001/12/11/communitycohesionreport.pdf. Accessed September 8, 2010.

Crossley, Nick. 2001. "The Phenomenological Habitus and its Construction." *Theory and Society* 30 (1): 81–120.

Eastmond, Marita. 1998. "Nationalist Discourses and the Construction of Difference: Bosnian Muslim Refugees in Sweden." *Journal of Refugee Studies* 11 (2): 161–81.

Griffiths, David, Nando Sigona, and Roger Zetter. 2005. *Refugee Community Organisations and Dispersal: Networks, Resources, and Social Capital.* Bristol: The Policy Press.

Gupta, Akhil, and James Ferguson. 1992." 'Beyond Culture': Space, Identity, and the Politics of Difference." *Cultural Anthropology* 7 (1): 6–23.

Hajdukowski-Ahmed, Maroussia. 2008. "A Dialogical Approach to Identity: Implications for Refugee Women." In *Not Born a Refugee Woman: Contesting Identities, Rethinking Practices,* edited by Maroussia Hajdukowski-Ahmed, Nazila Khanlou, and Helene Moussa. New York, Oxford: Berghan Books.

hooks, bell. 1989. *Talking Back: Thinking Feminist, Thinking Black.* Boston: South End Press.

Hollander, Jocelyn A., and Rachel L. Einwohner. 2004. "Conceptualizing Resistance." *Sociological Forum* 19 (4): 533–54.

Howe, Leo. 1998. "Scrounger, Worker, Beggarman, Cheat: The Dynamics of Unemployment and the Politics of Resistance in Belfast." *The Journal of The Royal Anthropological Institute* 4 (3): 531–50.

Hubbard, Phil. 2005. "Accommodating Otherness: Anti-asylum Centre Protest and the Maintenance of White Privilege." *Transactions of the Institute of British Geographers* 30 (1): 52–65.

Isin, Engin F. 2008. "Theorizing Acts of Citizenship." In *Acts of Citizenship,* edited by Engin F. Isin and Greg M. Nielsen. London: Zed Books.

Kelly, Lynnette. 2003."Bosnian Refugees in Britain: Questioning Community." *Sociology* 37 (1): 35–49.

Kundnani, Arun. 2007. *The End of Tolerance: Racism in 21st Century Britain.* London: Pluto Press.

Kuwee Kumsa, Martha. 2006. " 'No! I'm Not a Refugee!' The Poetics of Be-Longing among Young Oromos in Toronto." *Journal of Refugee Studies* 19 (2): 230–55.

Malkki, Liisa H.1995. "Refugees and Exile: From "Refugee Studies" to the National Order of Things." *Annual Review of Anthropology* 24: 495–523.

Massey, Douglas S., et al. 1998. *Worlds in Motion: Understanding International Migration at the end of the Millennium.* New York: Oxford University Press.

Miles, Robert. 1993. "The Articulation of Racism and Nationalism: Reflections on European History." In *Racism and Migration in Western Europe*, edited by John Wrench and John Solomos. Oxford: Berg.

Nyers, Peter. 2008. "No One Is Illegal Between City and Nation." In *Acts of Citizenship*, edited by Engin F. Isin and Greg M. Nielsen. London: Zed Books.

Piacentini, Teresa. 2008. "Contesting Identities in Exile: an Exploration of Collective Self-understanding and Solidarity in Refugee Community Organisations in Glasgow." *eSharp* 11 (Spring): Social Engagement, Empowerment and Change. http://www.gla.ac.uk/departments/esharp/issues/11/. Accessed August 2, 2010.

Polzer, Tara, and Laura Hammond. 2008. "Editorial Introduction: Invisible Displacement." *Journal of Refugee Studies* 21 (4): 417–31.

Portes, Alejandro, and Rubén G. Rumbaut. 1990. *Immigrant America: A Portrait.* Berkeley: University California Press.

Rex, John. 1970. *Race Relations in Sociological Theory.* New York: Schocken Books.

Rubin, Jeffrey W.1996. "Defining Resistance: Contested Interpretations of Everyday Acts." *Studies in Law, Politics and Society* 15: 237–60.

Schuster, Lisa, and John Solomos. 2004. "Race, Immigration, and Asylum: New Labour's Agenda and its Consequences." *Ethnicities* 4 (2): 267–300.

Scott, James C.1985. *Weapons of the Weak: Everyday Forms of Peasant Resistance.* New Haven: Yale University Press.

———. 1990. *Domination and the Arts of Resistance: Hidden Transcripts.* New Haven: Yale University Press.

———. 1998. *Seeing Like a State: How Certain Schemes to Improve the Human Condition Have Failed.* New Haven: Yale University Press.

Straw, Jack. 1998. "Preface by the Home Secretary," *Fairer, Faster, and Firmer: a Modern Approach to Immigration and Asylum*, Home Office White Paper. Cm. 4018. London: Home Office.

Temple, Bogusia, and Rhetta Moran. 2005. *Learning to Live Together: Developing Communities with Dispersed Refugee People Seeking Asylum.* York: Joseph Rowntree Foundation. http://www.jrf.org.uk/sites/files/jrf/1859352871.pdf. Accessed August 20, 2010.

Tyler, Imogen. 2006. " 'Welcome to Britain': The Cultural Politics of Asylum." *European Journal of Cultural Studies* 9 (2): 185–202.

Turton, David. 2003. "Refugees, Forced Resettlers, and 'Other Forced Migrants': Towards a Unitary Study of Forced Migration." *New Issues in Refugee Research*, Working Paper No. 94, Evaluation and Policy Analysis Unit. UNHCR, Geneva, Switzerland. http://www.unhcr.org/3f818a4d4.html. Accessed September 4, 2010.

Vertovec, Steven. 2006. "The Emergence of Super-Diversity in Britain." http://www.researchasylum.org.uk/?lid=154. Accessed October 4, 2010.

Walters, William. 2008. "Acts of Demonstration: Mapping the Territory of (Non-) Citizenship." In *Acts of Citizenship*, edited by Engin F. Isin and Greg M. Nielsen. London: Zed Books.

Zetter, Roger, and Martyn Pearl. 2000. "The Minority within the Minority: Refugee Community-based Organisations in the UK and the Impact of Restrictionism on Asylum-seekers." *Journal of Ethnic and Migration Studies* 26 (4): 675–98.

Figure 9.1. *Everydayness*, 2011. Fia Persson

9

Pushing the Boundaries of Asylum

Everyday Resistance in Swedish Clandestinity

MAJA SAGER

The rate at which asylum applications are rejected in Sweden has been increasing steadily since the beginning of the 1990s and, consequently, the number of people who find themselves compelled to become clandestine—to hide away from the authorities to avoid being deported—also has increased during this period.[1] Authorities and politicians regularly explain this development by claiming that an increasing number of asylum seekers do not have grounds for seeking the protection afforded by asylum. However, many others in the debate assert that, on the contrary, it is not the need for protection among asylum seekers that has decreased but that the practice of law and the legal procedures which assess credibility and the need for protection have become increasingly restrictive (see, e.g., Bexelius 2008; Dahlstedt and Mekonnen 2004; Khosravi 2010; Tamas 2009; Vestin 2006, about Swedish migration policies). This chapter develops the latter argument, taking a critical perspective upon Swedish and wider European migration policies and practices. I argue that migration policies produce clandestinity through exclusionary laws and practices and through a political goal of limiting refugee immigration.[2]

However, there is no simple and direct relation between rejection of an asylum application, on the one hand, and deportation or total exclusion from social rights and welfare entitlements on the other. Rather, the exclusion is implemented and experienced on a more multileveled basis through the interplay among: migration policies and labor market policies; social policies regulating undocumented migrants' welfare entitlements; individual and collective practices within welfare institutions that are actors in civil society; and movements of social protest. I explore the interplay of these different modalities and examine how they shape the varied experiences of being rejected and living clandestinely in Sweden. More specifically, I trace some instances of *everyday resistance* to exclusion and discuss the practices and relations of migrant experiences on the ground.

Clandestine and Clandestinity

I use the term *clandestine asylum seekers* to refer to asylum seekers who stay in Sweden after their asylum applications have been rejected and who consequently "hide" from the police and the authorities in order to avoid deportation. The concept refers only in part to the Swedish term *gömda asylsökande*, which literally means "hidden asylum seekers" and is the most commonly used term in Swedish public debate.[3] However, my research suggests that people in this situation are in most cases not hidden in a literal sense; it is only some people and families who end up actually *hiding* due to strong fear or special circumstances. The way I want to apply the term *clandestine*, in contrast with *hidden* (*gömda*), entails recognizing the agency involved in the chain of everyday acts and decisions that are necessary in order to avoid deportation. Clandestine refers to "being actively underground" rather than "hiding away." I also alter the word *clandestine* into the noun form "clandestinity" to describe the social and discursive space in which clandestine asylum seekers are located. This social and discursive space is marked by simultaneous inclusion and exclusion in relation to the Swedish welfare state. Needless to say, the position in clandestinity is temporary and marked by plurality in relation to nationality, "race"/ethnicity, gender, class, and sexuality, which creates diversity in the ways in which clandestinity is lived and how it dis/connects from/to the welfare state.

Methodological and Theoretical Framework

This project is based on an ethnographic study that I undertook for my PhD, "Everyday Clandestinity: Experiences on the Margins of Citizenship and Migration Policies" (2011), in which I explore a broad range of aspects of clandestinity. The data and analysis in this chapter is drawn from the material gathered through participatory fieldwork and interviews with clandestine asylum seekers and asylum rights activists in Sweden during 2006–08. I also build on my own experiences of being engaged in migrant activism from years before the project started.

Epistemologically, I take my point of departure from a standpoint perspective, and argue that valid forms of knowledge are produced from marginal social positions and within activist and social movements. However, my position *also* entails taking a poststructuralist approach which understands scientific knowledge as being partial and contextual. Theoretically, clandestinity needs to be conceptualized as a location marked by a complex interplay between inclusion and exclusion—a location inside the nation-state but yet not a part of it. Some important sources of theoretical interventions that can provide tools for theorizing this location are feminist critical theories on citizenship and welfare, and intersectional approaches to studies of citizenship, welfare, and social policy that focus on lived experience as a means of understanding the processes at stake.

Feminist and antiracist studies of social policy and welfare have been important in the feminist understanding of citizenship as a process, and the importance of "agency" as central for an analysis of both social policy and citizenship (Lister 2003, 6–7). Political scientist Ruth Lister (2003) and sociologist Nira Yuval-Davis (1997) are representative of feminist and antiracist approaches in expanding and nuancing understandings and practices of citizenship. This branch of feminist and postcolonial citizenship theory can be described as the analysis of the ways that formal citizenship translates—or does not translate—into substantial citizenship. But, in my analysis, I use these insights in "the other direction" and explore how positions characterized as being excluded from formal citizenship might still carry the possibilities of instances of active citizenship as routes toward (limited) forms of citizenship through participation. Lister works with the concept of "active citizenship" to grasp less formal aspects and expressions of citizenship (Lister 2003, 23–30). She quotes Ray Pahl to illustrate this concept, arguing that active citizenship is about "local people working together to improve their own quality of life and to provide conditions for others to enjoy the fruits of a more affluent society" (ibid., 24). Lister also suggests that this is a kind of citizenship practice that "disadvantaged people, often women, do for themselves, for instance through community groups, rather than a paternalistic top-down relationship" (ibid.). Active citizenship describes forms of everyday practice that creates participatory subjects resisting, for example, the construction of marginal groups as "objects" of humanitarianism.

Pushing the Boundaries

In "Everyday Clandestinity: Experiences on the Margins of Citizenship and Migration Policies," I demonstrated how a lack of rights and recognition when combined with deportability—that is, the pending risk of detention and/or deportation—shapes and limits people's lives in many and various ways (2011). Deportability intersects with gender, ethnicity, "race," sexuality, and nationality in ways that define subject positions on the labor market, in family life, in relation to the body, and even imaginations of the future. The ability to defend one's rights in relation to an employer or a partner, or the ability to reproduce and care for children, are all restricted and conditioned by the lack of legal permission to stay.

But along with the uncertainty and precarity that characterize the everyday experiences of clandestinity, one can trace migrants' ongoing and multiple practices of resistance and negotiation in regard to access to rights. Firstly, one encounters the resistance inscribed in the clandestine position itself—that is, the challenge made to sovereignty and to notions of belonging, which is inscribed in continuous residence of undocumented migrants. Secondly, one sees the ways in which undocumented migrants organize, both formally and informally, by way of political mobilization and network building. Finally, one can trace the different ways undocumented migrants find access to welfare services (healthcare, education, and childcare) through family, friends, NGOs, and activist networks.

In what follows, I theorize these practices and strategies as being forms of political struggle: struggles through which the boundaries of exclusion and belonging are negotiated in the everyday lives of asylum seekers. These boundaries are negotiated by asylum seekers constructing their own possibilities to remain in Sweden under livable conditions, and by the NGOs, activists, families, friends, and professionals who support them. I discuss how resistance and forms of active citizenship are taking place on three levels: in the everyday, through belonging in the local community, and through counterrepresentations.

At the center of the practical everyday work involved in pushing the boundaries of exclusion, we find the struggles for asylum and/or residence permits. Most of the asylum-seeking informants I talked to regarded themselves as refugees in need of protection from persecution of different kinds. They all understood that the situation they would find themselves in if they returned to their countries of origin was too dangerous and hazardous to consider. Most of the activist informants supported asylum assessments based on trust in migrants' accounts of their experiences and their fears of returning. The activists also shared beliefs in open borders and disapproval of the very processes through which the state categorizes and separates people into "worthy" and "non-worthy" asylum seekers and migrants. However, one of the central aspects of the struggle by migrants and activists is negotiation with these state processes and categorizations in the attempt to gain permanent residence permits or refugee status.

In the concrete terms of everyday life, this struggle is about a variety of activities: it is about trying to find lawyers to work with the cases, and gathering information about political developments and shifts in the countries of origin, and, in particular, finding material about the treatment of political/minority/religious groups in the states from which the asylum seekers come. It is also about constructing legal cases on the grounds of exceptionally distressing circumstances; it is about going over the possibilities of getting a residence permit through family reunification with a partner who is a citizen/permanent resident or through the labor migration scheme; it can be about trying to bring about a hearing at the Migration Court; about getting media attention for a case; it is about mobilizing protests related to individual cases or to groups of asylum seekers sharing the same situation. For the informants, this struggle is also expressed through the ongoing practice of networking and information sharing with activists, friends, their own diasporic community, and/or other asylum seekers. It is also illustrated by a constant awareness of debates on asylum policies and changes in legislation, as well as by hours spent by the television watching news and political debate shows on the topic. In addition to the work related to the legal process, the everyday practical work by and in support of asylum seekers is mainly about compensating for the lack of social rights and welfare entitlements through finding alternative routes to education, welfare services, and the labor and housing markets.

In the case of schooling and childcare, the activist informants knew about a few schools where teachers and principals always tried to provide a place for clandestine children and others where it was impossible, but most often they would have to contact schools and principals each time a clandestine child was in need of a place at a school. In other cases, an engaged teacher, school welfare officer, or principal from a school the child attended during the asylum process would try to make it possible for the child to stay or find a place somewhere else. The schools that wanted to include children who found themselves in these circumstances faced a series of administrative and security problems, such as how to register the children, their grades and their credits, and how to assure their safety. Among the informants' children, some of them had no access to schooling and others had found places in schools. For all of them, the children's access or non-access to schools were central in their accounts of their situation.

Another central aspect in these accounts—and in the accounts of the activists, as well—is the (non-) access to healthcare. In the bigger cities (Stockholm, Gothenburg, and Malmö) there are "underground clinics" run by medical NGOs, asylum rights networks, and individual healthcare professionals. At these clinics nurses, doctors, and other healthcare professionals volunteer to help undocumented migrants using the resources they manage to gather through both fundraising and through the connections they have with regular healthcare institutions.[4] However, those among the informants in my study who had been in need of medical care had actually turned to regular public healthcare. Undocumented migrants are entitled to emergency medical care, but are supposed to be charged for the care. However, among the informants who had accessed public healthcare, none had experienced this. All the same, some of the activist informants did speak of cases when people had been invoiced after visits to hospitals. With the exception of a few negative experiences when they had been turned away, most of the informants reported that they had been well received when seeking treatment. However, in a few cases, echoing experiences at the Migration Board, the informants had encountered a suspicious attitude from healthcare staff, and been accused of simulating and exaggerating their symptoms.[5]

While education and healthcare are areas of welfare that still remain a central (although unequally distributed and accessed) right of all citizens and permanent residents, both the housing market and the labor market are fields within the welfare state that are non-accessible and/or differentiated for both undocumented migrants *and* groups of citizens and permanent residents. So, while informal routes to schools and healthcare are constructed almost exclusively by/for undocumented migrants, the informal housing and labor markets have a broader "purpose" and are populated by broader groups of marginalized citizens and workers. Compared to other European welfare states, the informal housing and labor markets might be small in Sweden, but they still exist and they still offer their paradoxical "possibilities" to clandestine asylum seekers (Schierup, Hansen, and Castles 2006, 215–17).

The possible sources of income that my informants (both activists and asylum seekers) knew about, or had to rely on, were quite varied. The main source of income among the group of informants was economic support such as gifts or loans from friends and relatives or from activist groups, NGOs, religious congregations, or political parties (mainly the Left Party and the Liberal Youth, two parties that have special funds from which individuals and groups can apply for economic support). Alongside different kinds of gifts and loans, informal labor is an important source of income for this group who are excluded from the possibility of gaining formal employment. Among the informants in my study only a few had experiences from the informal labor market, but altogether the accounts of the activist informants, reports from trade unions, and documentation in the news media indicate that most clandestine asylum seekers (and undocumented migrants in general) are referred to the informal labor market for economic maintenance and survival (Schierup, Hansen, and Castles 2006, 216). As well as these two main sources of income, the informants told me about a couple of other potential revenue streams. One, for example, entailed gathering cans and bottles to return to shops in order to collect the deposit. However, the most inventive method was "job sharing." This involved an NGO/activist group (as a group) or a person with citizenship taking on a position but then allowing the asylum seeker to do the actual work and receive the money. Needless to say, these "incomes" were often below subsistence levels and the lack of money and nourishing food for the children was a central concern.

Finally, accommodation is another field of urgency for the informants. Some of the informants have been able to stay in the same place during their time in clandestinity, but others, finding only temporary accommodation, have had to constantly move around between apartments and rooms. The ways of finding accommodation, much like the ways of finding the economic means to exist, are either through friends, family members, or activists. Activists often find friends with empty rooms, or locate the temporarily empty apartments of others who are on vacation. The other option is to find a place to rent on the informal housing market. However, this often involves paying an overpriced rent and living under insecure conditions. Finally, some activists rented apartments in their own name and either paid the rent themselves or by using the money from activist networks. For the asylum seekers among the informants, the issue of accommodation was, of course, urgent and a source of constant worry. This was also the problem that seemed to take most time and energy to solve for the activists.

Some of these strategies are, at first sight, limited solutions that only reach individual families on a short-term basis. But, I want to argue that the struggle to gain welfare access on an individual level often is closely related to collective levels of struggle for access. An example of the way the engagement on the level of "individual needs" tends to spill over into other forms of politics can be seen, for example, in the ways representatives for underground health and medical clinics have become important actors and public voices in the asylum rights debate. As I mentioned above, the social rights of undocumented migrants is a topic that has a growing presence in public debate and, as a consequence of asylum advocacy, some of the rights to healthcare and education have been revised and partly expanded during the years I have been working in this area. This growing attention coupled with the mobilization of public opinion and demands for these expansions have developed mainly in civil society and in the groups of professionals working in the actual fields (doctors, nurses, psychologists, teachers, social workers, counselors, etc.). These individual actions seem to have opened up the discursive space for challenging the exclusion of migrants from welfare services and naturalizing the discourse on who has rights to welfare.

Resistance through Local Community—
Inclusion through Clandestinity

Paradoxically, at the same time that it is defined by exclusion, the position in clandestinity seems to have the potential to serve as a point of entrance to some (limited) kinds of community, belonging, and even active citizenship. In some of the informants' lives the contact with and support from asylum rights groups and other sectors of civil society have grown into a relative inclusion on the community level.[6] Parallel with the ways that individually orientated support on the level of welfare provision tends to lead to, and inspire, collective mobilization for expanded welfare rights for undocumented migrants, the same individual support also creates enhanced feelings of security and belonging through the actual networks of people (activists, friends, family, professionals from churches, schools, and healthcare) involved in the support work. In addition to having concrete needs for care, accommodation, and schooling met and solved in direct and instrumental ways, the informants also talked about their feelings of enhanced security through the sense of having a network of people around—of having gained a social place with people who express a will to at least try to support them. Let us consider an example of this clandestine belonging.

Ermir and Miranda are a young couple from Kosovo. They left Kosovo after the war and arrived in Sweden in 2002 with their two children who were one and three years old at the time. Their asylum application was rejected after three and a half years. They then decided to leave the refugee center where they had been waiting, and came to Malmö to stay clandestinely. In Ermir and Miranda's account of their time in Sweden, the importance of inclusion on the level of the local community is very much emphasized. They discuss how they and their children, upon arriving in Sweden, were reallocated from Malmö to a refugee center in a village in Småland. They had to stay there for the three and one-half years that the asylum process lasted, until they left for Malmö to avoid deportation. Although they moved to Malmö to become clandestine, they felt that many aspects of life in the city offered a greater level of community.

> MIRANDA: We are not clandestine! We were more clandestine when we were at the refugee reception center in the forest, but after we arrived in Malmö, we don't feel clandestine, and my children don't either.

Although Miranda and Ermir also express how they sometimes felt included and welcomed in the village, they mainly give accounts of the feeling of being hidden away in the refugee center in the forest, and of the unfair and even racist practices that they understood to be a result of a prevailing "culture of suspicion" (Lewis 2004, 28–32), which had developed from the close cooperation between the small community's local unit of the Migration Board, the Healthcare Clinic, and the Language School (*SFI*). So, although they were not clandestine during the years in refugee center, they felt very isolated, surveyed, regulated, and controlled by the local unit of the Migration Board. When Miranda and Ermir arrived in Malmö, they had friends from Kosovo who could support them emotionally and practically. Furthermore, they soon got in touch with activist networks that sustained them, and eventually they got involved in a political campaign for a general refugee amnesty during 2005 and 2006.

Apart from the political and theoretical implications of the refugee amnesty campaign on the level of national politics and asylum rights, it became a site for the creation of a local network that involved both clandestine asylum seekers and various actors from different parts of civil society—migrant associations, NGOs, activist groups, political parties, and religious congregations. Miranda and Ermir participated in demonstrations, flyer distribution, collecting signatures for the petition for amnesty, and in the planning and a performance that was developed by activists and a local theatre company, which aimed to provide the audience with testimonies from clandestine lives. Their work with the theater and their campaigning during these months can be understood as a practice of active citizenship and as inclusion through community building (Calhoun 2007; Lister 2003; Yuval-Davis 1997). This (along with the access to friends in the local Kosovo Albanian diaspora) is the context from which Miranda expresses her insistence that she and her family have not been clandestine during their time in Malmö.

Another aspect of relative inclusion on the level of the community—and hence a challenge to statist boundaries of exclusion—can be understood through the concept of "passing" (Lewis 2004, 18–20). Gail Lewis defines "passing" in terms of "a public presentation of self in a way that denies or disguises the identity or membership of a subordinated (and often despised, feared and hated) social group in an attempt to avoid the stigma, discrimination and ridicule that such individuals and groups often receive" (ibid., 20). She continues by arguing that, "'passing' becomes a way of negotiating the inequalities of citizenship and social power that result from what we might call the hierarchical ordering of difference" (ibid.). While the concept is more often applied in the context of the differentiation of identities such as in respect of gender, "race"/ethnicity, and sexuality, it is also relevant in the context of the temporary, juridically defined position of my informants. This is because despite the temporary nature of the position of clandestine asylum seekers, some of the informants, and other clandestine asylum seekers I have met in activist settings, bear witness to the feeling of having their exclusion *written all over their skin*. This creates a feeling that everyone can see that they are not allowed to be here, that they are bodies out of place, afraid, poor, or homeless (see Khosravi 2006). In this context, the moments of "passing" become important moments in a kind of "momentary resistance" that challenges the boundaries of exclusion. For Miranda and Ermir, who participated in the mobilization for general refugee amnesty, it was practices of active citizenship that made them pass as citizens. For other informants these moments could happen, for example, at their workplaces, where the work colleagues did not know about their status.

Through passing as an activist or a citizen, as a refugee with a permanent residence permit or as an asylum seeker still waiting "within" the system, my informants live moments outside clandestinity and inside the boundaries of belonging. Although one has to be careful not to romanticize such a relative form of citizenship, in the face of the consequences of exclusion from formal citizenship (or a permanent residence permit), it is important to highlight these openings and interstices in which clandestine asylum seekers can enact themselves as political subjects through active participation in political protest and mobilization.

Resistance through Counterrepresentations

The accounts of the informants I worked with relate partly to the material and practical circumstances they are exposed to in terms of migration authorities, the lack of residence permit, welfare institutions, and the non-access to those institutions. However, their accounts are also shaped by the ways in which clandestinity is discursively constructed through available representations of migrants, in terms of prevailing perceptions of both racialized others in Sweden in general and clandestine asylum seekers in particular. Antiracist scholars have pointed out how racism often takes expression in a form of "culture of suspicion" in policies and institutional practices that regulate access to welfare. The culture of suspicion seems to be explicitly present in the field of assessment of asylum status and applications for residence permits (Lewis 2004, 28–32). The asylum seekers in my study confirm this perceptual framing, giving testimonies about the feeling of not having been listened to or taken seriously.

In the context of a culture of suspicion and racist representations of asylum seekers, migrants' productions of counterrepresentations of themselves are central forms of resistance, which also took place within their interviews with me.

Adelina is from Kosovo and in her early thirties. In 2005, she and her two children had left Kosovo for a second time to escape from Adelina's abusive and violent husband. As they had claimed (and been rejected) asylum in Germany the first time they managed to flee, the Swedish authorities referred to the Dublin Regulation and wanted to return them to Germany.[7] Adelina knew that a return to Germany would mean another rejection and deportation to Kosovo, and decided to stay clandestinely with her children. Adelina's cousin lives in the same small town, and he and his family have supported them during the periods they had to stay clandestinely. During the interview, her cousin served as an interpreter but he also took part in the conversation.

Adelina and her cousin responded to my questions in a way that implicitly, but yet very clearly, related to the culture of suspicion that migrants encounter from authorities and in racist representations. These suspicions most often relate to ideas that asylum seekers are so-called economic migrants.[8] Adelina and her cousin reveal this through their ways of talking *against* these representations of asylum seekers as "economic refugees" or "asylum shoppers" who have come to Sweden to draw upon welfare support systems. During our two-hour conversation they often related to me as if my questions were coming from the place of suspicion and, with increasing impatience, returned several times to explain the nature of flight to me:

> MAJA: But how come, when you decided to leave Kosovo, you decided specifically to come to Sweden?
>
> ADELINA: When you have to . . . when you have the kind of problems with your family as I had, you don't care where you go. You just want to take off and be left in peace somewhere. So there was nothing special that made me go specifically to Sweden, it was all about leaving Kosovo.
>
> MAJA: But how come you ended up in Sweden? Was it a coincidence? Was this the only place it was possible to go at that moment?

Adelina and her cousin explained that a man in Sweden had promised to marry her to make it possible for her to leave Kosovo. The details about this are not important here, I only want to show how they often understood my questions as implying motives other than her actual need of protection for Adelina's arrival in Sweden:

> INTERPRETER: For her the only important thing was to leave.
>
> . . . .
>
> INTERPRETER: She ended up here [for various reasons], but for her the important thing was to get out of Kosovo.
>
> . . . .
>
> ADELINA: If I had anywhere to return in my home country, I would have returned immediately. I wouldn't have stayed here to hide away as though I was in a prison. And I haven't come here just because I wanted to . . . or to be clandestine or anything like that. . . . I escaped for the children's sake.
>
> . . . .

ADELINA: Listen, when you are down there [in Kosovo] . . . you are not interested in going exactly here. And you don't care what country your relatives or friends are in either.

Instead of accepting the dominant negative representations of asylum seekers to which they are implicitly relating, and instead of positioning themselves against "the rest" (or "other" asylum seekers), they both reacted strongly to my questions about Adelina's "choice" of Sweden as destination country and defended themselves against the perceptual framing of migrants as "welfare parasites" by arguing with vehemence against stigmatizing stereotypes.

Who Is Allowed to Be a Political Subject?

While understanding citizenship as *formal citizenship* is not enough to formulate and grasp the position of clandestine asylum seekers, a more community-oriented notion of belonging and of citizenship practices manages to grasp these activities and these groups and collectives as acts of citizenship. Through a multileveled understanding of citizenship, the actors involved in the contestation and pushing of the boundaries of exclusion can be understood as performing active citizenship—and this applies to both the citizens and the noncitizens involved.

However, despite the possibility of understanding asylum seekers' central role in these processes as a route toward partial inclusion in the local (activist) community, there seems to be a gap between the comprehension of these activities as held by citizen activists and the understanding held by noncitizen activists. This also extends to a similar gap between the understanding of citizen activists understood as "Swedish Swedes" and the struggles to challenge and negotiate the boundaries of exclusion that are practiced by nonwhite citizens. For example, activists organized in activist groups or NGOs get much more appreciation and attention than asylum seekers, immigrant associations, members of diasporic communities, and the families and relatives of asylum seekers, who also actively support clandestine asylum seekers—often much more than actors in civil society. This gap is made manifest in the ways some of the informants represent the movement with "idealized" personifications of Swedish asylum rights activists: heroic representations that are reproduced within the news media and other publications as well as in the general discourses within the movement itself.

In a book titled *Gömmarna* (*The Hiders*) Ingrid Segerstedt (1997) takes on the important task of documenting some of the activities practiced in civil society to challenge exclusionary asylum policies. *Gömmarna* is an important intervention in the defense of values of solidarity and inclusion that have been systematically challenged in Sweden by neoliberal policies and the emergence and increasing establishment of right-wing parties. The complex balancing act between inclusive activities and the distancing realized through polarized representations of "hiders" and "hidden" is also represented in the book. For example some passages demonstrate a stark polarization between the active citizen "hider" ('*gömmare*') and the passive asylum-seeking victim:

> Among those who carry out the obligations of democracy to the asylum seekers are the "refugee hiders" [*flyktinggömmarna*]. They are not undemanding but are however tolerant towards the refugees. They understand the asylum seekers' fear of being forced to go back to countries without freedom. Therefore, they want to help the asylum seekers through, among other things, learning thoroughly about the reasons for their flight. . . . We owe the hiders [*gömmarna*] many thanks for their courage to defend the weakest and most vulnerable today and in particular for speaking for the children, who have become the victims of wars and persecution. (Segerstedt Wiberg 1997, 8; my translation).

Here, the account attributes a lack of voice and power to asylum seekers while highlighting the active humanism of the hiders. It also focuses on the responsibility of activists to not be "undemanding" and to "thoroughly [learn] about the reasons for the flight." These kinds of representations, which also recur in the interviews with both activists and asylum seekers, are problematic because of the way in which they polarize the relation between citizens and noncitizens. Representations such as these, which ultimately identify the citizen as a representative of the Swedish state, reproduce notions of deserving and undeserving migrants. The binarisms reproduced in *Gömmarna* and other activist accounts reveal the pervasiveness of polarized representations of activist "do-gooders" (often represented as "Swedish Swedes") and powerless clandestine asylum seekers. Another problematic aspect of these heroic representations is that the protests, the support, and the networks from within diasporic communities or families are not interpreted as conscious acts of solidarity and political protests to the same degree as similar acts made by NGOs and activist groups. In short, citizens' acts of resistance or protest are channeled through their citizenship and thereby tend to be read as being "more political," while noncitizens' acts are either effaced or understood in terms of strategies for everyday survival.

However, during the first decade of the twenty-first century, the self-organization of undocumented migrants has increased, and, among other central issues, they have challenged this helper/helped relation. In particular, it is the mobilizations related to work and labor rights that have grown most strongly, and have become important sites for representations of undocumented migrants as a political collective and for claims of labor rights. These struggles, which originate in the local unions of the SAC in and around Stockholm, where undocumented workers have organized as undocumented *workers* rather than asylum seekers or any other category of migrants, reflect earlier developments of unions, workers', and anarchist movements in Europe (especially in Southern Europe).[9] Groups of clandestine asylum seekers with a focus on asylum rights have also challenged the helper/helped division through creating direct dialogues between themselves and politicians. For example, the group *Papperslösa Stockholm* continued struggling for migrant amnesty, after larger branches of the network in the campaign either ran out of energy or were happy (and therefore more or less silent) with the compromise that was the provisional legislation.

The representations of helper/helped are also challenged by some of the informants on the individual level. Miranda, for example, was angry about the ways some people approached her, having the feeling that some of them enjoyed her precarious situation:

> MIRANDA: I don't like it at all when people talk like that [imitating a pitiful voice] "Oooh! Poor you! And you are having a baby and you need this and that and that!" . . . I am not dying! I am normal. I live in a hidden way, but I am normal like you!

As I have shown above, clandestine asylum seekers are themselves often at the core of the movements of social protest. Finally, I want to frame this empirical discussion about the effacement of migrants' agency and self-representation with Peter Nyers's argument, which states:

> Through an impossible activism—"impossible" because the non-status do not possess the "authentic" identity (i.e. citizenship) that would allow them to be political, to be an activist—they make visible the violent paradoxes of sovereignty. Consequently, the risks taken by the taking abject foreigner—i.e. taking the risk to become a speaking agent—is risky for the sovereign account of the political as well. Not surprisingly, representatives of the sovereign order display a striking anxiety whenever the abject foreigner takes on the status of a political activist engaged in acts of self-determination (e.g. stopping his/her deportation). (Nyers 2003)

The effacement of migrants' political mobilization might, within these theoretical frames, be understood as an expression of the "anxiety" produced when this mobilization sheds light on the "violent paradoxes," defining their position/s in relation to the political.

Relations to the State

The asylum activist informants I worked with all talked about support practices at the individual level as being directly linked to demands for rights on a collective scale. Through generating knowledge and awareness of the consequences of exclusion from rights, and of the details in the legislation in welfare rights and institutional rules and practices that become obstacles for asylum seekers' access, their very involvement in support becomes the bridge to collectively formulated demands.

Maria is from the north of Sweden, she was in her mid-twenties and had been an activist in an asylum rights group based in Malmö for about five years at the time I interviewed her. She has had close contact with around twenty different asylum-seeking individuals/families during these years. Earlier in the interview, she shared a lot of practical information about the activist group's work with juridical counseling, administration of economic support, finding places for the families to stay, and contacting physicians and nurses who give free care to clandestine asylum seekers. At this point she has returned to reflect a bit more on the implications of this activism:

> MARIA: We are an organization that is not tied to the state, so we don't have to care about what the state . . . says or thinks. . . . And I think it is good that we work with both direct contacts with people *and* with the campaigning and creating of opinion in favor of migration and asylum rights. . . . If we only did the direct support to individual asylum seekers, it wouldn't feel like the right thing for me—although that might be what I have focused on mostly so far in the interview—because then it only becomes like upholding the system. . . . If we don't protest clearly and publicly against the unfair system, it is as if we give legitimacy to the system. So I think that it is important to do the two things. . . . And the other way around, it is about creating some kind of closeness. . . . If we were only in the streets shouting, it would become too distanced in some way, like a kind of escapism. Because here there are still people, here and now, who are desperate for someone who can support them in their struggle to be included. And, also, how can we know that our ideas are right if we don't keep in touch with the people we are trying to help? . . .
>
> Both these things [the practical work and the campaigning] give me strength in relation to each other. To meet people who are in this very exposed position, as one is as clandestine, that gives me strength to react or, rather, it almost forces me to react. And the other way around, to feel what I know I am talking about

in the campaigning work, I need this contact, to have seen how it is. . . .

I want this situation to be made more visible, and the best would of course be if people had the possibility to talk publicly about the situation themselves, but it isn't all clandestine asylum seekers who have the strength for that, or want to do it or dare to do it . . . and then I think I, with my experiences, can serve as some kind of voice or witness.

Here Maria describes how individually and practically oriented support to asylum seekers might link to a more collective struggle through the knowledge and community that are created through these more individual contacts. She also describes how the individual contacts form an important knowledge base that gives more legitimacy to her and other activists to speak about/for asylum seekers in the public debate. However, in her description Maria is constantly negotiating a tension that she sees in the role of the asylum rights activists and their activities, between the urge to "do something" in relation to an unbearable and emergent situation, and the risk of victimizing people and reinscribing the authority of the state and "the system" through these activities. Especially, she worries that a singlehanded focus on the juridical procedures—although the pursuing of a residence permit earlier has been described as the most foundational need for most clandestine and undocumented migrants—will have as a consequence increased legitimacy for the practices of asylum legislation.

This balancing act in relation to the state is also present in another way in my material. Let us consider Ismail and Floriana's approach to the asylum rights movement. Floriana and Ismail came with their children to Sweden from Macedonia in 2003. They had three children; a son and a daughter in their early teens and a son of around seven years old at the time the fieldwork was conducted. They had been hiding for more than a year at the time I interviewed them. When we were discussing their experiences of Sweden, Floriana and Ismail focused a lot upon the support they received from a range of Swedish citizens, as well as on the way that experience clashed with the exclusionary attitudes and policies they had encountered at the level of the state and its institutional arm, the Migration Board:

FLORIANA: Wherever we have been we have been so well received. That is why I can't understand how the Migration Board can be like that, when the people is totally different.

In the description offered by Floriana and Ismail it is rather the support and understanding they have met that describe their ideas about Swedish society, while the Migration Board is described as a separate ("evil" or "cold") actor. The inclusionary practices of activists, doctors, and psychologists are understood as representing the nation just as well as the exclusionary practices of the Migration Board.

While the arguments for actors in civil society taking action are about challenging the state and its institutions—in differing degrees, from anarchist renunciation of the state to moderate calls for reformed practice of the Alien Act—the everyday practices of these challenges offer a more blurred account of state boundaries. As an example, activists who give support in the juridical case can end up shoring up the exclusionary policies and practices of the state, through explaining the rationales behind the decisions and assessments. Furthermore, the practice of finding alternative routes to access to welfare rights also entails "helping" the state to make the effects of its policies less explicitly violent. Through solidarity and/or humanitarian actions that make the policies understandable, or make clandestinity more "livable" and humane, the active citizenship practices of civil society and individual civil servants can be read as providing the state with a more *humane face*. These acts can, of course, be read in different ways, and throughout the accounts given by the asylum seekers about their understanding of the actions of asylum rights activists, "disobedient" civil servants, or civil society, they often talk about these acts as contrasting strongly with their perception of migration authorities or the state proper. Others interpret the acts as something that makes them describe Sweden as "a good country." Another possible interpretation is that these experiences of care and solidarity provide a powerful contrast with state bureaucracy and create an inclusive environment. On the one hand, this allows one to name the injustices experienced and, on the other, permits a shift from isolated personal experience toward forms of shared, collective practices. Hence, these acts can be read as both working against and as working in concert with the state. In other words, migrant activism, whatever its intentions, always remains caught within a series of paradoxes. I want to conclude by arguing that while these paradoxes are inescapable, we must be attentive to them by giving a central role to the voices and active citizenship practices of migrants themselves as they "push the boundaries" from below.

Notes

My thanks go to the informants who generously shared their stories. I am also grateful to Professor Diana Mulinari, Lund University, for many interesting discussions about this article.

1. The number of undocumented migrants in Sweden is generally estimated as being somewhere between 20,000 and 50,000, while the estimated number of

clandestine asylum seekers in particular varies at anywhere between 10,000 and 20,000, depending on the "counting technique" utilized (*Social rapport* 2010, 270). Most estimates presented to the public come from journalists, activists, NGOs, and politicians rather than from the results of academic research. Further, except for the "practical" difficulties involved in "counting," asking for—and producing—numbers is problematic in relation to questions about *how* and *for what purposes* these numbers are being produced and used (Stenum 2008; Khosravi 2010).

2. Political scientist Peo Hansen traces a fundamental paradox in European migration policies between attempts to discourage and delimit refugee migration while at the same time opening borders to controlled, temporary labor immigration (Hansen 2008).

3. During the years that I have been working with this study, the concept *papperslösa*, which literally means "paper-less" but could be roughly translated to undocumented migrants, has become another popular concept.

4. See Baghir-Zada's (2009) study of healthcare provision for undocumented migrants in Sweden and the Netherlands.

5. Although the governing coalition of right-wing parties have made an agreement with the Green Party about extended rights to healthcare for undocumented migrants, and a governmental commission has recommended such an expansion of rights, the actual content in the legislation is still under negotiation at the time of writing. At the moment, the national legislation still only stipulates the right to subsidized care for children under the age of eighteen but the county councils have the possibility to grant adult undocumented migrants "emergency and other immediately necessary care"—and some of them have chosen to do so (Baghir-Zada 2009, 47ff). For an analysis of variations in both formal and actual access to care, see Baghir-Zada (2009) and for further analysis of the implications of undocumentedness in relation to non-access to healthcare, see Erika Sigvardsdotter (2012).

6. Here, it is pertinent to mention that I got in touch with the informants through the activist networks I was part in myself at the time. This means that I only got in touch with people who already had some kind of contact with civil society, and the study is limited to that group within the group of clandestine asylum seekers, and can only deal with the situation of undocumented migrants without these connections to civil society through secondary material and sources.

7. At the ECRE Web site, the Dublin Regulation is described as establishing "a hierarchy of criteria for identifying the EU Member State responsible for processing an asylum claim. Usually this will be the state through which the asylum seeker first entered the EU. The Regulation aims to ensure that each claim is examined by one Member State, to deter repeated applications, and to enhance efficiency." http://www.ecre.org/topics/asylum_in_EU/determining_responsibility. Accessed September 10, 2010.

8. In this interview, the informant chose to have a relative rather than a professional as an interpreter. He was Adelina's cousin and had been with the family during the difficult times. He had a lot of insights and emotions in relation to the situation himself. Sometimes he expressed his own opinion or put his own words to things rather than translating directly. For those occasions I present him as an "own voice" in the interview, and not only as a channel for Adelina's words.

9. The SAC, or the Swedish Syndicalist Union, a relatively small radical union that was the first to even acknowledge the presence of—and then organize—undocumented workers.

Works Cited

Baghir-Zada, Ramin. 2009. *Illegal Aliens and Health (care) Wants: The Cases of Sweden and the Netherlands*. Diss. Malmö: Malmö högskola.
Bexelius, Maria, 2008. *Asylrätt, kön och politik—en handbok för jämställdhet och kvinnors rättigheter*. Swedish Refugee Advice Centre.
Calhoun, Craig. 2007. *Nations Matter. Culture, History, and the Cosmopolitan Dream*. London and New York: Routledge.
Dahlstedt, Magnus, and Mekonnen Tesfahuney. 2004. "Rörlighetens paradoxer." In *Rasismer i Europa: migration i den nya världsordningen*, edited by Avtar Brah, Magnus Dahlstedt, and Ingemar Lindberg. Stockholm: Agora.
Hansen, Peo. 2008. *EU's migrationspolitik under 50 år. Ett integrerat perspektiv på en motsägelsefull utveckling*. Lund: Studentlitteratur.
Khosravi, Shahram. 2006. "Territorialiserad mänsklighet: irreguljära immigranter och det nakna livet." In *Om välfärdens gränser och det villkorade medborgarskapet*. SOU 2006: 37.
———. 2010. "An Ethnography of Migrant Illegality in Sweden: Included yet Excepted?" *Journal of International Political Theory* 6 (1): 95–116.
Lewis, Gail. 2004. "'Do Not Go Gently . . .': Terrains of Citizenship and Landscapes of the Personal." In *Citizenship. Personal Lives and Social Policy*, edited by Gail Lewis. Bristol: Open University/The Policy Press.
Lister, Ruth. 2003. *Citizenship: Feminist Perspectives*. 2nd ed. London: Macmillan.
Nyers, Peter. 2003. "Abject Cosmopolitanism: The Politics of Protection in the Anti-deportation Movement." *Third World Quarterly* 24 (6): 1069–93.
Sager, Maja. 2011. *Everyday Clandestinity: Experiences on the Margins of Citizenship and Migration Policies*. Diss. Lund: Lunds universitet.
Schierup, Carl-Ulrik, Peo Hansen, and Stephen Castles. 2006. *Migration, Citizenship, and the European Welfare State A European Dilemma*. Oxford: Oxford University Press.
Segerstedt Wiberg, Ingrid. 1997. *Gömmare och andra*. Lindelöws bokförlag.
Sigvardsdotter, Erika. 2012. *Presenting the Absent: An Account of Undocumentedness in Sweden*. Kulturgeografiska institutionen, Diss. Uppsala : Uppsala universitet.
Social rapport. 2010. Socialstyrelsen, Stockholm, 2010.
Stenum, Helle. 2008. "How Many Illegals in El Dorado? Governing Migrant Illegality and the Issue of Numbers." Conference paper, *Internationell Migration: Utmaningar och möjligheter. Ett interdisciplinärt samtal*. October 3, 2008. Ceifo, Stockholm University.
Tamas, Gellert. 2009. *De Apatiska*. Stockholm: Natur & Kultur.
Yuval-Davis, Nira. 1997. *Gender and Nation*. London: Sage.
Vestin, Sanna. 2006. *Flyktingfällan*. Stockholm: Ordfront.

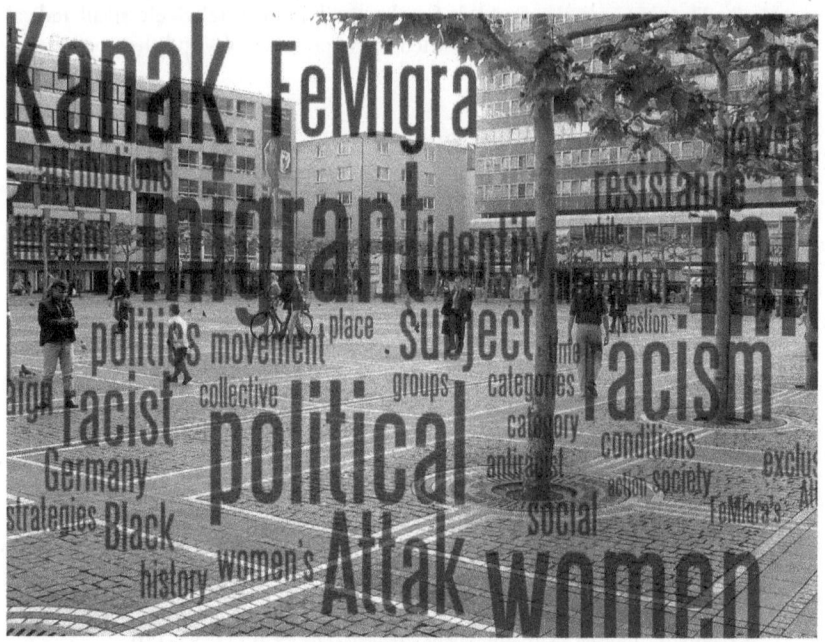

Figure 10.1. The original photograph of Konstablerwache, Frankfurt am Main, Germany taken and uploaded by User Melkom on http://upload.wikimedia.org/wikipedia/commons/b/bf/Konstablerwache%2C_Frankfurt.jpg. Accessed June 21, 2012. Graphic: Carmen Losmann/Petra Rostock.

10

Subjects that Matter?

Nonidentitarian Strategies of Pro-"Migrant" and "Migrant" Protest in Germany

Petra Rostock

There is a long history of "migrants"'[1] self-organized resistance against racism in Germany (Karakayalı and Spenkoch 1999).[2] Nevertheless, "migrants" were and often still are nonexistent as articulated political subjects (*FeMigra* 1994, 50–51; *Teile der FeMigra* 1992). Instead, "migrants" have been regularly stigmatized as culturally different and therefore inferior in the ongoing disputes over migration. Cultural differences between the inhabitants of Germany are essentialized as criteria for demarcation and exclusion while questions of social inequalities are obscured.

In the face of this culturalization of social and economic inequalities and under the impression of increasing racist violence in the aftermath of German reunification,[3] "migrants" increasingly self-organized in the 1990s. These self-organizations can be understood as an effort of collective self-defense to fight against racism not only in German society in general but also within the Left and women's movements. Since reunification, debates about German national identity had proliferated, pushing ahead a concept of national belonging grounded in ethnic descent and reinforcing the already existing boundaries between those included and those excluded from German society. In view of this compulsory identity logic, "migrants'" self-empowerment and political articulation seemed possible only by positively resignifying those ethnic and racial attributions by which they were excluded as "other" (Bojadžijev 2008, 252–54; Gutiérrez Rodríguez 2001, 22; Kaynar and Suda 2002, 169). At the same time, exactly those attributions that constitute discrimination have to be fundamentally challenged. Otherwise, resistance against discriminations that result out of essentialized ethnic, cultural, and/or religious attributions remain caught in a binary logic of "us" and "them," which suppresses existing exclusions and differences, reproduces group stereotypes and denies intersecting oppressions.

Considering this dilemma, I want to draw attention to pro-"migrant" strategies of political action, which try to avoid the binary logic of "them" and "us," of inclusion and exclusion by means of recontextualization and resignification of the excluding categories (Butler 1995b, 128). More precisely I ask: Can pro-"migrant" resistance be grounded in a subject position of, for example, "female migrant" not in the sense of a homogeneous collective identity but as a political category that needs to be occupied in order to challenge discrimination yet is never fully determined but remains open for redefinition?

I will explore this question by analyzing protest material of two German pro-"migrant" and "migrant" actors called *FeMigra* and *Kanak Attak*. Both assume a deliberately antinational and nonorigin-based perspective, rejecting identitarian politics. *FeMigra* as well as *Kanak Attak* strove to challenge binary categories of "us" and "them," the notion of "migrants" as "other" along with the conditions of enunciation and decision-making processes. While engaging in different times at different places, their actions similarly asserted migration as an integral part of German history and present. Thus, they tackle the hegemonic power of definition and shift the ground on which antiracist and pro-"migrant" politics has been founded in the past: *FeMigra* are feminist "migrants" who organized in the city of Frankfurt/Main to abolish racist exploitation and discrimination in general and within the feminist and Left movement, the academia, and municipal and federal policies in particular. Breaking away from their ascribed position as society's outsiders, *FeMigra* among others networked with different "migrant" self-organizations, demonstrated, and participated in antiracist and feminist events and publications. *Kanak Attak* was a network present in different West German cities. This actor not only called for the granting of citizenship and other privileges, but questioned the allegedly self-evident regulation of insiders and outsiders on a fundamental level employing a mix of theory, politics, and cultural and artistic practices.

I use protest material from these groups not to provide conclusive data but to offer a grounded means for conceptualizing my thesis that nonidentitarian strategies of political action are contingently and temporarily possible before they are again subjected to an identitarian reappropriation. To substantiate my thesis, for each of the two actors I will first look at the subject positions they occupy in order to resist and irritate the hegemonic discourse on "migrants" and migration in Germany. Subsequently, I analyze two case studies of protest activities from each group as a means of examining the strategies used by these two groups to resist the multiple effects of racism, sexism, and capitalism. To conclude, I will revisit the im/possibilities of nonidentitarian strategies of political action.

FeMigra: Walking the Tightrope

FeMigra was founded in 1991 as a feminist "migrant" political project in the context of a growing critique of the German women's movement by "migrant" women (Apostolidou 1980; Camlikbeli 1984; Gültekin 1985; Kaynar and Suda 2002). It was inspired by the writings of Black feminists such as bell hooks and the Combahee River Collective as well as the formation of a German Black movement which was largely pushed ahead by Black women (Hügel et al. 1993; Oguntoye et al. 1986). Referring to Black as a political category and having recognized themselves in the political writings of and about Black women, the women that formed *FeMigra* had initially understood themselves as Black. Yet, in their alliances with Afro-German/ Black women, they realized that the political category "Black" could not grasp their specific situation as "migrant" women with specific histories and experiences (Migrantinnengruppe—FFM 1992).[4]

The starting point of *FeMigra*'s interventions was their analysis that, by being perceived as "foreign" women by German society, they were constructed as either "same" or "other" with both images representing two sides of the same problematic: the stereotype of the "other" depicts "migrant" women as deficit, as political problem, or as victims of patriarchy, while "foreign" men are subjected to tropes of criminality and sexual deviance. At the same time, "migrant" women who do not fulfil the image of a deficit "foreigner" are monopolized especially by social work and in the women's movement as "emancipated women" in ways that elide the material inequalities faced by "migrants." Within this binary logic of inclusion and exclusion, "migrants" are either made invisible, the history and experience of migration and "migrants" is systematically suspended in public discourse and institutions. Or "migrants" become an object—of science,[5] education, social work. As political subjects who put up resistance against racist discrimination in Germany, "migrants" were nonexistent (Apostolidou 1994; *FeMigra* 1992, 1994; Gutiérrez Rodríguez 1997; *Teile der FeMigra* 1992).

Neither included in the political category of Black nor represented within the white Left and women's movement, *FeMigra* strove to create their own collective voice and language. Inspired by writers such as Gloria Anzaldúa, Cherrie Moraga, and Gayatri Chakravorty Spivak (*FeMigra* 1994, 61), they decided for what Spivak once coined "strategic essentialism" (1993, 3). Occupying and resignifying the subject position of *"Migrantinnen"* ("migrant women") was to challenge the hegemonic conditions of representation on both the level of speaking of (*Darstellung*) and the level of speaking for (*Vertretung*) (Spivak 1988). On the first level of representation (*Darstellung*), referring to the subject position of "migrant women" was to make visible the political position of "migrants" as denizens linked to Germany de facto being a country of immigration with restrictive migration policies. "Migrant women" in this sense was not understood as a natural identity but as a political status that was (and is) only possible due to the political conditions that create "migrants." The second level of representation (*Vertretung*) is exemplified in exactly the fact that *FeMigra* self-organized as "migrant women" claiming participation and the right to speak for themselves. Similar to the Combahee River Collective (The Combahee River Collective 1982 [1972]), their aim was to overcome their isolation by sharing their experiences and individual analysis of racism in Germany with other women affected by racism, and in fighting racism by developing political forms of resistance against racist attacks and discrimination (Apostolidou 1994; *FeMigra* 1992, 1994; Migrantinnengruppe—FFM 1992; Wiese 1997; Yurtsever-Kneer 2002, 2004). As one member of *FeMigra* explained:

> With our organization and our publications we originally intended to question the image of the "other women" or the migrant women as deficit beings. That is what we did: by making our voice visible through publications respectively by means of interfering in public events and by making clear that we are not to be talked about but have our own voice—and can thus speak for and about ourselves. (Wiese 1997, 44; my translation)

One example of a public event in which *FeMigra* critically intervened was the campaign "Women Take the City." From August to October 1992 the city of Frankfurt/Main's women's department organized different actions for women such as night walks or a visit to the central surveillance office of the public transportation where women could inform themselves about security measures in train stations. The aim of the campaign was to encourage women to move freely around the town. The final rally of the campaign took place at a central square, Konstablerwache, "a place that was everything else but women friendly at the beginning of the 90s" (Anonymous 2009; my translation).

FeMigra situated their protest against the "Women Take the City" campaign as well as against the city's and women's department's security discourse within their large-scale criticism of the racism inherent in German feminism and the women's movement (*Teile der FeMigra* 1992; *FeMigra* 1992; GIS et al. 1993; Gutiérrez Rodríguez 1993). For *FeMigra* Konstablerwache was not only a place that was avoided by most women but also the space where police control and violence against "migrants" was a daily occurrence, and a place which was closely associated with media campaigns against "criminal foreigners." By organizing the final rally of the campaign exactly at this place, the women's department did not distance itself from the racist discourse on "foreign criminals." Instead, it actively participated in it by implicitly constructing the perpetrators of violence against women as "foreign." For *FeMigra*, the campaign's partaking in the hegemonic discourse of "foreigners as criminals" exemplified the racism within the women's movement and white women's participation in and profit from racist power structures.

Moreover, it is important to consider the context of contemporary history: the "Women Take the City" campaign took place in a social climate of daily racist violence, of racist assaults and arson attacks that came from the midst of society (cf. note 3). Yet the constant threat of racist violence that Black, "migrant," and refugee women face was cut out of the women's department's campaign, thus ignoring the intersection of sexism and racism. In focusing only on sexist oppression, the subject of the campaign was white women whose experiences were universalized under the category "women." By protesting against the "Women Take the City" campaign, *FeMigra* attempted to reject identity attributions and the binary categories of "us" and "them" in at least two ways: Firstly, by posing the question of representation, namely, who speaks when, where, and how for whom. By publicly articulating the absence of Black, "migrant," and refugee women in the city's campaign, *FeMigra* gained agency. Yet they did not merely juxtapose an essentialized identity of "migrant women" against "white women." Reflecting on how representation is connected with the power to produce inclusion and exclusion into societal institutions and discourses (Castro Varela and Dhawan 2005, 24; Gutiérrez Rodríguez 2003, 26; Spivak 1988), their aim was to make room for difference. This included taking into account economic, political, and social differences between any women as within the subject position of "migrant women": being from different "migrant" generations, being confronted more or less with racism, being of European or non-European origin, being hetero or homosexual. Recognizing the complexity of power relations and one's own entanglements within them (Gutiérrez Rodríguez 1997; Wiese 1997; Yurtsever-Kneer 2004) was to keep "migrant women" a subject position open for reappropriation.

Secondly, contextualizing and deconstructing the category "women" was to render it "a site of permanent political contest" (Butler 1995a, 41), thus making room for strategic temporal alliances among different individuals and groups on selectively defined topics. "Women" was to be understood as a contested category comprised of a social category reproducing the intersection of racism, capitalism, and sexism; a political moment of collective organization and a geographical and political standpoint from which to reflect one's positionality, privileges, and entanglements. Differences and similarities should neither be made invisible nor should they be understood as obstacles but as products of exploitation and oppression and as cultural constructs. Different affections of exclusion mechanisms had to be recognized. And the reproduction of racist stigmatizations had to be prevented by any means (*FeMigra* 1994; GIS et al. 1993; Gutiérrez Rodríguez 1993; Wiese 1997).

Despite their negative experiences especially within the German Left and women's movement, *FeMigra* adhered to the possibilities of forming an antiracist movement. In the knowledge that particular interests might not cooperate but conflict, they called for a joint resistance of "migrant," Black, Jewish, and even white women and men against racist repressions (*Teile der FeMigra* 1992). Prerequisites for such a movement were white wo/men questioning their privileges, and sharing power and resources with "migrant" and Black wo/men respectively giving up part of their power and resources. In order to build such a movement, *FeMigra* actively engaged in different forums, such as the group of international students and the foreigners' department of the Student Union at the Goethe-University Frankfurt/Main, and organized a joint network against racism of migrants, Black, Afro-German, Jewish, and refugee men and women (Apostolidou 1994; Gutiérrez Rodríguez 1993; Wiese 1997).

To summarize, *FeMigra* strategically took and occupied the subject position "migrant women" by means of iteration and appropriated it for a political purpose for which it was not explicitly devised (Butler 1995b, 128, 134–35). While "migrant women" had not been a legitimate subject position but an excluded one, *FeMigra* was able to change the meaning of "migrant women." They did so by simultaneously articulating their experiences as "other women" that are excluded from mainstream feminist politics *and* contesting the category *women* in order to include their different experiences. Yet the difficulty remained: in order to speak of racism and sexism, exactly those attributions that were to be deconstructed had to be resignified first. Every resignification of the position of "migrant women" established, however temporarily, a certain fixed meaning to it again, excluding new forms of signification.[6] Thus, they were "always at risk of being resubordinated through the discourses naming and politicizing them" (Brown 396). In short, *FeMigra's* strategies can be summarized as "the constant tightrope walk from one place to the other and the permanent redefinition within the political scene" (*FeMigra* 1994, 61; my translation).

Kanak Attak: This Song is Ours

"[T]here are a number of competing stories and myths around the origins of Kanak Attak" (Heidenreich and Vukadinović 2008, 133), but it was possibly founded in 1997 by mostly West German antiracist, "migrant" or leftist activists (Karakayalı and Spenkoch,1999; Seibert and Glasenapp 2001). According to Nanna Heidenreich and Vojin Saša Vucadinović, two *Kanak Attak* activists, "Kanak Attak is neither an organization nor a political party; it is not even a fixed group" (Heidenreich and Vukadinović 2008, 200, 134; cf. ibid. for a more detailed description of *Kanak Attak's* development).

While *FeMigra's* starting point was the felt need to represent themselves as "migrant women" since until then they did not exist as agentic subjects within German society, *Kanak Attak* resulted out of the analysis of a failure of antiracist politics in Germany in the aftermath of German reunification. The hopes they had for a change of government after a continuous sixteen-year-long conservative government were soon disappointed. For *Kanak Attak*, the migration policy of the Social Democratic and Green coalition still proved to be racist and guided by utility criteria to select only economically, culturally, and politically useful "migrants" (*Kanak Attak* 1998a; Karakayalı and Spenkoch 1999; Seibert and Glasenapp 2001). While *Kanak Attak* detected continuity in racist power relations, it also criticized large parts of the "migrant" and antiracist movement for its conception of racism as homogeneous and unchangeable and the resulting failure to effectively counter racism.

According to *Kanak Attak*'s analysis, antiracist politics in the 1990s was often restricted to consciousness raising and unconnected to other sociopolitical protest such as workers' or students' strikes. Moreover, large parts of the "migrant" and antiracist movements only articulated themselves within the assigned spaces and discourses. This was reflected in what *Kanak Attak* called the "anti-racist division of labor." Instead of questioning the racist stratification into different status groups such as foreigners, refugees, asylum seekers, and others by connecting their claims such as the abolition of residence requirements with the general lack of "migrants'" mobility, the antiracist and "migrant" movements were split into exactly these status groups and their special needs (Bojadžijev 2001; Diefenbach and Grimm 2001; Goethe and Günther 1999; *Kanak Attak* 1998a; Karakayalı and Spenkoch 1999; Seibert and Glasenapp 2001).

Linked to this critique of "migrant" and antiracist politics was *Kanak Attak*'s attempt to foil identities:

> Kanak Attak is a self-chosen union of different people across the borders of assigned, quasi inherited "identities." Kanak Attak does not enquire about passports or heritage but opposes the enquiry after passport or heritage. Attacking the Kanakisation of certain groups of people through racist attributions with all its social, legal, and political consequences is our lowest common denominator. Kanak Attak is antinationalist, antiracist, and rejects any form of identity politics that result, for example, from ethnological attributions. (*Kanak Attak* 1998a; my translation; cf. also *Kanak Attak* 1998b)

In contrast to the strategic essentialism practiced by *FeMigra*, the *Kanak Attak* network operated with a queer attitude expressed in their motto "what is right has to be negotiated and decided in each situation" (Heidenreich and Vukadinović 2008, 149; *Kanak Attak* 1998a). *Kanak Attak* criticized the identitarian policies of "migrants" that articulate themselves only within the categories imposed on "migrants" by mainstream society. Yet, at the same time, they recognized the dilemma that agency for "migrants" was and is limited due to socio-material realities and societal hierarchies, whereas the retreat into an ethnic community may offer safety within a racist regime. Thus, *Kanak Attak* refused the denunciation of "migrants'" self-empowerment as merely identity politics because no tactics are ever completely identitarian and there is never one right political strategy (Bojadžijev 2001; Ayata 1999; Goethe and Günther 1999; *Kanak Attak* 1998a; Karakayalı and Spenkoch 1999; Seibert and Glasenapp 2001).

By investing in the subject position of "Kanake" (Kanaka), a term otherwise used as a racist address for "migrants" and mainly so-called guest workers, *Kanak Attak* took the resignification even farther than *FeMigra*. The subject position of "Kanake" first of all appeared in the name of the network—*Kanak Attak*—referring to a gesture of reappropriation shared by other "migrant" movements or naming practices that originated in the 1990s such as Kanak Hip Hip, Kanaster, etc. In conjunction with "Attak" it is to suggest "an in-your-face agitprop of attitude, which refuses to act within a discursive frame defined by the mainstream and its apologetic rhetoric" (Heidenreich and Vukadinović 2008,152, note 1).[7]

Since the subject position "Kanake" was a question of attitude and not of heritage or papers, it could include nonmigrants or ethnic Germans. It thus opened up space for a subject position that until then was neither politically relevant nor visible while, at the same time, constantly pointing to society's racism that cannot be overcome with better concepts. Moreover, resignifying the term *Kanake* included the attempt to overcome the aforementioned split in antiracist politics between different status groups of "migrants," thereby refusing to reproduce the separation into useful or useless groups of "migrants" carried out by government "migrant" policy (Goethe and Günther 1999; Karakayalı and Spenkoch 1999). Yet the subject position "Kanake" remained queered. It was never understood as a universal political position for any "migrant" existence (Bojadžijev 2001) but as a certain attitude, "a kind of copycat franchising through self-entitlement, simply by metaphorically signing the manifesto" (Heidenreich and Vukadinović 2008, 133–34), which served as a common promise despite differences with regard to political content (Seibert and Glasenapp 2001). And it served as a strategy to reject a collective identity by employing it as a linguistic but acting subject (*Kanak Attak* 1998a).

"This song is ours" was one of the slogans *Kanak Attak* frequently used to reinforce this acting subject, which possibly relates to a quote by Karl Marx that "the petrified social conditions could be forced to dance by singing to them their own melody" (Marx 1976, 381; my translation).[8] Singing the petrified social conditions' own melody meant rewriting German history from the perspective of "migrants" as history of migration and of racism but also of resistance against racism. This was done—among others—by staging the OPEL PITBULL AUTOPUT—Kanak History Revue.[9] The performance took place within the context of the first major public appearance of *Kanak Attak*. The event *Dieser Song gehört uns* (This Song Is Ours)[10] happened on April 13, 2001, at the theatre Berliner Volksbühne and included the release of a CD, "film screenings, panel discussions, and DJ sets" (Heidenreich and Vukadinović 2008,131).

The one-hour-long Kanak History Revue drew the bow of Germany's migration and racism history from the 1960s to the early 1990s, working with a mixture of cinematic and photographic archive records and personal accounts of histories of migration, racism, and resistance.[11] The revue's ongoing undulation between facts about the working and living conditions of "migrants" in Germany, for instance, the recruitment of so-called guest workers, personal accounts of racism in Germany, citations of government politics, and the celebration of "migrants'" resistance such as the numerous strikes organized by "migrant" workers revealed the continuity of German racist migration policy. Simultaneously, it pointed to how the migration regime is to no avail by defining resistance as an everyday practice that was there even before government regulations. The past is thus retrieved and reinscribed "not as a static fetishized phase to be literally reproduced, but as fragmented sets of narrated memories and experiences on the basis of which to mobilize" (Shohat 1992,109).

The aim of the revue, as much as of *Kanak Attak*'s other actions,[12] was to achieve the so-called "Kanak-Attak-Aha-Effekt" (Seibert and Glasenapp 2001) or "Kanak-Aha-Effekt" (Diefenbach and Grimm 2001). This was meant not to view the state as the sole producer of racism but instead to analyze racism as a societal condition, bound in numerous intersecting power relations. Thus, antiracism always needs to be situated in the context of social struggles in general. This was done in the revue by depicting "migrants'" resistance against racism as composed of various social struggles such as against housing or working conditions. Covering more than thirty years of German migration and racism history, the revue reflected how, just as racism is constantly changing, intensifying, or abating, so is resistance, and neither can be told as a linear history of failure or success.

Just as exemplified within the revue, *Kanak Attak* attempted to reject identity attributions in three ways: first of all, by depicting "migrant" and antiracist resistance not as a question of identity but as an everyday struggle and an attitude as Kanaka. Secondly, identity attributions were circumvented by twisting the everyday racist ascriptions that "migrants" have to face into a cliché about "the Germans." Thus, ethnic attributions were ironized. At the same time, *Kanak Attak* distanced itself from such ascriptions by working different languages into a kind of Esperanto slang, generally describing Germany either in Turkish as Almanya, or as the Federal Republic.[13] Thirdly, identity politics were overcome by discussing racism in a larger context of social conditions such as changing working conditions, or even the pension scheme.

Subjects that Matter? Nonidentitarian Strategies of Political Action Revisited

Against the negative images of "migrants" present in German society, both *FeMigra* and *Kanak Attak* tried to intervene into the hegemonic discourse by occupying and irritating categories. Yet, this was not done with the aim to construct a collective identity. Instead, the starting point of their resistance was a question of power: Who may—or can—speak for whom when, where, and how? And moreover, which subjects (not in the sense of an individual but as a political actor) are legitimate, or in Butler's words "intelligible" (1991, 55, 216)? Therefore, *FeMigra*'s and *Kanak Attak*'s activities can be conceptualized first of all as a politicization of processes of exclusion and inclusion between subjects that matter and those that do not.

In other words, the subject positions that *FeMigra* and *Kanak Attak* inhabited have to be understood as positions in a process of resignification within networks of power. To be able to grasp the power relations at work within any resignification process necessitates questioning the context of any however intended subversive positioning: "Who is represented by which use of categories, and who is excluded? Which kinds of political content are enabled by the usual employment of categories, and which are neglected or cut out?" (Butler 1997, 312). In short, do *FeMigra* and *Kanak Attak* succeed in overcoming the very exclusion of the "other" they criticize by means of recontextualization and resignification of the excluding categories (Butler 1995b, 128)?

As I have shown in the course of my essay, both actors engaged in the paradoxical activity of challenging exactly those categories that constitute them by means of relocating norms through iteration, "which brings into being or enacts that which it names, and so marks the constitutive or productive power of discourse" (Butler 1995b, 134): *FeMigra* relocated the subject position of "migrant women" to deconstruct feminism while, at the same time, reinventing an antiracist feminism. Occupying an attitude as Kanakas and retelling German history as a history of migration, racism, and Kanakas' everyday resistance strategies, *Kanak Attak* made nonsense of any attempt to regulate migration.

Yet, it has as well become apparent that any nonidentitarian moment is always on the brink of the very exclusionary effects of any identity politics. Occupying a however strategic or queered subject position as a strategy of resistance always bears the risk of this position not staying an open site of political contest but becoming an established and monopolized position. Because each time the attributions of "female migrants" and "Kanakas" are grabbed and resignified, this occupation contains another closing. Each appropriation of a category (temporarily) excludes those that do not partake. As an (unintended) effect of their employment of demanding theories in their analysis of German racism, access to *FeMigra*'s and *Kanak Attak*'s politics was limited to those "female migrants" and "Kanakas" with a certain intellectual education. But precisely at the paradoxical closures that are inherent in the spaces opened up by *FeMigra*'s and *Kanak Attak*'s politics, discourses are renewed, enabling yet other strategies of political action.

Nowadays, any pro-"migrant" resistance has to operate in the area of tension between a rigid normativity that still defines "migrants" (and other minorities) as the "other" and a flexible normalization that enables a societal integration if the "other" turns usable or consumable (Engel 2001, 2005). Within this area of tension, *Kanak Attak*'s and *FeMigra*'s strategies discussed here did at the same time overcome and reproduce the very exclusion of the "other." While they succeeded in a relocation especially of the term and position of "migrants," this position is still seldom one of agentic power. Although *FeMigra*'s and *Kanak Attak*'s analysis of and resistance against the racism inherent in German society has at some points been taken up, "Afro-Germans" and "migrants" still remain largely absent in German academia and society. What remains is the insight that exactly this moment of failure or fracture at the same time contains a promise: nonidentitarian strategies of political action might only exist for a moment but point to the possibility of collective action not in the name of a collective but in the knowledge of the excluded. And each renewed effect of exclusion, each identitarian closure also contains another opening for alternative subject positions and strategies of action.

Acknowledgments

I would like to thank Encarnación Gutiérrez Rodríguez, Dana Jirouš, Inga Luther, Helma Lutz, Laura Mestre Vives, Alexander Nöhring, Birgit Sauer, and Imogen Tyler for their helpful comments on earlier versions of the article.

Notes

1. Using the term *migrants* is a paradoxical activity: while I want to deconstruct the exclusionary mechanisms and attributions that (re)produce "migrants," I still (need to) use the terms to name exactly those that are excluded as "migrants."

Thus, I place "migrants" in quotation marks to show that the term is "under contest, up for grabs . . . to denaturalize the terms, to designate these signs as sites of political debate" (Butler 1995a, 54).

2. Migrants have self-organized since the beginnings of postwar migration but due to their systematic exclusion from political participation opportunities, most self-organizations focused on exile politics. In the 1960s and 1970s, work migrants protested against the racist working and living conditions in Germany, organizing (wildcat) strikes and demonstrations (Bojadžijev 2008; *FeMigra* 1994, 51; Karakayalı 2005; Kaynar and Suda 2002, 168; Mestre Vives 2006, 273).

3. Under the slogan "the boat is full," images of an alleged flood of asylum seekers and refugees and their misuse of German asylum law dominated the political and media debate in the 1990s. The anti-asylum campaign of the Kohl government was accompanied by daily right-wing terror that was supported by large parts of the German population and elites. The pogroms of Hoyerswerda (1991), Rostock-Lichtenhagen (1992), Mölln (1992), and Solingen (1993) have become synonyms for the racist horrors of reunified Germany. The government used the racist violence as a proof of the people's frustration with the "hybridization" of their culture and identity due to immigration and accepted the death of "migrants" for a public production of the will of the people to abolish the basic right of asylum.

4. Expert interview with Selçuk Yurtsever-Kneer, member of *FeMigra*, Dec. 21, 2010; expert interview with Encarnación Gutiérrez Rodríguez, member of *FeMigra*, Dec. 22, 2010.

5. As a white woman working in German academia, I myself cannot evade this objectivization for good. Though in my research I am trying to deconstruct exactly these objectivization processes, which produce certain people as the "other," I am still part of these processes. Thus, I constantly try to self-reflect my own positioning and make this reflection part of my work. What is most important is that such a reflection is not possible without relation to People of Color's critique of a white hegemonial setting (cf. Piesche 2009 [2005], 16).

6. Expert interview with Laura Mestre Vives, member of *FeMigra* on Oct. 14, 2010.

7. *Kanak Attak* activists Nanna Heidenreich and Vojin Saša Vucadinović tell the story of a *Kanak Attak* event, where "the audience actually discussed amongst themselves (with a great deal of bewilderment but surprisingly diplomatically) who or what Kanake is or should be: boys from the hood (who made up a large part of the audience, excited about the *Kanak Attak* idea), or postcolonial dykes and theory geeks (who had organised the evening)—or both or something else?" (Heidenreich and Vukadinović 2008, 146).

8. I owe gratitude to Dennis P. B. Luh for this analogy.

9. http://www.kanak-attak.de/ka/archiv/vb01/opa.htm. Accessed Oct. 11, 2010.

10. http://www.kanak-attak.de/ka/archiv/vb01/prog.htm. Accessed Oct. 11, 2010.

11. For a more detailed description of the revue cf. Heidenreich and Vucadinović 2008: 142–45. A five-part video recording of the revue can be viewed at http://www.kanak-attak.de/ka/media_video.shtml. Accessed Nov. 16, 2010.

12. *Kanak Attak* staged a number of other events (cf. http://www.kanak-attak. de/ka/archiv.html. Accessed Nov. 16, 2010), organized discussions, published numerous articles (cf. f.ex. http://www.kanak-attak.de/ka/text.html Accessed Nov. 16, 2010) and co-organized a larger campaign on the legalization of migrants (cf. http://www. rechtauflegalisierung.de Accessed Nov. 16, 2010).

13. Referring to West Germany as the Federal Republic was a Left language practice creating an analogy to the German Democratic Republic, thus distancing itself from the official language referring to West Germany only as Germany.

Works Cited

Anonymous. 2009. *Frauen nehmen sich die Stadt. Frauenreferat feiert 20-jähriges Jubiläum am 2. Oktober*. http://intranet.stadt-frankfurt.de/sixcms/detail.php?id=33853. Accessed June 25, 2009.

Apostolidou, Natascha. 1980. "Für die Frauenbewegung auch wieder nur 'Arbeitsobjekte'?" *Informationsdienst zur Ausländerarbeit* 2: 143–46.

———. 1994. "Quotierung für Migrantinnen." In *Gender Killer. Texte zu Feminismus und Politik*, edited by Cornelia Eichhorn and Sabine Grimm. Berlin: Edition ID-Archiv.

Ayata, Imran. 1999. "Heute die Gesichter, morgen die Ärsche." *Spex* 11. http://www.kanak-attak.de/ka/archiv/passagiere/presse/spex_11_99.htm. Accessed February 12, 2011.

Bojadžijev, Manuela. 2008. *Die windige Internationale. Rassismus und Kämpfe der Migration*. Münster: Westfälisches Dampfboot.

———, et al. 2001. "Legalisierung statt Rasterfahndung." *Jungle World Supplement Subtropen* 46. http://jungle-world.com/artikel/2001/45/24943.html. Accessed August 12, 2010.

Brown, Wendy. 1993. "Wounded Attachments." *Political Theory* 21 (3): 390–410.

Butler, Judith. 1991. *Das Unbehagen der Geschlechter*. Frankfurt/Main: Suhrkamp.

———. 1995a. "Contingent Foundations." In *Feminist Contentions. A Philosophical Exchange*, edited by Seyla Benhabib et al., New York and London: Routledge.

———. 1995b. "For a Careful Reading." In *Feminist Contentions. A Philosophical Exchange*, edited by Seyla Benhabib et al. New York and London: Routledge.

———. 1997. *Körper von Gewicht. Die diskursiven Grenzen von Geschlecht*. Frankfurt/Main: Suhrkamp.

Camlikbeli, Deniz. 1984. "Deutsche Frauen—türkische Frauen." *Informationsdienst zur Ausländerarbeit* 1: 19.

Castro Varela, María do Mar, and Nikita Dhawan. 2005. *Postkoloniale Theorie: Eine Einführung*. Bielefeld: transcript.

Diefenbach, Katja, and Sabine Grimm. 2001. "Der Kanak-Aha-Effekt." *Jungle World* 17. http://jungle-world.com/artikel/2001/16/25921.html. Accessed April 4, 2012.

Engel, Antke. 2001. "Die VerUneindeutigung der Geschlechter—eine queere Strategie zur Veränderung gesellschaftlicher Machtverhältnisse?" In *Jenseits der Geschlechtergrenzen. Sexualitäten, Identitäten, und Körper in Perspektiven von Queer Studies*, edited by Ulf Heidel et al. Hamburg: MännerschwarmSkript Verlag.

———. 2005. "Entschiedene Interventionen in der Unentscheidbarkeit. Von queerer Identitätskritik zur VerUneindeutigung als Methode." In *Forschungsfeld Politik*, edited by Cilja Harders et al. Wiesbaden: VS Verlag für Sozialwissenschaften.

FeMigra. 1992. "Offener Brief an den Magistrat und an das Frauendezernat der Stadt Frankfurt, an Migrantinnen- und Frauenprojekte." *diyalog* 2: 8–13.

———. 1994. "Wir, die Seiltänzerinnen. Politische Strategien von Migrantinnen gegen Ethnisierung und Assimilation." In *Gender Killer. Texte zu Feminismus und Politik*, edited by Cornelia Eichhorn and Sabine Grimm. Berlin: Edition ID-Archiv.

GIS (Gruppe internationaler StudentInnen) im Autonomen Ausländerinnen Referat/ KOZ-Kollektiv. 1993. "Sicher ist nicht sicher, daß Sicherheit sicher ist." In *Femigra-Texte*, edited by *FeMigra*. Frankfurt/Main.

Goethe, Tina, and Stephan Günther. 1999. "Am Ende von Dialog- und Multikultur. Gespräch mit Imran Ayata, Manuela Bojadžijev, und Serhat Karakayalı von der Gruppe Kanak Attak." *iz3w* 240. https://www.iz3w.org/zeitschrift/ausgaben/240_kulturalisierung/iz3w%20attak. Accessed February 12, 2011.

Gültekin, Neval. 1985. "Eine schweigende Minderheit meldet sich zu Wort." In *Sind wir uns denn so fremd? Ausländische und deutsche Frauen im Gespräch*, edited by Arbeitsgruppe Frauenkongreß. Berlin: sub rosa.

Gutiérrez Rodríguez, Encarnación. 1993. "Frauenpolitik im Kleide der Herrschaft." *Perspektiven* 2: 13–15.

———. 1997. "Eine Frau ist eine Frau ist eine . . . Migrantinnen in der deutschen Frauenbewegung." *Blätter des iz3w* 219: 26–28.

———. 2001. "Widerstand in der différance. Repräsentation, Vereinnahmung, und Gegenstrategien von MigrantInnen und Schwarzen Deutschen." *iz3w* 253: 22–23.

———. 2003. "Repräsentation, Subalternität, und postkoloniale Kritik." In *Spricht die Subalterne deutsch? Migration und postkoloniale Kritik*, edited by Hito Steyerl and Encarnación Gutiérrez Rodríguez. Münster: Unrast.

Heidenreich, Nanna, and Vojin Saša Vukadinović. 2008. "In Your Face: Activism, Agit-Prop, and the Autonomy of Migration; The Case of Kanak Attak." In *After the Avantgarde: Contemporary German and Austrian Experimental Film*, edited by Randall Halle and Reinhild Steingröver. Rochester: Camden House.

Hügel, Ika et al., eds. 1993. *Entfernte Verbindungen. Rassismus, Antisemitismus, Klassenunterdrückung*. Berlin: Orlanda.

Kanak Attak. 1998a. *KANAK ATTAK UND BASTA!* http://www.kanak-attak.de/ka/down/pdf/manifest_d.pdf. Accessed August 8, 2007.

———. 1998b. *KANAK ATTAK UND BASTA!* http://www.kanak-attak.de/ka/down/pdf/manifest_e.pdf. Accessed August 8, 2007.

Karakayalı, Serhat. 2005. "Lotta Continua in Frankfurt, Türken-Terror in Köln. Migrantische Kämpfe in der Geschichte der Bundesrepublik." *trend onlinezeitung* 09/05. http://www.trend.infopartisan.net/trd0905/t100905.html. Accessed August 17, 2011.

———, and Uli Spenkoch. 1999. "Dieser Song gehört uns! Interview mit Imran Ayata, Laura Mestre Vives, und Vanessa Barth von Kanak Attak." *diskus— Frankfurter StudentInnen Zeitschrift* 1/99. www.copyriot.com/diskus/1_99/3.htm. Accessed April 28, 2008.

Kaynar, Erdal, and Kimiko Suda. 2002. "Aspekte migrantischer Selbstorganisation in Deutschland." In *Landschaften der Tat. Vermessung, Transformationen und Ambivalenzen des Antirassismus in Europa*, edited by Ljubomir Bratić. St. Pölten: sozaktiv.

Marx, Karl. 1976. "Zur Kritik der Hegelschen Rechtsphilosophie." In *Werke, Band 1*, ed. Karl Marx and Friedrich Engels. Berlin/DDR: Dietz Verlag.

Mestre Vives, Laura. 2006. "Kultur als Zugang und Vermittler von politischer Bildung? Über die problematische Trennung von Kultur und Politik." In *Politische Bildung in der Einwanderungsgesellschaft. Zugänge—Konzepte—Erfahrungen*, edited by Heidi Behrens and Jan Motte. Schwalbach: Wochenschau.

Migrantinnengruppe—FFM. 1992. "Brief an Afrodeutsche/Schwarze Frauen—Teilnehmerinnen des Schwarzen-Frauen-Studienkongreß." In *FeMigra-Texte*, edited by *FeMigra*. Frankfurt/Main.

Oguntoye, Katharina et al., ed. 1986. *Farbe bekennen. Afrodeutsche Frauen auf den Spuren ihrer Geschichte*. Berlin: Orlanda.

Piesche, Peggy. 2009 [2005]. "Das Ding mit dem Subjekt, oder: Wem gehört die Kritische Weißseinsforschung?" In *Mythen, Masken, und Subjekte. Kritische Weißseinsforschung in Deutschland*, edited by Maureen Maisha Eggers et al. Münster: Unrast.

Seibert, Thomas, and Martin Glasenapp. 2001. "Der Kanak-Attak-Aha-Effekt. Die Überwindung der antirassistischen Arbeitsteilung—ein Gespräch mit Menschen von Kanak Attak." *ak—analyse & kritik. Zeitung für linke Debatte und Praxis* 451: 14.

Shohat, Ella. 1992. "Notes on the 'Post-Colonial.'" *Social Text* 31/32: 99–113.

Spivak, Gayatri Chakravorty. 1988. "Can the Subaltern Speak?" In *Marxism and the Interpretation of Culture*, edited by Cary Nelson and Lawrence Gossberg. Urbana: University of Illinois Press.

———. 1993. "In a Word: Interview." In *Outside in the Teaching Machine*, edited by Gayatri C. Spivak. London: Routledge.

Teile der FeMigra. 1992. "Sexismus und Rassismus." In *FeMigra-Texte*, edited by *FeMigra* Frankfurt/Main.

The Combahee River Collective. 1982 [1972]. "A Black Feminist Statement." In *All the Women Are White, All the Blacks Are Men, But Some of Us Are Brave: Black Women's Studies*, edited by Gloria T. Hull et al. Old Westbury, NY: The Feminist Press.

Wiese, Dorothee. 1997. "Selbstorganisation statt StellvertreterInnenpolitik. Interview mit Encarnación Gutiérrez Rodríguez von FEMIGRA." *Hamburger Frauenzeitung* 53: 44–46 (FFBIZ-Archiv, D, 200).

Yurtsever-Kneer, Selçuk. 2004. *Strategien feministischer Migrantinnenpolitik*. trend onlinezeitung 01/04 http://www.trend.infopartisan.net/trd0104/t110104.html. Accessed January 08, 2008.

———. 2002. "Arbeit im Sozialbereich, Prämissen. Vortrag." *Kofra. Zeitschrift für Feminismus und Arbeit* 20 (98): 4–5.

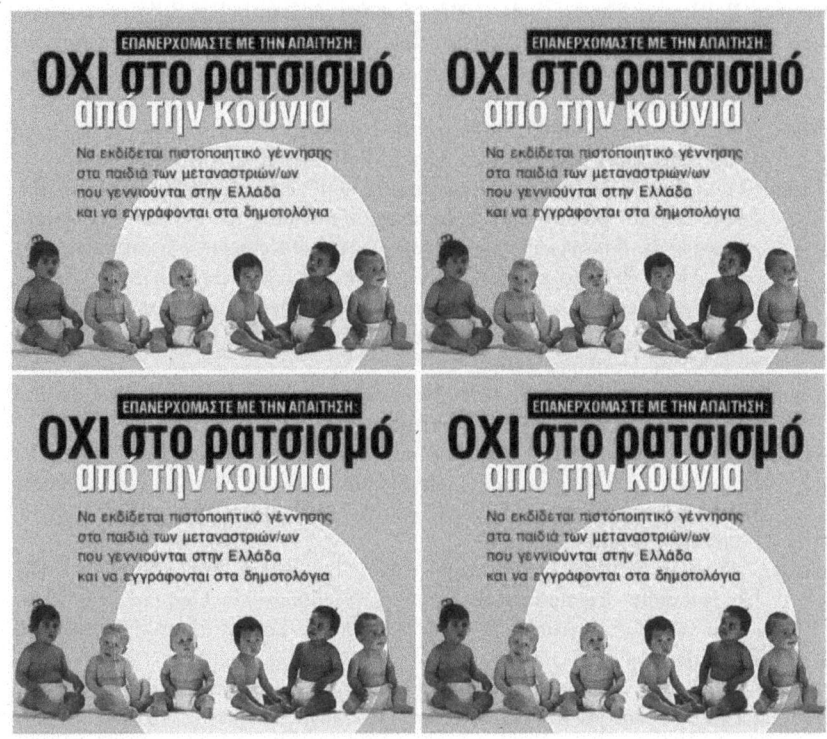

Figure 11.1. *No to Racism from the Baby's Cot*, 2005 campaign. Collage by Alexandra Zavos

11

Gender and the Politics of Anti-Racist and Immigrant Protest in Greece

Alexandra Zavos

Through a case study of three examples of protest—a Greek antiracist pamphlet, a campaign by migrant mothers for citizenship rights for their children, and a mass hunger strike by migrants demanding "papers"—I will consider how the intersecting dynamics of gender and "race" shape the political relationship between migrant and Greek activists in the antiracist movement in Athens. I am interested in teasing out the nuances of immigrant protest and analyzing the ways in which such protests depart from, impact, and resignify established cultural and political norms. For migrants' political subjectification, the discourse of gender—and the performativity it affords, refracted through the discourses of nation, "race," and culture—becomes an important site of struggle.

In my work as activist and social researcher, I have engaged with the political relationship between migrants and Greeks in the antiracist movement in Athens, taking a feminist approach that understands gender as a social relation of power fundamentally articulated to and implicated in all other relations of difference and inequality, including class, ethnicity, and "race." The significance of attending to gender lies not only in the analysis of the specific position of migrant women in Greece, but, even more importantly, in tracing how gender as a discursive regime encodes culturally and historically situated normative representations of masculinity and femininity to naturalize and order asymmetrical relations of power in specific sociopolitical and cultural contexts.

As many scholars have argued, representations of migrants in Europe are frequently stigmatizing and racializing (Silverstein 2005). Western imaginaries of national and cultural identity and difference, refracted in the figure of the "migrant woman" as doubly "other," articulate gender and particular notions of agency and entitlement. Importantly, the borders erected between Europe and its "others," in this case migrants, are not only spatial and territorial but also temporal; they establish the legitimacy of European dominance in terms of the quality of historical time, through ideas of progress, modernity, development. Europe's "others" are not only territorially located outside; they are also temporally located, as they are assumed to inhabit a less "advanced" historical time. The enforcement of the border entails violence that is not only material but also epistemic in the sense that migrant populations are often assumed to inhabit a premodern, backward, tribal, theo- or autocratic historical time. They are considered as less than full human beings, less than legitimate bearers of rights, less than sovereign subjects (Lewis 2006). This racialized politics of difference, which is inflected in particular ways through gender, legitimates European border controls, and is reproduced at numerous points including within migrant advocacy, activist, and antiracist movements (Lentin 2004).

In a previous study of antiracism in Greece, I have argued that the historically and culturally conditioned, yet disavowed, intersecting dynamics of gender and "race" inevitably shape the political relationship between migrant and Greek activists in the (leftist) antiracist movement (Zavos 2010a). While the movement contributed significantly to the politicization of migration and the engagement of public opinion and politicians with the adverse conditions that the majority of migrants experience in Greece, this politicization was established in terms that largely prevented migrants themselves, and most notably migrant women, from equal participation in oppositional political practices. Sexist and racialized borders were redrawn within the movement, reproducing gendered and ethnocentric hierarchies that placed migrants in feminized, subordinate, and dependent positions vis-à-vis Greek male, political patronage. Expanding on this argument in this chapter, I consider how migrants are both framed by but also use (and thereby also displace) or even depart from available discourses and strategies of struggle producing a multiplicity of significations and practices that disturb and extend culturally sanctioned political identities.

In the first section, I discuss representations of women migrants in antiracist discourse that constructs hierarchically ordered essentialized (political) identities through narratives that invoke stereotypes of the (female and feminized) migrant as victim. In the second section, I analyze the event of the first public demonstration organized by migrant women campaigning for the rights of children born in Greece as an example of a practice of citizenship that engenders a new politics of belonging and challenges existing (ethnocentric, racialized, masculinist) hierarchies and entitlements. In the final section, I consider the hunger strike of three hundred migrants struggling for papers and legal rights as an example of a biopolitical struggle that produces a condition of alienness that allows for the emergence of a politics of nonidentity.

Case 1: The Voiceless Victims of Globalization: Antiracist Solidarity as a Politics of Representation

> Migrant women constitute the most oppressed category of our society. They are paid less, they are hired with more difficulty and fired more easily, they are dependent not only on their employer, but on their husband or father as well—who usually secure their residence permit. . . . Foreign women are usually tragically isolated and excluded since they are subjected not only to the racism and the prejudices of the country they live, but also the backward (anachronistic) mores and the conservatism of their country of origin. . . . In ethnocentric, classist, and patriarchal societies the migrant woman suffers both from racism and exploitation as well as sexism.
>
> The slave trade of foreign women constitutes the most brutal form of social barbarism . . . the slave trade of foreign women is certainly directed by Greek-spirited policemen and foreign or native criminals, but it exists and proliferates because thousands of our fellow Greek countrymen, under all appearances reputable citizens and respectable family men, demonstrate an excess of brutality and exhibit an equivalent amount of barbarism. (Antiracist pamphlet *Solidarity to Migrants* 2004; my translation)

Antiracist pamphlets are part of larger antiracist campaigns or events, such as the Annual Antiracist Festival in Athens, staged by different leftist and antiauthoritarian groups. These texts capture the scope of as well as significant trends and shifts in the antiracist movement's discourses on migration and activism. While pamphlets showcase different groups', often competing, political and ideological profiles within the antiracist movement, what stands out is the remarkable continuity and overlap of arguments regarding the position and problems of migrants in Greece. The pamphlet I discuss here is among the few referring exclusively to migrant women, and it comes from a key leftist antiracist group, anonymized as "Support Action," whose work has impacted the direction of the whole antiracist movement in Greece.

Antiracism emerged in the Greek political context in the late 1980s, echoing wider European debates on ethnic minority rights, through the efforts of different strands of the Left and, to this day, bears the marks of leftist discourses and practices. In the wake of the fall of the Berlin Wall in 1989, which precipitated the movement of large numbers of Eastern European and Balkan migrants toward Greece (and other Southern and Northern European countries), leftist antiracism developed mainly into a solidarity movement concerned with fighting for migrants' legalization and the recognition of their social and political rights (Glarnetajis 2001).

The Greek antiracist movement exhibits an anticapitalist and workerist orientation, aiming its interventions toward the central and public political stage as well as the collectivization of the movement through the organization of large public events (such as demonstrations, protest marches, press conferences, as well as an annual antiracist festival, which showcases a variety of groups and organizations active in the movement). Migrants in antiracist discourse are mainly interpellated as exploited workers and victims of neoliberal capitalism, whose rights need to be defended and fought for by the antiracist solidarity movement; a call that confers on antiracism the prerogative of practicing a politics of representation vis-à-vis migrants. As I have suggested, this often involves silencing those populations whom the movement is ostensibly fighting for.

The Greek Migration and Antiracist Context

In the two decades since the fall of the Berlin Wall in 1989, Greece has seen a rise of incoming migration. Today, Greece is considered one of the main entry points of migration to Europe. The EU calculates that 90 percent of the people who enter Europe illegally are apprehended at the Greek borders,[1] catapulting Greece from the geographical margins to one of the geopolitical focal points of the European border and migration regime (Geddes and Lazarou 2008). Currently, more than 10 percent of the country's population are migrants, with long-term, temporary, or illegal status. There have been different waves of migration: in the decade following 1989, migration to Greece involved mostly people from Eastern European countries and the Balkans (particularly Albania and Bulgaria). Since the 2000s, migration from African, Middle Eastern, and Asian countries has predominated, including a large number of asylum seekers from Afghanistan (Triandafyllidou and Maroukis 2010). Migration in Greece has mainly been illegal, not only because of Greece's so-called porous borders, but also, importantly, because of the lack of a comprehensive migration policy; a lack that was both unintended—it is broadly claimed that "Greece was unprepared to deal with the large influx of migration"—and cultivated, to the extent that illegal migration fed into and sustained, if not enlarged, the country's extensive informal economy. Migration was legitimized in public discourse and in popular opinion on the basis of the economic advantages it offered the Greek economy, providing cheap and basically uninsured labor. Restrictive migration policies, as elsewhere in Europe, fixed migrants in conditions of precarity and vulnerability.[2] Migrants were mainly occupied in the agricultural, construction, and domestic labor sectors. Illegal migration, although exploited by the media, was not seriously targeted and controlled by government policy since it fed directly into the large informal sector of the Greek economy (Pavlou 2007).

Measures to regularize the presence of migrants in the country included three ad hoc legalization procedures (in 1998, 2001, 2006), following what has been termed a "Southern European" migration model applied in Italy, Spain, and Portugal as well (Baldwin-Edwards 2004). Since 2010, a new Code of Greek Nationality (Law 3838/2010) has been introduced to complement and regulate previous unsystematic arrangements. According to the new legislation, it will be possible for some, but not all, categories of migrants to be granted citizenship rights. Emphasis is placed on nationalizing and integrating second-generation migrants, which include children of migrant parents, born in Greece or having attended Greek education for a number of years. This development has been greeted as, in part, a victory of the antiracist solidarity movement, especially of the campaigns staged by migrant and Greek antiracist groups who demanded equal rights for children born in Greece.

Gender as Add-on and Moral Category in Antiracist Discourse on Migration

As I have argued in my analysis of antiracist discourse (Zavos 2010b), gender functions as a signifier of vulnerability and victimhood as well as of oppression and backwardness, thereby affording the antiracist solidarity movement an ethical and political prerogative in its interventions on behalf of migrants. Located exclusively in references to the social category "women migrants," gender in antiracist narratives is rendered as a (specifically) female attribute highlighted against the background of the universal subject of migration, who is invoked as genderless but by inference assumed to be masculine. Thus, gender appears as an add-on identity, rather than as constitutive category (such as class, or "race"). References to gender in antiracist literature are minimal and are restricted to the representational motif of women migrants' victimization. The plight of migrant women is not only linked to racism and exploitation they are subjected to in receiving countries, but also to traditional patriarchal social relations in their countries of origin from which they cannot escape. Migrant women are represented, tout court, as the most insecure, exploited, oppressed, vulnerable, and victimized social group, suffering both at the hands of their Greek employers, or pimps, as well as their own, conservative, and sexist menfolk, who keep them under control in conditions of dependency. References to their isolation and/or incarceration in the home, be it their employer's or their family's, serve to highlight migrant women's supposed inaccessibility and invisibility as social actors. Hence, migrant women can only become visible as victims, through their assumed weakness, and are, thus, firmly fixed into positions of fatalistic and inescapable subordination. In spite of emancipatory invocations, migrant women are infantilized and feminized as "passive" and apolitical subjects without agency against the background of an ideal national, paternal, and "active" political subjectivity.[3]

The fact that gender when present in antiracist discourse is invested with moral rather than political meaning is most clearly observed in accounts of trafficking and sexual exploitation of migrant women. In language that calls up moral outrage, denunciation, and incrimination, trafficking and female migrant prostitution are conflated as "slave trade" and represented not only as exploitative, abusive, and criminalized work but also as an ethical aberration (Anderson and Andrijasevic 2008). Descriptions of trafficked women as passive victims of male violence to be used, bought and sold at will, without any resistance or agency on their part, are normative in public antitrafficking discourse. Antiracist, feminist, and mainstream discourses appear to collude in representing migrant women as sex slaves rather than agentic subjects, thereby engendering them politically inoperative (Andrijasevic 2007). Gender signals either a lack (in the case of women) or an excess (in the case of men) of power. Power when understood as emerging not through social and political antagonisms and struggles but as a property of gendered bodies is more difficult for women migrants to contest. Relations of power are recast as moral qualities—the barbaric perversion of "bad" men. "Good" men, on the other hand, such as those to be found among the rank and file of antiracist activists, are not implicated in abuses of power. The effect of this disavowal, couched in terms of moral outrage, of complicity in the articulation of power relations and the gendered displacement of power from the political field, is a political elision: rendering migrant women as voiceless victims denies them political agency while, at the same time, secures the antiracist movement moral imperative to intervene and speak on their behalf.

Importantly, references to trafficking also signal a telling metonymic projection. In the place of the violated female body are positioned not only specific sexually abused women, but the countries from which they come. As feminist theorists have argued (Pettman 1996; Yuval-Davis 1997), gender is a fundamental social relation *and* code in the legitimation of nationalism as a natural expression of political sovereignty. Gender solidifies the imaginary construction of the nation-state as a self-evident, universal, and ahistorical form of societal organization, modeled on the heterosexual family unit. The inscription of the nation as a family articulates the performance of sexualized gender roles to the hypostatization of national identity and the safeguarding of national sovereignty. References in antiracist discourse to trafficked women's exploitation on the basis of their national identity, rather than their precarious legal status, illustrate the conflation of nation and family; if the women of a country are violated, it is assumed that the whole country is violated as well, as if women were the agents of a country's integrity and wholeness. In this sense, antiracist discourse, far from challenging nationalist assumptions, reproduces them. Through the representation of migrant women as passive, backward, and dominated subjects, gender functions as a signifier of migrants' "otherness" and legitimizes antiracist politics as a politics of representation; in other words, as a politics framed by the imaginary, and executed within the purview of the nation-state.

Case 2: "We are your children. We want our rights": Performing a Politics of Belonging

In late November 2005, the United African Women's Organization, a migrant women's activist group in Athens, launched the campaign "No to Racism from the Baby's cot," demanding papers and citizenship rights for children born in Greece to migrant parents. During the inaugural demonstration, African migrant children chanted: "Greek women and men, we are your children! We want our rights!" This slogan caused considerable unease among Greek antiracist demonstrators and the children were advised by Greek activists to adopt the politically correct slogan: "Equal rights to all children."

In this section I turn to migrant women's public performances. In contrast to prevailing representations of victimhood and backwardness, the complex and controversial positioning of migrant women in antiracist mobilizations points to the potential emergence of new political subjectivities and discourses that confound and subvert established hierarchies of the leftist antiracist movement and engender new practices of citizenship. Importantly, the presence of migrant women crosses several normalized and normative boundaries: the gendered inscription of the public domain, and of politics, as a masculine domain; the gendered order of discourse, where only masculinist, abstract, and universalizing narratives are "properly" political; and, finally, the racialized/nationalized culture of political engagement, where—if women do engage in public politics—it is mainly native (Greek) women. In the following incident, migrant women engage in a social poetics that strategically invokes common and culturally legible identity discourses to establish recognition and visibility with Greek audiences. They reiterate nationally salient cultural codes to establish claims of belonging for themselves and their children, and, at the same time, through this act, transgress the patrolled borders of the racially purged and culturally homogenized national political community. Identifying migrant women's agency in such acts of performative appropriation of available discourses and terms of address is important for recognizing the different ways in which they actively wield power and recast national and political imaginaries.

The Campaign "No to Racism from the Baby's Cot"

In the fall of 2005, a group of mainly African migrant women formed the United African Women's Organization to mobilize for migrant women's and children's rights. With the help and support of feminist, antiracist, and other migrant activist groups, they launched their first campaign, "No to racism from the baby's cot." The campaign was set off by a demonstration on December 3, 2005, starting in Omonoia Square, the commercial and trade center of Athens where a large number of migrants live and work.

The demonstration began with a small gathering of mainly black African migrant women, from different countries, and their children, singing, shouting slogans, and distributing leaflets demanding the legalization of children born in Greece to migrant parents and their right to obtain proper birth certificates and citizenship rights. The posters prepared for the occasion appropriated the theme of a well-known Benetton advertisement depicting a group of babies, black and white, to which the slogan "No to racism from the baby's cot" was added. The children had been instructed to sing traditional Greek Xmas carols with English verses adjusted for the occasion, in addition to the well-known tune of John Lennon's song "All we are saying is give peace a chance" with the lyrics "All we are asking is give *us* a chance." After an hour of singing and some public announcements, the protest march started with the children at the front singing the above-mentioned songs and shouting the slogan: "Greek women and men, we are your children. We want our rights." I followed the march on the side of the children, taking pictures. As we progressed, an older Greek male activist approached me and asked me to intervene and instruct the children to stop shouting that particular slogan on the grounds that "it is not only inaccurate, it is also inelegant." Rather, he insisted, they should shout the more politically sound slogan "Equal rights for all children."

Reiteration and Mimicry as Enactments of Citizenship

The "No to racism from the baby's cot" protest in 2005 presented a significant departure from antiracist protocol. Up until that moment, demonstrations for migrants' rights had been organized by Greek antiracist groups with migrants and their organizations in supporting roles. In contrast, this mobilization originated with migrant women in the first place, and was organized and orchestrated by them, independently of Greek activist leadership. The presence of mainly African women migrants and their children, and their leading position in the demonstration, presented a novel sight, since such occasions were usually saturated by the visibility of Greek activists and migrant men. Apart from the challenges of visibility and public presence it occasioned, the event raises several questions regarding forms of political mobilization of migrants: firstly, the possibility of the enactment of citizenship as the right to have rights by those who do not have rights; secondly, the subversive use of mimicry as a foundation of belonging; thirdly, the invocation of universality in the interpellation, and disciplining, of proper political subjects.

The issue of citizenship as practice, also referred to as citizenship from below, has been the topic of some debate both in feminist as well as in migration and postcolonial studies, and has been variously conceptualized as informal citizenship (Sassen 2008), inclusive citizenship (Kabeer 2005), multilayered citizenship (Yuval-Davis 1997), flexible citizenship (Ong 1999), acts of citizenship (Isin 2008), or citizenship in motion (Mezzadra 2003). The focus of these approaches is to reimagine citizenship outside the frame of legal, formal status, determined by and attached to entitlements conferred in the context of and by the institutional powers of the nation-state, to citizenship as practice that not only demands the recognition of rights to discriminated or excluded groups, but through its various (public and private, political and informal) enactments challenges the legitimacy and universality of the nation-state as the frame of political agency. Such a practice is always multiple, dispersed, scalar, and involves social actors and social networks who may or may not enjoy formal rights, but, who, nevertheless through the enactment of "the right to have rights," establish a claim for being part of, actively participating in, and, thereby, transforming (a) political community.

The event can be reasonably regarded as such a practice of citizenship, not only because it explicitly articulated a demand for citizenship rights to be recognized to migrant children, but also because it directly enacted the right to belonging and entitlement through the enunciation of a doubled discourse captured in the main slogan "Greek men and women, we are your children. We want our rights." This slogan welded together two registers of identity, a familial and a legal one. Strategically invoking an identity discourse that references a familial bond, which is also a national bond, and at the same time a universal human rights discourse, the slogan articulated a complex term of address that both referenced an understanding of cultural intimacy in the Greek case, the construction of insiderhood around familial ties. At the same time it surpassed this frame by simultaneously referring to a higher-order abstract foundation of rights, thereby reframing the position of the African migrant appellant as an insider entitled to recognition.[4]

Regarding the use of mimicry as subversive political strategy (McClintock 1995), the performance can be seen to represent a strategic reiteration and displacement of culturally sanctioned discourse, which produced a disturbing hybrid figure that was simultaneously both "like us" and "other." As McClintock suggests, mimicry need not only be understood as inadvertent disruption of the discourse of power, emanating from its own contradictions, but also as a form of agency; a way in which the disempowered use the tools of their subjection to claim presence. The choice of songs, posters, and slogans presented an important shift from the traditional leftist antiracist repertoire, which systematically draws on workerist and/or cultural identity narratives, and provoked impressions ranging from the familiar to the embarrassing. In using symbols from mainstream popular culture, including a Benetton poster, Xmas carols, and the famous John Lennon song, migrant women strategically appropriated and resignified common and evocative, visual and oral narratives and images. This move, as well as the foregrounding of children as the main appellants, could be seen as an attempt to render their claims legible and appealing to a wider audience than the one usually solicited by leftist antiracist discourses. However, the controversial slogan's ambiguous meaning bore more disquieting implications for the activists. On the one hand, it placed migrants in the position of children to be protected, thereby evoking sympathy rather than antagonism. On the other hand, it reframed migrant children as part of the "Greek" family, as Greek children. Thus, the slogan both referenced and subverted the dominant national imaginary of racial and cultural purity, homogeneity, and distinctiveness, by alluding to it and, at the same time, recasting its intimate racial and ethnic boundaries and embodiments. It resignified the Greek family as a potentially multicultural and, moreover, "black" family; a significant and signifying anomaly in terms of the narrative of homogenous uninterrupted Greek lineage. It is this racial transgression that constitutes an act of subversive mimicry as it disrupts the discourse of Greek national identity as self-evidently "white" by doubling it as "black," thereby also implying the possibility of not only cultural mixing, but racial miscegenation.

As Michael Herzfeld argues, "Nationalism and cultural intimacy are entwined in mutual dependence." Cultural intimacy, as an index of nation, references a collective space of identification based on "the sharing of known and recognizable traits that not only define insiderhood but are also felt to be disapproved by powerful outsiders" (Herzfeld 2005, 132). Breaching the boundaries of cultural intimacy evokes shame and unease in the "host" body politic because it lays bare the potentially compromising aspects of collective identity which are shared by insiders yet outwardly disavowed: "Embarrassment, rueful self-recognition: these are the markers of what cultural intimacy is all about. They are not solely personal feelings, but describe the collective representation of intimacy" (ibid., 6). This was exhibited in the Greek male activist's reaction to the controversial slogan. He found himself in a fraught position being simultaneously the bearer of two competing interpellations; a conflict that accounted for annoyance and nervousness. On the one hand, as a Greek, he was connected to the community of his co-nationals, with whom he finds himself in political antagonism. On the other hand, as an antiracist activist, he was linked to the community of migrants, who are, nevertheless, positioned as outsiders to the national community. His admonition to "stop this inelegant slogan," prompted by shame, reveals precisely his intimate cultural knowledge that there is a trait that defines community, in spite of political commitments. This trait, which the slogan brings to the surface and disturbs, is the articulation of nation and family and the use of the latter as a model for the former.

The main antagonism between Greek antiracist and migrant women's political standpoints expressed a tension between invoking programmatic universal premises, on the one hand, and staging an affective appeal, on the other. While Greek antiracist activists based their politics on abstract and normative presuppositions such as a united workers' identity, or class membership, or even human rights, migrant women were more concerned to articulate a personal claim of inclusiveness and to blur the boundaries between "insiders" and "outsiders," "self" and "other." In the Greek male activist's disciplinary intervention to impose the correct antiracist address, the borders between those who are recognized as proper and entitled political subjects and those who are not were redrawn within and by the antiracist movement, albeit in the name of universality rather than difference.

Case 3: Hunger Striking for Rights: The Body and the Politics of the Nonidentity

In late January 2011, three hundred male migrants from Northern African countries, who had been long-term residents in Greece but had not yet been able to secure official residence and work permits, started a hunger strike in order to force the government to recognize their rights and grant them legal status. After surviving forty-five days of food abstinence in conditions of extreme hardship that critically endangered their lives, during which fierce debates divided Greek public opinion, political parties as well as the antiracist movement itself, the government conceded to reconsider the cases of the three hundred appellants and grant them partial rights of mobility and work.

If up until now, the presence of migrants in Greece was tolerated by official and popular opinion on the basis of economic rationalizations, the current economic, social, and political crisis has turned the tables against them. As the economy sinks into ever-deepening recession, the presence of migrants is tolerated less and less; migrants are targeted not only by official policies but also attacked by public opinion, now almost exclusively invoking migrants as "illegals." Far-right political discourses have become mainstream. Since the advent of the economic crisis in late 2009, racist violence against migrants, involving attacks against individuals and families on the street, places of residence, places of worship, refusals to service migrants in local stores, evictions, "broom" operations, and deportations, has risen exponentially. Government policy today flounders between enforcing deportations, exerting pressure on migrants' communities to discourage influx, announcing plans to build a concrete wall in the Evros-Turkey border zone, zero-asylum, but also granting some citizenship rights to long-term residents and second-generation migrants, and reconsidering the criteria for renewal of residence and work permits, which systematically been used to retain migrants at the brink of illegality.

In the context of this tense but also stagnant situation, in January 2011, three hundred migrants, who had been long-term residents in Greece but had not yet been able to secure official residence and work permits, decided to go on hunger strike. Their intention was to force the government to recognize their rights and grant them legal status, which would allow them, among other things, to travel back to their countries of origin, or to any other country for that matter, a possibility foreclosed to most undocumented migrants and asylum seekers apprehended in Greece because of the EU mandated Dublin II Regulation.[5] The hunger strike, the magnitude of which was unprecedented within recent European history, required the significant mobilization of social and political resources, drawn mainly from the Greek leftist, antiracist, and anarchist movement, which was, however, not only unprepared for dealing with the demands of the situation but also split as to the appropriateness and timeliness of the undertaking. It was initially organized, for practical and political reasons, as an occupation of one of the empty buildings of the Athens Law School, which, as a public university, is granted, under the Greek Constitution, asylum from police intervention. The occupation of a public educational institution by a group of migrants was received with great ambivalence, if not outright hostility, by mainstream public opinion, large parts of the Left not excluded, because it was seen as an abuse, if not desecration, either of sanctified national institutions (the university representing a national achievement), or of the public good (the public university as national university representing a social good of/for the Greek people), or of hard-won and inalienable civic freedoms (such as university asylum) by subjects who were considered not entitled to (or worthy of) staking a claim on what was considered the Greek people's property, right, or legacy. After a week of failed negotiations and repeated ultimatums, the government staged a police siege of the occupied university building, threatening to apprehend and immediately deport all migrant hunger strikers as well as press charges against Greek activists. The hunger strikers were forced to move to a private building in the center of Athens, its use granted for the occasion by a "personal friend" of one of the members of government, because no other appropriate or available public building could be found in the whole city. In other words, a "familial" (domestic) solution was sought to an obviously thorny, and potentially nationally compromising, political issue. The hunger strike continued for forty-five days, amidst furious debates as to its effrontery, legitimacy, efficacy, and "independence" (i.e., whether or not it was opportunistically "staged" by Greek activists or directed by the migrants themselves).

As an event and a particular performance of a struggle for rights, the hunger strike produced intense popular discomfort and split not only the mainstream public, the Left, and the antiracist movement, but migrants' communities as well, all of whom contested, but were also confounded by, what was considered the audacity, folly, or resolution of the three hundred migrant hunger strikers and, in particular, the way they put their life on the line. As a political act that involved confrontation with the state, and with an institutional regime of power and injustice, through the medium of the body, in fact, through the deprivation and emaciation of the (robustness, physical strength, and health/integrity) of the body, the hunger strike was hailed as both outrageous and courageous. In effect, it was apprehended as a largely alien and mostly unintelligible (even reprehensible) practice, implicitly constituting an affront to, or disregard for a culturally, and religiously, upheld reverence for the sacredness of life and a caricature of (heroic and masculinist) struggle. On the one hand, the migrants were seen as usurping the hunger strike from political prisoners (ironically, of course, the hunger strikers, as illegal migrants, had been themselves incarcerated in Greece, albeit through state indifference rather than through state persecution). On the other hand, they were seen to engage in a more "passive" than "active" form of resistance, a feminized performance of "nonrational" and "desperate" struggle embodied through fragility and weakness, but, also, a religiously inspired self-sacrifice, since as Northern Africans, they were presumed Muslims.

Precisely because of its incomprehensibility, the hunger strike presented a profound cultural, political, and gendered stake. Its significance and value lie not so much in the immediate political gains accrued, which are disputed, but rather in the disruptions of "normal" and "proper" politics, practices, and bodies that the affective and semantic dissonances it evoked engendered. It manifested, both for mainstream society as well as the antiracist movement, the impossibility of communication within the premise of a common cultural code and common values; what has been called a "monolingual address" (Sakai 1997, 74). The experience and expectation of community, be it national or political, as an aggregation of people that speak the "same language" and communicate based on the assumption of fixed and preestablished common identities, "us" and "them" spatially located "inside" and "outside," was confounded. In the ensuing confusion emerged the possibility (or necessity) of a different kind community based on a "heterolingual address" (ibid., 75), that is, on a form of enunciation that does not assume immediacy or transparency of meaning but rather one where we address ourselves to each other as foreigners, as distant subjects engaged in continuous translation rather than communication. It is therefore precisely the confrontation with the noncommunicable *within* the national or political community, that which defies identification and therefore necessitates translation, which, on the one hand, lays bare the workings of power, as it is culturally and materially encoded but, on the other hand, engenders the conditions of possibility for the emergence of a "non-aggregate community" that is, a community not based on the assumption of sameness.[6]

Conclusion

If the slogan "Greek and foreign workers unite" represents a discursive landmark for the leftist antiracist movement, referring to a shared struggle premised on the assumption of unity between Greeks and migrants on the basis of a common and universal worker consciousness (or identity) and common oppression, the cases of migrant-led mobilizations I have been discussing point to a very different imaginary constitution and enactment of political subjectivity. Rather than accepting the interpellation "victims," "foreigners," and/or "workers," available within leftist antiracist politics of representation, migrants sometimes claim rights not through recourse to notions of identity and sovereignty but rather by performing a politics of belonging that blurs the boundaries between "outsider" and "insider," "us" and "them." I want to argue that we might understand these forms of migrant protests as forms of embodied politics, which renders migrants as political actors through enactments of their collective vulnerability.

Notes

This chapter is based on work I did for my PhD ("The politics of gender and migration in an antiracist group in Athens," 2010, Manchester Metropolitan University) and is informed by subsequent research on gender and migration in Greece, undertaken in the context of the FP7 funded research programs GEMIC (www.gemic.eu) and MIGNET (www.mignetproject.eu).

1. http://www.civitas.org.uk/wordpress/2011/01/05/3770/. Accessed Aug. 29, 2011.

2. As discussed by Nicholas de Genova (2002) and Sandro Mezzadra (2003), immigration regimes, including different legal procedures, border technologies and migration policies, in both the United States and Europe, produce migrant "illegality" as a conditional legal status by which to control migrant labor. As De Genova claims, "Once we recognize that undocumented migrations are constituted in order not to physically exclude them but instead, to socially include them under imposed conditions of enforced and protracted vulnerability, it is not difficult to fathom how migrants' endurance of many years of 'illegality' can serve as a disciplinary apprenticeship in the subordination of their labour, after which it becomes no longer necessary to prolong the undocumented condition" (429).

3. Notions of migrants' quasi-atavistic attachment to traditional social norms, in spite of sociocultural mobility, and of their resistance toward a more liberal Western way of life could be seen to derive from Western feminist emancipation narratives, which inadvertently signal a historically founded colonial European imaginary regarding the superiority of the "West" vis-à-vis its "others"; the invoked passivity, authoritarianism, and implied irrationality of migrants assumes a Western rational agentic subject in the background, against which migrants, as non-Western subjects, are measured, found wanting, and paternalistically guided. It is precisely liberal feminist precepts, which are deployed today in various institutional contexts (e.g., German and Dutch naturalization tests) to justify institutionalized racist discrimination against migrants, especially Muslims, who have to henceforth prove that they are amenable to European values in order to gain the right to claim European citizenship.

4. For a discussion of the tensions and contradictions involved in mobilizing universal human rights discourses to advocate for women's rights, see Hesford and Kozol (2005).

5. The Dublin II Regulation (Regulation 2003/343/CE) presents a case in point where the "illegal" movement of migrants can confound and cancel international agreements. The regulation stipulates that asylum claims can only be processed at the country of first entry to Europe and illegal migrants apprehended in other countries must be accordingly redirected. Because Greece has a de facto zero-asylum policy, as well as being administratively inept to deal with the growing number of asylum applications, many EU countries no longer redirect migrants/asylum seekers back to Greece, as it is now clear that their claims will not, or cannot be processed here. For example, on January 21, 2011, Belgium was indicted and fined by the European Human Rights Court for sending back an Afghan refugee/asylum seeker to face "the inhuman and degrading circumstances" in Greece. Subsequently, other European countries, such as Denmark, Finland, Norway, and Switzerland declared that they would stop returning refugees to Greece (http://www.nytimes.com/2011/01/27/world/europe/27iht-asylum27.htm). The persistent "illegal" movement of migrants who try to escape incarceration in Greece has effectively canceled the Regulation.

6. "In a nonaggregate community, therefore, we are together and can address ourselves as 'we' because we are distant from one another and because our togetherness is not grounded on any common homogeneity" (Sakai 1997, 7).

Works Cited

Andrijasevic, Rutvica. 2007. "Beautiful Dead Bodies: Gender, Migration, and Representation in Anti-Trafficking Campaigns." *Feminist Review* 86 (1): 24–44.

Anderson, Bridget, and Rutvica Andrijasevic. 2008. "Sex-Slaves and Citizens: the Politics of Anti-Trafficking." *Soundings* 40 (1): 135–45.

Baldwin-Edwards, Michael. 2004. "Immigration into Greece, 1990–2003. A Southern European Paradigm?" *European Population Forum 2004*, Geneva, January 12–14. http://www.mmo.gr/pdf/publications/publications_by_mmo_staff/UNEC%20paperV3.pdf. Accessed August 29, 2011.

De Genova, Nicholas. 2002. "Migrant 'Illegality' and Deportability in Everyday Life." *Annual Review of Anthropology* 31: 419–47.

Geddes, Andrew, and Elena Lazarou. 2008. "Europeanization of Migration Policy and Narratives of Migration Management in Greece." Paper presented at the ESRC Seminar Series *Migration Management and Development*, University of Sussex, 18–19 September.

Glarnetajis, Nikos. 2001. "Taking a Look at the Antiracist Movement in Greece." In *Migrants in Greece*, edited by Athanasios Marvakis, Dimitris Parsanoglou, and Miltos Pavlou. Athens: Ellinika Grammata.

Herzfeld, Michael. 2005. *Cultural Intimacy: Social Poetics in the Nation-State*. 2nd ed. New York: Routledge.

Hesford, Wendy, and Wendy Kozol. 2005. "Introduction." In *Just Advocacy? Women's Human Rights, Transnational Feminisms, and the Politics of Representation*, edited by Wendy S. Hesford and Wendy Kozol. New Brusnwick: Rutgers University Press.

Isin, Engin F. 2008. "Theorizing Acts of Citizenship." In *Acts of Citizenship*, edited by Engin Isin and Greg Nielsen. London: Zed.

Kabeer, Naila, ed. 2005. "Introduction: The Search for Inclusive Citizenship: Meanings and Expressions in an Interconnected World." In *Inclusive Citizenship. Meanings and Expressions*. London: Zed.

Lentin, Alana. 2004. *Racism and Antiracism in Europe*. London: Pluto Press.

Lewis, Gail. 2006. "Imaginaries of Europe. Technologies of Gender, Economies of Power." *European Journal of Women's Studies* 13 (2): 87–102.

McClintock, Anne. 1995. *Imperial Leather: Race, Gender, and Sexuality in the Colonial Contest*. New York: Routledge.

Mezzadra, Sandro. 2003. "Citizenship in Motion." *Makeworlds*. http://www.makeworlds.org/node/83. Accessed August 29, 2011.

Ong, Aihwa. 1999. *Flexible Citizenship: The Cultural Logics of Transnationality*. Durham: Duke University Press.

Pavlou, Miltos. 2007. "'Greece, Greece, we are your Children!' Macropolitical Challenges of Migration for the State and Society." In *Transformation of Migration*

Policy, edited by Charis Kontiadis and Theodoros Papatheodorou. Athens: Papazisisis.
Pettman, Jan Jindy. 1996. "Boundary Politics: Women, Nationalism and Danger." In *New Frontiers in Women's Studies: Knowledge, Identity, and Nationalism*, edited by Mary Maynard and June Purvis. London: Taylor and Francis.
Sakai, Naoki. 1997. *Translation and Subjectivity: On "Japan" and Cultural Nationalism*. Minneapolis: University of Minnesota Press.
Sassen, Saskia. 2008. *Territory, Authority, Rights: From Medieval to Global Assemblages*. 2nd ed. Princeton: Princeton University Press.
Silverstein, Paul. 2005. "Immigrant Racialisation and the New Savage Slot: Race, Migration and Immigration in the New Europe." *Annual Review of Anthropology* 34: 363–384.
Triandafyllidou, Anna, and Thanos Maroukis, eds. 2010. *Migration in 21st Century Greece*. Athens: Kritiki.
Yuval-Davis, Nira. 1997. *Gender and Nation*. London: Sage.
Zavos, Alexandra, 2010a. *The Politics of Gender and Migration in an AntiRacist Group in Athens*. PhD thesis, Manchester Metropolitan University.
———. 2010b. "Gender, Migration and Anti-Racist Politics in the Continued Project of the Nation." In *Gender and Migration: Feminist Interventions*, edited by Ingrid Palmary, Erica Burman, Khatidja Chantler, and Peace Kiguwa. London: Zed.

Figure 12.1. At the Court of Women on Poverty in the U.S. (May 2012), the all-woman *bomba* ensemble, *Las Bomberas de la Bahia*, performed songs and dances of protest created by seventeenth and eighteenth-century African slaves in Puerto Rico, 2012. Austin Long-Scott.

12

Immigrant Protest and the Courts of Women

Marguerite Waller

While much of our work is activist in nature, as with women, with rural, urban and tribal communities and through the numerous campaigns that we have initiated and been part of, it is rooted essentially in a more reflective praxis that is able to integrate the more aesthetic and the analytical. For it has grown around a vision which has always sought the continuities in politics, in art and all other dimensions of life; all the while avoiding the extreme specialization which informs both mainstream and alternative institutions.

—Center for Informal Education and Development Studies (CIEDS)

This essay shifts the focus from Europe and North America to sites in the Global South where thinking about migration has evolved as an integral part of investigating the violence of European colonialism and its neocolonial permutations, development, and "globalization." My first encounter with the Courts of Women, at the NGO Forum in Huairou, China, in 1995, introduced me to a form of political praxis that puts on trial the metaphysical and political systems that make immigration a judicial issue in the North. Trying to imagine what it would mean to rethink migration and immigration without taking the nation-state for granted has led me on a journey across time and space in search of a story, rich in coherence and connection, that confounds linear narrative and statist logic.

To introduce this story, I begin with a different, though not unrelated, story. In the early 1990s, I was a member of a women's political art-making collective called Las Comadres, active in the Tijuana/San Diego border region. Members of the group supported one another's individual projects, developed a major collaborative installation and performance that gained national recognition, and, in all of our activities, took a deeply critical stand on the North American Free Trade agreement (NAFTA) that threatened to devastate rural Mexican livelihoods. We supported a border open to people moving between Mexico and the United States (as the region's inhabitants had done since long before the border was created in 1848), and, through our art and our direct actions, we particularly reached out to those San Diegans who had forgotten, or who had never known about, the complex histories of this borderland involving the U.S. annexation of Northern Mexico in 1848 and, before that, the Spanish conquest and colonization of the indigenous people living in what are now Mexico and California. Our artistic and protest strategies recalled these histories and parsed the logics of the region's legacies of colonialism, militarism, and occupation. Through these lenses, it seemed inevitable that the proposed "free trade" agreement, opening the Mexico labor market to U.S. corporate development and its consumer market to cheap, subsidized, duty-free U.S. corn, but clamping down on the movement of Mexicans themselves across the border, would exacerbate rather than ease the pressure to go North (Waller1994; Mancillas, Wallen, and Waller 1999). As it happened, the flooding of the Mexican market with U.S. corn wiped out Mexican corn growers, resulting in pressure on young women to migrate to factory towns along the border to work for very low wages under dangerous conditions. These wages were (and are) insufficient to live on, let alone to support a family. Men and women of all ages were forced in increasing numbers, then, to cross the border without documents in search of some way to make a living. Within a very few years, furthermore, even the low wages paid for factory work in Mexico were undercut by wages in China, India, and Southeast Asia, with the result that many of the assembly plants built in Mexico in the 1990s have since shut down.

I begin with the story of Las Comadres and NAFTA to remind myself of, and to alert readers to, the difficulties of writing about political action that seeks to reimagine the political itself. When an American university student wrote her Masters thesis on our group, we felt misrepresented—subverted and silenced—by the result. We felt that she had construed our experiments, our discoveries, our ways of interacting with one another and within our communities, according to the very academic and political frames we were trying to leave behind. She had also left out the feel, the texture, the affect of our motivations, our successes and failures, and even the circumstances of our coming together. In writing about the World Courts of Women, a project located and coordinated in the Global South, I risk following in the footsteps of that student whose work so disappointed us. At the outset, then, let me emphasize that my intention is *not* to represent, define, or theorize the Courts of Women per se, a project that the project's organizers in Bangalore and Tunis already carry out brilliantly across multiple media and languages. Rather, I propose to explore how the "new political imaginary" embodied by the Courts, an imaginary rooted in the anticolonial struggles of the South, opens new ways and spaces for thinking about immigration and immigrant protest (Kumar 2005). Particularly, as recurring clashes escalate in scope and intensity between the human rights of immigrants and the violent repression and deportation of immigrants in the name of national sovereignty and security, the epistemology of the Courts is suggestive of the kinds of political praxis in which both state and nonstate actors might engage.

The Courts are well documented. Indian-born Corinne Kumar, the founder and guiding spirit of the Courts of Women, and her colleagues in two NGOs, the Bangalore-based Asian Women's Human Rights Council and the Tunis-based El Taller International, have filmed and recorded the forty Courts of Women convened throughout the global South since 1992, producing DVDs and books that include detailed transcripts, reflections, and analyses of the proceedings. These are readily available through the Web sites of both organizations. One can see, hear, and read the testimony of witnesses, the responses of audiences, the work of the "wise men and women" jury members, who listen, learn, and reflect on the significance of testimonies.[1]

One challenge presented by these materials for a reader or viewer not accustomed to the Courts' instantiation of the "postcolonial baroque" is that these materials may overwhelm (Glissant 1997, 77–85). They are densely layered, or palimpsestic, and their logic is, as Gloria Anzaldúa says of her hard-won *mestiza* consciousness, not "convergent" but "divergent, characterized by movement away from set patterns and goals and toward . . . one that includes rather than excludes" (Anzaldúa 1987, 79). The Courts themselves and the archive they have produced are organized around connections rather than categories, specifics rather than generalizations. On a metaconceptual level, they bring different epistemes or "cosmovisions" into relation with one another rather than mapping out positions and dynamics in terms of a single unifying ideological system.[2] In drawing upon this rigorous and meticulous archive of feminist political praxis in the Global South to reflect upon the paradoxes and challenges of immigrant protest in the Global North, I am therefore confronted with a translation problem that, in a sense, mirrors the non-fit between the diverse and ever-changing circumstances of immigrants and the exigencies of state sovereignty (Brown 2010).

But the impurities of translation are as relevant as they are problematic. The Courts' modes and methods, I will suggest, clarify why and how conventional forms of protest often legitimate and intensify state violence. They also explain why efforts to put immigrant rights on the agendas of either sending or receiving nations are unlikely to succeed. Such realizations come into focus, though, only if and when one is willing to suspend the overarching frame of statist politics. One of the consequences of the Courts' approach is that the results of their proceedings are not foreseeable and that, even in retrospect, they are difficult to codify or quantify in the conventional terminology of "outcomes."[3] Nevertheless, the Courts of Women are increasingly recognized by other political projects that have made their way to a similar epistemological jumping-off place. In December 2010, Kumar was invited to Chiapas, Mexico, to discuss the Courts with members of the indigenous Zapatista Movement and the Faculty of the University of the Earth at their end of the year *Encuentro*. In November 2011, Kumar spoke at the General Assembly of Occupy London and in May 2012 at Occupy Oakland in California.

In their refusal to formulate demands in state-form idioms, in their commitment to asking questions, to opening rather than closing avenues of analysis and agency, the Courts of Women decenter nation-state epistemologies, producing spaces for the emergence of a trans-, extra-, or perhaps pre/post-national political praxes. As Kumar explains the convergence between the Courts of Women and Zapatista projects: "The peasants of Chiapas, Mexico . . . [i]n their profound and careful organization, in their political imagining and vision . . . do not offer clear, rigid, universal truths of power, politics, and patriarchy. They sum up their vision in three little words, 'Asking we walk.' The asking, in itself, challenges master narratives, masters' houses, houses of reason" (Kumar 2005, 191).

The work of the Courts of Women has its roots in the Centre for Informal Education and Development Studies (CIEDS) collective in Bangalore, India. Founded in 1975 by a group of mostly university-educated friends, including Kumar, who felt they needed to go beyond the political paradigms available to them if they were going to engage the complex circumstances of poverty in postcolonial India, CIEDS has grown into a diverse, mutually porous collection of organizations and programs. One of them, *Vimochana* (Liberation), is a women's forum out of which, in turn, the idea for a transnational umbrella organization, the Asian Women's Human Rights Council (AWHRC), emerged in the early nineties. The AWHRC has made organizing and facilitating the Courts of Women one of its core activities, along with related fact-finding missions, networking among women's grassroots projects in the Global South and indigenous groups worldwide, and opening lines of communication from the grass roots to the national and international political classes. By contrast to many European and North American groups, Vimochana addresses contemporary forms of violence rhizomatically, as an ever-shifting network of interrelated issues, rather than analyzing them in terms of discrete categories: domestic, state, ethnic, development, nuclear, environmental, military, sexual, etc. (Deleuze and Guattari 1987, 3–25).

Kumar began urging a reconceptualization of human rights that moves outside dominant rights discourses after the first several Courts identified the principle of "universal human rights" as itself a primary factor in obfuscating the nature and degree of the violence of our times (Kumar 2005, 169–70, 174–75).[4] Among other limitations, the discourse and praxis of individual human rights, with its roots in Enlightenment notions of the sovereign subject, has worked to exclude the collective rights of peoples, including ethnic and indigenous groups, increasingly threatened with extinction in the name of "development" (Ezeilo 2007; Klein 2007; Perkins 2004; Roy 2002, 2009; Shiva 1988, 2002). Making nation-states responsible for ensuring human rights and making citizenship the prerequisite for such protection have compounded this exclusion, leading to the emergence of the nation-state as one of the greatest violators of human rights. In the name of "protecting" its citizens and of the greater common good, extremes of repression, exploitation, injury, incarceration, and displacement have been committed by the signatories of the 1948 Declaration (Kumar 2005; Tyler 2006; Doctors Without Borders 2009; Human Rights Watch 2011).

Madhu Bhushan, a member of CIEDS, and Ashis Nandy, a long-time friend of the collective, emphasize the importance of Gandhi's legacy to the mode of protest embodied in the Courts of Women. Gandhi's vision of community and nationhood, radically different from what became India's post-Independence reality, was developed in light of his experiences of British colonialism in South Asia, and, significantly, of his early adult years as a young lawyer in South Africa. In her essay, "An Open Letter to Gandhi," Bhushan reminds us that Gandhi elaborated a notion of nation comprising a decentralized, deterritorialized network of interdependent villages and a form of postcolonial government that would not merely replicate the European nation-state:

> The village for you was not a geographical and territorial space. *It was an event, a dream, a happening, a culture; a set of values. It was a node in a network of oceanic circles that overlapped and spread out in its ever widening circles.* (Bhushan 2007, 122; italics Bhushan's)

The context of this evocation by Bhushan is a discussion of the intrinsic violence of the centralized, territorialized, hierarchical nation-state system, the rejection of which, she notes, was an important part of Gandhi's anti-imperial, anticolonial philosophy.

Ashis Nandy also foregrounds Gandhi's disaffection from European nation-statehood, noting the irony of Gandhi's enshrinement in both right-wing and left-wing authoritarian political imaginaries. Putting the chaotic legacy of the Mahatma to good use, though, he appreciates how these reifications actually blind both states and authoritarian "revolutionaries" to the nature of the legacy they would like to co-opt. Gandhi's political strategies are misperceived and undervalued by both Left and Right, precisely because of the nonviolence of these tactics, which do not translate into power within a dominant paradigm that still equates power with violence. As Nandy argues, "The tyrants undervalue him, because he has no arms to back him up and the professional revolutionaries make fun of him because he talks of nonviolence" (Nandy 2007, 139). For Nandy, this underestimation makes Gandhian transformations of state violence into displays of state weakness extremely potent and widely applicable, especially as they unravel the legal and ideological dissimulations of that violence. By the late twentieth century, he notes, Gandhi's militant nonviolence had made its way into contexts as disparate as the U.S. civil rights movement, the Polish Solidarity movement, the People Power Revolution in the Philippines, the Burmese uprising against the military regime, and, coming full circle, the Truth and Reconciliation Commission in South Africa where Gandhi's methodology of *satyagraha*, or insistence on an inclusive truth that does not require violent enforcement, first took shape.

To appreciate Gandhi's legacy in terms of this nonteleological, cross-cultural mesh of likenesses requires a nomadic rather than a linear historiography (Deleuze and Guattari 1987). Rigorously displacing the seizure and exercise of political control by which nation-states are created and maintained and the relations among nation-states so created as the framework of historical understanding, this transnational, postcolonial historiography opens a field of connections and relations congruent with the geometry of the "network of oceanic circles" (Bhushan 2007, 122). If the *nation-states* evoked by Nandy do not themselves incarnate Gandhi's philosophy, this is no surprise, and it does not mean that Gandhi's *satyagraha* approach has been unsuccessful. On the contrary, given the inherent violence of the nation-state, it would be unrealistic and illogical to expect it to embody a practice designed to disempower such violence. It is only when the nation-state is privileged as the *arche* or ultimate historiographical framework of political analysis that Gandhi's practice might appear to have landed in history's dustbin.

Because the Courts of Women focus on violence, rather than on the state per se, and because they address particularly the forms of violence suffered by women for which there are no legal remedies at the local, national, or international level, they are able to pursue connections beneath the fragmentation and disconnection of state epistemologies. They practice a historiography that investigates the "private" sphere, relegated by the nation-state to the nonhistorical, in relation to the public sphere, undoing the "minoritizing" effects of legal discourses that exclude "domestic affairs," whether of households or of states, from the calculus of human rights (Sedgwick 1990, 82–86). At the World Court of Women Against Racism, held in Durban, South Africa, in 2001, witness Pregs Govender concisely identified the internalization of this minoritizing effect on women and other deprivileged positions as itself a fundamental issue, testifying: "We have begun to believe that we are fragments; that our stories are disconnected from each other; the enemies are safely ensconced within our minds and hearts, and none of us escapes" (AWHRC/El Taller 2002b, 10).

In order to piece together these fragments, we need to think about the kinds of spatial as well as historiographical frames within which such a collaborative activity can take place. Bhushan's conflation of space and time in her description of Gandhi's "village" as "an event, a happening, a dream" reminds us, by contrast, of the homogeneous empty space and linear time that Benedict Anderson (1983) and others attribute to nation-states. The space of nation, as Anderson has described it, is constructed as a bordered enclosure of uniformly mappable territory, with no tactile qualities, no smell, taste, or memories—not the kind of place created by people as they live in relation to one another

By contrast, theorist/activists such as Vandana Shiva and Silvia Federici appreciate the social as well as the material support offered by a variety of "commons," in which there is a sense of co-production, of shared care and responsibility, of interacting with, rather than owning, land and its resources. They call attention no less urgently to the ecological and human rights crises that the increasing enclosure of the commons—including now water, air, and communal knowledges of agricultural and medicinal biodiversity—by neoliberal market forces is precipitating (Shiva 1988, 2002; Federici 2010).

Of less concern in the literature on development is the effect of enclosure on those excluded from the commons by their positions of relative wealth. Activist/architect Jean Robert, a friend of both the Zapatistas and the Courts of Women, was struck early in his career by several instances of clients becoming profoundly depressed or going mad in their expensive, custom-built Bauhaus homes. Commenting on the hegemony of a kind of space composed of non-overlapping frames, all subject to a single rule of measurement, which revolutionized early modern European painting, mapping, navigation, architecture, and urban planning, Robert marvels at its destructive reach. This sociohistorical construction of what he calls "*a priori* space" (which he believes did not exist before the European Renaissance) always already implies enclosure (Robert 2007, 341). It can only be appropriated—fenced in, controlled, and exploited—a conclusion also reached by Shiva as she thinks beyond "the colonial paradigms that have emerged over the last 500 years of colonial rule" (Shiva 1997, 6). Robert emphasizes that the effects of this "*a priori* space" are psychologically and epistemologically, as well as politically and ecologically, devastating. It has:

> Induced . . . people to reduce the world's inexhaustible perceptual richness. . . . I have the impression that *a priori* space is . . . a strange malady, because those who are infected by it in turn affect reality, render it shallow, cause it to dwindle and fade, make it uninhabitable *for themselves and for others*. Above all, I get the impression that things and people *lose their relatedness to each other and fall apart*. (Robert 2007, 341; italics mine)

The Courts of Women acknowledge the centrality of this space in the production of both gendered violence and state/corporate violence against indigenous and minority communities. Their organizers attend no less carefully to the space in which their own proceedings unfold. The ability of their diverse participants to respond with care and creativity to one another and to the forms of violence being brought to the Courts' attention depend upon how effectively the Courts themselves produce a social and perceptual commons that dissolves hierarchies of class, of belonging and unbelonging, of visibility and invisibility.

The bearing of these nonstatist understandings of history, place, and by implication, "the human" on our concepts of justice and rights is direct and startling. Archbishop Desmond Tutu of South Africa has described the truth and reconciliation process in postapartheid South Africa as a deliberate departure from the colonizers' retributive justice. In keeping with the isolating and fragmenting space of the nation-state, retributive justice pits the accuser and the accused against one another, leaving out the victim almost entirely. The need for communities to heal through the reweaving of relationships is not even a consideration. Thus, the opportunity for transgression to lead to transformation is lost. Punishing the crime amounts instead to a performance of state sovereignty, a reinscription of mastery within a Cartesian space of enclosure.

The restorative justice of the Truth and Reconciliation Commission, on the other hand, was premised on the "African principle of *Ubuntu*." Tutu explains, "In our understanding a person can be a person only in relationships, not in isolation. Ubuntu [African Communalism] says I am human only because you are human. If I undermine your humanity, I dehumanize myself" (Tutu 2007, 171). This relational understanding of the human, which allows for infinite variations in the interaction among participants, endows everyone with agency. In so doing, the TRC worked to create and expand a postapartheid community that could move on from the violence of apartheid rather than perpetuating it. The nation-state of South Africa in 2011 is not what was hoped for in 1995, but like Gandhi's *satyagraha*, the historical significance of the Truth and Reconciliation Commission depends upon one's historiographical frame.

The *Aporia* of Migrant Rights and National Sovereignty

Although it was not their point of departure, over the course of the first several Courts of Women and by the time of the 1995 United Nations Fourth World Conference on Women and its parallel Nongovernmental Organization (NGO) Forum, the AWHRC had come to the realization that the dominant concept of "human rights," enshrined in the 1948 United Nations Universal Declaration of Human Rights, was itself a fundamental part of the problem. Not "universal" but universalizing, it was deeply rooted in historically and geographically local European Enlightenment notions of truth, personhood, and society, which defined all other systems of knowledge and social organization as deficient and inferior (Harding 1998, 1–22). Kumar, in her remarkable critique of the Western concept of human rights, emphasizes the imbrication of the nation-state in this discourse:

> It hegemonized all peoples, tribes, minorities, ethnic groups into the one polity of the *nation-state*. It made all citizens of the state—faceless citizens mediated and manipulated by the market. It portrayed the one civilization of universal man, flattening all diversities, ignoring all historical specifications, homogenizing all aspirations into universal norms of freedom, liberty, and equality.
> *And all this was done with great violence.* (Kumar 2005, 169; italics Kumar's)

I will return to the complicity of gender categories in this state-form episteme in a moment, but here we need to appreciate the connections among human rights discourse, sovereignty, and state violence. In order to become a person with rights, one must first be successfully subsumed by and within a sovereign nation-state, a process that in itself can be both epistemologically and physically violent:

> [I]n the name of human rights, the nation-states . . . may . . . legitimate the most inhuman conditions of life, the most brutal repressions of its own people, which are then seen as the *internal* concern, the *law and order*, the *national security* of these sovereign states. . . .

> [T]he human rights discourse and praxis legitimate what is described as state violence and state terror.... [I]t also legitimates ... the violence of poverty, of famine, of malnutrition, of multinationals, of militarization, of ecological destruction, and of technological terrorism. (ibid., 170)

Kumar here references and relates to each other not only histories of conquest, expansion, colonization, and exploitation, but patterns of domestic repression and exploitation—the roundup of Muslim American citizens after the attack on the New York World Trade Center, the destruction of social safety nets by governments around the world at the behest of financial institutions such as the International Monetary Fund, the destruction of the homes and livelihoods of millions by big dams and oil drilling—all done in the name of protecting the rights and the "greater common good" of the nations' people.

"There are very specific issues related to women who are victims," Kumar further points out. Specifying them allows us to perceive the connections between the position of women in the nation state and that of other denationalized groups, including immigrants and refugees (Kumar 2005, 172–73). Radhika Mohanram, for example, draws attention to the intersection between colonial and gender politics in nineteenth-century Britain. Like colonial subjects, British women were, by law, people without rights who yet resided under the legal jurisdiction of the imperial nation-state (Mohanram 2007, xxiii, 26–56). Immigrants, refugees, and asylum seekers today in many ways fill the niche of the nineteenth-century female citizen and the colonial subject in materializing sovereignty (Tyler 2006; Brown 2010). As the critical literature on gender and nation elaborates in much greater detail, the patriarchal bourgeois family was the template of the European nation-state, whose essence and identity—whose sovereignty—were underwritten by binarisms between male and female, private and public, domestic and foreign. There are really two relationships at stake. There must be subjects in relation to whom there can be a sovereign—be it a person or a governmental apparatus—and there must be other sovereigns (male heads of household, other sovereign states) who identify with and mirror one another. The domestic inside, be it intrafamilial or intrastate, becomes a "private" sphere that cannot be interfered with by an "outside" foreign power. According to the Universal Declaration of Human Rights, it is the responsibility of the sovereign powers to enforce rights domestically (including in their colonies), but since this is the same sovereign power that determines what constitutes well-being in the domestic sphere (like the Victorian *paterfamilias* who legally "protected" his female and minor dependents), there is a fundamental denial of rights built into the paradigm, a denial deeply rooted in nineteenth-century European gender relations.[5]

To bring the operation of this intersection of gender and patriarchal sovereignty into focus, Kumar cites the compound forms of violence encountered by women who are also refugees (who now number in the tens of millions): "[W]omen who crossed the border at Djibouti were either raped by border guards or city police or were forced into a liaison with a man who offered a *measure of protection* from random abuse in exchange for certain services" (Kumar 2005, 174; italics mine). Similar stories are told by refugees crossing the Mediterranean from Africa to Europe, along the U.S.-Mexico border, among women entering the E.U. from non-E.U. former Soviet bloc countries, from "postconflict" zones such as Bosnia and Kosovo, from Iraq and Afghanistan, and from many other parts of the world (Higate and Henry 2009; Jurschick 2003; Siapno 2009). Sexual abuse by border authorities, trafficking and forced prostitution by international peacekeepers, and other forms of militarized sexual violence are *not* considered either violations of international human rights or war crimes because they are not seen judicially as "political." "I think they are two different issues and two different problems, and they shouldn't be confused or conflated. . . . [Y]ou must draw a distinction between rape used as a form of warfare . . . and rapes committed by individual peacekeepers because of their own individual criminality," suggested former chief prosecutor of the International Criminal Tribunal in The Hague and distinguished South African jurist Richard Goldstone at a conference devoted to accountability for crimes against women (Joan B. Kroc Institute 2005, 46). For Kumar and various of Justice Goldstone's interlocutors, this distinction is part of the problem. "[T]he *crimes are privatized.* Refugee politics do not deal with the specific violence against the women refugees, which women experience from all sides—from their *enemies*, from their own men, and from those who claim to help them" (Kumar 2005, 174; italics Kumar's). Women's studies professor Huma Ahmed-Ghosh responded to Goldstone, "When the U.N. peacekeeper rapes, it is not because he has a criminal record. It is mainly because he has the power to do that. We cannot trivialize it by individualizing it" (Joan B. Kroc Institute 2005, 46).

In practice, throughout the 1990s and into the first decade of the twenty-first century, such crimes have been treated at the highest levels of the United Nations as both outside their jurisdiction and a distraction from the serious business of building new nation-states (in which sexual violence against women will continue to be treated as nonpolitical) and monitoring the "political" rights of refugees (Jurschick 2003; Waller 2010). On the ground, many male sexual abusers see themselves unproblematically as benefactors (Higate and Henry 2009, 149, 153–54). If refugee politics *did* deal with the specific violence against the women refugees, which in terms of the nation-state paradigm is both "inside" and "outside," "domestic" and "foreign," "private" and "public," then these binaries would implode (at least in theory), with enormous ramifications for the future of nation-states. A focus on violence against women migrants and refugees in effect raises the question of whether women's human rights, and by implication human rights generally, are compatible with *any* current model of nation-state organization.

Kumar thus pinpoints a disconnect, or what deconstructive philosophy would call an *aporia*—a kind of uncrossable chasm or disjunction—within the Western political imaginary itself. Though they share the same Enlightenment genealogy, the principle of national sovereignty—with its distinction between the domestic and the foreign—and the principle of "universal human rights" have been held in productive tension through many nationalist revolutions and wars of national independence, but they do not cohere. Their historical codependence in the West seemed to political theorist Hannah Arendt to have, in fact, definitively unraveled in the aftermath of the Holocaust and two world wars. In her classic discussion from the late forties of the "right to have rights," she notes that this is a dimension of rights that "we became aware of . . . only when millions of people emerged who had lost and could not regain these rights because of the new global political situation" (Arendt 1966, 296–97). They could not regain these rights because no nation-state would grant them citizenship, and the American and French revolutions had made citizenship the bedrock of rights (while using "the rights of man" in Moebius-loop fashion to legitimate the state). Even as Eleanor Roosevelt in her role as U.S. Ambassador to the United Nations was promulgating the landmark "Universal Declaration of Human Rights" in 1948, it was clear to Arendt and others that national sovereignty—also claimed as a "universal principle"—was predicated on the power to exclude "noncitizens" from access to whatever powers and protections it might afford its citizens.

This *aporia* has significant implications for the theory and methodology of immigrant protest, for the same reasons that it did for anticolonial protest in India. Political and ideological responses to the treatment of immigrants (both documented and undocumented) by nation-states and to these states' immigration policies are everywhere triggering, even strengthening, anti-immigrant enactments of national sovereignty. "[S]overeignty is nowhere more absolute than in matters of emigration, nationality, and expulsion," Arendt wrote in *The Origins of Totalitarianism* (1966, 278). Since World War I, she observed, in a paradoxical effort to reassert the sovereignty compromised in multiple ways by the war, European states had embarked on a frenzy of creating "rightless" populations over which they gave their police forces "unrestricted and arbitrary domination" (ibid., 289). As a consequence, when the Nazis invaded other countries during World War II, she notes, they had little trouble enlisting the help of local police in organizing arrests and deportations of minority populations (ibid.). Extrapolating from Arendt's analysis, we might expect that in the twenty-first century, in an age of accelerating corporate integration that has reduced the scope of national sovereignty almost entirely to military and police functions, the demand for rights by, and on behalf of, "denationalized" people would be used to justify and intensify state violence. Indeed, as scores of Courts of Women witnesses as well as scholars and human rights workers have testified, the treatment of those marked in some way as immigrants (particularly but by no means exclusively those without papers) by police and military on every continent has become increasingly violent, inhumane, and, from the point of view of addressing the causes of migration, irrational (Tyler 2006; Doctors Without Borders 2009; Christian Solidarity Worldwide 2010; Human Rights Watch 2011; di Maio 2012). In the United States under President Barack Obama, the number of deportations has increased from a little more than two hundred thousand a year to almost four hundred thousand (Slevin 2010). In violation of international agreements, the UK is forcibly repatriating asylum seekers, including minors, to active war zones (Human Rights Watch 2011). Thus, if we remain within the political imaginary of the nation-state, immigrant protest appears to be on a collision course with the very institution to which the demand for rights is being addressed.

Moving Toward a New Political Imaginary

The master's tools will never dismantle the master's house.

—Audre Lorde

With their deep roots in anticolonial protest and non-Western cultures, the Courts of Women engage the modern nation-state differently, not as a sovereign entity but as an epiphenomenon of a political imaginary that, like any social construct, is mutable and porous, embedded in what postcolonial theorist Édouard Glissant has called the "baroque poetics of relation" (Glissant 1997, 79). As Glissant articulates this shift, "Relating realms of knowledge (questions and solutions) with each other cannot be categorized as either a discipline or a science but, rather, as an imaginary construct of reality that permits us to escape the pointillistic probability approach without lapsing into abusive generalization" (ibid., 100). By focusing on relationality, the Courts of Women and also the series of volumes edited by Kumar, called *Asking We Walk: The South as New Political Imaginary*, disable the fracturing inside/outside, us/them: the "pointillistic" binary logic of the nation-state. As the title of the project suggests, these projects are about *connecting* realms of knowing—the rational with the intuitive, compassion with reason, logic with poetry. For the 1995 Fourth UN World Conference on Women, for example, the AWHRC in collaboration with a transnational network of women's groups made "violence against women," in Vimochana's inclusive sense of this designation, the theme of their two-week World Court of Women on Violence Against Women, a centerpiece of the NGO Forum that paralleled the UN Conference. They thus circumvented sharp divisions among the world's feminisms—particularly those of "developing" countries focused on globalization and those of "developed" countries for which the imperialist effect of globalization was still a major blind spot—that threatened to short-circuit dialogue at this historic gathering. By not hierarchizing some positions over others, the succession of testimonies, analyses, and reflections offered listeners a sense of their interconnectedness with one another. As Glissant's metaphorics imply, this relational analytic endows everyone with agency.

A media image that became iconic of the NGO Forum offers a microcosmic example of the intellectual, emotional, and physical interactions enabled by this approach. A gathering of three thousand Women in Black, brought together late one afternoon during the NGO Forum by the AWHRC and their affiliates, stood in silent vigil for an hour to protest violence in their own cultural and political contexts. The Women in Black consist of self-organized local groups worldwide who have been inspired by the weekly silent vigils begun in Jerusalem in 1988 to protest state violence (Svirsky 2001, 243; Kumar 2005, 197). Women in Black do not have membership lists nor are they centrally coordinated with one another, but the practice has been taken up on every continent. As the NGO Forum vigil drew to a close and people began to talk to one another, the Chinese police tried to clear the intersection where it had taken place. Moved by their collective action and excited to be meeting one another face-to-face, many Women in Black did not feel that the event had run its course, and responded to the order to disperse by sitting down. This action effectively disabled the police. To enforce their order, they would have had to commit the very violence against women that was being protested, which would have created shocking headlines around the world and graphically validated the women's point. A textbook case of *satyagraha*, this powerful moment—blurring the distinction between "planned" and "spontaneous"—epitomizes collective agency.[6] The planning processes of the Courts of Women are, in effect, about catalyzing such a release, about deactivating "enclosure" or "pointillism" and materializing everyone's capacity to connect with, and to contribute his or her "truth" of perception and feeling to a community of other people engaged in the same process. The Courts, however, also seek to provide occasions for this kind of transformation that do not appear threatening (within sovereignty's narrow field of vision) to the nation-state.

Amina Mama, a Cape Town University professor (now professor of women's studies at U.C. Davis) who grew up in Nigeria, noted an important corollary of this affect/effect of the distinctive way the AWHRC orchestrates "political" action through and around the Courts of Women. As an "expert witness" for the 2001 World Court of Women Against War, for Peace in Cape Town, South Africa, she was struck by how social identities became porous under these circumstances, noting a new level of communication across personal and professional boundaries:

> I spent several days preparing myself for this occasion. After what we have seen and heard today, I must confess that I am unprepared. On reflection I would say that *no amount of preparation would have been enough*. In fact one should never be prepared for such horrors as have been presented before us here today, because they are and should be, unacceptable. . . . It has been difficult to go through today. It is a day on which the *borders between testifiers and witnesses have been dissolved*, to such an extent that most of us called here as experts could equally have been giving testimonies, and I daresay, that there are members of the jury of wise women and men who could also have been giving testimonies. I, for example, listened with empathy and pain, as my own memories that I have forced back for many years were resurrected. Horrors seen in childhood, during the outbreak of a civil war in my hometown, came back as I listened to women here, and I am deeply humbled by the courage of all those who have spoken so far. (AWHRC and El Taller International 2002a, 230; emphases Mama's)

As subject positions come to appear arbitrary, contingent, and unstable, differences among people take on a new quality, the likeness among ontological statuses translating into an appreciation of difference as an epistemological resource, the way out, so to speak, of no less contingent, historical, enclosures.

Lawrence Liang, a Bangalore-based lawyer, legal studies scholar, and several-times jury member, who has worked extensively with South Asians in Europe, spoke in greater detail at a Roundtable on the Courts of Women about the epistemological significance of these shifts in subjectivities and discursive parameters.[7] For him, a further significant effect of the Courts is their revelation of the lack of freedom, the strict discursive, behavioral, and performative limits enforced by conventional court systems. Memory lapses, breakdowns of language, tears, witnesses testifying with their supporters by their sides, not to mention interludes of singing, dancing, and poetic visuals, would be seen as intrusions threatening the coherence of the central narrative in a regular court. In the Courts of Women, though, this access to the human fragility and vulnerability underlying systems of thought and social organization is precisely what is sought. The testimony of the witnesses begins a process of foregrounding and responding to the forms of violence that hegemonic discourses of law and order, citizen and noncitizen, sovereignty and security both legitimate and occlude.

To the question of the effectiveness of the Courts of Women, Liang responded by citing Walter Benjamin's essay, "The Storyteller," concerning the decline of storytelling and the ability to share experiences in the wake of World War I. Soldiers, Benjamin wrote, returned surprisingly silent, not richer, but poorer in communicable experience:

> For never has experience been contradicted more thoroughly than strategic experience by tactical warfare, economic experience by inflation, bodily experience by mechanical warfare, moral experience by those in power. A generation that had gone to school on a horse-drawn streetcar now stood under the open sky in a countryside in which nothing remained unchanged but the clouds, and beneath these clouds, in a field of force of destructive torrents and explosions was the tiny, fragile human body. (Benjamin 1968, 84, quoted by Liang in El Taller International et al. 2010, 72 [unpublished report])

Those tiny fragile humans are precisely the ones, Liang pointed out, who challenge the evasions of "unspeakability." Their injuries and their traumas expose the violence that depends upon its not being articulated. "There is more than logic at work" in the ways these figures catalyze new knowledges, new imaginaries, and different courses of action in the midst of devastation (Liang, in El Taller International et al. 2010, 72). Trauma and its disruptions of memory, thought, language, and feeling confound the binary oppositions between mind and body, reason and feeling, modern and traditional, rich and poor, male and female that camouflage the violence of "development" and "globalization."[8]

Through the *Aporia* of Protest

> I have learned and dismantled all the words to construct a single one Home.
>
> —Mahmoud Darwish

In her Prologue to the proceedings of the "World Court of Women against War, for Peace" Madhu Bhushan, a member of the CIEDS Collective, juxtaposes Mahmoud Darwish's lines about the loss of his home in Palestine in 1948 with Hannah Arendt's proposal that the figure of the refugee holds the key to understanding relations among nation-states, international political economy, and a general "uprootedness or homelessness of the modern age" (AWHRC and El Taller International 2001a, 23). From different angles, the Courts of Women increasingly call attention to a story unfolding beneath the stories of "growth," "development," "scientific progress," and the "greater common good": a story about a war being waged against the livelihoods of a majority of the world's people whose sustainable ways of life are rebranded as "poverty" and targeted for destruction.

Let me conclude, then, with one more story, this one told by Farida Akhter, a Bangladeshi activist, theorist, and member of the AWHRC. Akhter, whose innovative involvement with women's health, labor, and environmental initiatives have been carried on multiple levels, including advocacy, publishing, policy research, and education, recasts immigration literally from the ground up. Taking the *aporias*—the internal contradictions—of nation-state-focused immigrant rights activism as her starting point, Akhter begins with state-sponsored violence against migrants as the catalyst for a reconceptualization of the notion of security. If states criminalize immigrants, making the lives especially of trafficked women and children "unbearable" even or especially in the process of "rescuing" them, the "refusal of states to address socio-political, environmental, ecological, food, health and housing, or in short the human, security concerns is equally criminal," she argues (Akhter 2007, 87–88). National security paradigms also show a complete lack of interest in ensuring the security of people on the move, she adds (ibid., 88). Noting these yawning gaps in the security state's approaches to immigration, Akhter and her associates decided to follow immigrants back to the point where they became emigrants, analyzing the migration pressures on the men, women, and children of a particular community of Bangladeshis living precariously on "chars" (new land formed by rivers from silt eroded from elsewhere) of the Brahmaputra River. Already migrants due to the destruction by erosion of their own villages upriver, the inhabitants of the chars did not have land ownership and could not therefore be involved in agriculture or in livelihoods that agriculture would support. Adult men sought agricultural work in other parts of the country and were away three months out of four. Young children, both male and female, also had to leave the villages to find jobs. Brokers came to the area to buy small children to be sold in Bangladesh's cities as bonded labor, and girls were vulnerable to various versions of forced migration including trafficking and what are deceptively called "marriages without dowry" (Akhter 2007, 96–97). Purchasing food and other household needs while the men were away placed families in debt, which immediately consumed whatever cash was brought back from elsewhere.

Resistance against these pressures called for collaboration among activist groups and NGOs working in what are usually thought of as distinct areas. The interests these groups ranged from biodiversity-based farming to the study of the impacts of WTO agreements and TRIPs on sustainable agriculture and food security and the prevention of trafficking. Gaining access for the char people to land, forming farmers' groups, and introducing forms of agricultural production and livestock keeping that produced enough food—both cultivated and uncultivated—to feed the villages meant that men no longer had to migrate seasonally to work for cash, families' debts were thus reduced, and, significantly, women's roles in agricultural production—particularly seed and livestock keeping—were restored. With less debt pressure and a more secure standing in the family and the community, women and girls became far less vulnerable to trafficking. The agricultural activity also involved the children, reducing the pressures on them to leave as well.

"It was not enough to create awareness against trafficking, if we could not talk about security of food and livelihood," Akhter writes. "We called it food sovereignty, the right to produce food" (Akhter 2007, 97–98). For Akhter, the *dignity* that comes with food sovereignty is no less important than increased material security. Concurring with Kumar's critique of the statism of the "Universal Declaration of Human Rights," she points out that, unlike conventional, state-form "rights," dignity is community-based. The community approach, unlike the "rights" approach, is not primarily about protecting "victims" and punishing "abusers." (In fact, distinguishing between victims and abusers would be difficult in many circumstances.) Though it goes without saying that she supports interventions to protect migrants at their destinations, she emphasizes the insensitivity of these interventions to the initial conditions that destroy or guarantee security:

> If means are still available or survival, particularly if food sources are not destroyed and the social relations are still in place for reciprocal support, people hardly take decisions to move out of the village. What is important to understand is that separation of the people from the land and releasing labor to make them available for capital is a violent act. (Akhter 2007, 86)

Bringing the micro example of the char people to bear on the global level, she argues that dignity itself is therefore one of the most effective deterrents of the many levels of violence involved in migration. Sex-ratio imbalances, the profitability of trafficking and forced sex work, and the perception that global capital has the right to destroy livelihoods in order to have an ample supply of raw materials and cheap labor are each in their own way *effects* as well as causes of losses of dignity. "We are indeed asking to open up the horizon of our investigation and rearrange our analytical tool box," Akhter emphasizes (ibid., 87).

"The solution has to be drastic and it has to be protected first and foremost from the sabotage of rhetoric that dismisses any alternative as unreal, impractical," wrote the late South African antiapartheid activist and director of the Institute of Black Research at the University of KwaZulu, Natal, Fatima Meer (2007, 81). Meer was writing from her experience battling a state apparatus that until the eleventh hour even many sympathetic observers thought could not be dismantled within the foreseeable future (Waller 2006, 528). There seems no reason why the historically contingent corporate nation-state should be less immune to "rupture and transformation" than its mid-twentieth-century avatar, apartheid. A great deal is at stake. If this transnational project can find ways to unfold outside the barely three hundred-year-old paradigm of the corporate nation-state, reconceptualizing rights to prioritize the dignity and livelihoods of people, whether on the move or not, then it may help prevent not only great violence and political injustice, but also the ecological crises that would render nation-state sovereignty definitively irrelevant.

Notes

1. Further information about the CIEDS Collective, the AWHRC, and El Taller International may be found at the following Web sites: http://www.ciedsindia.org, www.awhrc.org, and www.eltaller.org. Books and DVDs documenting specific Courts of Women are available from either the AWHRC or El Taller International.

2. Well versed in precolonial, colonial, and postcolonial Indian history, Kumar has also listened closely to indigenous thinkers in Africa, Australia, North and South America, and South Asia, whose cultures were, and largely still are, excluded from the international nation-state-based community of the United Nations from which the 1948 Universal Declaration of Human Rights emerged. The term *cosmovision* is used by Mexican religious studies scholar Sylvia Marcos to bring nonsecular epistemes into dialogue with European binary logic in her work on gender in pre-Columbian Mesoamerican religion (Marcos 2006, 21, 31, 38, 96).

3. For a concise description of the outcomes of the Courts of Women, see Kumar 2005, 196. The first Courts of Women included the Court of Women on Domestic Violence (held in Lahore, Pakistan, in 1993 and focusing on dowry burning, acid throwing, battering, rape, crimes of honor), the historic Court of Women on Violence of War Against Women, held in Tokyo, Japan, in 1994 and focusing on women victims of the wars in Asia from World War II (the "comfort women") to Vietnam, Cambodia, and the U.S. military bases in the Pacific; the Court of Women on Crimes Against Dalit Women, held in 1994 in Bangalore, India; the Court of Women on Reproductive Rights and Genetic Engineering, held in 1994 in

Cairo during the U.N. International Conference on Population and Development; the Court of Women on the Violence of Development, held in Bangalore, India, in 1995 (Kumar 2005, 192–95).

5. The Preamble of the UDHR concludes, "The General Assembly, Proclaims this Universal Declaration of Human Rights as a common standard of achievement for all peoples and all nations, to the end that every individual and every organ of society, keeping this Declaration constantly in mind, shall strive by teaching and education to promote respect for these rights and freedoms and by progressive measures, national and international, to secure their universal and effective recognition and observance, *both among the peoples of Member States themselves and among the peoples of territories under their jurisdiction*" (United Nations 1948; italics mine).

6. California writer Anthony Cristofani characterizes his experience of the police raid of Occupy L.A. in December 2011 in terms of just such a transformation of subjectivity: "I watched these people . . . become 'a people' . . . [e]xercising what for many of us was a new understanding of public space as ours, not theirs" (Cristofani 2011).

7. Liang has done extensive work on the use of intellectual property law to dispossess rural and indigenous people of their access to sustainable, subsistence food production through the Alternative Law Forum, a nonprofit collective he co-founded in Bangalore.

8. The critique of binary logic and its relation to neoliberal economics and its attendant militarism, environmental devastation, and wholesale displacement of people is a large and complex topic, which has been explored extensively by a wide range of scholars, social critics, and public intellectuals, including Arundhati Roy, Vandana Shiva, Naomi Klein, Sandra Harding, Gilles Deleuze and Félix Guattari, and, one could argue, French philosopher Jacques Derrida. I have discussed the effects of this logic in relation to such issues as "first world" feminist imperialism, sex trafficking, and globalization policymaking (Waller 2005; 2006; 2010).

Works Cited

Akhter, Farida. 2007. "Dignity: Security of Movement, Security of Livelihood." In *Asking We Walk: The South as New Political Imaginary: Book One: In the Time of the Earth*, edited by Corinne Kumar. Bangalore, India: Streelekha Publications.

Anderson, Benedict. 1983. *Imagined Communities: Reflections on the Origin and Spread of Nationalism*. London and New York: Verso.

Anzaldúa, Gloria. 1987. *Borderlands/La Frontera: The New Mestiza*. San Francisco: Spinsters: Aunt Lute.

Arendt, Hannah. 1966. *The Origins of Totalitarianism*. San Diego, New York, London: Harcourt.

Asian Women's Human Rights Council and El Taller International. 2002a. "Amina Mama, South Africa: Expert Witness." In *Singing in Dark Times: Women Remember. World Court of Women Against War, for Peace. Cape Town, South Africa, March 6–9, 2001*. Bangalore: Asian Women's Human Rights Council and El Taller International.

———. 2002b. *World Court of Women Against Racism/NGO Forum, World Conference Against Racism, Racial Discrimination, Xenophobia and Related Intolerance, Durban, South Africa, August 30, 2001*. Bangalore: Asian Women's Human Rights Council and El Taller International.

Benjamin, Walter. 1968 "The Storyteller: Reflections on the Works of Nikolai Leskov." In *Illuminations*, translated by Harry Zohn, edited by Hannah Arendt. New York: Harcourt, Brace, Jovanovich.

Bhushan, Madhu. 2007. "An Open Letter to Gandhi." In *Asking We Walk: The South as New Political Imaginary: Book Two: In the Time of the River/In the Time of the Wind*, edited by Corinne Kumar. Bangalore, India: Streelekha Publications.

Christian Solidarity Worldwide. 2010. "Egypt Forcibly Returns Eritrean Refugees." http://dynamic.csw.org.uk/article/asp?t=news&id=756. Accessed June 10, 2011.

Cristofani, Anthony. 2011. "Cops 'Peacefully Evacuate' Occupy L.A." http://theragblog.blogspot.com/2011/12/anthony-cristofani-cops-peacefully.html. Accessed January 2, 2012.

Brown, Wendy. 2010. *Walled States, Waning Sovereignty*. Brooklyn: Zone Books.

CIEDS (Center for Informal Education and Development Studies). 2011. "Overview." http://www.ciedsindia.org/overview.htm. Accessed August 10, 2011.

Deleuze, Gilles, and Félix Guattari. 1987. "Introduction: Rhizome" and "Nomadology:—The War Machine." In *A Thousand Plateaus: Capitalism and Schizophrenia*, translated by Brian Massumi. Minneapolis: University of Minnesota Press.

Di Maio, Alessandra. 2012. "The Black Mediterranean: Migration and Revolution in the Global Millenium." Public Lecture presented at UCLA, May 7, 2012.

Doctors Without Borders. 2009. "Migrants and Asylum Seekers Endure Inhuman Conditions in Malta." http://www.msf.org.uk/exposing_appalling_conditions_malta_20090416.news. Accessed July 9, 2010.

El Taller International, Center for Informal Education and Development studies (CIEDS Collective), Vimochana and the Asian Women's Human Rights Council. 2009. "Angsana Report: Towards New Notions of Justice: International Roundtables/Reflections on the Courts of Women" (unpublished report).

Ezeilo, Joy Ngozi. 2007. "Amazons Go to War Without Weapons: Women and the Conflict in Escravos, Niger Delta." In *The Wages of Empire: Neoliberal Policies, Repression, and Women's Poverty*, edited by Amalia Cabezas, Ellen Reese, and Marguerite Waller. Boulder and London: Paradigm Publishers.

Fasheh, Munir. 2007. "Bombardment by Rootless and Cluster Words." In *Asking We Walk: The South as New Political Imaginary: Book Two: In the Time of the River/In the Time of the Wind*, edited by Corinne Kumar. Bangalore, India: Streelekha Publications.

Federici, Silvia. 2010. "Feminism and the Politics of the Commons." In *Uses of a WorldWind, Movement, Movements, and Contemporary Radical Currents in the United States*, edited by Craig Hughes, Stevie Peace, and Kevin Van Meter. Oakland: AK Press. Available at http://www.the commoner.org. Accessed June 23, 2012.

Fortress Europe. 2012. "Death by Policy: The Fatal Realities of 'Fortress Europe.'" http://www.unitedagainstracism.org/pages/underframeFatalRealitiesFortress Europe.htm. Accessed June 26, 2012.

Glissant, Édouard. 1997. *Poetics of Relation*, translated by Betsy Wing. Ann Arbor: University of Michigan Press.

Harding, Sandra. 1998. *Is Science Multicultural? Postcolonialisms, Feminisms, and Epistemologies*. Bloomington and Indianapolis: Indiana University Press.

Higate, Paul, and Marsha Henry. 2009. *Insecure Spaces: Peacekeeping, Power, and Performance in Haiti, Kosovo, and Liberia*. London, New York: Zed Books.

Human Rights Watch. 2011. "World Report 2011: European Union." http://www.hrw.org/en/world-report2011. Accessed June 12, 2011.

Joan B. Kroc Institute for Peace and Justice. 2005. "Final Report on the Global Women's Court of Accountability." http://catcher.sandiego.edu/items/peace studies/Global Court-FinalReport.pdf. Accessed June 24, 2012.

Jurschick, Karin, dir. 2003. *The Peacekeepers and the Women*. Women Make Movies.

Klein, Naomi. 2007. *The Shock Doctrine: The Rise of Disaster Capitalism*. New York: Picador.

Kumar, Corinne. 2005. "South Wind: Towards a New Political Imaginary." In *Dialogue and Difference: Feminisms Challenge Globalization*, edited by Marguerite Waller and Sylvia Marcos. New York and Basingstoke: Palgrave Macmillan.

Lorde, Audre. 1984. "The Master's Tools Will Never Dismantle the Master's House." In *Sister Outsider: Essays and Speeches by Audre Lorde*. Freedom, CA: The Crossing Press.

Mancillas, Aida, Ruth Wallen, Marguerite Waller. 1999. "Making Art, Making Citizens: Las Comadres and Postnational Aesthetics." In *With Other Eyes: Looking at Race and Gender in Visual Culture*, edited by Lisa Bloom. Minneapolis, London: University of Minnesota Press.

Marcos, Sylvia. 2006. *Taken From the Lips: Gender and Eros in Mesoamerican Religions*. Leiden and Boston: Brill.

Meer, Fatima. 2007. "The Global Crisis: A Crisis of Values." In *Asking We Walk: The South as New Political Imaginary: Book One: In the Time of the Earth*, edited by Corinne Kumar. Bangalore, India: Streelekha Publications.

Mohanram, Radhika. 2007. *Imperial White: Race, Diaspora, and the British Empire*. Minneapolis and London: University of Minnesota Press.

Nandy, Ashis. 2007. "Gandhi after Gandhi after Gandhi." In *Asking We Walk: The South as New Political Imaginary: Book Two: In the Time of the River/In the Time of the Wind*, edited by Corinne Kumar. Bangalore, India: Streelekha Publications.

Perkins, John. 2004. *Confessions of an Economic Hit Man*. San Francisco: Gerrett-Koehler.

Robert, Jean. 2007. "Place in the Space Age." In *Asking We Walk: The South as New Political Imaginary: Book Two: In the Time of the River/In the Time of the Wind*, edited by Corinne Kumar. Bangalore, India: Streelekha Publications.

Sedgwick, Eve Kosofsky. 1990. *Epistemology of the Closet*. Berkeley, Los Angeles: University of California Press.

Shiva, Vandana. 1988. *Staying Alive: Women, Ecology, and Development*. London: Zed Books; New Delhi: Kahli for Women.

———. 1997. "The Enclosure of the Commons." *Third World Network*. http://twnside.org.sg/title/com-cn.htm. Accessed June 22, 2012.

———. 2002. *Water Wars: Privatization, Pollution, and Profit*. Cambridge: South End Press.

Siapno, Jacqueline. 2009. "Human Safety, Security, and Resilience: Making Narrative Spaces for Dissent in Timor Leste." In *Timor Leste: How to Build a New Nation in Southeast Asia in the 21st Century*, edited by Christine Cabasset-Semedo and Fréderic Durand. Bangkok: IRASEC (Institute of Research on Contemporary Southeast Asia). Available as a free e-book at http://www.irasec.com.

Slevin, Peter. 2010. "Deportation of Illegal Immigrants Increases under Obama Administration." *Washington Post*. http://www.washingtonpost.com/wp_dyn/content/article/2010/07/25/AR2010072501790.html. Accessed June 26, 2012.

Svirsky, Gila. 2001. "The Impact of Women in Black in Israel." In *Frontline Feminisms: Women, War, and Resistance*, edited by Marguerite R. Waller and Jennifer Rycenga. New York and London: Routledge.

Tutu, Desmond, and Mukund Padmanabhan. 2007. "Future and Forgiveness: Interview with Archbishop Desmond Tutu." In *Asking We Walk: The South as New Political Imaginary: Book Two: In the Time of the River/In the Time of the Wind*, edited by Corinne Kumar. Bangalore, India: Streelekha Publications.

Tyler, Imogen. 2006. "'Welcome to Britain': The Cultural Politics of Asylum." *European Journal of Cultural Studies* (9) 2: 185–202.

———. "Naked Protest: the Maternal Politics of Citizenship and Revolt." *Citizenship Studies* 17 (forthcoming).

United Nations. 1948. "The Universal Declaration of Human Rights." http://www.un.org/en/documents/udhr/. Accessed April 16, 2012.

Waller, Marguerite. 1994. "Border *Boda* or Divorce *Fronterizo*?" In *Negotiating Performance: Gender, Sexuality, and Theatricality in Latin America*, edited by Diana Taylor and Juan Villegas. Durham and London: Duke University Press.

———. 2006. "Addicted to Virtue: The Globalization Policy Maker." *Social Identities: Journal for the Study of Race, Nation and Culture* (12) 5: 575–94.

———. 2010. "Vertigo in the Balkans: Karin Jurschick's *The Peacekeepers and the Women*." In *Visions of Struggle in Women's Filmmaking in the Mediterranean*, edited by Flavia Laviosa. New York and London: Palgrave Macmillan.

Figure 13.1. Solidarity Leaflet (front), 2012. Courtesy of The Anti-Raids Campaign in London

13

Migrant Resistance and the Anti-Raids Campaign in London 2012

Anti-Raids Campaign Coalition

This afterword is a short introduction to the anti-raids campaign, a coalition of community-based groups of migrants and precarious workers started in 2012 in response to raids of migrant people by the UK Border Agency and the police in London. Included here is the migrant "bust-card" (the pocket guide for migrant rights), which was produced in the context of the campaign, as well as an info-sheet with tips on acting in solidarity with migrants who are stopped and searched by immigration officers and the police.

This campaign has become urgent after the large-scale raid on February 25, 2012, of a concert at "The Coronet," a music venue in Elephant and Castle (South London) mostly attended by Latin Americans: numerous police vans appeared on the site and while people were waiting to enter the building, immigration officials and police officers started checking the papers and the migration status of those in the queue. The result was that ninety people were detained in immigration removal centers, some of whom were deported a few days later. Additionally, six Latin Americans have recently been arrested at a school in Kent, and there are frequent raids on bus stops in neighborhoods populated by migrants from different backgrounds across the city. Anecdotal evidence suggests that more than four thousand raids have been conducted in London in the sole month of February at work and public sites.[1]

The immigration raids signal an intensifying persecution of migrants who do not have the correct documents to reside in the UK. It is important to highlight that in this period of political and economic crises, increased pressure on migrants and the spreading of fear in migrant communities in

London is creating a situation where migrant workers are being pushed even farther underground. This results in worsening conditions for migrant laborers, such as lower pay, precisely at a time when employers are in particular need of exploitable labor. Migrants are being made ever more vulnerable also through changes in the law that make their residency status more precarious (with shrinking legal channels to enter and work in the "low skilled" job sectors). Additionally, as mentioned above, increased efforts are going into tracking migrants down and expelling them, regardless of their local lives, or the dangers they may face upon being deported.

In the face of brutal raids and deportations of friends, lovers, and comrades, some immediate questions arise: What are the rights of migrants when they are stopped on the street? How can they act in these circumstances to avoid intimidation and harassment by the police? How can they challenge racial profiling when they are stopped just because of their appearance? What are the rights of migrants when they are in detention? How can passers-by witnessing a "stop and search," or a raid act in solidarity? These are some of the questions that the anti-raids coalition in London tried to respond to through the creation of the "migrant bust-card" and with the launch of a larger political campaign aimed at involving migrants and non-migrants against the increased racist attacks on the Latino community and beyond.

The coalition at the base of this anti-raids campaign originated from the urgency to find some answers to these questions, and to develop some tools for action in relation to them. A collaboration between the "Latin American Workers Association" (LAWAS) and "Precarious Workers Brigade" (PWB) had already existed for a few years, with some of the PWB members actively involved in migrant workers' rights groups in London such as "No One is Illegal" and "No Borders" activist networks. In March 2012, the existing alliance took a more definite form with the launch of a campaign: during an event organized by LAWAS, a public statement denouncing the persecution of the Latin American community was read out, and the urgency of coordinating efforts became clearer. An unconventional coalition that has since been growing has become an intense and productive collaboration between different political realities and groups including LAWAS, Precarious Workers Brigade, Stop Deportations and Southwark Action, The Prisma, No Borders, and South London Solidarity Federation.

Migrant Bust Card

The launch of the bust card took place on the second of June 2012, when a colorful, folded sheet of A4 with step-by-step guides of what to do when faced with a raid was given, as well as advice about possible actions to take if a person ends up in detention. The card was launched initially

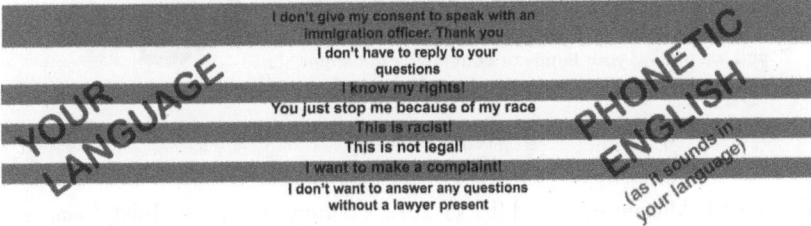

Figure 13.2. Migrant Bust Card (front), 2012. Courtesy of The Anti-Raids Campaign in London

This Migrant Bust Card has been created based on personal experiences.
**It provides minimal and necessary information to avoid detention during a immigration raid on the streets and a step by step guide on how to act
promptly in the event you are detained.**

If you are taken to a detention centre

They will take away phones with camera and internet access.
But You have the right to keep a phone without camera or a SIM card.

- You will receive documents with **reference numbers** from the Home Office, or a Port Reference from the Detention Centre.
- **These numbers will be required** by lawyers and immigration officers
- Keep these documents handy and in order at all times!
- Share this information with people that you trust!
- To obtain legal help, you should register ASAP at the '**welfare office**'. If there isn't one at your detention centre, you can do this in the **library**.
- You have the right to an interpreter in your language at this stage.

There's two ways to get out

1. Bail

You have the right to apply for this **from the day of arrival** at the detention centre.
You will need two guarantors, and complete an application with the help of a lawyer or organization
A Judge will make a decision about your situation

2. Temporary Admission

You may apply for this if you have been in detention **seven days**.
Fill in the applications at the welfare office or library. For this application **no you don't need a lawyer or guarantor**, but you must provide an address or valid reasons to get out
(personal relationships or children with EU citizenship.
You may also use articldes **3 and 8** of the Universal Declaration of Human Rights
Article 3 : Everyone has the right to life, liberty and security of person.
Article 8 : All are equal before the law and are entitled without any discrimination to equal protection of the law. All are entitled to equal protection against any discrimination in violation of this Declaration and against any incitement to such discrimination.
The application is sent directly to UKBA officers in the detention centre where you are held.
Bear in mind that the address will be asked so the authorities can make sure that you have a place to go back to.
But remember, if you think that by giving away an address
you are putting your family or community in danger
you don't have to provide this information!

Read and study the information on this card! Share it with family and friends! Exercise the sentences in english ! For more information you can also visit www.freemovement.org.uk

Figure 13.3. Migrant Bust Card (back), 2012. Courtesy of The Anti-Raids Campaign in London

Figure 13.4. Migrant Bust Card (front, Spanish), 2012. Courtesy of The Anti-Raids Campaign in London

¡nadie es ilegal!
estos son nuestros derechos

Guía de bolsillo para el migrante detenido

Esta tarjeta de apoyo al migrante ha sido creada en base a experiencias personales. Esta tarjeta provee de información mínima y necesaria para evitar una detención o a actuar prontamente si te llevan detenida.Ten en cuenta que esta tarjeta NO pretende ser un documento de ayuda legal experta. En caso de detención, no entres en pánico, mantén la calma, revisa los puntos y contactos aquí presentados y busca ayuda.

Si te llevan a un centro de detención

Decomisarán teléfonos con cámara y acceso a internet (**tienes derecho a mantener un teléfono sin camara o retener una tarjeta SIM**)

Recibirás documentos con números de referencia del Ministerio del Interior (**Home Office**) o del centro de detención (**Port Reference**)

Estos números serán requeridos por abogados y agentes de migración

¡ Asegúrate de mantener estos documentos a mano y en orden en todo momento !

Comparte estos datos con personas de confianza

Para obtener ayuda legal, regístrate cuantos antes en el **'welfare office'** (oficina de bienestar) Si no hay, házlo en la **'library'** (biblioteca).

En esta instancia tienes derecho a un interprete

Hay dos formas para salir

1. Bajo Fianza

Tienes derecho a solicitar esto **desde el primer día** de tu llegada al centro de detención
Se requiere tener 2 (dos) **garantes** y llenar un formulario con ayuda de una organización o abogados.
Un Juez o Jueza decidirá sobre Tu situación

2. Con Admisión Temporal

Tienes derecho a solicitarlo **si has estado detenido por más de siete (7) días**
Puedes llenar los formularios en welfare office o library. Para esta solicitiud **no necesitas abogados ni garantes**, pero si debes proveer una dirección, o motivos válidos para salir (relación personal, dependientes o niños con ciudadanía de la Comunidad Europea. También puedes usar los artículos 3 y 8 de la Declaración Universal de Derechos Humanos.

Artículo 3 : Todo individuo tiene derecho a la vida, a la libertad y a la seguridad de su persona
Artículo 8 : Toda persona tiene derecho a un recurso efectivo ante los tribunales nacionales competentes, que la ampare contra actos que violen sus derechos fundamentales reconocidos por la constitución o por la ley.

El formulario se envía directamente a los oficiales de UKBA en el centro de detención donde te encuentras.

Ten en cuenta que dirección será pedida para que la ley se asegure de que tienes un lugar a donde volver.

Pero recuerda, si crees que dando tu direccion puedes **poner en peligro a tu familia o tu comunidad,**

¡no tienes que proveer esta informacion!

Lee y estudia la información aquí presentada! ¡Compártela con amigos y tu familia! ¡Ejercita las frases en inglés! Para más información sobre detención (en inglés) www.freemovement.org.uk

Figure 13.5. Migrant Bust Card (back, Spanish), 2012, Courtesy of The Anti-Raids Campaign in London

Figure 13.6. Solidarity Leaflet (back), 2012. Courtesy of The Anti-Raids Campaign in London

in Spanish, Portuguese, and English and, as a result of the launch, it has been further translated into Tamil, Arabic, Hindi, Mandarin, and Shona in process. The launch also included a theatre performance by members of LAWAS who performed typical cases of migration controls based on personal experiences, followed by a role-play involving the audience in exercising the tips written on the card. This was an inspiring example of the possible ways to distribute the migrant bust-card and make it operational, while providing a model of dissemination across different migrant communities in the capital.

Some of the organizations in this campaign have a history of working with and supporting immigrants on issues of migration controls, exploitation, and labor rights. Yet as is often the case in London, efforts are scattered and often remain isolated. On the contrary, the main aim of this campaign is to create a stronger nexus between communities, enabling strong solidarity and mobilization across and beyond those affected by raids within an increasingly hierarchical postcolonial border regimes, where the government claims to wanting to expel all those migrants earning less than £35,000 a year and reduce the number of immigrants from sixty thousand to thirty thousand entering the UK annually.[2]

It is important to highlight that the emerging alliances were born out of everyday collaboration in the community, such as the self-managed language classes organized weekly by LAWAS and where local activists, migrants and non, had a chance to learn the art of literal and cultural translation, gathering their skills, artistic, political, and social capacities, while pointing to existing potentials for acting together in and against this moment of crisis, austerity, and racist repression by the state. Bringing together the struggles of migrant and precarious workers of different citizenship and employment statuses, this campaign hopes to invent ever more unexpected connections and shared forms of self-organization.

Emerging from its early stages, this campaign aims to gain more momentum, focus and participation, encouraging different communities to get involved and contribute ideas and strategies.

For more information on the campaign, and to download the bust cards in different languages, please visit:

www.lawas.org.uk
precariousworkersbrigade.tumblr.com
london.noborders.org.uk/node/606

Text written collectively by the Anti-Raids Campaign, June 2012.

Notes

1. http://www.theprisma.co.uk/2012/03/12/immigrants-and-detentions-in-the-uk-police-round-ups-how-when-and-where/.
2. http://www.guardian.co.uk/uk/2012/feb/29/skilled-migrants-lose-right-settle.

Figure 14.1. *Report Non-Humans*, 2009. A *D-9* movie bus bench poster. Photo courtesy of Kamil Turowski

Afterword

The Human Waste Disposal Industry
or Immigrant Protest in Neoliberal Times

Imogen Tyler and Katarzyna Marciniak

Along the fault-lines of the world disorder piles of human waste are rising.

—Zygmunt Bauman, "The Crisis of the Human Waste Disposal Industry"

Borders and prison—walls and cages—are global crises. Walls and cages are fundamental to managing the wealth, social inequalities, and opposition to the harms created by capitalism and the present round of colonial dispossession.

—Jenna M. Loyd, Matt Mitchelson, and Andrew Burridge, *Beyond Walls and Cages*

Wasted Lives

The short black comic film *Asylum* (2011, directed by Joern Utkilen)[1] depicts the lives of two migrants, Alfred Islami (Mihai Arsene) and Wan Yun Ji (Andy Cheung), living through the interminable time of an immigration detention center in Scotland. Immigration detention, *Asylum* reveals, is characterized by *an excess of time*. In the absurdist tradition of Samuel Beckett's *Waiting for Godot* (1953), the detainees "can only kill time, as they are slowly killed by it" (Bauman 1998, 88). Alfred Islami dreams of running a biodynamic farm and spends time reading about biodynamic farming methods, acting out his farming fantasies with the few props, chairs,

Figure 14.2. Wan Yun Ji and Alfred Islami contemplate another day in "Dungwood" Immigration Detention Centre in Scotland. Still from *Asylum*, 2011, directed by Joern Utkilen

pot-plants, rubber gloves at his disposal and attempting to procure potatoes and cows from detention officials. Alfred shares a shabby room in the detention center with Wan Yun Ji (Andy Cheung). While Alfred spends his time playing farmer in order to "kill time," Wan Yun Ji engages in repeated acts of self-harm, including cutting his wrists in a failed suicide attempt and throwing himself through the glass window of his detention center room. These different strategies of survival represent attempts not only to *pass time* but to sustain some semblance of agency and self-determination. These are activities that stave off (the seemingly inevitable) psychological deterioration into zombie-like "dead but undead" states of being, which overwhelm detainees around them (Figure 14.3).

Zygmunt Bauman argues that one of the major characteristics of global capitalism is the manufacture of ever greater numbers of "wasted humans" within and at the borders of sovereign territories (Bauman 2004, 5). As Loïc Wacquant details, the three major characteristics of human waste production are: labor precariousness, which produces "material deprivation, family hardship, temporal uncertainty and personal anxiety" (Wacquant 2008, 24–25); the relegation of people to decomposing neighborhoods in which public and private resources are dwindling; and heightened stigmatization "in daily life as well as in public discourse" (ibid.). The rise of neoliberal social and economic policies since the 1970s has accelerated "human waste production" (see Tyler 2013). Growing numbers of *wasted*

Figure 14.3. Zombification in detention. Still from *Asylum*, 2011, directed by Joern Utkilen

lives are no longer containable within the "dumping grounds" and shanty towns of the South, but are visible as shadow populations at and within the borders of wealthy nations—slum-dwellers, illegal workers, rough-sleepers, immigration detainees.

Bauman suggests that the world is now characterized by two classes of people: tourist-consumers, those with agency who are free to consume and move, and vagabonds, disposable populations who get stuck and whose lives are often wasted. What distinguishes these two classes is mobility, the relative freedom to move across borders. As Abby Peterson summarizes, for the tourists "distances are easily bridged . . . and borders are easily crossed" (Peterson 2010, 16). By way of contrast, when vagabonds attempt to cross borders:

> they travel surreptitiously, often illegally, sometimes paying more for the crowded steerage of a stinking unseaworthy boat than others pay for business-class gilded luxuries and are frowned upon, and if unlucky, arrested and promptly deported, when they arrive. (Bauman 1998, 89)

In the case of unwanted migrants, immigration detention centers are factories of human waste production which strip people of their human dignity and reproduce them as dehumanized, deportable beings. Utkilen's *Asylum* is a meditation on the human waste disposal industry. From the name of the detention center, "Dungwood" (Figure 14.4), a reference to Dungavel Immigration Removal Centre in Scotland, to Islami's explanations of the shit-based science of biodynamic farming, to Wan Yun Ji's poem "Shit Hole" (Figure 14.5), this film is about the production of *wasted lives*. It is a story told from the perspective of migrants interpellated as illegal, deportable waste. Through a black comic lens, it examines what it might mean to find oneself constituted as disposable, and what the conditions for surviving such an abject classification might be.

The protagonists of *Asylum* resist and survive the human waste removal center. While Islami fails to persuade the detention center manager to allow him to transform Dungwood into a biodynamic farm, by the end of the film he has succeeded in obtaining a "live potato." Wan Yun Ji is in a wheelchair after throwing himself through the window, but has found love (and a possible route out of imprisonment) with a Scottish nurse who cared for him in hospital. In the final scene of the film we see Islami planting his potato in the grounds of the detention center with Wan Yun Ji beside him. Embracing the philosophy of biodynamic farming, they have both found ways to resist their designation as human waste. The moral of *Asylum* seems to be that there is always some value, some life, some comedy and some hope, to be extracted from the shit holes in which people find themselves.

Immigrant Protest: Politics, Aesthetics, and Everyday Dissent has brought together a series of interviews, art works, and scholarly essays that, through a focus on protest and resistance, variously reflect upon the disenfranchise-

Figure 14.4. Dungwood Removal Centre. Still from *Asylum*, 2011, directed by Joern Utkilen

Figure 14.5. Wan Yun Ji reads his poem "Shit Hole" to zombified detainees in the English Language Class at "Dungwood" Immigration Detention Centre.

ment of migrant populations. While we are witnessing the intensification of the production of wasted lives, we are also living in a period of intensive resistance to the processes of disenfranchisement. This is a time when people around the world are questioning deepening inequalities, the impoverishment of democracy, the marketization of welfare, the proliferation of surveillance cultures and the militarization of borders. It is in this context that *Immigrant Protest* has sought to explore and document some of the diversity and vitality of protests against border regimes in a range of local and national contexts. Yet what it has also highlighted is the difficulty of resistance and the creative means through which migrants, artists, and activists engage in protest.

What connects all the contributions to this collection is the "No One Is Illegal" protest. This is the call for the equality of all humans and a shared, collective and utopian vision of a future world without borders, prisons, and cages, visions of a future in which "human illegality" would be unthinkable. However, in order to think "No One Is Illegal," we need to further unpack the question of human illegality. What does it mean to be classified as illegal? How is illegality produced, by whom and for what purposes? How is it experienced? What is the relationship between criminality and illegality? Who profits from illegality? While we cannot answer these questions in depth here, at the end of the process of editing this book after talking and working with academics, artists, and activists about illegality, borders, citizenship, and protest for many years, what is clear is that these questions remain the pivotal ones with which to intervene in and challenge "the human waste disposal industry." As Jenna Loyd, Matt Mitchelson, and Andrew Burridge write in the introduction to their brilliant collection *Beyond Walls and Cages: Prisons, Borders, and Global Crisis*, undoing criminality and illegality involves the development of "an abolitionist analytic and practice which can connect movements against state violence" (Loyd, Mitchelson, and Burridge 2012, 8). We want to end by telling the story of

Lamia,[2] and her experiences of the human disposal industry. We will focus on the cruel and absurd ways in which the legal production of illegality has emerged as "a 'recession-proof' business" (Feltz and Baksh 2012, 143).

The Value of Waste: The Economics of Illegality

Lamia, a migrant worker from North Africa, was detained in a dawn-raid by British border officials at the hostel in which she lived. Her arrest was triggered when she applied for a casual cleaning job at a local hospital. It transpired that Lamia had overstayed a three-month tourist visa. Lamia had been living in the UK for three years, working primarily as a cleaner, dog walker, and occasional child minder in private family homes. On her arrest she was transported in a prison van by migrant "detainee escort services," a job contracted by the British government to the private company *Reliance Security Group*, to a temporary holding facility at a police station before being moved to Yarl's Wood Immigration Removal Centre. From this moment in Lamia's story it is important to begin to note how her newly determined status as "illegal" enabled her to be systematically transformed into a commodity. For example, once migrants are caught in Britain's detention estate, they are frequently moved in, out, and between different places of incarceration—cycles of *arrest and release* that can last years. For companies like *Reliance, mobility determines profit* and the greater the number of migrant detainee movements within the immigration detention estate the more profit accrues to securities companies. This is a multi–million pound business as according to the then minister of state for immigration, Damien Green, in 2011 alone:

> Around 80,000 journeys were undertaken. . . . These include transferring detainees from police stations, prisons and other places of detention into immigration removal centres, taking them to ports and airports for removal, to hospitals for medical appointments, courts for appeal hearings and embassies for documentation interviews. It also includes the transfer of detainees between different immigration removal centres. (Green 2011)

As Nick Gill (2009) argues, the management of irregular migrants captured within the detention estate is characterized by a complex and often seemingly random combination of forced movements and enforced periods of stillness (migrants are often compelled to stay in specific housing, in designated towns and cities as well as being imprisoned in secure detention facilities). Despite the governmental rhetoric, these mobility controls are not designed to "seal the borders" so much as to *extract profit from border creation*. Indeed, in the space of a decade, an unbelievably profitable *detain and release network* has emerged, controlled by global securities companies. These controls form what Sandro Mezzadra (2004) describes as "a system of dams," which enable the transformation of illegality from a status into a commodity which/who can be bought and sold in a global marketplace. As the investigative journalists Renee Feltz and Stokely Baksh argue in "Business of Detention," an account of the rise of immigration detention business in the United States:

> Immigrant rights advocates cheered when the Obama administration announced in August 2009 that it would stop holding immigrant children inside a former medium-security prison run by the nation's largest private prison company. But by then, immigration detention contracts with the federal government had become a key part of the Corrections Corporation of America's expansion plan. . . . The company expects detention, which has tripled in the twenty-first century, to provide a "recession-proof" business (Feltz and Baksh 2012, 143).

An analysis of the entangled relationship between governmental policy and the economics of immigration detention reveals that increasingly immigrants are systematically transformed "into profitable 'products'" (ibid., 146).

Lamia ended up in Yarl's Wood, a detention center run under contact by the global securities company SERCO—the company who manages Australia's notorious immigration detention estate. The average daily overall cost to the British Government and its taxpayers of keeping a single person in detention per day is estimated to be £120 ($188 or E140) (Silverman et al. 2012). While detention is supposed to be a short-term solution, employed in the forty-eight-hour window prior to deportation, Lamia was still detained several weeks later. In order to continue to buy expensive top-up phone cards, to keep in touch with friends and family in the outside world, Lamia took on a cleaning job in the detention center. Paradoxically, Lamia had been detained because she was working, illegally, as a cleaner. She had been paid the minimum wage (currently £6/$9 an hour) as an illegal worker. Ironically, once detained, normal labor laws do not apply to illegal migrants, and SERCO paid Lamia 50p ($.75) an hour (see also McVeigh 2011). A job description leaked by a migrant worker from inside SERCO reveals the post of "Laundry Assistant" at wages of 50p an hour (Figure 14.6). Exploited detainee labor reduces SERCO's running costs and further increases the profit to be made from this growth market in "migrant illegality." Serco's motto is "Bringing Services to Life."

Lamia was finally released from detention after twelve weeks, at which stage SERCO would have billed the British government approxi-

JOB DESCRIPTION

POSITION TITLE	Laundry Assistant
LOCATION	Dove/Avocet/Crane
REPORTING RELATIONSHIP	Unit Officers

ROLE

To maintain cleanliness of the area, help other residents with the machines as required and ensure area is tidy at all times.

PRINCIPLE DUTIES AND ACCOUNTABILITIES

- To attend to the laundry room Three times a day. You are to attend these duties at 14.00hrs – 14.30hrs (mid-afternoon cleaning), 19.00hrs – 19.30hrs (early evening cleaning), and 20.30 - 21.00hrs at the end of your working day you must check the laundry room and water the flowers in the unit garden.
- Assist with making up bedding packs.
- Empty bins in laundry, wipe down machines and clean the floor at 14.00hours and at the end of the working day (9.00pm).
- Identify any abandoned clothing and advise staff accordingly.
- Restock sanitary dispensers when necessary.
- Water plants in the garden on the unit you work on. This will be required to be done last thing in the evening to prevent the flowers getting burnt by the sun.

PAYMENT

- Payment will take place daily apart from Friday, Saturday and Sunday this will be paid the following Monday
- You will receive £1.50 per day
- You are required to work a total of one and a half hours per day

This position reports to: Unit Officers

Reviewed by: Amanda Haywood

Figure 14.6. A photocopy of job description produced by Serco for Immigration Detainees, published online at "Yarl's Wood echós H-Block and Attica" http://stop-deportations.wordpress.com/2012/09/10/yarls-wood-echos-h-block-and-attica/

mately £100,000 for her incarceration. Lamia was unsure why she had been released. She had received no legal advice while detained. Now destitute, Lamia began an asylum claim primarily because other inmates at the detention center informed her that this was the best way to secure temporary accommodation while she found work. It was probably the only way to survive without living on the streets and/or sex work. Lamia was given a single room in a shared house with other asylum applicants while her claim was processed. The property was leased by a notorious slum landlord to SERCO, who had been awarded a £175m contract to provide accommodation to asylum seekers as part of the Border Agency project "Commercial and Operational Managers Procuring Asylum Support Services" (COMPASS). This policy shift saw a seismic change as contractual obligations for housing and support services to asylum seekers were redirected from local government authorities to private for-profit contractors. Three global securities firms have been the primary beneficiaries of COMPASS, G4S, SERCO, and *Reliance*, all "multinational security companies with abhorrent track records of abusing migrants and refugees in their care" (Corporate Watch 2012).[3] In 2013, SERCO, dubbed by activists as "the company running Britain," posted profits of £203 million on £5 billion of revenue (Crook 2013).

Because Lamia's asylum claim was made retrospectively, because she was from a "safe country" of origin, and because her asylum claim was unfounded, she was again detained, this time when she signed on at her local reporting office, one of fifteen reporting centers located across the UK. Soon after this detention, Lamia was re-released on bail. However, she absconded from her bail address in order to escape the grips of the market in illegality which she had become caught up in. Lamia is currently working in the hospitality trade in a different city and intends to move to another country when she can afford to purchase a forged passport.

Neoliberal economic policies such as privatization, deregulation, unrestricted foreign investment, and the contracting out of state-run services are dependent upon the porosity of borders to flows of capital, including the availability of pools of precarious migrant labor. Thus, there is a major discrepancy between policies seemingly aimed at curbing immigration and limiting movement, and the demand for cheap irregular migrant labor. It is in the context of this "double agenda" between the imperatives of state formation and neoliberal economics, between the imperatives of securing the borders and opening the borders, that irregular migrants are capitalized. "Illegality," as Nicholas de Genova argues,

> is lived through a palpable sense of deportability—the possibility of deportation, which is to say, the possibility of being removed from

the space of the . . . nation-state. The legal production of "illegality" provides an apparatus for sustaining . . . migrants' vulnerability and tractability—as workers—whose labor-power, inasmuch as it is deportable, becomes an eminently disposable commodity. (de Genova 2004, 161)

Lamia's case reveals the degree to which illegality makes her vulnerable to precarious working conditions not only outside but within the detention estate. What this story also reveals is some of the ways in which global securities companies are extracting profit from the market in human waste production. As more and more bureaucratic systems of determination, detention, and deportation emerge so international global securities companies penetrate farther into the fabric of the state in response to the "problem" of migrant illegality. At the same time, while huge amounts of taxpayers' money are handed to multinationals to manage the borders, most irregular migrants determined to be illegal are not deported but remain in limbo "under excruciatingly vulnerable socio-political conditions" (de Genova, 2011). As Hein de Haas argues, "Policies to 'fight illegal migration' are bound to fail because they are among the very causes of the phenomenon they pretend to combat" (de Haas 2008, 16).

Conclusion: An Accumulation of Small Acts

One of the major themes of this book has been in/visibility and, in particular, the centrality of representations and perceptual frames in creating value and prescribing *differential values* to human lives. Peter Nyers highlights the material risks of visibility for undocumented people caught in the "abject diaspora," the "deportspora" (Nyers 2003, 1070): "For people without status, everyday activities (working, driving, and going to school) are at risk of being transformed into criminal and illicit acts with dire consequences" (Nyers 2008, 166–67). The various forms of migrant protest and resistance explored in this book are a reminder that even the most marginal populations, including migrant workers without formal rights and protections, have the capacity to intervene within systems of classification that constitute them as deportable or illegal.

The intensification of the migrant protests documented in this book form one tiny part of a growing number of uprisings, movements, and moments by disenfranchised people and their allies against neoliberal social and economic policies around the world. *Immigrant Protest* has sought to map the diversity and vitality of migrant protests against border and citizenship regimes in a range of places, mediums, and contexts. We have highlighted some of the extraordinary and creative means through which migrants, citizens, artists, activists, and scholars engage in acts of resistance in a range of exceptional and everyday contexts. The recording and restaging of migrant protests in books such as this is a critical part of "No One Is Illegal" movement—a movement that urgently requires the invention of "new idioms of the political, and of belonging itself" (Berlant 2011, 262). As art activist Irina Contreras notes in a beautiful essay about her work titled "Cycles of Invisible Resistance": "There are ways in which the rigor of research and storytelling reclaims something. This work cannot fix everything, but it feels like part of a process, a step towards healing" (Contreras 2012, 329). We know that equality and justice require transformations in the relations "between words and things, between words and the visible" and a reorganization of "the sensory configuration of what is given to us and how we can make sense of it" (Rancière 2008, 174). Documenting resistance and protest involves the creation of new aesthetics of migration, which, in turn, can be used to question the inclusive/exclusive logic of citizenship and the language and economics of illegality.

Notes

1. Thanks to Brigit Morris-Colton for drawing my attention to this film, and to the Director Joern Utkilen for supplying a copy.

2. Lamia's story is a composite of several migrant stories assembled from both primary and secondary sources, a decision made in part to protect identities.

3. Activist John Grayson has detailed the conditions of some of the slum housing that migrants in West Yorkshire have been forced to live in when the contract for housing moved from the local authority to securities giant G4S.

Works Cited

Bauman, Zygmunt. 2002. "The Crisis of the Human Waste Disposal Industry." *Tikkun* 17 (5): 41–47.
———. 2003. *Liquid Love: On the Frailty of Human Bonds*. Cambridge: Polity.
———. 2004. *Wasted Lives: Modernity and Its Outcasts*. Cambridge: Blackwell.
———. 1998. *Globalization: the Human Consequences*. New York: Columbia University Press.
Berlant, Lauren. 2011. *Cruel Optimism*. Durham: Duke University Press.
Contreras, Irina. 2012. "Descado en Los Angeles: Cycles of Invisible Resistance." In *Beyond Walls and Cages: Prisons, Borders, and Global Crisis*, edited by Jenna M. Loyd, Matt Mitchelson, and Andrew Burridge. Athens and London: University of Georgia Press.
Corporate Watch. 2012, December 22. "Asylum Seekers to Be Housed by Prison Guards." *Corporate Watch*. http://www.corporatewatch.org/?lid=4159. Accessed June 18, 2013.

Crook, F. 2013, March 15. "Who Wins at Payment by Results? Ask Shareholders at Serco, the Company Running Britain." http://www.opendemocracy.net/ourkingdom/frances-crook/who-wins-at-%E2%80%98payment-by-results%E2%80%99-ask-shareholders-at-serco-company-running-. Accessed June 18, 2013.

Feltz, Renee, and Stokely Baksh. 2012. "Business of Detention." In *Beyond Walls and Cages: Prisons, Borders, and Global Crisis*, edited by Jenna M. Loyd, Matt Mitchelson, and Andrew Burridge. Athens and London: University of Georgia Press.

Foucault, Michel. 2008. *The Birth of Biopolitics: Lectures at the Collège de France, 1978–1979*. Edited by Michel Senellart, translated by Graham Burchell. New York: Palgrave Macmillan.

de Genova, Nicholas. 2004. "The Legal Production of Mexican/Migrant Illegality." *Latino Studies* 2 (2): 160–85.

Gill, Nick. 2009. "Longing for Stillness: The Forced Movement of Asylum Seekers." *M/C Journal* 12 (1). http://journal.media-culture.org.au/index.php/mcjournal/article/viewArticle/123. Accessed June 11, 2013.

Green, Damien. 2011. Hansard, HC, 5 September 2011, c241W http://www.publications.parliament.uk/pa/cm201011/cmhansrd/cm110905/text/110905w0009.htm. Accessed July 10, 2013.

de Haas, Hein. 2008. "The Myth of Invasion: The Inconvenient Realities of African Migration to Europe." http://www.heindehaas.com/Publications/de%20Haas%202008%20-%20inconvenient%20realities.pdf. Accessed June 1, 2012.

Loyd, M. Jenna, Matt Mitchelson, and Andrew Burridge, eds. 2012. "Introduction: Borders, Prisons, and Abolitionist Visions." In *Beyond Walls and Cages*. Athens: University of Georgia Press.

McVeigh, Karen. 2011 (January 2). "Yarl's Wood detainees paid 50p an hour." *The Guardian*. http://www.guardian.co.uk/uk/2011/jan/02/yarls-wood-detainees-paid-50p-hour. Accessed June 18, 2013.

Mezzadra, Sandro. 2004. "Citizenship in motion." *Generation Online*. http://www.generation-online.org/t/tmezzadra.htm. Accessed June 10, 2012.

Nyers, Peter. 2003. "Abject Cosmopolitanism: The Politics of Protection in the Anti-deportation Movement." *Third World Quarterly* 24 (6): 1069–93.

———. 2004. "Introduction: What's Left of Citizenship?" *Citizenship Studies* 8 (3): 203–15.

———. 2008. "No One Is Illegal Between City and Nation." In *Acts of Citizenship*, edited by Engin F. Isin and Greg Nielsen. London: Zed Books.

Peterson, Abby. 2010. "The Use-Value of Human Waste and the Currency of Waste-Disposal Sites in Liquid Modernity." In *Bauman's Challenge: Sociological Issues for the 21st Century*, edited by Mark E. Davis and Keith Tester. New York: Palgrave Macmillan.

Rancière, Jacques. 2008. "Aesthetics Against Incarnation: An Interview by Ann Marie Oliver." *Critical Inquiry* 35 (Autumn): 174–90.

Silverman, Stephanie J., and Ruchi Hajela. 2012. (May 22). *Immigration Detention in the UK*. The Migration Observatory: University of Oxford: http://migrationobservatory.ox.ac.uk/briefings/immigration-detention-uk. Accessed April 11, 2013.

Tyler, Imogen. 2013. *Revolting Subjects: Social Abjection and Resistance in Neoliberal Britain*. London: Zed.
Utkilen, Joern, dir. 2011. *Asylum*. The Bureau, Hopscotch Films, Imagine Pictures Limited.
Wacquant, Loïc. 2008. *Urban Outcasts: A Comparative Sociology of Advanced Marginality*. Cambridge: Polity.

Notes on Contributors

The Anti-Raids Campaign Coalition started in 2012 by a coalition of community-based groups of migrants and precarious workers in response to raids of migrant people by the UK Border Agency and the police in London. The anti-raids campaign has developed tools such as the bust-card and solidarity leaflet in multiple languages so that people know their rights. The campaign is supported by a growing coalition of groups including Latin American Workers Association, Precarious Workers Brigade, Stop Deportations and Southwark Action, The Prisma, No Borders, and South London Solidarity Federation.

Azra Akšamija is a Sarajevo-born Austrian artist and architectural historian, currently Assistant Professor in Art, Culture and Technology at the Massachusetts Institute of Technology (MIT). She holds undergraduate and graduate degrees in architecture from the Technical University Graz, Austria (Dipl.Ing. in 2001) and Princeton University (M.Arch. in 2004), and received her Ph.D. from MIT (History, Theory and Criticism of Art and Architecture / Aga Khan Program for Islamic Architecture) in 2011. In her interdisciplinary practice, Akšamija investigates the potency of art and architecture to facilitate the process of transformative mediation in cultural or political conflicts, and in so doing, provide a framework for researching, analyzing, and intervening in contested socio-political realities. Akšamija's academic inquiry informs her ongoing artistic explorations She works with different types of media, including text, clothing, video, sculpture and new media. Her interdisciplinary projects have been shown in leading international venues such as at the Generali Foundation Vienna, Valencia Biennial, Liverpool Biennial, Sculpture Center NY and Manifesta 7. Recent exhibitions include the Royal Academy of Arts London (2010), Jewish Museum Berlin (2011), and the Fondazione Giorgio Cini as a part of the 54th Art Biennale in Venice. Website and contact: azraaksamija.net

Bruce Bennett is Lecturer and Director of Film Studies at the Lancaster Institute for the Contemporary Arts, Lancaster University UK. In addition to co-editing *Cinema and Technology: Cultures, Theories, Practices* (Palgrave Macmillan, 2008), he has published work on James Cameron, Georges Bataille and general economy, contemporary Chinese cinema, transnational cinema and the visual culture of the war on terror. A monograph, *The Cinema of Michael Winterbottom: Borders, Intimacy, Terror*, was published by Wallflower Press/Columbia University Press in 2013. Email: b.bennett@lancaster.ac.uk.

Rozalinda Borcilă is a Romanian artist, writer, and migrant justice organizer living in Chicago. Her work is situated at the intersection of art, experimental pedagogy and grassroots organizing, directed towards exploring and intervening into the conditions under which we live/work/know. This implies attending to the material and subjective spaces of power, to the ways in which the aesthetic is mobilized within the circuits of capital and a critique of the ways in which the institutionalization of "social practices," "relational esthetics," and "community art" works to deflect possibilities for radical critical/creative imagination. She is engaged in several autonomous collectives and has developed extensive programming around the histories and practices of collectivism within a counter-capitalist horizon. Websites: http://www.borcila.com, http://www.messhall.org, http://www.elastictestproject.com, http://www.6plus.org, www.moratoriumondeportations.org. Email: rborcila@yahoo.com.

Simon Faulkner is Programme Leader in Contemporary Art History at Manchester Metropolitan University, UK. His past research has been on aspects of British Art in the mid-twentieth century and relationships between visual culture and British colonialism during this period. His current research is focused on relationships between visual culture and conflict, with a particular emphasis upon the Israeli-Palestinian conflict. Email: S.Faulkner@mmu.ac.uk.

Katarzyna Marciniak is Professor of Transnational Studies in the English Department at Ohio University. She is the author of *Alienhood: Citizenship, Exile, and the Logic of Difference* (University of Minnesota Press, 2006), co-author of *Streets of Crocodiles: Photography, Media, and Postsocialist Landscapes* in Poland (Intellect, 2010), co-editor of *Transnational Feminism in Film and Media* (Palgrave, 2007), co-editor of a special issue of *Feminist Media Studies* on "Transcultural Mediations and Transnational Politics of Difference" (2009), and, with Imogen Tyler, co-editor of a special issue on "Immigrant Protest" for *Citizenship Studies* (2013). Her interdisciplinary work on immigration and foreignness and their relation to transnational discourses in cinema, media, and visual culture has been published in *Camera Obscura, Cinema Journal, Citizenship Studies, differences, European Journal of Cultural Studies, Feminist Media Studies,* and *Social Identities*. She has a longstanding interest in pedagogies of dissent and her article, "Pedagogy of Anxiety," published in *Signs*, was the winner of the 2010 Florence Howe Award for Outstanding Feminist Scholarship. She is also Series Editor of Global Cinema, a new book series from Palgrave. Email: marcinia@ohio.edu.

Teresa Piacentini works as a GRAMNet Post Doctoral Researcher based in the School of Education at the University of Glasgow. Her current research involves developing a pedagogical model for effective translation in intercultural health care settings, using drama and role play. She was awarded her doctorate in Sociology in 2012 from the School of Political and Social Sciences at the University of Glasgow. Her ethnographic research explored the associational practices of African asylum seekers, refugees and migrants in Glasgow, focusing on subjective relations to place and space and how these are shaped by broader social processes, as well as processes of 'settlement,' belonging, identification and group mobilization in exile. Since 2000, she has also worked as a community interpreter in and around Glasgow mainly for asylum seekers and refugees from a number of Francophone African countries. Email: teresa.piacentini@glasgow.ac.uk.

Alex Rivera is a filmmaker and digital media artist. Over the past fifteen years he has made work that illuminates two parallel realities: the globalization of information through the internet, and the globalization of families, and communities, through mass migration. His work uses a highly stylized language and has won multiple awards at the Sundance Film Festival and been screened at the Museum of Modern Art, The Berlin International Film Festival, The Guggenheim Museum, PBS, and other international venues. Rivera is a Sundance Fellow, USA Artist Fellow, Rockefeller Fellow, and the 2012 Rothschild Lecturer in the History of Science Department at Harvard University. Website: alexrivera.com. Email: alex@alexrivera.com.

Petra Rostock, political scientist, is currently a Ph.D. scholar at the Goethe Graduate Academy (GRADE), Goethe University Frankfurt/Main, Germany. In 2006–2009 she was a Research Fellow in the Department of

Political and Social Science at Free University Berlin, Germany. Involved in pro-migrant activities as well as intercultural and antiracist political education, her research interests include Critical Migration Research, Gender and Queer Studies, Postcolonial Studies, Questions of Identity, Subjectivity and Difference. Email: petrarostock@gmx.de.

Maja Sager is a post-doctoral researcher at the Centre for Gender Studies, Lund University, Sweden and at the Sociology Department, Lancaster University, UK. She completed her PhD, "Everyday Clandestinity: Experiences on the Margins of Citizenship and Migration Policies," in 2011. The project analyzes the ways in which undocumented migrants experience the Swedish welfare state. Her post-doctoral work is a comparative study in Sweden, Denmark and the UK which will further explore how undocumented migrants with support from civil society challenge the exclusion from social rights and create alternative forms of belonging and inclusion. She has published the article "'Gömdhet' på arbetsmarknaden: kopplingar mellan arbetsmarknad, migrationspolitik och asylrätt" in the anthology *Arbete: intersektionella perspektiv* edited by Paula Mulinari and Rebecca Selberg (2011). She is part of a research network (Irreguljär migration och irreguljära migranter) that connects researchers working with undocumented migrants' rights in Sweden. Email: maja.sager@gmail.com.

Lena Šimić, performance artist, born in Dubrovnik, Croatia, lives in Liverpool, UK. Lena has completed practice as research PhD "(Dis)Identifying Female Archetypes in Live Art" at the Lancaster Institute for the Contemporary Arts at Lancaster University in 2007 and has worked as a Lecturer in Drama and Theatre Studies at Liverpool Hope University. Recent solo and collaborative performances and arts projects include *790 Recreations* (If Only festival at the Bluecoat, 2012), *Blood & Soil: we were always meant to meet...*(West Everton Community Council 2011), *Masha Serghyeevna* (the Bluecoat 2009) and *Sid Jonah Anderson by Lena Simic* (MAP Live, Carlisle, 2008). Lena is currently co-organizing The Institute for the Art and Practice of Dissent at Home, an art activist initiative run from a spare bedroom of her council house. Lena toured her performances nationally and internationally; her and the Institute's work has been presented at the National Review of Live Art in Glasgow, Leeds Met Studio Theatre, V&A Museum, Artsadmin in London, Arnolfini in Bristol, Odin Teatret in Denmark, Teatro Guiñol in Santa Clara, Cuba amongst others. Email: lenasimic@hotmail.com.

Imogen Tyler is a Senior Lecturer in Sociology at Lancaster University in England. She specializes in researching social identities and marginalization and is the author of numerous journal articles on immigrant identities, social class and gender. She has a longstanding interest in activism, protest and resistance. She is the author of the monograph *Revolting Subjects* (Zed Books, 2012). Her work has also appeared in *Australian Feminist Studies, Citizenship Studies, European Journal of Cultural Studies, Feminist Media Studies, Feminist Review, Feminist Theory, International Journal of Cultural Studies, Media/Culture,* and *Oxford Literary Review*. She is a co-editor of a special issue of *Feminist Review* on "Birth" (2009), the co-editor of special issue of *Studies in the Maternal* on "Austerity Parenting" (2012), and, with Katarzyna Marciniak, the co-editor of a special issue of *Citizenship Studies* on "Immigrant Protest" (2013). Imogen is a member of the research group www.asylum-network.com. Email: i.tyler@lancaster.ac.uk.

Marguerite Waller is Professor of Women's Studies and Comparative Literature at the University of California, Riverside. She writes on feminist theory, contemporary women's activism, cinema and new media, border art, and European Renaissance literature. Among her publications are *Petrarch's Poetics and Literary History* and the co-edited volumes *Frontline Feminisms: Women, War, and Resistance* (Routledge 2001), *Dialogue and Difference: Feminisms Challenge Globalization* (Palgrave 2005), *The Wages of Empire: Neoliberal Policy, Repression, and Women's Poverty* (Paradigm Publishers 2007), and *Postcolonial Cinema Studies* (Routledge 2012). As a member of Las Comadres, a transnational feminist art-making collective, she has participated in many forms of immigrant protest, and she has co-organized several conferences facilitating transnational dialogue between activists and academics. Email: mwaller@ucr.edu.

Alexandra Zavos has been researching gender and migration in Greece, where she has also been engaged in feminist anti-racist politics. She obtained her PhD from Manchester Metropolitan University on "The politics of gender and migration in an anti-racist group in Athens." She is currently based in Athens at the Center for Gender Studies, Panteion University, where she has been working for the EC FP7 funded projects GEMIC (www.gemic.eu) and MIG@NET (http://www.mignetproject.eu). Some of her research has been published in *Das Argument* (2006), the *Annual Review of Critical Psychology* (2008), and in *Feminist Review* (2010, with Helen Kambouri). Book chapters include the edited collection *Gender and Migration: Perspectives and Interventions* (2010, London, Zed), and the Greek collection *The Gender of Migration* (2009, Athens, Metaixmio). Email: azavos@otenet.gr.

Index

Abdel-Majid, Mouna, 156–57
abjection, 11, 18, 21, 48, 61, 119, 289
Acland, Charles, 117
active citizenship, 191–92, 197
activism, 5–6, 10, 12–13, 15–16, 48, 55–56, 67–68, 118–19, 156–57, 163, 190, 192–98, 200–206, 225–27, 281
acts of citizenship, 13, 20, 78–79, 185–87, 200, 233, 240, 288
Acts of Immigrant Protest, 9, 13, 23, 145
aesthetics, 6, 8–10, 13, 18, 46–49, 55, 61, 147–48, 165–67, 280, 288
Akhter, Farida, 259–62
Akšamija, Azra, xi, 9–10, 12, 24–28, 30, 32, 34–42
Ali, Kecia, 40–41, 43
alienhood, 3, 20, 44, 47, 49, 97–99, 101, 103–11, 113, 115, 117, 119, 121, 140, 142
Allen, Lori A., 153, 156, 166
Aloni, Udi, 150, 166
Anderson, Benedict, 175, 184, 230, 240, 249, 262
Anderson, Bridget, 230, 240, 249

Andersson, Ruben, 18–19
Andrijasevic, Rutvica, 230, 240
Andrzejewski, Julie, 121
anger, 13, 83–84, 89, 91, 122–25, 132–33, 135, 138, 140–41
anthropological cinema, 104
antiracist, 16, 210, 214–17, 225–33, 235–37, 239–41
Anti-Raids Campaign Coalition, 227, 267–68, 274
Anzaldúa, Gloria, 87, 89, 95, 211, 245, 262
aporia, 251, 254, 258–59
Apostolidou, Natascha, 211–12, 214, 221
Arendt, Hannah, 175, 185, 254, 262
art, xi–xii, 7–10, 12, 17–18, 25–26, 47–50, 52–58, 60, 63, 65–69, 71, 74–75, 89–90, 243–44, 281
Art and Practice of Dissent at Home, 63, 71
Asian Women, 16, 246, 262–63
asylum, 74–75, 170–72, 175, 181, 184, 186–87, 189, 191–93, 195, 197, 199, 201–3, 205–7, 277–80, 285
asylum applications, 15, 189–90, 196, 239

asylum seekers, 5–6, 14–15, 74, 78, 134, 169–84, 189–90, 192–95, 198–206, 215, 220, 228, 236, 285, 287–88
Autonomy of Migration, 20–21, 222
Avatar, 12, 97–119
avatar activism, 106, 115, 118
AWHRC (Asian Women's Human Rights Council), 245–46, 251, 256, 259, 261–63
Ayata, Imran, 216, 221–22
Azoulay, Ariella, 166

Baldwin-Edwards, Michael, 240
Bangalore, 16, 245–46, 257, 261–65
Barth, Vanessa, 222
Bauman, Zygmunt, 134, 140–41, 277–79, 287–88
Bazin, André, 98–99, 118
Beckett, Samuel, 277
Becoming British (art project), 10–11, 62–75, 77, 79, 95
Behdad, Ali, 4, 19, 124, 130, 140–41
Benjamin, Walter, 258, 263
Bennett, Bruce, 1, 12, 14, 97–98, 100, 102, 104, 106, 108, 110, 112, 114, 116–18
Berger, Martin A., 166
Berlant, Lauren, 56, 60, 287
Bexelius, Maria, 189, 207
Bhushan, Madhu, 247–49, 258, 263
Biemann, Ursula, 123
Bil'in, 14, 152, 156–57, 159, 161–67
Bloch, Alice, 171, 185
Bloemraad, Irene, 21
Blood & Soil (art project), 70, 73–77
Bojadžijev, Manuela, 209, 215–16, 220–22
Borcilă, Rozalinda, 5, 9–10, 46–48, 53, 60
border patrol, 2, 88, 129
borders, 3–4, 6, 10–11, 48–49, 66–67, 81–85, 87–90, 93–95, 122–24, 127–32, 151, 244, 277–79, 281, 285–88
The Borders Trilogy, 85, 93–94

Bosch, Carlos, 123
Bourdieu, Pierre, 185
Brewer, Jan, 1
Britain, 10–11, 21, 63–67, 71–75, 77–78, 119, 172, 186
Brit Pop, 67
Brown, Wendy, 214, 221, 245, 252, 263
Brun, Catherine, 172, 185
Buñuel, Luis, 3
Burridge, Andrew, 20, 277, 281, 287–88
Butler, Judith, 18, 20, 60, 210, 213–14, 218, 220–21

Calhoun, Craig, 197, 207
California, 17, 82, 84, 244
Cameron, James, 117–18
Camlikbeli, Deniz, 211, 221
Canada, 8, 129–31
Cantle, Ted, 172, 185
Carnevale, Fulvia, 159, 166
Carnevale, Graciela, 59–60
Castles, Stephen, 194, 207
Castro, Varela, 213, 221
checkpoints, 150, 152–53, 155
child, 66–67, 95, 193, 282–83
children, 63–64, 66, 70, 109, 123–24, 192–94, 196, 198, 201, 204, 206, 225–26, 229, 231–34, 259–60
Christen, Claudia, 78
cinema, 3, 6, 11, 21, 49, 103, 115, 118–19, 137, 166
Cissé, Madjiguéne, 7
citizens, 5–6, 8, 10–11, 15–16, 45–47, 71, 87, 140–41, 191, 194, 197–98, 200–201, 231–33, 236, 251
citizenship, 11, 16–17, 20–21, 63–72, 74–75, 77–79, 139–40, 185–87, 190–91, 197–98, 200–202, 207, 231–33, 240, 288
citizenship in motion, 233, 240, 288
Citizenship Studies, 20–21, 79, 95, 265, 288
clandestine, 15, 189–92, 195–99, 203, 205

Index

class, 7, 10, 13, 49–50, 75, 124, 126, 135–36, 138, 140, 143, 190, 229, 250, 279
classroom, 13, 77, 121–22, 124, 135–37, 139, 142
colonial violence, 12, 97, 116
Combahee River Collective, 211–12, 223
commons, 60, 249, 263–64
communities, 17, 20, 27–29, 32, 40–41, 43, 73, 75, 84, 130–31, 184, 195–97, 235–38, 260, 274
community, 15, 27–29, 31–32, 41–43, 72–73, 84, 130–31, 173–76, 183–87, 191–93, 195–97, 235, 238, 259–61, 267–68
Contreras, Irina, 287
counterrepresentations, 192, 198
Courts of Women, 16–17, 243, 245–47, 249–51, 253, 255–59, 261–63, 265
Cristofani, Anthony, 262–63
Crossley, Nick, 185
culture of suspicion, 196, 198
Cyranek, Rebecca, 78

Dahlstedt, Magnus, 189, 207
Davis, Oliver, 166
dead labor, 93–95
Decena, Carlos Ulises, 95
De Genova, Nicholas, 5, 20, 95, 239–40, 285–86, 288
De Giorgi, Alessandro, 46, 60
De Haas, Hein, 20, 286, 288
Deleuze, Gilles, 247–48, 262–63
DeLuca, Kevin, 155, 162, 166
demonstrations, 14, 18, 40, 48, 79, 148, 152, 156, 159–64, 166, 187, 197, 220, 228, 232–33
denizen, 211
deportation, 11, 15, 17, 54, 58, 185, 189–91, 196, 198, 202, 255, 265, 268, 283, 285–86
Derrida, Jacques, 86, 95
detention center, 17, 58, 140, 171, 185, 191, 268, 275, 278–80, 282–83, 285–86

Dhawan, Nikita, 221
Diefenbach, Katja, 215, 217, 221
discrimination, 18, 38–39, 180, 209–10, 212
displacement, 10, 14–15, 115, 150, 174, 234, 247, 262
diversity, 29, 33, 171, 186, 190, 251, 281, 286
Doctors Without Borders, 247, 255, 263
documentary, 55, 83–84, 97–98, 114–15, 123, 158
Do Mar, María, 221
Doty, Roxanne L., 89, 95
dress, 32–33, 35, 46, 69
The Dr. Phil Show, 123
Dyer, Richard, 113–14, 118

East European, 49–50, 147, 149, 151, 153, 160
Eastmond, Marita, 185
Einwohner, Rachel, 170, 175, 185
Ellis Island, 4, 20
Elsaesser, Thomas, 113–16, 118
El Taller International, 258, 261, 263
emotions, 12, 122–23, 132–33, 135–36, 142, 173, 196–98, 202, 206, 256, 258
Engel, Antke, 219, 221
Engin, Isin, 13, 20, 78–79, 95, 141, 185–87, 240, 288
environment, 37, 68, 99–100, 138
equality, 149–50, 153, 161, 167, 251, 281, 287
ESOL (English for Speakers of Other Languages), 69, 72–73
ethnographic films, 102, 104–5, 114–16
Europe, 31, 51, 60, 98, 202, 213, 225–26, 228–29, 239–40, 247–48, 253
Everyday Acts of Resistance, 14, 169, 171, 173, 175, 177, 179, 181, 183, 185, 187
exclusion, 9, 15–16, 39–40, 183, 185, 190–92, 195, 197–98, 200, 203, 209–11, 213, 218–19, 247

Eyre, Chris, 131, 141
Ezeilo, Joy Ngozi, 263

families, 84, 86, 88, 91, 93, 124–25,
    190, 192, 196–201, 203, 206, 227,
    230–31, 235–36, 260
Fasheh, Munir, 263
Faulkner, Simon, 6, 14, 115–16, 118,
    147–48, 150, 152, 154, 156, 158,
    160, 162, 164, 166
Federici, Silvia, 56, 60, 249, 263
FeMigra and Kanak Attak, 15, 209–16,
    218–20, 222–23
feminist, 7, 191, 210–11, 221, 230,
    232–33, 245
Ferguson, James, 174, 185
Fernández-Kelly, Patricia, 20
film, 1–4, 11–13, 81, 83–85, 89, 91–94,
    97–98, 100–107, 111–17, 123–24,
    126–29, 131–33, 137–38, 140–42,
    280
flexible citizenship, 233, 240
food, 74, 126, 173, 179–81, 259–60,
    281
Fore, Dana, 117
foreigners, 46–47, 64, 66, 71, 73, 78,
    121, 211–12, 214–15, 238
Fortress Europe, 263
Foucault, Michel, 288
Frankfurt/Main, 210, 221–23
free trade, 84, 95, 130, 134
Frommer, Paul, 117
Frozen River, 13, 123–25, 127, 129,
    132, 135, 137–38, 141

Gambia, 71, 74–75
Gandhi, 247–49, 263–64
Geddes, Andrew, 228, 240
gender, xi, 7, 16, 121, 124, 133, 142,
    190–91, 197, 225–26, 229–30,
    238–41, 252–53, 261, 264–65
Genet, Jean, 158, 166
Getino, Octavio, 115, 118
Gill, Nick, 282, 288
Giroux, Henry, 137
Givoni, Michal, 167

Glarnetajis, Nikos, 228, 240
Glasenapp, Martin, 214–17, 223
Glasgow, 14–15, 168–70, 172–73, 175,
    184
Glissant, Édouard, 245, 255–56, 264
globalization, 83, 124, 133–34, 139–41,
    227, 243, 256, 258, 287
Global North, 5, 7, 10–11, 140, 245
Global South, 5, 11, 16–17, 59,
    243–46
Goethe, Tina, 215–16, 222
Gómez-Peña, Guillermo, 49, 60, 87,
    89, 95
Grabar, Oleg, 31, 43
Gray, Margaret, 95
Greece, 5–6, 16, 70, 225–29, 231–40
Green, Damien, 282
Gregg, Melissa, 136, 142–43
Griffiths, David, 185
Griffiths, D.W., 105, 174–75, 184–85
Grimm, Sabine, 215, 217, 221–22
Grimonprez, Johan, 166
groups, 15, 28, 67–68, 73–75, 78,
    87–89, 173–78, 193–95, 206, 210,
    213–16, 227–28, 232, 244, 260
Guattari, Felix, 247–48, 262–63
Guénoun, Solange, 166
Gültekin, Neval, 211, 222
Günther, Stephan, 215–16, 222
Gupta, Akhil, 185
Gutiérrez, Rodríguez, 209, 211–14, 222

Hadith, 27–28
Halberstam, Judith, 135, 141
Hallward, Peter, 166
Hammond, Laura, 178, 186
Hanafi, Sari, 167
Hansen, Peo, 194, 206–7
Haraway, Donna, 108, 116, 118
Harding, Sandra, 251, 262, 264
Hasan, Asma Gull, 39, 43
Hawara checkpoint, 152, 154–55, 158
healthcare, 15, 192–96, 206
Heidenreich, Nanna, 214, 216–17, 220,
    222
Henry, Marsha, 118, 253, 264

Herrera, Josue, 44
Herzfeld, Michael, 234, 240
Hesford, Wendy, 8, 20, 239–40
Higate, Paul, 253, 264
hijab, 38–41
Hoffman, Eva, 122
Hollander, Jocelyn, 185
home, 27, 63, 71, 91, 93, 173–74, 180, 182, 184, 246, 252, 258–59, 282, 285, 287
Home Office, 177, 180, 185–86
Howe, Leo, 185
Hubbard, Phil, 185
Hügel, Ika, 211, 222
human disposal industry, 282
human rights, 6, 20, 75, 139, 152, 158, 166, 240, 245, 247, 249, 251–52, 254–55, 260–62, 264–65
human waste production, 277–81, 286–87
hunger strike, 226, 235–37
Hunt, Courtney, 13, 131, 142

Ibarra, Juan, 57, 59
identity, 28, 41, 43, 45–47, 112–15, 121–22, 124, 170–75, 184–85, 209–10, 212–13, 215–18, 225–26, 231, 233–35
identity politics, 215–16, 218
Ifekwunigwe, Jayne, 122, 141
Illegal, 95, 120, 127, 132, 186, 268, 281, 287–88
illegality, 14, 16, 20, 46–48, 95, 236, 239–40, 281–83, 285–86
Immigrant Protest, xi, 5–10, 12–13, 16–19, 45, 47, 49, 51, 53, 55, 57, 59, 245, 253–55, 280–81
immigrant rage, 3, 12–13, 20, 49, 91, 121–22, 140
immigrant rights, 17, 21, 246, 283
immigrants, 1–5, 7, 10, 19–20, 37–38, 42–43, 72–73, 75, 87–91, 102, 121–23, 181–82, 245, 254–55, 274
undocumented, 3–8, 15, 87–88, 92, 190, 194, 197–98, 200, 202–4, 206, 282, 285

inclusion, 16, 21, 28, 174, 178, 183, 191, 195–97, 200, 210–11, 213, 218, 233, 240
inclusive citizenship, 233, 240
indigenous peoples, 97, 102–3, 107, 109, 114, 130, 244, 246–47, 262
informal citizenship, 233
interpreter, 198–99, 206
in/visibility, 6–9, 14, 286
irregular migrants, 3, 5–8, 282, 285–86
Irwin, Robert, 43
Isin, Engin, 13, 20, 67–68, 78–79, 89, 95, 141, 182, 185–87, 233, 240, 288
Islam, 21, 26–29, 31, 33, 38, 41–43
Israel/Palestine, 13–14, 116, 147, 149–51, 153–61, 163–67, 265
Ivory Coast (Africa), 171, 173

Jarrar, Khaled, 152–53, 155, 158, 165–66
Jenelik, Brett, 55
Jenkins, Henry, 116, 118
jungle, 106, 110–12, 221
Jurschick, Karin, 253, 264
jus sanguinis, 74
jus soli, 74

Kabeer, Nalia, 233, 240
Kanak Attak, 15, 210, 214–23
Karakayali, Serhat, 209, 214–16, 220, 222
Kavanagh, James H., 166
Kaynar, Erdal, 209, 220, 223
Kearns, Paula, 72
Kelly, Lynnette, 185
Kelsey, John, 166
Khatib, Mohamed, 161
Khosravi, Shahram, 189, 197, 206–7
King Kong, 105–6, 117
Klein, Naomi, 247, 262, 264
Kosovo, 196, 198–200, 253, 264
Kozol, Wendy, 8, 20, 239–40
Kreuzpaintner, Marco, 124
Kroc Institute, Joan B., 253, 264
Kumar, Corinne, 16, 245–47, 251–56, 261–65

Kundnani, Arun, 185
Kurashige, Scott, 59–60
Kuwee Kumsa, Martha, 185

labor, xi, 16, 81–83, 91–95, 149, 153–54, 167, 191, 193–94, 201–2, 215, 259, 274
Lang, Fritz, 82
Las Comadres, 243–44, 264
Latin Americans, 267–68
lawyers, 173–77, 192
Lazarou, Elena, 228, 240
Lee, Jessica, 59–60, 114, 118
legal status, 5, 7, 182–83, 235–36
Léger, Marc James, 37, 43
Lentin, Alana, 226, 240
Lewis, Gail, 197, 207
Lewis, Reina, 37–38, 43, 196
Liang, Lawrence, 258, 262
Life in the UK: Citizenship Test, 64, 68–69, 73, 75, 77
Lister, Ruth, 191, 197, 207
Liverpool, 11, 63–65, 72–73, 75, 78
living labor, 93–95
Lorde, Audre, 255, 264
Loyd, Jenna M., 20, 277, 281, 287–88

Machete, 1–5, 21
Malkki, Liisa H., 186
Malmö, 193, 196–97, 203, 207
Mama, Amina, 257, 262
Mancillas, Aida, 244, 264
Marciniak, Katarzyna, 1–6, 8, 10–14, 16, 18, 20, 48–50, 61, 63, 81, 95, 121–22, 128–30, 140–42, 277–78
Marcos, Sylvia, 129, 140, 142, 261, 264
marginalization, 40, 170–71, 175, 180–82
Maroukis, Thanos, 228, 241
Marx, Karl, 216, 223
Massey, 175, 186
Massey, Robert, 175, 186
Mathison, Dirk, 119
May, Todd, 166
McCarthy, Tom, 123
McClintock, Anne, 234, 240

McLaren, Peter, 137
Meer, Fatima, 261, 264
Mestre Vives, Laura, 219–20, 222–23
Mexico, 4, 11, 81–84, 86–87, 93, 95, 244, 246, 253
Mezzadra, Sandro, 233, 239–40, 283, 288
migrancy, 8, 10
Migrancy Research Group, xi
migrant activism, 9, 190, 205
Migrant Artist Mutual Aid, 78
migrant artists, 11, 73–74
migrant bodies, 95, 123, 134
Migrant Bust Card, 268–72
migrant communities, 181, 267, 274
migrant experiences, 10–11, 190
migrant illegality, 15, 46, 49, 52, 207, 283, 286
migrant labor, 19, 268
migrant movements, 4, 7, 15, 215–16, 239, 274
migrant organizations, mainstream NGO, 6, 15–16, 48, 51–52, 197, 232
migrant parents, 229, 231–32
migrant populations, 8, 13, 51, 226, 281
Migrant Protest, 5, 9, 15, 18, 55, 97, 209, 238, 286–87
Migrant Resistance, 14, 267, 275
migrant rights, 6, 251, 267–68
migrants, 6–9, 12–20, 49–51, 89–92, 94–95, 181–83, 192, 202, 209–21, 225–29, 231–33, 235–40, 267–68, 274–75, 279–82
  illegal, 228–29, 237, 239, 283
  new, 171, 175
  placed, 226, 234
  second-generation, 213, 229, 236
migrant woman, 226–27
migrant women, 16, 72, 211–14, 218, 225–27, 229–35, 286
migrant workers, 217, 268, 282–83
migration, 11–12, 16, 18, 20–21, 46, 49, 51, 207, 209–11, 217–18, 221–22, 226–29, 238–41, 243, 274

migration policies, 189–91, 207, 215, 239–40
mimicry, 232–34
Minneapolis, 20–21, 61, 118, 142, 167, 241, 263–64
Mirzoeff, Nicholas, 108–9, 112, 118
Mitchelson, Matt, 20, 277, 281, 287–88
Modou, Pa, 11, 71, 74–75, 77
Mohanram, Rahika, 252, 264
Mohanty, Chandra, 133, 140, 142
Moran, Rhetta, 171, 186
mosques, 10, 25, 27–30, 32, 35, 41–43
motherhood, 63, 78
movement, women's, 209, 211–13
Mukherjee, Bharati, 8, 20
multilayered citizenship, 233
Murawska-Muthesius, Katarzyna, 50, 61
Muslim groups, 25, 28, 38, 40–41
Muslim women, 38–41

NAFTA (North American Free Trade agreement), 11, 84, 244
Nama, Adilifu, 101–2, 118
Nandy, Ashis, 247–48, 264
National Asylum Support System (NASS), 179, 184
nationalism, 1, 67, 87–91, 105, 123–24, 130, 135–36, 150–51, 186, 230–31, 234–35, 240–41, 245–56, 259, 261–62
nationality, 65–66, 139, 182, 190–91, 254
Nava, Gregory, 82
Neoliberalism, 51–52, 79
Ngai, Mae, 87, 95
NGOs (Nongovernmental Organization), 14–15, 179, 192, 194, 197, 200–201, 206, 245, 251, 260
Nielsen, Greg M., 13, 20, 67, 78–79, 185–87, 240, 288
noborders, 6, 21, 71, 274
NoName Collective, 52, 54
nonviolence, 161, 248
No One Is Illegal, 6, 186, 268, 281, 287–88

Nyers, Peter, 7, 20, 115, 118, 170, 172–73, 182, 184, 186, 202, 207, 286, 288

Oguntoye, Katharina, 211, 223
Ong, Aihwa, 233, 240
Operation Gatekeeper, 11, 87
Ophir, Adi, 167
orientalism, 21

Padmanabhan, Mukund, 265
Pahl, Ray, 191
Palestinians, 13–14, 147, 150–56, 158–61, 164–65
Papadopoulos, Dimitri, 6, 9, 20
Pavlou, Miltos, 229, 240
Pearl, Martyn, 174, 187
pedagogy, 13, 48, 60, 121, 123, 125, 127, 129, 131, 133, 135, 137, 139, 141, 143
Peeples, Jennifer, 155, 162
performance, 6, 9, 46, 49, 52–54, 65–70, 75, 77–78, 86–87, 89, 116, 148–49, 161–63, 231, 234
Perkins, John, 247, 264
Peterson, Abby, 279, 288
Pettman, Jan Jindy, 230, 241
photographs, 46, 152–53, 165
Piacentini, Teresa, 6, 14–15, 169–70, 172, 174, 176, 178, 180, 182, 184, 186
Piesche, Peggy, 220, 223
police, 15, 17, 88–89, 122, 133, 148–51, 154, 190, 255–56, 267–68, 275
policies, social, 189, 191, 207
political action, 11, 147, 210, 219, 244, 253, 257
Political Aesthetics, 10, 45, 47, 49, 51, 53, 55, 57, 59, 61
political agency, 6, 8–9, 107, 153, 158–59, 230, 233
politics, 5–6, 8, 15–16, 18–19, 21–22, 49–50, 85–86, 147–50, 165–67, 197–98, 210–11, 218, 225–27, 231–32, 245–46
noborder, 17, 19

politics of belonging, 226, 231, 238
politics of dissensus, 165
Politics of Visibility, 13, 147, 149, 151, 153, 155, 157, 159, 161, 163, 165, 167
Polzer, Tara 178, 186
Portes, Alejandro 175, 186
postcolonial, 4, 7–8, 102, 105, 114, 140–42, 191, 220, 233, 245–48, 261, 264, 274
precarious lives, 14, 169, 184
Price, David, 104, 119
protests, 5–11, 13–14, 16–18, 48, 54–56, 68, 86–87, 112, 116, 147, 159–60, 182, 201, 210, 280–81
   political, 7, 155, 198, 201, 215, 254–55

race, 50–51, 101, 105, 112–13, 119, 121, 123–24, 126, 139, 143, 190–91, 225–26, 229, 240–41, 264–65
racial cinema, 101
racialization, 49–51
racism, 97, 105, 132, 185–86, 198–99, 209–10, 212–19, 224, 227, 229, 231–32, 240, 249, 263
racism history, 138, 215, 217, 220
rage, 12–13, 49, 121–23, 125, 127, 129, 131, 133, 135–37, 139, 141, 143
Rally for Immigrant Rights, 17, 21
Rancière, Jacques, 8, 18, 21, 47–48, 61, 148–50, 153–54, 158–59, 166–67, 287–88
Ratcliffe, Krista, 121, 142
recognition, 7, 9, 13, 45, 47, 170, 191, 228, 231, 233–34
Reeb, David, 158, 163, 166
refugees, 5–6, 75, 78, 115, 118, 170, 172, 174–75, 179, 181–86, 196, 198, 201, 214–15, 252–54
representation, 6–9, 12, 27, 29, 33, 43, 47, 112, 158–59, 211–13, 227–28, 231, 235, 238, 240
resist, 16, 18–19, 49, 56–57, 160, 169–70, 174, 177, 179–80, 182, 210, 280, 287

resistance, 6, 13–16, 21, 55–56, 141, 167, 169–87, 192, 198, 209–12, 217–19, 237, 239, 280–81, 286–87
Rex, John, 172, 186
Rieder, John, 112, 119
Rigby, Joe, 6, 21
rights, 11–14, 16–18, 66–67, 116, 176–77, 191–92, 195, 203, 226, 228, 231–37, 250–52, 254–55, 260, 262
Rivera, Alex, xi, 11, 80–86, 88, 90, 92, 94, 277–78
Robert, Jean, xii, 1, 3, 21, 43, 186, 249–50, 264
robots, 82–83
Rockhill, Gabriel, 166–67
Rodriguez, Robert, 1, 3, 5, 7, 19, 21
Roei, Noa, 160, 167
Rony, Fatimah Tobing, 3, 21, 102–6, 114–16, 119
Roosevelt, Eleanor, 254
Rostock, Petra, 6, 15–16, 209–10, 212, 214, 216, 218, 220, 222
Routledge, Paul, 155, 167
Rubin, Jeffrey, 170, 186
Rumbaut, Rubén G., 175, 186

Sager, Maja, 6, 15, 189–90, 192, 194, 196, 198, 200, 202, 204, 206–7
Said, Edward, 8
Sakai, Naoki, 238, 240–41
Saleh, Nabi, 156–57, 166
Sans-Papiers, 5, 7–8, 20, 134
Sassen, Saskia, 233, 241
Schierup, Carl-Ulrik, 194, 207
Schlembach, Raphael, 6, 21
schools, 5, 100, 109, 126, 177, 193–94, 196, 258, 267, 286
Schuster, Lisa, 171, 185–86
Scott, James, 186
Secure Communities, 11, 88–89
security, 90, 95, 196, 245, 258–59, 265
Sedgwick, Eve Kosofsky, 264
Segerstedt, Ingrid, 200–201, 207
Seibert, Thomas, 214–17, 223
Seigworth, Gregory, 136, 142–43

sexism, 132, 210, 213–14, 227
shipping containers, 94–95
Shiva, 247, 249–50, 262, 264
Shohat, Ella, 5, 21, 217, 223
Shut Down ICE, 53–54, 56–58
Siapno, Jacqueline, 253, 265
Sibley, David, 39, 43
Sigona, Nando, 185
Sigvardsdotter, Erica, 206–7
Silverstein, Paul, 225, 241
Šimić, Lena, 9–11, 62, 64–66, 68, 70, 72, 74–75, 78
Skeggs, Beverley, 138–39, 142
Sleep Dealer, 12, 80–83, 85
Slevin, Peter, 255, 265
Smith, Anthony D., 28, 43
smuggling, 13, 66, 123, 127, 130–31
Sobchack, Vivian, 137, 142
social change, xi, 58–59, 142, 176–77, 181, 183
society, civil, 195, 197, 200, 205–6
Solanas, Fernando, 115, 118
soldiers, 78, 110, 153, 160–61, 163–64, 258
solidarity, 6, 16–17, 58, 178–80, 183, 200–201, 205, 266–68, 273
Solomos, John, 186
South Africa, 247, 249–51, 257, 262–63
sovereignty, 17, 46, 68, 192, 202, 230–31, 238, 245, 250–56, 258, 260–61, 263
Sowe, Fatoumata, 78
Spielberg, Steven, 123
Spivak, Gayatri Chakravorty, 9, 21, 102, 115, 119, 140, 142, 211, 213, 223
Stam, Robert, 5, 21
state violence, 246, 248, 251–52, 255, 281
Stenum, Helle, 206–7
stereoscopic cinema, 103, 115
Stockholm, 193, 202, 207
strategic essentialism, 211, 215
Straw, Jack, 171, 186
struggles, 6–7, 9, 13–14, 20, 54, 159, 165, 181, 192–93, 195, 200, 202–3, 225–26, 230, 237

subjects, 15–16, 46–47, 65–66, 122–23, 147–48, 170–71, 209, 211, 213, 215, 217–19, 221, 223, 249, 252
Suda, Kimiko, 209, 211, 220, 223
Survival Mosque (art project), xi, 24, 35–38
suspicion, 3, 88, 127, 198–99
Svirsky, Gila, 256, 265
Sweden, 6, 15, 189–90, 192, 194, 196, 198–200, 203–7
Swyngedouw, Erik, 10–11, 21

Tamas, Gellert, 189, 207
Tamimi, Bilal, 156, 158
Taylor, Ella, 132, 142, 241
technologies, 6, 9, 11, 18, 47, 51, 81, 89–90, 101–3, 107, 159
Temple, Bogusia, 171, 186
terrorism, 3, 127, 252
Tesfahuney, Mekonnen, 207
testimonies, 197–98, 245, 256–58
trafficking, 16, 133, 230, 253, 260
transnational, 6–7, 16, 18–19, 49–50, 86, 98, 116, 123, 138, 240, 248, 256, 261
Tsianos, Vassilis, 6, 9, 20
Turkish immigrant culture, 33
Turowski, Kamil, 8, 20, 276
Turton, David, 171, 178, 186
Tutu, Desmond, 250, 265
Tyler, Imogen, 1–2, 4, 6, 8, 10, 12, 14, 16, 18, 20, 48–49, 63–64, 66, 68, 277–78

Udel-Lambert, Miriam, 42–43
undocumented migrants, 9, 15, 87, 192–95, 201–2, 204–6, 286
United African Women's Organization, 231–32
United Nations, 253–54, 261–62, 265
United States, 3–5, 12, 17, 19–20, 25, 40–42, 46, 82, 84, 87, 91, 98, 102, 122–23, 130–31
Universal Declaration of Human Rights, 252, 254, 260–62, 265
Utkilen, Joern, 277–80, 287, 289

veil, 19, 33–34, 37–38, 41, 43
Verson, Jennifer, 70–72, 75, 79
Vertovec, Steven, 172, 186
Vestin, Sanna, 189, 207
violence, 3, 6, 12, 16–17, 46, 108, 110, 116, 212, 243, 247–48, 251–54, 256, 258, 260–61
visibility, 6–10, 25, 50, 52, 94, 107–8, 147–49, 151, 153–55, 157–61, 163, 165, 167, 173–74, 233
Vukadinović, Vojin Saša, 220, 222

Wacquant, Loïc, 278, 289
Wallen, Ruth, 244, 264
Waller, Marguerite, 6, 16–17, 129, 140, 142, 243–44, 246, 248, 250, 252–54, 256, 258, 260–65
Walls and Cages, 17, 20, 277, 281, 287–88
Walters, William, 67, 79, 173, 187
Warschawski, Michel, 167
Watkins, Megan, 137, 143
Wearable, 10, 25–27, 29, 32–33, 38, 41–43
Wearable Mosques, 10, 25–27, 29, 32–33, 38, 41–43
West Bank, 14, 146–48, 150, 156, 159–60, 163

white trash, 50, 52, 113, 124, 126–27, 138, 142–43, 213
Why Cybraceros?, 12, 83, 91–92
Wiese, Dorothee, 212–14, 223
Wodiczko, Krzysztof, 37, 43
women, 15–17, 20, 38, 40, 73, 78, 123–24, 127, 129, 132–33, 171, 173, 211–14, 230–31, 240–65
women migrants, 226, 229–30, 254
workers, guest, 216–17
Wray, Matt, 126, 143
Wrench, John, 186
Wyman, Julie, 60

xenophobia, 3, 29, 110, 132, 263

Yans, Virginia, 4
Yarl's Wood Immigration Removal Centre, 282
Yurtsever-Kneer, Selçuk, 212–13, 220, 223
Yuval-Davis, Nira, 230, 233, 241

Zapatista, 246, 249
Zavos, Alexandra, 6, 16, 224–26, 228–30, 232, 234, 236, 238, 240–41
Zetter, Roger, 174, 185, 187
Žižek, Slavoj, 104, 119
Zolberg, Aristide, 4